WITHDRAWN
UML LIBRARIES

The Red Tape Cutter's Handbook:

A Working Tool for Dealing with Bureaucracies

The Red Tape Cutter's Handbook:

A Working Tool for Dealing with Bureaucracies

Carol Lea Clark

Facts On File, Inc.
460 Park Avenue South
New York, N.Y. 10016

The Red Tape Cutter's Handbook:

A Working Tool for Dealing with Bureaucracies

© Copyright 1982 by Facts On File, Inc.

All rights reserved. No part of this book may be reproduced or utilized in any form or by any means, electronic or mechanical, including photocopying, recording or by any information storage and retrieval systems, without permission in writing from the Publisher.

Library of Congress Cataloging in Publication Data
Clark, Carol Lea.
   The red tape cutter's handbook.

   Includes index.
   1. Administrative agencies—United States—Handbooks, manuals, etc.   2. Administrative law—United States—Handbooks, manuals, etc.   3. United States—Executive departments—Handbooks, manuals, etc.   I. Title.
JK464 1981.C55   353.04′02′02   81-21193
ISBN 0-87196-389-2   AACR1

Printed in the United States of America
10 9 8 7 6 5 4 3 2 1

Dedication

For Patrick, my husband, mentor, and friend.
For my parents, Morris and Rose Usry, who have always helped and believed.
For my daughter Amber, who has grown with this book.
Without these four the book would not have been written.

Introduction

Bureaucracy is all around us. We meet it when we are born and when we die; we encounter it in education, in the armed forces and in many of the professions and jobs we choose. In fact, we experience it every day. If we drive a car, we must be licensed, if we own a dog, it must be licensed. We listen to TV and radio stations licensed by the federal government and we are employed in factories where safety conditions are monitored by Uncle Sam. Private bureaucracies also control our lives. Various trade organizations monitor consumer complaints for their type of business.

Although the federal government and some state governments have offices to aid people trying to deal with the vast maze of government regulation, there is not one easily available source explaining where to go to get the things done. *The Red Tape Cutter's Handbook* fills this gap. Here, in an easy A to Z format, is the citizen's guide to dealing with both government and private bureaucracy. Obviously we cannot answer or anticipate all questions or problems an individual may have. Each entry has been chosen with the life and experience of the average American consumer and businessman in mind. Entries focus primarily on citizen and consumer problems as well as those of small businesses. Thus *The Red Tape Cutter's Handbook* tells you how to get a birth certificate, or get help with a complaint about auto repair. It will tell you who controls professional hockey and what organization your daughter will have to join if she wants to be an Olympic figure skater. It will even tell you what documents you need if you want to travel to Israel. It will not, however, tell you how to get a snow survey or a permit to mine on government land, or what documents you need to travel to Mongolia since these problems do not face the average individual.

To find the answer to your question simply look it up by key word. For example, if you want to find out how to complain about programming on children's TV, look up "Television: Children's Programming." If you want to find out who registers automobiles, look up "Automobiles: Registration. Most entries give you a national organization to contact. However, in a large number of consumer, tourist or tax questions you will be referred to specific state entries. This was done because each state bureaucracy is organized differently and offers different consumer services.

The information in *The Red Tape Cutter's Handbook* is accurate as of December 1981. Please remember, however, that under the Reagan administration the government bureaucracy is changing rapidly. Many of the agencies cited are operating on limited funds or on grants that may run out in a few months. Therefore, if you are dealing with the regional office of an agency and cannot get a reply to your question, contact the Washington office which may still be in operation.

In writing this book I have discovered that the description of civil servants as "neither servants nor civil" does not apply. Most of the government employees I contacted went out of their way to help me. To them I owe thanks. I also want to thank all the people at Facts On File who made this book possible. And to Pat and Amber a special note of gratitude for their patience.

February 1982   Carol Lea Clark

A

ABORTION

As a result of Supreme Court rulings in 1973 and 1976, women can legally have abortions during the first three months of pregnancy. Currently, the decision about whether to have or not to have an abortion rests with the pregnant woman and her doctor. A state can prevent an abortion only if the fetus is able to live outside the womb. A minor has the right to decide whether to have an abortion or not.

Federal funds cannot be used to pay for an abortion except in cases of pregnancies that were the result of incest or rape or if the life of the mother would be endangered by carrying the fetus to term. States decide whether to provide funding for other abortions.

Information on how to obtain an abortion can be obtained from a physician or a clinic. Planned Parenthood offers information and counseling and abortion services. Contact its local office or Planned Parenthood Federation of America, Inc., 810 7th Ave, New York, N.Y. 10019, Tel. 212-541-7800. For information about state and federal funds for abortions consult the local Medicaid office or write Division of Public Inquiries, Social Security Administration, 8401 Security Blvd., Baltimore, Md. 21235, Tel. 301-953-3600.

ACCOUNTANTS

To work as a certified public accountant (CPA) an individual must have a certificate issued by the state board of accountancy. All states require that applicants pass the CPA exam prepared by the American Institute of Certified Public Accountants to qualify for certification. Three quarters of the states require that CPAs have college degrees and most states require that applicants have two years of public accounting experience. Some will accept a master's degree in accounting as a substitute for the public accounting experience. Obtain specific requirements from the state board of accountancy, located in the state capital.

Accountants can work in public accounting without certification as long as they do not call themselves CPAs although states put restrictions upon what services accountants can perform without the certificate. Check with the state board of accountancy.

Applications for the national CPA examination can be obtained only through the state board of accountancy, though information about the test can be obtained

1

from the American Institute of Certified Public Accountants, 1211 Avenue of the Americas, New York, N.Y. 10036, Tel. 212-575-6200.

Because the test is nationwide, a CPA from one state can obtain a reciprocal certificate in another state if he meets the educational and experience requirements for the second state.

ACUPUNCTURE

Most states do not regulate the practice of acupuncture. Only New York and California restrict its use to licensed medical practitioners. These states view it as an experimental technique that should be restricted to research in order to determine its effectiveness. Questions about acupuncture practitioners in these states should be directed to the state board of licenses that regulates medical practitioners.

The Food and Drug Administration (FDA),under authority of the Food, Drug and Cosmetic Act, requires labeling of acupuncture needles and other paraphernalia as prescription medical devices. The label must bear the name and address of the manufacturer and a statement that the acupuncture device is experimental and should be used only for research or under the direct supervision of licensed medical or dental practitioners. The investigation must be approved by the appropriate institutional review committee, or conditions for such use must be in accordance with state law.

Questions or complaints about acupuncture devices can be referred to the Consumer Communication Management Staff, Office of Policy Coordination, Food and Drug Administration, 5600 Fishers Lane, Rockville, Md. 20857, Tel.: 301-443-2170.

ADDITIVES: FOOD

Two federal agencies regulate food additives in products that cross state lines. Direct additives are those added to foods by the manufacturer to increase nutritional value or preserve or beautify the product. Meat products fall under the jurisdiction of the Department of Agriculture. Other food products are controlled by the Food and Drug Administration. Additives deemed safe fall into two categories; those in use before 1958 (when Congress began requiring the manufacturer to pretest new additives) are deemed GRAS (Generally Recognized as Safe) or given *Prior Sanction.* Those tested after that date are placed on the *Approved* list. If the FDA finds an additive on the market harmful, it is *Banned;* if serious doubts arise about the item it is placed on an *Interim* list. The substance on the *Interim* list may be sold until its danger is conclusively proven.

The FDA also regulates indirect additives. These are substances used in packaging which might leech into the food or are chemicals present in animal feed that find their way into the final product. The FDA sets tolerance levels for these substances, usually determined in parts per million or billion.

Complaints and questions about food additives should be directed to the Consumer Communication Management Staff, Office of Policy Coordination, Food and Drug Administration, 5600 Fishers Lane, Rockville, Md. 20857, Tel. 301-443-2170.

ADOPTION

Adults who wish to adopt children can generally apply to either public or private agencies. Most states have a child welfare agency that places children with families without charging a fee. The children referred by these agencies are frequently older, handicapped or from minority groups. Prospective adoptive parents who want special types or younger children usually must register with a private adoption agency and be placed on a waiting list before an adoption study is even done. Some private agencies also place older, handicapped or minority children. Private agencies generally charge a fee. Check the telephone directory under adoption agencies or call the local child welfare or child protective services agency.

Prospective adoptive parents must satisfy the requirements of the adoption agency. Criteria may include age, income (financial stability), religion (only in church-sponsored agencies), length of marriage (usually two to five years) and health. Most agencies today also consider single parents. After application the individual or couple undergoes an adoption study. The agency will then make a recommendation on the individual's or couple's suitability to adopt.

After a couple or an individual's application has been approved, the agency will match the parent(s) with a child or children. Caseworkers will provide assistance during the adjustment period and in family court until the adoption is finalized.

Consent for an adoption is required from the natural parents if they are alive, unless a court has removed the child from their custody due to neglect or abuse. If the child is illegitimate, notice is generally given to the natural father even though his consent is not required. The child's consent must be given if he or she is over a certain age, usually 10 to 14, depending on the laws of the individual states. Consent is also required from the authorized institution that has custody of the child.

It is usually necessary to retain a lawyer to file an adoption petition. This petition must be made to the court (usually family court), and a judicial hearing is held in which the court considers the qualifications of the adoptive parents and decides on their petition. State laws usually mandate a probationary period either before or after the court hearing, during which time the child lives with the family.

After the adoption is formalized for most legal purposes the child is treated as the natural child of the adoptive parents. Generally, the child's original birth certificate and all papers relating to the court action are sealed. A new birth certificate is issued bearing the adoptive parent's names. Recently, however there has been an increasing trend to give adopted children access to these papers.

In all states an adopted child may inherit from the adoptive parents in the absence of a will. In the following states an adopted child may still inherit from the natural parents in the absence of a will: Alabama, Arkansas, Indiana, Louisiana, Maine, Mississippi, Montana, Rhode Island, South Dakota, Texas and Vermont. The same applies to the Commonwealth of Puerto Rico. For further information contact the local state department of social services of the U.S. Department of Health and Human Resources, Office of Human Development, Children's Bureau. P.O. Box 1182, Washington, D.C. 20013, Tel. 202-755-7418.

See also: FOSTER PARENTS

ADVERTISING: COMPLAINTS

Complaints about national advertising, especially advertising that the consumer considers in poor taste, should be made first to the manufacturer or distributor of the product. Complaints about claims made in national advertising also may be referred to the National Advertising Review Board, 845 Third Ave., New York, N.Y. 10022, Tel. 212-832-1320. The board is part of the national organization of Better Business Bureaus. It will investigate the complaint and recommend that the advertising should or should not be changed. If the advertiser does not comply with its recommendations, the board may issue press statements or refer the matter to a government agency.

The Federal Trade Commission is the government agency responsible for monitoring and acting to curb deceptive advertising. Complaints should be directed to the Federal Trade Commission, Bureau of Consumer Protection, 414 11th St. NW, Washington, D.C. 20580; Tel. 202-724-1499.

AERIAL PHOTOGRAPHS

Aerial photographs for every region of the United States are available from different agencies within the Department of Agriculture. To obtain an aerial photograph, outline the section desired on a road map or other map and request the index numbers for the photographs covering that region. The photographs are then ordered by index number. Forms and catalogs are available from each of the agencies on request. Charges vary depending on the kind of photo, the enlargement and the material desired. For most photographs contact: Aerial Photography Field

Office, P.O. Box 30010, Salt Lake City, Utah. 84130, Tel.: 801-524-5856. For high altitude and satellite imagery contact: Eros Data Center, User Services, Sioux Falls, S.D. 57198, Tel.: 605-594-6151.

AERONAUTIC CHARTS

Aeronautic charts of the United States and foreign areas are available from the National Ocean Survey of the National Oceanic and Atmospheric Administration. Charts must be ordered by catalog number from *Aeronautical Charts and Related Publications*, or from agents listed in the catalog.

Contact the Department of Commerce, Distribution Division, 14 Pennsylvania Ave. NW, Washington, D.C. 20230, Tel. 202-377-2000.

AERONAUTICS

See SPACE EXPLORATION

AGING

See ELDERLY

AIRCRAFT ACCIDENTS

Civil aircraft accidents in the United States are investigated by the National Transportation Safety Board which issues public recommendations based on the findings of the probe. The recommendations may result in changes in safety standards for aircraft, for air traffic control or for any other area relating to aircraft in the United States. This includes the performance of other government agencies such as the Federal Aviation Administration or the Civil Aeronautics Board. The reports are made officially to Congress but are available to the public. For further information contact the National Transportation Safety Board, 800 Independence Ave. SW, Washington, D.C. 20594, Tel. 202-472-6100.

AIR FARES

The Civil Aeronautics Board (CAB) is the federal agency authorized to supervise airfares. Each carrier is required to file the proposed change with related rules concerning refunds etc. The Board may review fares on its own initiative or after receiving a complaint. The CAB has deregulated fares, and airlines are no longer required to charge the same fares for the same routes. Consult the specific airline or a travel agent for information. Complaints about an air fare should first be taken to the airline concerned. If that does not solve the problem consult the Civil Aeronautics Board, Bureau of Consumer Protection, 1825 Connecticut Ave. NW, Washington, D.C. 20428, Tel. 202-673-5930. CAB offices are also located in Des Plaines, Fort Worth, Miami, Anchorage, New York, Los Angeles and Seattle.

AIRPLANE PILOTS: PRIVATE LICENSE REQUIREMENTS

The Federal Aviation Administration is the licensing agency for private pilots. Private pilots are defined as those which do not work for hire or receive wages for transporting goods or passengers. An individual can get a private license in either of two ways: by attending an "approved school" or by receiving instruction from a licensed pilot or a flight school. All instructors are certified by the FAA. If an individual attends an approved school, that is, one which has submitted its curriculum and maintenance inspection to the FAA, he or she can receive a license after 35 hours of flight time and 35 hours of ground instruction. Should an individual choose the second procedure, he needs 40 hours of flight time plus ground instruction. Prior to soloing, the student takes a physical administered by the FAA designated medical examiner. In order to obtain a license he must pass a written examination and a flight test. To fly in instrument weather, he must pass an instrument rating test. An individual can apply for a license through an FAA designated pilot examiner or through the Flight Standard District Office, P.O. 17325, Dulles International Airport, Washington, D.C. 20041, Tel. 202-557-5360.

AIR POLLUTION

Transportation exhaust, primarily from the automobile, contributes about half of the total air pollution. Other fuel combustion, such as in public utilities, contributes about 30 percent and solid waste disposal about five percent. The rest comes from miscellaneous sources.

The Environmental Protection Agency (EPA) is responsible for controlling air pollution. Other federal agencies, such as the National Highway Traffic Safety Administration and the Federal Power Commission are also involved with the problem.

State governments also have their own agencies concerned with air pollution. These enforce air quality control according to state regulations. Local governments may have clean air ordinances as well.

States are divided by EPA into "air quality control regions" composed of areas that have common pollution problems because of geographical characteristics, weather or patterns of population and industry. The regions are designed to make cooperation easier between federal, state and local agencies concerned with air pollution. The EPA prepares reports on each region's pollution problems. These reports are available to the public upon request.

Regional EPA, state and local agencies are required to develop a plan for reducing air pollution to acceptable levels. The plan may include requiring permits with emission standards for new industrial plants, a motor inspection program or controls on transportation.

Inquiries or complaints about air pollution should, therefore, be directed to the regional EPA office (address in the appendix), and the state and local air quality control agencies in the air quality control region.

Contact the regional office of the EPA to find one's region and the appropriate state and local agencies or the Environmental Protection Agency, 401 M St. SW, Washington, D.C. 20460, Tel. 202-755-2673.

AIR TRAFFIC CONTROL

The Federal Aviation Administration operates and maintains the equipment at air traffic control centers and towers in the United States. For further information contact the local FAA office listed in the telephone directory under U.S. government or the Department of Transportation, Federal Aviation Administration, 800 Independence Ave. SW, Washington, D.C. 20591, Tel. 202-426-3711.

AIR TRAFFIC CONTROLLERS

The Federal Aviation Administration employs civilian air traffic controllers for federal airports. The entry level position is air traffic controller trainee. New trainees are selected through the competitive federal civil service system. Applicants must be under 31 years of age and must pass a written test that measures ability to learn and perform the air controller's duties. Applicants must also have three years of work experience or four years of college or a combination of both. The

health of the applicant must be excellent, and vision must be correctable to 20/20. Those applicants who have had sufficient experience as military controllers, pilots or navigators may be hired without taking the written test. For further information contact any Civil Service Commission Job Information Center listed in the telephone directory under U.S. government.

AIR TRAVEL: DELAYED AND CANCELLED FLIGHTS

Airlines do not guarantee their schedules. However, when a flight is cancelled, federal regulations require that the airline arrange transportation on the next available flight to the destination at no additional charge. If a flight is delayed for more than four hours, the carrier must provide certain amenities: a telephone call or telegram to the destination, a hotel room if necessary, cab or limousine fare between the airport and the hotel, and food at an airport restaurant. Should the airline fail to provide these, contact the airline's consumer office for expenses incurred. Or contact the Civil Aeronautics Board, Bureau of Consumer Protection, 1825 Connecticut Ave. NW, Washington, D.C. 20428, Tel. 202-673-5930.

AIR TRAVEL: LOST BAGGAGE

In most cases airlines are required to compensate a passenger for lost baggage. A claim must be made within 45 days of loss, but it

7

is best to notify the airline before leaving the airport. Liability is limited to $750 for a domestic flight. Additional compensation can be obtained by paying for "excess valuation" at the time of check in. Most airlines will pay some money at the airport for emergency purchases if luggage is misplaced or lost. Most will pay for rental equipment if the airline misplaces sporting equipment. It generally takes from six weeks to three months for the airline to pay for lost articles. Should the airline fail to grant compensation, contact the Civil Aeronautics Board, Bureau of Consumer Protection, 1825 Connecticut Ave. NW, Washington, D.C. 20428, Tel. 202-673-5930.

AIR TRAVEL: OVERBOOKING AND BUMPING

In most cases the Civil Aeronautics Board requires that each passenger who is involuntarily bumped be paid compensation. The airline must pay the fare to the destination plus compensation of $37.50 minimum and $200 maximum. If the airline cannot arrange another flight that is scheduled to arrive at the destination within two hours of the original flight arrival time (four hours on international flights) the amount of compensation doubles. The airline must also give the passenger a written statement explaining how it decides who is to be bumped in the case of an oversold flight. If a

passenger's expenses resulting from being bumped are greater than the airline is willing to pay, it may be possible to negotiate a higher settlement with that airline's consumer department or to take the airline to court. For further information contact the Civil Aeronautics Board, Bureau of Consumer Protection, 1825 Connecticut Ave. NW, Washington, D.C. 20428, Tel. 202-673-5930.

AIR TRAVEL: ROUTES

The routes on which an airline can or must provide service are regulated by the Civil Aeronautics Board (CAB). At present the CAB must approve any application by an airline for a new scheduled route if the airline is determined to be "fit, willing and able" to provide the service and if the service is "consistent with public convenience and necessity." New route applications are presumed to be in the public interest unless shown to be otherwise. Subsidies are provided to airlines for "essential" service to communities on established routes that cannot be operated at a profit.

The airlines are in the process of being deregulated as a result of the Airline Deregulation Act of 1978. As the CAB's authority is phased out, both the determination of an airline's fitness for a route and the subsidy program will be transferred to the Federal Aviation Administration (FAA). In 1985 the CAB will have ceased to exist unless Congress has taken action to the contrary.

Until then, questions and complaints about air routes can be directed to: Civil Aeronautics Board, Consumer Assistance Division, 1825 Connecticut Ave. NW, Washington, D.C. 20428, Tel. 202-673-6047.

AIR TRAVEL: SAFETY

The Federal Aviation Administration administers safety regulations for both private and commercial aircraft. It also issues and enforces minimum standards for the manufacture, operation and maintenance of aircraft, and rates and certifies airmen and airports that serve carriers certified by the Civil Aeronautics Board. The agency inspects navigation facilities as well. Complaints about safety should be addressed to the Department of Transportation, Consumer Liaison, Federal Aviation Administration, 800 Independence Ave. SW, Washington, D.C. 20591, Tel. 202-426-1960.

The National Transportation Safety Board (NTSB) has responsibility for determining the probable cause of aircraft accidents and making recommendations to Congress to improve safety regulations for the aircraft industry. All NTSB accident reports are available to the public. For further information contact the Office of Public Affairs, National Transportation Safety Board, 800 Independence Ave. SW, Washington, D.C.

20594, Tel, 202-472-6100.

AIR TRAVEL: SMOKING

Airlines based in the United States must provide a seat in the nonsmoking section for any passenger who asks for one, (if the passenger arrives within the time specified) and the Civil Aeronautics Board requires that the crew ensure that no one smokes in the nonsmoking section. No smoking is allowed throughout the aircraft when the no-smoking signs are lit.

Foreign airlines are not required to provide nonsmoking sections, but many do. Passengers requiring seats in a nonsmoking section should check with the foreign airline before making reservations.

A passenger refused a seat in the nonsmoking section may report the incident to the airline's consumer office and/or the Civil Aeronautics Board. The CAB records complaints but generally takes no further action. The airlines generally make an adjustment or at least an apology. Contact the individual airline or the CAB, Consumer Assistance Division, 1825 Connecticut Ave. NW, Washington, D.C. 20428, Tel. 202-673-6047.

ALABAMA

The agency responsible for consumer protection in Alabama is the Attorney General's Office of Consumer Protection. The Office investigates and mediates individual complaints and investigates business practices of particular businesses or industries indicating patterns of fraud. Unlike some other state consumer protection agencies, the Alabama agency will not advise whether or not a business is reputable.

Because the State of Alabama does not have a consumer protection law, the Attorney General's Office of Consumer Protection must, in most cases, use mediation as the primary means of resolving consumer complaints. When a complaint is received by the Office, the information is reviewed to determine what action should be taken. If the complaint seems legitimate, a letter will be sent with a copy of the complaint requesting a reply from the business stating its position in regard to the complaint. When the business replies, the staff will try to determine a fair and amicable settlement. If the Office cannot help, the complainant will be referred to another agency, advised to consult with a private attorney or take the complaint to Small Claims Court. Contact the State of Alabama Office of the Attorney General, Consumer Protection Division, 560 South McDonough St., Montgomery, Ala. 36104, Tel. 205-832-5936, Toll free tel. 800-392-5658.

There is no central licensing department in Alabama which administers the licensing of occupations and professions. Individual boards determine licensing re-

quirements, grant licenses, and review complaints. For information about licensing or complaints about a licensee, contact the Office of Consumer Protection, which will send your letter on to the proper licensing board.

The Alabama Development Office offers consulting services to businesses interested in moving to or expanding in the state. Contact the Alabama Development Office, 3734 Atlanta Highway, Montgomery, Ala. 36130, Tel. 205-832-6960.

Alabama offers city or county revenue or general obligation revenue bond financing to businesses in Alabama.

The corporate income tax is 5% for business corporations and 6% for banks and financial corporations. The sales tax is 4%.

Individual income tax rate ranges from 1.5% for amounts under $1,000 to 5% for income over $5,000.

Tourist information can be obtained from the Alabama Development Office, 3734 Atlanta Highway, Montgomery, Ala. 36130, Tel. 205-832-6810 or the Bureau of Publicity and Information, State Highway Building, Montgomery, Ala. 36130, Tel. 800-633-5761.

ALASKA

The Alaska Consumer Protection Office in the Office of the Attorney General investigates consumer complaints received by its office.

Where there is evidence of an unfair trade practice, the office will seek an assurance of voluntary compliance or injunctive relief where it appears necessary. In cases where there is no unfair trade practice involved but there is a dispute between consumer and business, the office will attempt to mediate the dispute.

The Consumer Protection Office informs consumers with complaints that the office cannot act as an attorney for individual consumers; when the attorney general's office sues a business, he sues for the state to stop the practice and collect fines. A consumer is also advised that it may be in his best interest to consult a private attorney, the legal services attorney, or file a claim in the small claims court at the same time. Contact the Consumer Protection Office at the main office, 1049 W. 5th St., Suite 101, Anchorage, Alaska 99501, Tel. 907-279-0428, or a branch office in Fairbanks, Juneau, or Ketchikan.

The Alaska Department of Commerce and Economic Development, Division of Occupational Licensing, licenses occupations and businesses through the following licensing boards: electrical administrators, physicians, concert promoters, nursing, marine pilots, mortuary science, guides, dental examiners, dispensing opticians, construction contractors, collection agencies, chiropractic examiners, architects, engineers, land surveyors, psychologists and psychological associates, welding, veterinary, public accountancy, state nursing home administrators, optometry, pharmacy and physical therapy.

Requirements for licensing of each occupation or business can be obtained from the specific board, care of the Department of Commerce and Economic Development, Division of Occupational Licensing, Pouch D, Juneau, Alaska 99811, Tel. 907-465-2535. Complaints about practitioners in the above occupations or businesses can be sent directly to the Division of Occupational Licensing. Such complaints will be investigated by specialists and forwarded to the board concerned with action. Each board has the authority to revoke licenses issued by that board in case of misconduct. Other penalities, such as financial compensation or criminal prosecution, must be pursued through the courts.

The Department of Economic Development also offers consulting services to businesses interested in moving into the state. Contact the Department of Commerce and Economic Development, Pouch D, Juneau, Alaska 99811, Tel. 907-465-2500.

Alaska offers state, city or county revenue bond financing to assist new or expanding industry in the state. It also offers state loans for building construction and equipment.

The state corporate income tax rate is 5.4% for business corporations and 7% for banks and financial corporations. There is no sales tax.

Individual income taxes in Alaska range from 3% for income under $2,000 to 14.5% for income in excess of $200,000.

Tourist information about Alaska can be requested from the Division of Tourism, Department of Economic Development, Pouch E, Juneau, Alaska 99811, Tel. 907-465-2010.

ALCOHOLISM

Most states have an office of substance abuse that can offer information on programs for the prevention and treatment of alcoholism. Check the telephone directory under the state listing for alcohol, mental health or substance abuse. The National Clearinghouse for Alcohol Information can also supply the names of local education and treatment programs. For further information contact the Department of Health and Human Services, Alcohol, Drug Abuse and Mental Health Administration, National Clearinghouse for Alcohol Information, P.O. Box 2345, Rockville, Md. 20852, Tel. 301-468-2600.

The following organizations offer education about and treatment for alcoholics:

Alcoholics Anonymous, Inc.
468 Park Ave. South
New York, N.Y. 10016
212-686-3100

Veterans Administration
Alcohol and Drug
Dependent Service
810 Vermont Ave. NW
Washington, D.C. 20420
202-389-2073

The Salvation Army
120 West 14th St.
New York, N.Y. 10011
212-620-4900

ALIENS

According to the Immigration and Naturalization Service, aliens are any individuals not citizens of the United States. The Immigration and Naturalization Service divides aliens into several categories.

Immigrants are those aliens who have been admitted for permanent residence. These individuals can remain in the United States indefinitely. They can work, own property and move about freely as long as they follow the laws requiring annual registration and notification of address changes.

All immigrant aliens are required to have alien registration receipt cards (Form I-551). These cards are issued at the immigrant alien's port of entry. Aliens who wish to come to the United States for permanent residence should apply for an immigrant visa at the United States Embassy or Consulate in their home country.

Nonimmigrants are aliens who have been temporarily admitted to the United States for specific purposes and specific periods of time. Nonimmigrant alien visas are issued according to status: foreign government officials on official business and their families and servants; visitors for business or pleasure; alien students admitted to attend specified schools; temporary workers, including agricultural workers; intracompany transferees and their families and similar individuals. Except for aliens admitted specifically to work, nonimmigrant aliens may not accept employment in the United States. Students and cultural and other exchange visitors, however, may accept certain employment with written permission.

Illegal aliens have not been admitted into the United States for either temporary or permanent residence. Illegal aliens are deportable. Aliens who are in the U.S. illegally, either because of illegal entry, or expired visa, may apply to the Immigration and Naturalization Service to be declared permanent resident aliens. Deportation may be suspended and adjustment of status made in cases where aliens meet certain statutory requirements.

All nonimmigrant aliens who are legally admitted to the United States receive a Form I-94 at their port of entry. This form states the terms of entry and the length of time the alien may legally stay in the United States. All aliens who are subject to registration and are in the United States on January 1

of any year must notify the Immigration and Naturalization Service of their correct address before February 1 of that same year. Changes of address must be reported within 10 days. Address notification forms can be obtained from any U.S. post office.

Federal law restricts the number of immigrants into the U.S. to 290,000 in any one fiscal year, with the limit of 20,000 in any fiscal year for natives of any one foreign state.

Immigration quotas are set by law. Twenty percent of the total number of openings is available to qualified immigrants who are unmarried sons or daughters of citizens of the United States; 20 percent to qualified immigrants who are the spouses and unmarried sons or daughters of permanent resident aliens; 10 percent of the total plus any openings not used by the above go to members of the professions or those who, because of exceptional ability in the sciences or arts, will substantially benefit the United States and whose services are sought by an employer in the United States; 10 percent of the total immigration quota, plus any openings not filled by the first three categories goes to qualified immigrants who are the married sons or daughters of citizens of the U.S.; 24 percent of the total number, plus any openings not filled by the first four categories goes to the brothers or sisters of citizens of the United States; 10

percent of the total number is next available for skilled or unskilled labor not of a temporary or seasonal nature and of whom there exists a shortage in the United States. The remaining 6 percent can be made available by the attorney general for the conditional entry of refugees from any communist or communist-dominated country or country where there has been a natural disaster.

Questions about United States laws regarding all categories of aliens can be referred to the nearest regional or district Immigration and Naturalization service office or the Immigration and Naturalization Service, Department of Justice, 425 I St. NW, Washington, D.C. 20536, Tel. 202-655-4000.

ANGUILLA-ST. KITTS-NEVIS

Anguilla, St. Kitts and Nevis are under the same administration, and regulations are the same for the three islands. Proof of citizenship is needed for U.S. citizens traveling to any of these islands. A passport or visa is not required. There are no health requirements for entry unless arriving from an infected area. Pets may be brought to the islands if permission is obtained from the local government. A letter requesting permission should be sent to the Government Veterinarian Officer, Basseterre, St. Kitts, West Indies. The mone-

tary unit is the East Caribbean dollar. Persons traveling on business must declare all money in their possession upon arrival, but otherwise there are no restrictions on the import or export of currency. English is the official language of the islands. To drive a car, an International Driving License is required.

Anguilla, St. Kitts and Nevis are members of the British Commonwealth. Most imports are covered by an open general license and there are few exchange regulations.

For further information contact a British diplomatic mission or the Caribbean Tourism Association, 20 East 46 St., New York, N.Y. 10017, Tel. 212-682-0435.

ANIMAL EXPERIMENTS

Federal legislation has set minimum standards of humane treatment of dogs, cats, primates, rabbits, hamsters and guinea pigs in dealer's premises and in laboratories. The U.S. Department of Agriculture enforces standards and inspects laboratories.

The actual conduct of animal experiments is still outside the specific mandatory provisions of federal law. Requirements stress that it is the responsibility of the institutional veterinarian to prevent suffering through the humane design of experiments or through the use of drugs to relieve pain or anxiety.

Suspected cruelty to experimental animals should be reported to inspectors of the Department of Agriculture. Contact the nearest USDA office or the Department of Agriculture Animal and Plant Health Inspection Service, 14th St. and Independence Ave. SW, Washington, D.C. 20250, Tel. 202-447-3977.

ANIMAL WELFARE

All states have some form of law banning cruelty to animals, though they vary widely in content. The following categories are most often found in state laws relating to animal welfare: cruelty, transportation, fighting, experimentation, disposal, licensing and regulation of pets, licensing of facilities handling animals, poisoning, abandonment, endangered species, trapping and humane slaughter.

Cities or counties generally are responsible for providing some type of animal shelter, though the shelter may be operated by a nonprofit organization such as the American Society for the Prevention of Cruelty to Animals or the Humane Society.

Information about a state's provisions for animal welfare can be obtained from local authorities, the state veterinarian's office, the local animal welfare agency or the following national organizations: American Society for the Prevention of Cruelty to Animals, 441 East 92nd St., New York, New York 10028, Tel.: 212-876-7700 or the

Humane Society of the United States, 2100 L St. NW, Washington, D.C. 20037, Tel. 202-452-1100.

See also: ANIMAL EXPERIMENTS, ANIMALS: CRUELTY TO

ANIMALS: CRUELTY TO

Cruelty to animals is a criminal offense in all states. Any citizen who witnesses an incident can call the police to intervene or can swear out a warrant for criminal prosecution by a local law enforcement agency after the event. If the police—or a particular police officer—refuse to act on a cruelty to animals complaint, a person can call the local prosecutor's office (usually located in the county courthouse) to act on the cruelty case and can report the lack of police action.

The identity of the complainant will be revealed only if he or she agrees to be identified and to appear in court. Many cruelty to animal complaints are settled out of court by an investigation of the cruelty and recommendations on how to correct it.

Cruelty to animals can also be reported to the local humane society or the American Society for the Prevention of Cruelty to Animals. Both will generally offer assistance. For information on local legislation contact the local humane society or the ASPCA Humane Law Enforcement Division, 441 East 92nd St., New York, N.Y. 10028, Tel. 212-876-7700; or The Humane Society of the United

States, 2100 L St. NW, Washington, D.C. 20037, Tel. 202-452-1100.

ANIMALS: STRAY

Stray animals should be reported to the local humane society or the American Society for the Prevention of Cruelty to Animals. Strays that appear dangerous should be reported to the local police.

ANTIGUA

Proof of identity is required for U.S. citizens traveling to Antigua; neither valid passport nor visa is required. There are no health requirements if arriving from the United States or nearby islands, but a yellow fever innoculation is needed if arriving from an infected area. Pets are not allowed and are subject to quarantine if brought to the island. The local currency is the East Caribbean dollar (EC$). Business travelers must declare all money in their possession upon arrival, but otherwise there are no restrictions on the import or export of currency. Antigua levies a departure tax of EC$5 if leaving for a nearby island or EC$8 if going to another destination. The official language is English. To drive a car obtain a temporary license from the local police, which is available upon presentation of a valid license and a fee of EC$10.

Antigua is a member of the British Commonwealth. Most imports are covered by an open general license and few exchange restrictions are in force.

For further information contact a British diplomatic mission or the Antigua Department of Tourism and Trade, 610 Fifth Ave., New York, N.Y. 10020, Tel. 212-541-4117.

ANTI-SEMITISM

The Anti-Defamation League of the B'nai B'rith seeks to combat anti-Semitism and racism and fights discrimination in housing, education and employment. For further information contact B'nai B'rith International, 1640 Rhode Island Ave. NW, Washington, D.C. 20036, Tel. 202-857-6663.

APPLIANCES: COMPLAINTS

Complaints about appliance safety should be referred to the Consumer Product Safety Commission. Complaints can be taken either by telephone or in writing. They are forwarded to a staff investigator who decides whether or not the complaint should be pursued. Complaints not investigated are entered on the CPSC data base for use should that product ever come under investigation.

Complaints about appliance safety or other problems with appliances can also be sent to the Major Appliance Consumer Action Panel (MACAP), which is sponsored by the Association of Home Appliance Manufacturers, Gas Appliance Manufacturers Association and the National Retail Merchants Association. The panel is a group of independent consumer experts who review consumer complaints and comments.

MACAP forwards individual complaints to a senior executive of the manufacturer of the product involved. If the action taken by the company does not satisfy the consumer, MACAP may make specific recommendations to the manufacturer. Major appliances under MACAP's jurisdiction include: compactors, dehumidifiers, dishwashers, garbage disposal units, gas incinerators, home laundry equipment, microwave ovens, ranges, refrigerators and freezers, room air conditioners and water heaters.

Contact MACAP at 20 North Wacker Dr., Chicago, Ill. 60606, Tel. 312-984-5858, toll free: 800-621-0475, or the Consumer Product Safety Commission, Washington, D.C. 20207, Tel. 202-634-7700, toll free: 800-492-2937.

APPLIANCES: STANDARDS

The National Bureau of Standards develops safety standards for appliances and rates energy efficiency. For further information contact the Department of Commerce, National Bureau of Standards, Washington, D.C. 20234, Tel. 301-921-3181.

ARBITRATION: CONSUMER

Many consumer complaints in the United States are resolved by arbitration between the complainant and the company or individuals against whom the complaint is made. Arbitration is voluntary and depends on the agreement of the parties to arbitrate.

The American Arbitration Association (AAA) settles disputes between consumers and businesses, companies or professionals. An arbitration clause is frequently used in contracts. It provides for arbitration of any controversy arising from the contract. The AAA suggests the following wording for such a contract clause:

Any controversy or claim arising out of or relating to this contract, or the breach thereof, shall be settled by arbitration in accordance with the Rules of the American Arbitration Association, and judgment upon the award rendered by the Arbitrator(s) may be entered in any Court having jurisdiction thereof.

Even if a contract does not contain the arbitration clause, or if there is no written contract, AAA can still arbitrate the dispute if both parties agree.

The AAA does not decide cases, but it provides a list of from which the parties involved can select impartial arbitrators and mediators. In addition, AAA will supply full administrative services at reasonable fees. It will supply independent arbitrators who use specific rules and procedures determined by AAA who frequently serve without compensation, offering their judgment as a public service. The administrator assigned by AAA sees the case through each step from initiation to final settlement. AAA settlements are binding in courts of law.

Contact the regional AAA office or the American Arbitration Association, 140 West 51 St., New York, N.Y. 10020, Tel. 212-977-2000.

See BETTER BUSINESS BUREAUS

ARCHITECTS

Each state, including the District of Columbia, requires that architects be licensed by its state architectural registration board according to its state regulations. The National Council of Architectural Registration Boards (NCARB) serves as a clearinghouse for states' regulations for legal registration or licensing. All 50 state boards are members of NCARB and work together to standardize the examination of applicants.

Applicants for a license must have either a bachelor of architecture degree combined with three years of experience in an architect's office, or a master's degree in architecture combined with two years of such experience. Most states also allow additional experience to substitute for part or all of the required formal education.

All qualified applicants for licenses must pass a lengthy examination. Two sections are offered: the qualifying test and the professional examination. A large majority of states require the holder of an accredited or ap-proved degree in architecture to pass only the professional examination. Most require applicants for licensure without a professional degree in architecture to pass the qualifying test as well as the professional test. Individuals should check with their particular state architectural registration board for exact requirements, since education and experience requirements do vary from state to state. Architects who are not licensed may work under the supervision of a licensed architect.

Architects who have been licensed in one state can apply to NCARB for certification. If the architect is approved for certification and pays the required fee, NCARB will keep on file the individual's education, training, experience and current state registration or licensure. The architect can then have his or her NCARB records transmitted to any member state registration board in support of an application for reciprocal registration in that state.

NCARB is in the process of establishing registration procedures on an international basis. NCARB currently has reciprocity agreements with the United Kingdom and Australia.

The American Institute of Architects is another professional organization with over 35,000 architects in 200 local chapters. The institute attempts to shape policy on national issues, to promote a code of ethics and to offer continuing education and training for architects.

Complaints about architects' services should be made to the state architectural registration board. Consult the entry on the individual state for the address of the state agency administering the state licensing boards, or consult NCARB for the proper address. States boards have procedures for reviewing or investigating complaints and disciplining or revoking the license of an architect who has violated state laws. Civil or criminal penalties against an architect, however, cannot be obtained through the state board. Consult a lawyer.

Contact The National Council of Architectural Registration Boards at 1735 New York Ave. NW, Suite 700, Washington, D.C. 20006, Tel. 202-783-6500. Contact the American Institute of Architects at 1735 New York Ave., NW, Washington, D.C. 20006, Tel. 202-626-7300.

ARGENTINA

A valid passport is required for all U.S. citizens traveling to Argentina. A tourist visa is not necessary unless a stay of longer than three months is planned. Visas are required for business travelers, however, and may be obtained at the Argentine Embassy in Washington or any of the consulates in Baltimore, Chicago, Houston, Los Angeles, Miami, New Orleans, New York or San Francisco. The address of the Embassy of the Argentine Republic is 1600 New Hampshire Ave. NW, Washington, D.C. 20009, Tel. 202-387-0705. Persons traveling on business should present a letter from their company with their visa application detailing the nature of their business. A business visa is usually valid up to three months. A vaccination certificate is required for entry into Argentina. Persons bringing pets must provide a certificate of shots to the Embassy or consulate along with a photo of the animal not earlier than 10 days before the planned arrival in Argentina. There is a fee of $8 to get the pet into the country.

Tourists may bring any amount of foreign currency or pesos (the Argentine currency) in or out of the country. Spanish is the most prevalent language but English is becoming increasingly widespread. An International Driving License is required for driving, which must be stamped upon arrival by the Automovil Club Argentino.

Individuals planning to import or export should have a resident agent in Argentina to deal with the local industry and the government. The government has restricted some imports by placing high tarriffs on them. All trade agreements are subject to Argentine law, and foreign exchange is controlled by the Central Bank. Argentina is a member of the Latin American Free Trade Association (LAFTA) and the Organization of American

States (OAS). Credit cards, though accepted at major hotels and shops are not generally used in Argentina.

The U.S. Embassy in Argentina is located at 4300 Colombia, Buenos Aires, Argentina 1425, Tel. 774 7611. Tourist information can be had by calling 212-397-1413.

For further business information contact the Argentine-American Chamber of Commerce, McAlpin House, 50 West 34 St., New York, N.Y. 10001, Tel. 212-564-3855.

ARIZONA

In Arizona consumers can refer their complaints involving misrepresentation and deceptive business practices in connection with the sale of goods and services to the Office of the Attorney General, Consumer Fraud/Financial Fraud Division, 1700 W. Washington, Room 207, Phoenix, Ariz. 85007, Tel. 602-255-5763. Complaints about quality of workmanship are not handled by this Division because they are generally not fraud, and those complaints should be pursued privately through small claims courts or the Better Business Bureau.

When the Division receives a complaint it will contact the company or business involved and ask that they provide the Division with a response.

The Consumer Fraud/Financial Fraud Division cannot take court action on one individual's behalf, but will investigate and take action on businesses which are the subject of numerous complaints.

The Division has a branch office located in Tucson.

There is no special department of licensing in Arizona which administers licensing boards. Each occupation or profession has a licensing board which sets licensing requirements, licenses applicants, and receives complaints about licensees. Inquiries about licensing or complaints about licensees can be referred to the Arizona Office of the Attorney General, Consumer Fraud Division, which will send the letter on to the proper licensing board.

Businesses interested in moving to, or expanding in Arizona, can contact the Arizona Governor's Office of Economic Planning and Development, Phoenix, Ariz. 85007, Tel. 602-255-3833.

Arizona offers city or county revenue bond financing to industry expanding in or moving to Arizona.

The corporate income tax rate in Arizona is 2.5% for amounts up to $1,000 increasing to 10.5% for corporate income over $6,000. The state sales tax is 4% for retailers.

The individual income tax ranges from 2% for income under $1,000 to 8% for income over $6,000.

Request tourist information about Arizona from the Office of Tourism, Governor's Office of Economic Planning and Development, Phoenix, Ariz. 85007, Tel.

602-255-3618.

ARKANSAS

The Consumer Protection Division of the Attorney General's Office is the major state government agency responsible for protecting the citizens from consumer fraud.

The Division receives, reviews and investigates consumer complaints, with the purpose of settling disputes between consumers and businesses. Consumers who think that they have been defrauded or deceived can write or call the Consumer Protection Division and talk with a counselor. If there appears to be a violation of Arkansas law, the counselor will send the complainant a written consumer complaint form.

When a complaint is received in writing it is assigned to an investigator who talks with the business or individual against whom the complaint was filed, and with the complainant. The investigator will recommend either that the business settle the complaint and help with the settlement or will recommend that the consumer drop the complaint.

If the business is unwilling to settle a complaint considered valid by the Division, the investigator will turn the complaint over to an attorney in the Division who will decide whether or not the Consumer Protection Division will file a lawsuit against the business. If the Division decides to pursue a lawsuit it does not cost the con-

sumer anything, and the Division will request the court to order the business to give the consumer back his money.

Complaints handled by the Arkansas Consumer Protection Division generally involve possible violations of the state consumer protection code which prohibits false or deceptive practices in the advertisement of goods or services; pyramid schemes; failure or refusal of a retailer to give a customer purchasing an appliance or mechanical equipment the record of warranty and a statement of service availability; failure to identify flood, water, fire or accidentally damaged goods and the type of damage and other practices which constitute consumer fraud.

Contact the Consumer Protection Division, Office of the Attorney General, Justice Building, Little Rock, Ark. 72201, Toll free Tel. 800-482-8982. In Pulaski County call 371-2341.

There is no central licensing authority in Arkansas or central administrative board. Licensing is handled by a number of Boards and Commissions which are responsible for setting standards and requirements, as well as establishing fees in their particular field. Any requests for information about licensing in Arkansas or complaints about licensees can be sent to the State of Arkansas, Office of the Governor, State Capitol, Little Rock, Ark. 72201, Tel. 501-371-2345. Several caseworkers are on the governor's staff to assist citizens in their contacts with state government and will refer inquiries to the proper commission or board.

Industries moving to Arkansas can receive financing in the form of municipal and county bonds for up to 100% of the cost of construction at favorable interest rates. Arkansas also offers state funded pre-employment and on-the-job training programs designed to keep start-up or major expansion cost to a minimum.

The Department of Economic Development will help interested businesses find a site or existing facility and act as a consulting team, free of charge, on all aspects of operation in Arkansas. Contact the Department of Economic Development, One State Capitol Mall, Little Rock, Ark. 72201, Tel. 501-371-1121.

Request tourist information about Arkansas from the Department of Parks and Tourism, #1 Capitol Mall, Little Rock, Ark. 72201, Tel. 501-371-1191.

ARTHRITIS

Arthritis affects 30 million Americans in one form or another. The Arthritis Foundation, founded in 1948, seeks the cause of the disease and cure. The 73 chapters of the foundation support research, finance training for medical specialists, provide community services to patients and their families work to improve treatment techniques and Inform

doctors of the latest developments in the study of arthritis. Local chapters provide information and sponsor community services, including clinics. In addition, they can refer individuals to local arthritis specialists.

Contact the local chapter or write the Arthritis Foundation, 3400 Peachtree Road, N.E., Suite 1101, Atlanta, Ga. 30326, Tel. 404-266-0795.

ATHLETICS: (AMATEUR)

The international governing body for amateur athletics is the International Amateur Athletic Federation. The governing body in the United States is the Amateur Athletic Union (AAU), which has developmental programs in 22 sports. The AAU is the Olympic governing body for eight sports: track and field, aquatics, bobsledding, boxing, judo, luge, weightlifting and wrestling. Sports not under the AAU jurisdiction usually have their own governing bodies (see individual sports).

The National Collegiate Athletic Association regulates collegiate athletics in the United States. It conducts regional and national collegiate athletic contests and cooperates with other amateur athletic organizations in the promotion and conduct of national and international events. Contact the National Headquarters of the Amateur Athletic Union at 3400 West 86th St. Indianapolis, Ind. 46268, Tel. 317-872-2900, or the National Collegiate Athletic Associa-

tion, U.S. Highway 50 and Nall Ave., P.O. Box 1906, Shawnee Mission, Kan. 66222, Tel. 913-384-3220.
See also: Athletics: Wheelchair, Special Olympics and specific sport

ATHLETICS: WHEELCHAIR

Sports for those confined to wheelchairs is organized and governed by the National Wheelchair Athletic Association (NWAA). The association governs all wheelchair sports in the U.S. except wheelchair basketball which is under the aegis of the National Wheelchair Basketball Association of the U.S.

The NWAA develops all rules governing wheelchair athletics; maintains wheelchair athletics records and rules on claims for new records. It also selects sites for national championship meets and sanctions regional meets.

Wheelchair sports governed by the NWAA include archery, field events, slalom, table tennis, swimming, track, weightlifting and the pentathalon. Member athletes of the NWAA compete in regional events and the annual National Wheelchair Games. National champions are eligible for the U.S. Wheelchair Paralympic team which competes in the international wheelchair olympics, and the Pan American Wheelchair Games which consist of teams from North, South and Central American countries.

The NWAA has 15 regions in the U.S. with membership ranging from the junior division for youngsters between 8-and-14-years-old to the masters division for adults over 40-years of age.

Membership in the NWAA is open to all men and women in wheelchairs, and officials and coaches either involved in or interested in wheelchair sports. Affiliate membership is open to any interested individual. Members must pay an initiation fee and annual dues. The NWAA is located at Nassau Community College, Garden City, N.Y. 11530. The telephone number is 516-222-7560.
See also: Special Olympics

AUSTRALIA

A valid passport and a visa are required for U.S. citizens traveling to Australia for a stay of up to six months. Visa applications must be accompanied by a passport and one photograph. Business travelers will also need a letter from their company detailing the nature of business to be conducted and with whom, and the projected length of stay in Australia. There are no health requirements for entry. It is not advisable to bring pets as they are subject to a quarantine of at least six months. The local currency is the Australian dollar and there are no restrictions on the amount of local or foreign currency that can be taken in or out of the country. English is the official language of Australia. To drive a car, an American driver's license will suffice.

Agents and import companies generally handle exports to Australia. Licenses are not required for most goods and foreign exchange is usually arranged through letters of credit.

The Embassy of Australia is located at 1601 Massachusetts Ave. NW, Washington, D.C. 20036, Tel. 202-797-3959. There are consulates in Los Angeles, Chicago, New York, Honolulu and San Francisco.

The U.S. Embassy in Australia is located at Moonah Place, Yarralumla, Canberra, Australia, Tel. 733711. There are American consulates in Sydney, Melbourne and Perth.

For additional tourist information contact the Australian Tourist Commission, 1270 Avenue of the Americas, New York, N.Y. 10020, Tel. 212-489-7550.

For business information contact the Australian Trade Commission, Australian Consulate General, 636 Fifth Ave., New York, N.Y. 10111, Tel. 212-245-4000.

AUSTRIA

A valid passport is required for travel to Austria. Whether traveling on business or pleasure, no visa is needed for a stay of up to three months. For longer stays a visa is necessary along with a letter from the Austrian company describing the nature of the business. Apply for visas at the Embassy of Austria, 2343 Massachusetts Ave. NW, Washington, D.C. 20008, Tel. 202-483-4474, or at Austrian consulates located in Chicago, Los Angeles and New York. No vaccination certificates are required for entry unless an individual is arriving from an infected area. Pets are allowed as long as owners have proof of the required shots. The currency is the Austrian schilling. Any amount of schillings or of foreign currency may be imported into Austria, but only 15,000 schillings may be exported. German is the official language.

There are no restrictions on trade and no import licenses are required, but it is advisable to have a resident agent to deal with the local businesses and government.

The American Embassy in Austria is located at IX Boltzmanngasse 16 A-1091, Vienna, Austria, Tel. 222-31-55-11.

For further tourist information contact the Austrian National Tourist Office, 545 Fifth Avenue, New York N.Y., Tel. 212-697-0651.

For further business information contact the Austrian Trade Commission, 845 Third Ave., New York, N.Y. 10022, Tel. 212-421-5250.

AUTISTIC CHILDREN

The National Society for Autistic Children is a national organization which offers help to families with autistic children. It is located at 101 Richmond St., Huntington, W. Va. 25702, Tel. 304-523-1912. Another is the Council for Exceptional Children, 1920 Association Drive, Reston, Va. 22091, Tel. 703-620-3660.

The National Institute of Mental Health, 5600 Fishers Lane, Rockville, Md., Tel. 301-443-3724, has information on state and local programs.
See also: Children: Social Security Benefits, Disabled Children: Education

AUTOMOBILES: ABANDONED

Abandoned vehicles should be reported to the local police department. Include the color, make and license number in your report. If the car has been reported stolen, the police will notify the owner. Abandoned cars will be removed from the street after a period of time if they have not been claimed.

AUTOMOBILES: COMPLAINTS

Complaints about new cars should be first addressed to the dealer who sold the vehicle. If no satisfaction is obtained, contact the consumer division of the auto-maker. The National Automobile Dealers Association sponsors a series of consumer action panels which also handle complaints, but as a last resort. Generally, AUTO-CAPS, as they are called, will not deal with a case unless the consumer shows that he or she has made a sincere effort to settle the problem through all other appropriate channels. Complaints to an AUTOCAP should be made in writing. For information about AUTOCAPS in a particular region, contact the National Automobile Dealers Association, 8400 West

Park, Dr., McLean Va. 22101, Tel. 703-821-7000.

AUTOMOBILES: FUEL ECONOMY

Mandatory automobile fuel economy standards for model years 1978 and beyond are set by the National Highway Traffic Safety Administration. The administration assesses penalties to manufacturers who do not comply with the minimum standards and allows credits to those who exceed the average fuel economy standards. 400 Seventh Street SW, Washington, D.C. 20590, Tel. 202-426-1828.

AUTOMOBILES: LEASING

Car leasing agreements are under the jurisdiction of the Federal Trade Commission (FTC). Individual complaints cannot be handled by the commission but are compiled, and a sufficient number of complaints about a particular car dealer or general practice of dealers may cause the FCC to investigate.

Car leasing is also regulated by the states. Consumer complaints will usually be handled individually by the consumer protection division in each state. In addition, the state attorney general's office might be interested in investigating cases of unfair business practices. Contact the state consumer protection division (See individual state entries), the nearest FTC regional office or the Federal Trade Commission, Pennsylvania Ave. at Sixth St. NW, Washington, D.C. 20580, Tel. 202-523-3830.

AUTOMOBILES: REGISTRATION

Cars are generally registered through the state or county department of motor vehicles. Applications for certificate of title are processed by the same department.

Car license plates are issued each year by a state, or decals provided to update them. Owners of cars must pay the fee for a new license plate or decal each year.
See also: LICENSE PLATES: SPECIAL

AUTOMOBILES: REPAIR

Most states do not require mechanics to be licensed, but a few states, auto manufacturers, oil companies and other industry-related groups do test mechancs' skill and proficiency and do certify competency.

Before taking cars for repairs drivers should call the local consumer affairs office or Better Business Bureau to see if any complaints have been lodged against a particular service or to ask if a firm guarantees its work. If the auto repair shop fails to make satisfactory repairs and ignores complaints, contact the city, state or local consumer office. Another source of help are AUTOCAPS, auto dealer associations that handle automobile consumer complaints.

Contact the National Automobile Dealers Association, 8400 West Park Dr., McLean Va. 22101, Tel. 703-821-7000.

AUTOMOBILES: SAFETY

The U.S. Department of Transportation's National Highway Traffic Safety Administration regulates motor vehicle safety. NHTSA issues standards based on the level of performance required under specific tests that apply to all vehicles, domestic and foreign, manufactured for sale in the United States. The administration enforces compliance with the standards through a testing program, through manufacturer recall campaigns, through imposition of civil penalties and through court action when necessary.

NHTSA operates a 24-hour, toll-free hotline for consumer inquiries and complaints. Consumers who want to report a problem are mailed a postage-paid questionnaire. When the questionnaire is completed and returned, it is given to the agency's safety defect identification program; a copy is also mailed to the manufacturer of the vehicle with an accompanying letter requesting assistance in resolving the problem. Many consumer complaints have been resolved because of this intervention, even though NHTSA cannot investigate individual consumer complaints.

Vehicle recall information is also available from a hotline operator, as are referrals to other federal, state and local agencies that may be able to help.

For further information contact the Department of Transportation, National Highway Traffic Safety Administration, 400 Seventh St. SW, Washington, D.C. 20590, Tel. 202-426-0670. The toll-free number is 800-424-9393; in Alaska and Hawaii 800-426-0123.

AUTOMOBILES: USED

The seller of a used car is required by federal law to disclose the number of miles the car has been driven and to sign a statement that the odometer has not been altered in any way. If a buyer finds that the odometer has been tampered with, he or she can sue for damages plus court costs and attorney's fees. Consult a private attorney. Further details about federal odometer laws can be obtained from the National Highway Traffic Safety Administration (NHTSA). Unfortunately, the NHTSA cannot handle individual complaints.

Contact the NHTSA at 400 Seventh St. SW, Washington, D.C. 20590, Tel. 202-426-1828.

B

BAHAMAS

A tourist going to the Bahamas needs no passport or visa, only proof of citizenship (birth certificate or voter registration card) for a stay of up to one month. For longer stays, an extension is obtainable in the Bahamas. A business traveller needs a Work Permit if he is expecting to actually transact business while there. Work Permits are obtainable through the Bahamian Embassy or consulate or from the Director of Immigration, Immigration Dept., P.O. Box 831, Nassau, Bahamas. There are no health requirements for travel to the Bahamas. Those wishing to bring pets, will have to apply to the Bahamian Agriculture Department, which will take several weeks to process an application before issuing a permit. The currency in the Bahamas is the Bahamian dollar. There is no limit on the amount of foreign or local currency allowed into the country, but an individual may only take out 70 Bahamian dollars. English is the official language of the Bahamas. An International Driving License is required. For residence or permission to work in the Bahamas, a visa must be obtained from the Embassy of the Commonwealth of the Bahamas, 600 New Hampshire Ave., NW, Washington, D.C. 20037, Tel. 202-338-3940.

The Bahamas is a member of the British Commonwealth and restricts certain imports. The imports that are allowed need licensing, which is usually handled by resident agents. All foreign exchange transactions are handled through authorized local banks which are subject to Bahamian law.

The American Embassy in the

Bahamas is located at the Mosmar Building, Queen St., P.O. Box N-8197, Nassau, Tel. 809-322-1700, Telex 20-138.

For further tourist information contact the Bahamas Tourist Office, 30 Rockefeller Plaza, New York, N.Y. 10020, Tel. 212-757-1611.

BANK ACCOUNTS: FEDERALLY INSURED

The Federal Deposit Insurance Corporation (FDIC) was established in 1933, and its supervisory program has resulted in a reduction of bank failures. From 1934 to 1942 failures averaged 43 per year. From 1948 to 1980 bank failures ranged from zero to 16 per year, with a total of 178 for the 38 year period.

The FDIC provides insurance coverage for total bank deposits up to a statutory limitation of $100,000 per person per bank in various accounts such as savings and checking. Individuals in a joint account are still restricted to the $100,000 total despite the number of persons or the amount in the account.

To be insured by FDIC a bank must meet high standards of safety and soundness in its banking practices. Regular bank examinations are made by federal or state agencies to ensure adherence to these standards.

Unless a bank failure occurs, bank depositors usually are not involved with the insurance protection or bank supervisory program

except to know that insurance coverage exists. FDIC is either involved on a consistent basis with the banks that it supervises or is informed by other supervisory agencies when a bank develops serious problems that could lead to liquidation. If an insured bank then experiences financial difficulties requiring that they be closed in order to liquidate their assets, FDIC will make payments up to $100,000 per person within a few days after the final closing. Depositors are notified by the bank or FDIC of the procedure to recover their insured deposits. If a depositor has more than $100,000 on deposit in an insured bank that has closed, he or she will share in any proceeds from the liquidation of the bank along with other general creditors on a pro rata basis.

A bank's membership in FDIC can be terminated if a bank continues to engage in unsound banking practices. Notice is always given to depositors before termination of FDIC insurance. The insurance protection does not stop immediately after the FDIC terminates membership but continues up to two years on deposits existing at the date of FDIC termination and covers the maximum amount, less withdrawals.

The FDIC insures deposits in national and most state banks, including commercial and mutual savings banks. Savings and Loan Associations are insured by the Federal Savings and Loan Insurance Corporation. Credit unions are covered by the National Credit Union Administration.

Contact the FDIC through its local offices in major cities, or the Federal Deposit Insurance Corporation, 550 17th St. NW, Washington, D.C. 20429, Tel. (toll free) 800-424-5488.

See also: SAVINGS AND LOAN ASSOCIATIONS, CREDIT UNIONS, BANK SUPERVISION

BANK LOAN

To obtain a personal bank loan the applicant should contact the loan officer at the particular bank. The loan officer will want to know the applicant's salary, what the loan money will be used for, and any collateral that the applicant has for the loan. The bank will also want to establish a payment schedule and will check the applicant's credit history through a credit bureau.

By federal law the bank is required to disclose the annual percentage rate on the loan. Discrimination in obtaining credit is prohibited by federal law on the basis of age, sex, marital status, race, color, religion, national origin or receipt of public assistance. If the applicant is denied a bank loan, the law requires that the bank send notification in writing and that it give the applicant the right to request the reason for the denial.

A special office in the Federal Reserve Bank, the Division of Consumer Affairs, handles consumers' complaints about bank loan applications or payments. The division will respond within 15 days, answering questions or reporting on the status of the complaint. The Federal Reserve will forward complaints to another agency if it does not supervise the institution involved.

Contact the Federal Reserve Bank serving the district in which the bank is located or the Division of Consumer Affairs, Board of Governors of the Federal Reserve System, Twentieth St. at Constitution Ave. NW, Washington, D.C. 20551, Tel. 202-452-3000.

See also: CREDIT RECORDS

BANKRUPTCY

Bankruptcy is a declaration by a federal district court that an individual or company is insolvent. Almost anyone can declare bankruptcy voluntarily. Creditors also can commence an action for voluntary bankruptcy if the creditor is insolvent and has committed an act of bankruptcy such as an assignment for the benefit of creditors.

Bankruptcy is a formal and technical action beginning with a proceeding to have the debtor declared a bankrupt. The courts will then usually appoint a receiver to gather the property of the bankrupt. The assets of the bankrupt include all the debtor's property owned on the date bankruptcy is filed as well as any property transferred to defraud creditors. Wages or other assets not yet earned are not included. The debtor is al-

lowed to keep certain posses-
sions. These vary from state to
state and under special federal
laws.

The bankruptcy discharges the
debtor from all of his debts that
can be discharged by law. The
bankrupt will remain responsible
for such debts as taxes, child support and the costs of the proceedings.

An individual does not legally
need a lawyer to file for bankruptcy. The papers necessary for
filing may be obtained from a legal
stationery store. The court will
charge a filing fee for processing.
It is often wise to have a lawyer to
prevent future problems. Consult
a lawyer or a legal aid society for
further information.

BANKS: ACCOUNTS IN FOREIGN BANKS

There is no federal restriction
on United States citizens holding
foreign bank accounts. A U.S. citizen who has authority over an account in a foreign bank, however,
must file an annual report regarding the account if its aggregate
value in the previous year ex-
ceeded $1000.

The principle purpose for collecting this information is for
criminal, tax or regulatory investigations or proceedings. This information may be released to any department or agency of the federal
government upon the request of
the head of the department or
agency involved in such an investigation or proceeding.

Failure to file a report or filing a
fradulent report with the Treasury
Department can result in civil or
criminal penalties, including a fine
of not more than $500,000 or im-
prisonment of not more than five
years.

Treasury Department Form
90-22.1 is used for reporting a foreign bank account.

Contact the Department of the
Treasury, P.O. Box 28309, Central
Station, Washington, D.C. 20005
Tel. 202-566-2000. See also: Swiss
Bank Accounts

BANKS: COMPLAINTS

The Office of Bank Customer Affairs receives, investigates and
disposes of consumer complaints
against state-chartered banks
supervised by the Federal Deposit
Insurance Corp. (FDIC). The office
can recommend that the FDIC institute proceedings against member and non-member banks which
flout its regulations on equal
credit opportunity, fair housing
lending, bank advertising, etc.
Complaints should be directed to
the FDIC, Office of Bank Customer
Affairs, 550 17th St. NW, Washington, D.C. 10429, Tel. 202-389-4512.

BANKS: PRIME RATE

In commercial banks the prime
rate is the interest rate charged
leading corporate clients for the
very best credits of short-term maturity. The prime rate is determined by each bank as a part of its
lending policy and is influenced
by the general level of money

rates, the availability of excess reserves, and business conditions.

The prime rate charged by the Federal Reserve Bank on eligible commercial paper and on advances to member banks secured by U.S. Government securities influences the prime rate charged by commercial banks.

See also: BANK LOANS

BANKS: SAVINGS ACCOUNTS

Commercial banks, savings banks, savings and loan institutions and credit unions all offer savings accounts. The interest compounded on savings accounts varies from institution to institution and on different types of accounts in the same institution. Federal regulations allow interest rates to be computed in more than 50 ways, making it difficult to determine which type of savings accounts offers the most interest.

Federal laws sets the maximum interest rates that banks and other savings institutions can pay, but there is no minimum. It is advisable to compare interest rates and the methods of computation before deciding where to open a savings account.

Complaints and questions about savings accounts can be referred to the Federal Reserve System. The Federal Reserve System supervises only state-chartered banks that are members of the Federal Reserve System but will refer inquiries about other institutions to the appropriate agency. Mail inquiries and complaints to the Director, Division of Consumer Affairs, Board of Governors of the Federal Reserve System, 20th St. and Constitution Ave. NW, Washington, D.C. 20551, Tel. 202-452-3204

BANK SUPERVISION

Banks in the United States are generally examined by the responsible regulatory agency at least every 18 months. Banks with known supervisory or financial problems receive a full-scale examination at least once every twelve months.

The Federal Deposit Insurance Corporation is responsible for supervising and regulating insured, state-chartered banks that are not members of the Federal Reserve System and insured, state-licensed branches of foreign banks. The Office of the Comptroller of the Currency and the Board of Governors of the Federal Reserve System supervise national banks, federal branches of foreign banks and state-chartered banks that are members of the Federal Reserve System. State banks are also supervised and regulated by state banking authorities.

Each examination covers the adequacy of the bank's capital, the quality of its assets, the availability of adequate funds, the effectiveness of external and internal controls, the use of sound accounting procedures, the adequacy of fidelity bond coverage against extraordinary losses resulting from dishonest acts of officers or employees and the overall quality of the bank's management.

Examiners from the regulatory agencies offer bank managers constructive suggestions for improving policies and practices. Should a bank persist in practices that the regulatory agency considers unsound or in violation of a law or regulation, the regulatory board may issue a cease and desist order against the bank or one or more of its officers. Further penalties could be ordered by a court if necessary, and, in extreme cases, criminal proceedings could be initiated by the regulatory agency.

Banks are also required to prepare annual reports of income and condition for the regulatory agency. These are available to the general public upon request to the bank concerned. Individual depositors are not generally involved in bank supervision, but they may be interested in the bank's assets, liabilities and other financial information available in the bank's annual report. This information can be relied upon as accurate, since it is also examined by the regulatory agency concerned.

Contact the state banking department for state supervised banks or the appropriate federal agency for further information.
See also: BANK DEPOSITS: FEDERALLY INSURED, BANKS: STATE, BANKS: NATIONAL, BANKS: ACCOUNTS IN FOREIGN BANKS, SAVINGS AND LOAN ASSOCIATIONS.

BAPTIST CHURCHES

Baptists are the largest Protestant denomination in the United States, with over 23 million members in the various conventions that make up the denomination. The largest organization in the denomination is the Southern Baptist Convention, which has over 13 million members. Baptists are united in their belief that baptism should only be performed on believers and that total immersion is necessary. The organization of each convention varies. Generally, the various conventions within the denomination are organized in district associations and state conventions. An executive committee, chosen by the state and local groups, coordinates national work within each convention.
For further information contact the Executive Committee of the Southern Baptist Convention located at 460 James Robertson Pkwy., Nashville, Tenn. 37219, Tel. 615-244-2355; the National Baptist Convention of America located at 1230 Hendricks Ave., Jacksonville, Fla. 32207, Tel. 904-396-2351; and the American Baptist Churches in the U.S.A. located at Valley Forge, Penn. 19481, Tel. 215-768-2000.

BARBADOS

A valid passport or a birth certificate is required for a visit to Barbados for a stay of up to six months. For a stay longer than six months an individual must apply for a visa at the Immigration Department in Barbados. Those traveling on business must apply at the Barbados Embassy or a consulate for a visa with a letter from their company detailing the nature of their business. The Embassy of Barbados is located at 2144 Wyoming Ave. NW, Washington, D.C. 20008, Tel. 202-387-7373. Consulates are located in Boston, Atlanta and New York City. No shots are required for travelers coming from the United States. Pets are not allowed and are subject to quarantine in England. Up to $5,000 may be brought into Barbados. Over that amount must be declared upon arrival. The monetary unit on the island is the Barbados dollar. These are easily reconverted to American dollars before leaving Barbados. Those planning to drive will need a Barbadian permit which is available at the airport or at a local police station. These are valid up to one year and cost $10. The language of Barbados is English.

The government of Barbados is trying to balance their trade deficit by providing incentives for foreign investment. Barbados is a member of the Caribbean Common Market (CARICOM), and imports that are available from other member countries may be restricted from nonmembers. A local agent is not necessary but advisable. Import licenses are required.

The American Embassy in Barbados can be contacted at P.O. Box 302, Bridgetown, Barbados, Tel. 63574, Telex 259.

Further tourist information can be obtained from the Barbados Tourist Board, 800 Second Ave., New York, N.Y., Tel. 212-986-6516.

For additional business information contact the Barbados Industrial Development Corp., 800 Second Ave., New York, N.Y. 10017, Tel. 212-867-6420.

BARBERS

All states require barbers to be licensed, but the qualifications for licenses vary. In most cases the applicant must have completed the eighth grade in school, must have passed a physical examination, must be at least 16 years old (or 18 in some states) and must have completed a course of education at a state-approved barber school.

Most barber school programs last nine to 12 months, and may either be part of a public high school or technical school or be a private school.

Many states also require the beginning barber to take an examination for an apprentice's license and to serve one or two years as an apprentice barber before taking the examination for a registered barber's license. The apprentice barber is allowed to work only under the supervision of a licensed barber.

For licensing requirements contact the state board of barber examiners at the address listed for the state licensing board. Information about barber schools is available from the National Association of Barber Schools, 304 South 11th St., Lincoln, Neb. 68508, Tel. 402-474-4244.

BASEBALL

Professional Baseball in the United States is generally considered Major League Baseball, although there are a number of minor leagues and semi-professional organizations. Minor league teams are generally affiliated with a Major League organization for the training of new players. Major League Baseball consists of two leagues, the National League and the American League. There are 12 National League teams in 12 cities and 14 teams in the American League. Each league has its own president. Teams are operated by private, for-profit corporations. Organized Baseball is governed by the commissioner's office. The current commissioner is Bowie Kuhn. The commissioner is chosen by a vote of the team owners. The commissioner's office compiles schedules and statistics, determines rules and regulations, and oversees team rosters.

Major League Baseball teams cannot be sold without approval of the commissioner and a vote of the team owners.

The offices of The Commissioner of Baseball are located at 75 Rockefeller Plaza, New York, N.Y. 10019, Tel. 212-586-7400.

BASKETBALL

Professional basketball in the United States is controlled by the National Basketball Association (NBA). The NBA has 23 teams in 23 cities and is also affiliated with the Continental Basketball Organization, a semi-professional league which acts as a farm system from which players are recruited. The NBA administers all areas of the sport. It schedules games, does public relations for the sport, mediates disputes between teams and recruits players from minor league or amateur teams around the country. It also operates a training program for referees. The sale of any team must be approved by the NBA's Board of Governors. The Association is headed by a commissioner who currently is Lawrence F. O'Brien.

The offices of the National Basketball League are located at 645 Fifth Ave., New York, N.Y. 10011, Tel. 212-826-7000.

BATTERED ADULTS

Emergency shelters and counseling are offered in many cities to adults who have been battered by their spouses. In many cases, however, facilities are available only to women and only on a very limited basis. For information contact the local branch of the Salvation Army, the YWCA, the National Organization for Women or the American National Red Cross. Crisis intervention centers and hotlines, usually listed in the telephone directory, can also provide this information.

BELGIUM

A valid passport is required for traveling to Belgium. Whether going for business or pleasure no visa is needed for a stay of up to three months. For students or those needing work permits for longer stays visas may be applied for at the Embassy of Belgium, 3330 Garfield St. NW, Washington, D.C. 20008, Tel. 202-333-6900, or at the various Belgian consulates located in Atlanta, Chicago, Houston, Los Angeles, New York, and San Francisco. There are no health requirements except for pets, who need a rabies and good health certificate. Any amount of foreign currency or Belgian francs may be taken in or out of the country. An American driver's license is acceptable. Belgium is a bilingual country. Flemish, which is a variant of Dutch, is spoken by the Flemings and French is spoken by the Walloons. Brussels is officially a two-language city. English is widely spoken in major hotels, restaurants and shops.

Belgium does a great deal of trading with the United States, and the rules are quite relaxed. Licenses are not required for most imports, and exchange is easily handled through the Institut Belgo-Luxembourgeois du Change.

The American Embassy in Belgium is located at 27 Boulevard du Regent, B-1000 Brussels, Belgium, Tel. 513-3830.

For further tourist information contact the Belgian National Tourist Office, 720 Fifth Ave. New York, N.Y., Tel. 212-758-8130.

For further business information contact the Belgian American Chamber of Commerce in the U.S. Inc., 50 Rockefeller Plaza, New York, N.Y. 10020, Tel. 212-247-7613.

BERMUDA

Proof of citizenship is needed for travel to Bermuda. No passport or visa is necessary. A traveler must also have sufficient funds and a return ticket. There are no health requirements for entry into Bermuda for U.S. citizens. A pet may be brought in provided the owner gets permission from the Bermudian authorities. Write to the Bermuda Department of Tourism, 630 Fifth Ave., New York, N.Y. 10111, Tel. 212-397-7700 for the necessary forms. It will take several weeks for the permit to be granted. Any amount of foreign currency may be taken in or out of the country, but no Bermudian dollars may be imported or exported. The official language of Bermuda is English. There are no cars for rent on the island, but persons over 16 can rent a moped. No driver's license is required.

Bermuda is a free port and a member of the British Commonwealth. Except for a few items, all imports are covered under one comprehensive license. Foreign exchange transactions of more than BD$100 require a permit from the Foreign Exchange Control Department.

Bermudian affairs are handled by British Embassies and consulates. Further tourist information can be obtained from the Bermuda Department of Tourism (address above). The U.S. Embassy in Bermuda is located at Vallis Building, Front Street, Hamilton, Bermuda, Tel. 295-1342.

BETTER BUSINESS BUREAUS

Better Business Bureaus were established at the beginning of the century in an effort to build public confidence in business by fostering better business practices. They are funded mainly by national or local membership dues. Local bureaus provide the following services for consumers: general information about a company; help in resolving a complaint against a business, including binding arbitration if both parties agree; and, information or charitable organizations soliciting in an area.

Information about a particular company is based on the bureau's record of complaints against that company and the company's response to those complaints. Additional information on nationwide companies may be obtained from the national bureau network. When a consumer complaint is received by a bureau, a consumer service specialist takes it up with the business firm involved. In most cases the complaint is then settled by mutual agreement between the complainant and the company. Binding arbitration is also offered by most bureaus as an alternative. If a firm fails to respond to a complaint or will not resolve a complaint satisfactorily after several requests, that fact is placed in the company's file at the bureau.

A bureau's response to consumer questions varies from locality to locality. Many are diligent in giving accurate information on a company. Others are reluctant to term a company less than adequate. The complaint procedure is also complicated. Complaints must be made in writing or on a bureau form before the organization will act.

There are currently almost 150 Better Business Bureaus in the United States. For information on them and bureau programs contact the council of Better Business Bureaus, 1515 Wilson Blvd., Arlington, Va. 22209, Tel. 703-276-0100.

See also ADVERTISING COMPLAINTS: CHARITIES; ARBITRATION: CONSUMER; CONSUMER FRAUD; CONSUMER INFORMATION: NATIONAL

BICYCLING

The major national organization of recreational bicyclists in the United States is the League of American Wheelmen, P.O. Box 988, Baltimore, Md. 21203, Tel. 301-727-2022. The governing body for competitive bicycling is the United States Cycling Federation (USCF). The USCF sponsors the annual state and national championships and is responsible for selection of the teams for the Olympic and Pan American games. For further information contact the United States Cycling Federation, 1750 E. Boulder, Colorado Springs, Colo. 80508.

BIRTH CERTIFICATES

Upon a child's birth (see birth registration) the state, county or city bureau of vital statistics, which is usually part of the state department of health, issues a birth certificate. The certificate records the child's name, sex, date and time of birth. Also recorded are the father's name and mother's maiden name. It is not possible to tell from a birth certificate whether a child is legitimate or illegitimate.

Copies of the child's birth certificate can be ordered from the agency recording the birth. Information certifying the date of a person's birth can also be obtained by the U.S. Bureau of the Census. For a fee the bureau will check its records from past census statistics and provide a statement that can be used as a substitute for a birth certificate. Contact the Department of Commerce Public Information Office, Bureau of the Census, Washington, D.C. 20233, Tel. 301-763-7273.
See also: CENSUS: POPULATION

BIRTH CONTROL

See: ABORTION, FAMILY PLANNING, GENETIC COUNSELING, INFERTILITY

BIRTH REGISTRATION

Births are generally registered by the doctor or hospital shortly after birth. If the birth was at home without a doctor in attendance, the parents can register the birth. Births are generally registered at the city, county or state bureau of vital statistics. This is usually part of the state health department. The information is generally forwarded to a central registry at the state health department office in the state capital.
See also: BIRTH CERTIFICATES

BIRTHS AND DEATHS OVERSEAS: REGISTRATION OF

Births and deaths of American citizens abroad should be registered as soon as possible with the nearest United States embassy or consulate. Documentary evidence of citizenship held by parents or deceased should be produced.

Information about deaths of American citizens abroad may be obtained from the Department of State, Office of Special Consular Services, 2201 C St. NW, Washington, D.C. 20520, Tel. 202-655-4000.

BLINDNESS

Persons who are blind are eligible for social services and other assistance from many public and private sources. See BLIND: SOCIAL SERVICES FOR THE; SOCIAL SECURITY, SUPPLEMENTAL SECURITY INCOME, BOOKS FOR THE BLIND AND PHYSICALLY

DISABLED, REHABILITATION, CHILDREN: SOCIAL SECURITY BENEFITS.

Every state has a state commission for the blind which offers social services to blind residents of the state such as educational assistance, summer camps for children, counseling, and other assistance. Contact the state commission for the blind, usually located in the state capital.

The American Foundation for the Blind, 15 W. 16th Street, New York, N.Y. 10011, Tel. 212-620-2000, offers a clearinghouse for services for the blind.

See also: BOWLING: BLIND

BLIND: SOCIAL SERVICES FOR THE

State commissions for the blind utilize both state and federal funds to provide services to blind children and adults. The primary goals of these commissions are self sufficiency in employment and living. The following essential services may be offered by the state commission for the blind: eye medical care including counseling and guidance; parent and child counseling for children; evaluation of rehabilitation potential; physical and mental restoration; vocational and other training (including the provision of books, tools and other training material); maintenance; transportation; services to family members; interpreter services for the deaf; reader services; orientation and mobility services; telecommunications, sensory and other technological aids and devices; placement in suitable employment; post employment service to help a handicapped individual maintain employment; occupational licenses, tools, equipment, initial stock and supplies; and other services which can reasonably be expected to benefit a handicapped individual in terms of employability.

To be eligible for social services such as the above, the individual must have a visual disability that constitutes a handicap to employment and the agency must determine that there is reasonable expectation that the services of the agency will benefit the individual in terms of employability.

Many of these services are available only to persons below a certain income level, but some are provided with no such requirement.

Contact a commission for the blind office in your state, usually located in large cities or the state capital.

BLOOD DONORS

The Red Cross or local hospital will generally welcome any type blood for transfusion purposes. The need is particularly acute during the summer and the holiday season. They prefer volunteer donors because of the greater risk of hepatitis from commercial donors. Most healthy adults from 18 to 65 are suitable for donors. For information on hours of operation call the local Red Cross office.

BOATING: LICENSES

Persons operating small pleasure craft for their own use do not have to be licensed. Those carrying people for hire must be licensed. Requirements vary depending on the size of the boat. Operators of a vessel less than 65 feet long or under 15 gross tons and carrying six persons or less must have a motor boat operator's license. Those in boats that are large or carrying more passengers must meet the manning levels determined by the Coast Guard on its certificate of inspection. For further information contact the local Coast Guard office (listed under U.S. government in the telephone directory) or the U.S. Coast Guard, 2100 Second St. SW, Washington, D.C. 20593, Tel. 202-426-1587.

BOATING: RECREATIONAL

The National Boating Federation, founded in 1966, represents those interested in recreational boating in American waters. It is an alliance of state, regional and national recreational boating organizations. It represents, promotes and protects boating and related recreational activities; encourages programs of education, development and conservation of water resources and provides a medium of exchange of boating information and creates unity among recreational boaters through national, state and regional associations. It also acts as liaison among boaters, boating organizations and federal and state agencies. It may be contacted at 629 Waverly Lane, Bryn Athyn, Pa. 19009, Tel. 215-947-0158.

BOLIVIA

A valid passport and a tourist card are required for travel to Bolivia. A traveler can get a tourist card upon arrival at a Bolivian airport, at a Bolivian diplomatic mission or at an airline that serves the country. A tourist card is valid for up to 90 days. Business travelers must bring a letter from their company detailing the nature of their business and confirming financial responsibility for the traveler. All visitors must register with Bolivian Immigration authorities. This is done automatically if one stays at a hotel. Otherwise registration is at the Ministry of Immigration, Calle Junin esq. Avenida Arce, La Paz. All business travelers must report to the Immigration authorities upon arrival. Proof of a smallpox vaccination is required, and visitors are advised to have protection against typhoid, yellow fever and malaria. Pets are allowed if accompanied by a health certificate. The monetary unit is the Bolivian peso. Any amount of foreign or local currency may be brought in or out of the country, but visitors should expect difficulty changing pesos back to dollars. There is a large Indian population in Bolivia. Most of the people speak Spanish, but outside the cities the Indian languages Quechua and Aymara are spoken. An International Driving License is required.

Any foreigner wishing to trade with Bolivia must have a resident agent inside the country. All agreements with agencies are subject to Bolivian law. There are restrictions on some imports, especially if they are goods that are manufactured locally. There are no restrictions on foreign exchange. The Embassy of Bolivia is located at 3006 Massachusetts Ave. NW, Washington, D.C. 20036, Tel. 202-232-4804. There are consulates in Chicago, Los Angeles, Miami, New Orleans, New York and San Francisco.

The American Embassy in Bolivia is located at Banco Popular Del Peru Building, Corner of Calles Mercado y Colon, La Paz, Bolivia, Tel. 50251.

BOOKS FOR THE BLIND AND PHYSICALLY DISABLED

A network of regional and subregional libraries, in cooperation with the Library of Congress, provides free library services to people who cannot read or use standard printed materials because of visual or physical impairment. Books and magazines in braille and recorded form (talking books) are delivered by postage free mail and returned the same way. In addition specially designed phonographs and casette players are loaned free to those borrowing talking books.

To obtain this service, an individual must send a statement describing his or her disability to the library serving the area. He or she must also send a statement signed by a medical doctor, optometrist, nurse, therapist or professional on the staff of a hospital, institution or public agency describing the disability. For further information contact the Library of Congress, Division for the Blind and Physically Handicapped, 1291 Taylor St. N.W., Washington, D.C. 20542, Tel. 202-882-5500.

BOWLING: AMATEUR

The American Bowling Congress, an organization of male bowlers, provides standard rules and approves equipment to be used in tournaments. It also sponsors annual competitions. The Women's International Bowling Congress provides similar services for women bowlers. For further information contact the American Bowling Congress, 5301 South 76th St., Greendale, Wisc. 53129, Tel. 414-421-6400 or the Women's International Bowling Congress at the same address, Tel. 414-421-9000.

BOWLING: BLIND

The American Blind Bowling Association sponsors leagues and tournaments for blind bowlers throughout the United States. There is an annual national tournament in which prizes and trophies are awarded. Persons can also join the association as individual members. Any legally blind person is eligible if he or she is at least 18 years of age. Sighted persons can become auxiliary members. For further information contact the American Blind Bowling Association, 150 N. Bellaire Ave., Louisville, Ky, 40206, Tel. 502-896-8039.

BOWLING: PROFESSIONAL

The Professional Bowlers Association, organized in 1958, now has more than 2,000 members. The organization sponsors numerous tournaments, including the televised Pro Bowlers Tour. It also sponsors over 85 tournaments in six geographical regions of the country in which nontouring professional bowlers compete.

Membership is offered to regional professional bowlers under the title Resident Pro II. This gives the bowler the privilege of competing in high-level competition on weekends and the ability to qualify for a limited number of spots in those national tournaments held in the bowler's region. Requirements for membership include a minimum score of 190 for 66 games in an established league for each of the two most recent years, or a tournament record that has been approved by the Regional Director. Qualification as a touring pro bowler, of course, is more stringent, including minimum scores in recognized tournaments.

A schedule of events sponsored by the Professional Bowlers Association and information about membership is available from the association.

Contact the Professional Bowlers Association, 1720 Merriman Road, Akron, Ohio 44313, Tel. 216-836-5568.

BOXING: AMATEUR

Golden Gloves competitions for amateur boxers have been held yearly since 1929. Tournaments are held locally and are authorized by the Golden Gloves organization. Local winners advance to regional, state and national competition. Competitions are held in the following weight classes: 106 lb., 112 lb., 125 lb., 132 lb., 139 lb., 147 lb., 156 lb., 165 lb., 178 lb. and Heavyweight Class (175 lb. and over).

Amateur boxers interested in competing can contact the local organization of the Golden Gloves Association of America, 1704 Moon N.E., Albuquerque, N.M. 87112, Tel. 505-294-8659.

BOXING: PROFESSIONAL

The two major sanctioning bodies for professional boxing in the United States are the World Boxing Association and the World Boxing Council. These organizations are composed of member commissions by state, city and country. Each sanctions fights leading to a world championship. The two rarely agree on who is the reigning champion, and the struggle for control of the sport is still going on. For further information contact the World Boxing Association, Rodrigo Sanchez, P.O. Box 471, Panama, Republic of Panama. The World Boxing Council is located in Mexico City.

BOY SCOUTS

The Boy Scouts of America offers educational programs in character development, social training and physical fitness to boys ages eight through ten (Cub Scouts), ages eleven through seventeen (Boy Scouts) and ages fifteen through twenty (Explorers). The group is lead by adult volunteers and was founded in 1910. Current membership is 3,200,000 boys and 1,200,000 adults. The group also conducts studies on youth problems and maintains museums and a library of 8,000 volumes related to social studies, youth work and history. They publish several magazines, Boys' Life, Exploring Magazine and Scouting Magazine. Contact the local Boy Scout organization or the Boy Scouts of America, National Council, 1325 Walnut Hill Lane, Dallas, Tx. 75261, Tel. 214-659-2000.

BRAZIL

A valid passport and a visa are required for U.S. citizens traveling to Brazil. Tourists must present a passport valid for six months beyond the date of entry into Brazil, a round trip ticket and one photograph for a visa good for a stay of up to 90 days. Business travelers need a passport, three photographs, a health certificate not older than three months from a local doctor, a letter of good conduct from the local Police Department and a letter from his company detailing the nature of business to be conducted and confirming financial responsibility for the applicant. The visa is also good for 90 days. There are no health requirements necessary beyond the certificate presented for the visa, but yellow fever and typhoid shots are advised. Pets may be brought into the country provided a veterinarian's health certificate and rabies vaccination certificate has been validated by a Brazilian consulate. The local currency is the cruzeiro, and there are no limits on the amount of local or foreign currency which may be taken in or out of the country. The official language is Portuguese, but various minority groups also speak English, Spanish, French, Italian, German and Japanese. To drive a car, an International Driving License is required.

Trade with Brazil is conducted through agents, local retailers and distributors or Brazilian subsidiaries of foreign companies. All goods require import licenses and some luxury items are prohibited.

The Embassy of Brazil is located at 3006 Massachusetts Ave. NW, Washington, D.C. 20008, Tel. 202-797-0200. There are consulates in New York, Atlanta, Chicago, Dallas, Houston, Los Angeles, Miami, New Orleans and San Francisco.

The U.S. Embassy in Brazil is located at Avenida das Nacoes, Lote 3, Brasilia, Brazil, Tel. 223-0120. There are U.S. consulates in Rio de Janeiro, Sao Paulo, Recife and Porto Alegre.

For further tourist information contact the Brazilian Government Trade Bureau, 551 Fifth Ave., New York, N.Y. 10017, Tel. 212-682-4693. Import information is available from the same address or by calling 212-682-6036.

BRIDGE: CONTRACT

Approximately 200,000 members belong to the American Contract Bridge League (ACBL) in over 5000 local clubs. The league sets the rules used in duplicate and rubber bridge throughout the world, sanctions tournaments and selects the players who will represent the league in international competition. It is a member of the World Bridge Federation.

Over 900 tournaments are sanctioned by the ACBL each year. Master points are awarded to the winners and high finishers on a basis that provides awards commesurate with the importance of the event and the degree of success achieved by the individual players.

Contact the local club or the national headquarters of the ACBL at 2200 Democrat Road, Memphis, Tenn. 38116, Tel. 901-332-5586.

BROADCASTING STATIONS: COMPLAINTS

The Federation Communication regulates the numer and type of radio and TV stations. Complaints about stations and their responses to the needs of their communities should be made to the Federal Communications Com-

mission, Complaints Division, Broadcast Bureau, 1919 M St. NW, Washington, D.C. 20554, Tel. 202-632-7000.

BROADCAST TECHNICIANS

Broadcast technicians in both television and radio are required to have a Radiotelephone Operator's License from the Federal Communications Commission (FCC). By law the chief engineer of the station must have a first class Radiotelephone Operator's License, as must any technician operating the transmitter. Technicians with lower class licenses, such as second or third class licenses, may perform less responsible functions, such as operating the control room board during programs.

Radiotelephone Operator's Licenses are obtained by passing examinations given by the FCC. College and technical schools give courses preparing students for the examinations, but an individual may take the initial test for a third class license based on his or her own independent study. Further information about qualifying as a broadcast technician is available from the local or national FCC office.

Contact: the Federal Communications Commission, 1919 M St. NW, Washington, D.C. 20554, Tel. 202-655-4000.

BURIAL

The funeral industry in the United States has traditionally

been regulated by the states, and the regulation has been uneven and sometimes less than rigorous. Funeral homes or funeral directors are usually licensed by a state board. The boards will also accept and investigate complaints from individuals. They have the power to revoke licenses where appropriate.

The Federal Trade Commission has issued regulations for the funeral industry to encourage disclosure of prices and to discourage misleading or false claims by funeral companies. Complaints are kept on file for use should the FTC initiate an investigation as a result of numerous or exceptional complaints. Contact the state licensing agency for the proper licensing board or the Federal Trade Commission, Pennsylvania Ave. at Sixth St. NW, Washington, D.C. 20580, Tel. 202-523-3625. Individual complaints generally cannot be investigated.

Individuals with complaints can also contact their state consumer agency (address in individual state entry), or consult a private attorney.

See also: CEMETERIES: ARMED FORCES, DEATH CERTIFICATES, DEATH: SOCIAL SECURITY BENEFITS, DEATH WITHOUT FUNDS FOR FUNERAL, FUNERAL DIRECTORS AND EMBALMERS.

BUSINESS: ADVISORY SERVICES

The Service Corps of Retired Executives (SCORE) and the Active Corps of Executive (ACE) give assistance to new and existing small businesses and nonprofit community organizations. The program, directed by the Small Business Administration, offers free management counseling and workshops for those in business or thinking of opening a business. There is no cost for the service. The executives who participate are volunteers. The only criteria for using the service is that the business be classified as a "small business" under federal definition. For information contact your local office of the Small Business Administration (listed in the telephone directory under United States Government), or the Small Business Administration, Service Corps of Retired Executives and Active Corps of Executives, 1030 15th St. NW, Washington, D.C. 20008, Tel. 202-653-6958.

BUSINESS COMPLIANCE LOANS

The Small Business Administration offers direct and guaranteed loans to small businesses that face hardships because of required compliance with federal safety and inspection standards. For further information contact the local SBA office or the Small Business Administration, 1441 L St. NW, Washington, D.C. 20416, Tel. 202-653-6365.

BUSINESS: GOVERNMENT CONTRACTS

The General Service Administration operates a nationwide chain of Business Service Centers which provide information and counseling for business firms wanting to sell to the federal government. Service centers are located in Los Angeles, San Francisco, Denver, Washington, D.C. Atlanta, Chicago, Boston, Kansas City, Mo., New York, Philadelphia, Fort Worth, Houston and Seattle. Check the telephone directories in those cities under U.S. government, General Services Administration.

The Small Business Administration also aids business in obtaining government contracts. It maintains a roster of small firms for referral to government purchasing agents and issues certificates of competency to small businesses that are low bidders on contracts and need to have their credit ability to perform and production capacity verified. For further information contact the local Small Business Administration or the Small Business Administration, 1441 L St. NW, Washington, D.C. 20416, Tel. 202-653-6365.

BUSINESS: LEASE GUARANTEES

The Small Business Administration had a lease guarantee program for small businesses in which the government insures the landlord that rent payments will be met.

For information on how to qualify contact the local SBA office or the Small Business Administra-

tion 1441 L St. NW, Washington, D.C. 20416, Tel. 202-653-6365.

BUSINESS: MINORITY FEDERAL ASSISTANCE

Both the Minority Business Development Agency of the Commerce Department and the Office of Associate Administrator for Minority Small Business and Capital Ownership Development offer the minority businessman management and technical assistance and information about the federal programs available to him. For further information contact the Commerce Department, Minority Business Development Agency, Main Commerce Building, Washington, D.C. 20230, Tel. (202) 377-5061 and the Small Business Administration, Office of Associate Administrator for Minority Small Business and Capital Ownership Development, 1441 L St. N.W. 20416, Tel. 202-653-6407.

Many states also have programs for minority businesses. See individual state entries for further information.

BUSINESS: OVERSEAS GOVERNMENT AID

The Federal government offers several types of aid to U.S. firms interested in starting overseas operations, including technical assistance, loans, loan guarantees and investment insurance. The U.S. Commerce Department's Domestic and International Business Administration offers advice and counseling. The Overseas Private Investment Corporation (OPIC) mobilizes and facilitates the participation of U.S. private capital and skills in the economic and social development of developing friendly countries, complementing the development assistance objectives of the U.S. government.

OPIC operates two programs in over 90 developing countries: financing in conjunction with U.S. private investment, and insurance for U.S. investments against the political risks of expropriation, inconvertibility of local currency and war or revolution. Assistance is available to new ventures that are financially sound or to expansion of existing businesses in developing countries. Most OPIC assistance is for businesses in countries where the per capita annual income is less than $1000. In countries where the per capita annual income is greater, assistance is generally restricted to companies smaller than the "Fortune 1000." An exception to this guideline is energy development in non-OPEC countries and mineral projects, which may receive OPIC assistance without limitation on the size of the investor.

OPIC financing is available through a variety of loans and loan guarantees for medium- to long-term funding. Such funding uses the project itself as security for the loan, so a sponsor is not required to pledge its own general credit assets. There must, however, be adequate cash flow to pay all operating costs, to service the debt and to provide the owners with an adequate return on the investment. OPIC usually requires a ratio of 60 percent debt to 40 percent equity in projects that it finances. Loans in the past have ranged from $100,000 to $4 million.

Both the project and OPIC's participation must be approved by the host country. A wide variety of enterprises are eligible including manufacturing, agricultural production, fishing, forestry, mining, energy development, commercial hotels and tourist facilities. In some cases OPIC will share costs with a U.S. firm for a feasibility study of an opportunity that the firm has identified through its own reconnaissance in the host country.

The sponsor of a potential project interested in OPIC financing should provide OPIC with preliminary information in summary form, including location and business of the proposed project; identity, background and financial statements of the sponsors; planned sources of supply, anticipated output and markets; proposed financing plan; statement of the contribution the business is expected to make to the country where it is located.

For more information contact the Overseas Private Investment Corporation, 1129 Twentieth St. NW, Washington, D.C. 20527, Tel.: 202-632-1804, the nearest Commerce Department field office or the Domestic and International

Business Administration Department of Commerce, Fourteenth St. between Constitution Ave. and E St. NW, Washington, D.C. 20230, Tel.: 202-377-2000.

BUSINESS DISPUTES OVERSEAS

The Trade Complaint Service of the International Trade Administration investigates problems an American company may have in dealing with a foreign business. The American company must have tried to resolve the claim on its own before the agency will act. The agency, using the U.S. commercial attache in the area, attempts to push adjustment through the appropriate organizations in the foreign country. The Service does not act as a lawyer or a collection agency. It will, however, provide a list of local lawyers if the dispute goes to court. For further information contact the Department of Commerce, International Trade Administration, Trade Complaint Service, Main Commerce Building, Washington, D.C. 20230, Tel. 202-377-5087.

BUSINESS LOANS: SMALL BUSINESS

The Small Business Administration provides guaranteed, direct or immediate participation loans to small businesses for construction, equipment, supplies and materials. It also provides working capital. To qualify, a business must meet the qualifications for being

defined as "small business." For information on this and other requirements contact the Small Business Administration, 1441 L St. N.W., Washington, D.C. 20416, Tel. 202-653-6365.

Many states also have programs to aid small businesses as do municipalities. Contact the state agencies listed under each state entry for further information.

See also: DISASTER LOANS

BUS LINES: INTERSTATE

The Interstate Commerce Commission regulates interstate bus companies. Complaints about a particular carrier should first be made to the carrier in question. If there is no satisfaction, the consumer may file a complaint with any ICC field office or the Interstate Commerce Commission, 12th St. and Constitution Ave. NW, Washington, D.C. 20423, Tel. 800-244-9312.

C

CABLE TELEVISION: COMPLAINTS

The Federal Communications Commission regulates the construction and operation of cable television systems. Operators of these systems must obtain a certificate of compliance from the Commission before commencing operation or adding additional television broadcast signals to existing operations. Complaints about the service should be addressed to the Federal Communications Commission, Cable Complaint Service, 1919 M St. NW, Washington D.C. 20554, Tel. 202-632-9703.

CALIFORNIA

In the state of California the Department of Consumer Affairs has authority to protect the consumer from fraudulent or deceptive practices in the sale of goods or services. It also educates and informs the consumer how to make a rational choice in the marketplace. The department is responsible for responding to complaints concerning: unfair methods of competition and unfair or deceptive acts and practices by any person in the conduct of any trade or commerce; the production, distribution, sale, or lease of goods and services undertaken by any person which might endanger the public health, safety, or welfare; or violations of state laws relating to businesses and professions licensed by any agency in the department.

The Complaint Mediation Unit of the Department of Consumer Affairs mediates consumer complaints and also provides self-help guidance for resolving complaints, including providing suggested steps for consumers to resolve their complaints if the mediation does not result in a solution agreeable to the consumer.

The Legal Services Unit of the Department of Consumer Affairs will bring suit against a particular company when there is a pattern of consumer complaints.

The Department of Consumer Affairs also regulates the licensing of businesses and occupations through the following boards: behavioral science examiners, dental examiners, guide dogs for the blind, medical quality assurance, nursing home administrators, optometry, pharmacy, registered nursing, veterinary medicine, vocational nurse and psychiatric technician, accountancy, chemistry, collection and investigative services, architectural examiners, contractors license board, geologists and geophysicists, landscape architects, professional engineers, pest control, athletic commission, automotive repair, barber examiners, cosmetology, electronic and appliance repair, employment agencies, fabric care, funeral directors and embalmers, home furnishings, certified shorthand reporters.

These boards license applicants dependent on requirements of the individual board. Contact the board concerned through the Department of Consumer Affairs. The boards also accept consumer complaints, and will investigate, discipline or revoke licenses when appropriate.

Contact the Department of Consumer Affairs, 1020 N St. Sacramento, Calif. 95814, or one of the regional offices located in major California cities.

The Department of Economic

and Business Development provides services to assist businesses in site selection in California, and offers information about business development loans and loan guarantees. For assistance in plant location and capital investment for new and expanding businesses, contact the Department of Economic and Business Development, Office of Business and Industrial Development, 1120 N. St. Sacramento Calif. 95814, Tel. 916-322-5665, Toll free tel. 800-952-5502.

California offers financing through privately sponsored development credit corporations and also offers financial incentives for establishing industrial plants in areas of high unemployment. For information on state services to businesses contact the Chamber of Commerce, P.O. Box 1736, Sacramento, Calif. 95808, Tel. 916-444-6670.

California's personal income tax rate increases from 1% for income less than $2,240 to 11% for income in excess of $17,430.

The corporate income tax is 9.6%, with a minimum tax of $200. Banks and financial corporations pay 11.6% income tax.

Request tourist information from the Parks and Recreation Department, 1416 9th St. Sacramento, Calif. 95814, Tel. 916-445-6477.

CALL FOR ACTION

Call for Action is a referral and action service maintained by a number of broadcast organizations. The service refers consumers to specific agencies that may help them with their problems and follows up complaints if satisfaction has not been obtained. For a list of stations participating in this service contact Call for Action, 575 Lexington Ave. New York, N.Y. 10022, Tel. 212-355-5965.

CAMPAIGN FUND DISCLOSURE: FEDERAL CANDIDATES

Candidates for federal offices, are required to file periodic reports regarding campaign funds with the Federal Election Commission (FEC). These reports are made available to the public within 48 hours after receipt at the FEC's offices, and are maintained on file.

The FEC periodically audits candidates and committees to assure that they have disclosed the required information. If it finds a violation the FEC may file a civil suit against the suspected offender. Any criminal enforcement is handled by the Justice Department. For further information contact the Federal Election Commission, 1325 K St. N.W., Washington, D.C. 20005, Tel. 202-523-4110, toll free (800) 424-9530.

CAMPAIGN FUNDS: AMOUNTS

Under the election law a private citizen may contribute no more than $1,000 to an individual candidate for primaries and an additional $1,000 for general election. An individual can contribute no more than $25,000 to political campaigns in a year. See also: CAMPAIGN FUND DISCLOSURE: FEDERAL CANDIDATES.

CANADA

U.S. citizens do not need either a passport or a visa to travel to Canada. There are no health requirements for entry. Pets may be brought into the country with a recent certificate of vaccination against rabies. The local currency is the Canadian dollar and there are no limits on local or foreign currency which can be taken in or out of the country. English and French are the official languages of Canada, with French being spoken mainly in the Province of Quebec. An American driver's license will suffice to drive a car in Canada.

Trading with Canada is handled through many different channels—directly to retailers or wholesalers, distributors or agents. There are few licenses required and there are no exchange controls.

The Embassy of Canada is located at 1746 Massachusetts Ave. NW, Washington, D.C. 20036-1985, Tel. 202-785-1400. There are Canadian consulates in most major American cities.

The U.S. Embassy in Canada is located at 100 Wellington St., Ottawa, Ontario K1P 5TI, Canada, Tel. 613-238-5335.

CAPTIONED FILMS FOR THE DEAF

Captioned films and instructional materials for the deaf are available on free loan from the U.S. Office of Education. Films are loaned to agencies, schools, organizations, and groups of deaf persons.

Contact the Media Services and Captioned Films Branch, Division of Educational Services, Bureau of Education for the Handicapped, Office of Education, Department of Health and Human Services 400 Maryland Ave. SW, Washington, D.C. 20202, Tel. 202-245-8795.

CARPETING

Since many carpets carry no manufacturer guarantee, one of the main considerations in buying a carpet is the reputation of the dealer. The local Better Business Bureau can give information about the retailer's past record of consumer relations. Complaints about carpet retailers can also be sent to the state consumer agency (see individual state listing), which will generally attempt to mediate the complaint.

The Carpet and Rug Institute, a trade association of carpet and rug manufacturers, also offers assistance to consumers who have complaints about carpeting. The institute will supply an address of the carpet manufacturer when the consumer provides the name. Its staff experts in the area of carpet care and maintenance are sometimes able to resolve the consumer's problem by simply providing the necessary information. Contact the Carpet and Rug Institute, P.O. Box 2048, Dalton, Ga. 30720, Tel.: 404-278-3176.

CAR SEATS: CHILDREN'S

The Physicians for Auto Safety makes recommendations about the car seats produced for children as safety devices. Its recommendations are based on detailed testing done at the University of Michigan. For further information contact the Physicians for Auto Safety, 50 Union Ave., Irvington, N.Y. 07111, Tel. 201-926-1930.

See also: SAFETY: CONSUMER PRODUCTS, PRODUCT SAFETY: RETAILER'S RESPONSIBILITY and individual state entries.

CEMETERIES: ARMED FORCES

The Veterans Administration is responsible for burials in national cemeteries. Burial is available to any deceased veteran of wartime or peacetime service who was discharged under conditions other than dishonorable at all Veterans Administration national cemeteries having available grave space. Burial is also available in a national cemetery to the eligible veteran's wife, husband, widow, widower, minor children, and in some cases, to unmarried adult children.

The Arlington National Ceme-

tery is under jurisdiction of the Department of the Army, and burial is limited to specific categories of military personnel and veterans except in the case of cremated remains.

In both Veterans Administration cemeteries and Arlington National Cemetery headstones and markers are provided for the gravesites of those interred. Any Veterans Administration office can provide information about burial. Applications should only be made at the time of the death of the individual to be interred.

For information about burial in Arlington National Cemetary contact the Superintendent, Arlington National Cemetery, Arlington, Va. 22211, 202-695-3253.

The American Battle Monuments Commission provides to the public upon request the exact location and other information about the place of interment or memorialization of the war dead. The Commission will also give information about the best routes and modes of travel in-country to the cemeteries and memorials in foreign countries. Contact the Director of Operations and Finance, American Battle Monuments Commission 40014, Forrestal Building, Washington, D.C. 20314, Tel. 202-693-6089.

CENSUS: POPULATION

The Bureau of the Census in the U.S. Department of Commerce is responsible for providing a census of population in the United States every 10 years. The Bureau collects, tabulates and publishes a wide variety of statistical data about the people and the economy of the United States.

In addition to the decennial census of population and housing, in 1985 a mid-decade census of population will be taken and repeated ever 10 years thereafter. The Bureau also conducts censuses at the request and expense of states and local governments.

Some of the topic areas on which census data can be requested are: agriculture, business, construction, economic surveys (transportation, enterprise statistics, county business patterns, minority-owned businesses), energy, foreign trade, governments, industrial minority statistics, manufacturing, mineral industries, retail trade, selected service industries and wholesale trade.

Published census statistics are issued in bound volumes and on microfilm in the monthly *Data User News* and in brochures. The findings are summarized in the annual *Statistical Abstract,* the *Pocket Data Book* and in a number of almanacs and abstracts.

Census materials may be used or obtained at regional offices in: Atlanta, Boston, Charlotte, Chicago, Dallas, Denver, Detroit, Kansas City (Kans.), Los Angeles, New York City, Philadelphia and Seattle. Census materials are also available for use in local libraries

or can be borrowed through interlibrary loan. Extensive materials are available in over 1,300 government and census and census depository libraries.

Census information about individuals is available for 1790 through 1900. This information is available on microfilm at the National Archives, its branches and in a number of libraries in various parts of the U.S. The schedules on individuals from 1910 to the present are confidential for 72 years. Statistical data only is available for those years. Specific information from these records is available only to the person involved, his or her legal heirs or a legal representative. These transcripts may be used by individuals who do not have birth certificates and want to prove their ages. They can also sometimes be used as proof of citizenship or of relationship to a certain person. Requests for transcripts of census information for 1910 to the present should be made at an office of the Bureau of the Census or directly to the Bureau of the Census, Personal Census Services Branch, Pittsburg, Kan. 66762, Tel. 913-231-7100.

Questions about unpublished census data can be directed to the Bureau's Data User Services Division, Customer Services Staff, Bureau of the Census, Washington, D.C. 20233, Tel. 202-655-4000.

A complete list of publications can be obtained from the Bureau of the Census. Materials may also be ordered through the U.S. Department of Commerce or the Superintendent of Documents, Government Printing Office, North Capitol at H St. NW, Washington, D.C. 20402, Tel. 202-275-2051.

Contact the Public Information Office, Bureau of the Census, Washington, D.C. 20233, Tel. 202-763-4040, or the National Archives and Records Service, Eighth St. at Pennsylvania Ave. NW, Washington, D.C. 20408, Tel. 202-523-3134 for the location of the nearest library with 1790-1900 census information.

CEREBRAL PALSY

Direct services are provided to both children and adults with cerebral palsy and to their families by local affiliates of the United Cerebral Palsy Associations. Services include medical diagnosis, evaluation and treatment, special education, career development, social and recreational programs, parent counseling, adapted housing for the disabled, advocacy and community education.

The national organization serves as a lobbying group, encouraging legislation beneficial to the handicapped. It also provides assistance for local UCP groups.

UCP Research and Educational Foundation has an extensive research program for the prevention and treatment of the disease. It awards fellowships and traineeships to support scientific research in the field. Affiliates of UCP conduct their own fund-rais-

ing drives, retaining 75 percent of the funds for local programs.

Contact local UCP groups or the United Cerebral Palsy Associations Inc., 66 East 34th St. New York, N.Y. 10016, Tel: 212-481-6300.

CHARITIES

Regulation of charities in the United States tends to be uneven and ineffectual. There are no meaningful federal regulations for charities. A tax-exempt status from the Internal Revenue Service does not mean that the IRS has certified the charity's legitimacy. It means only that the organization has a stated benevolent or educational purpose and is operated on a nonprofit basis. Tax-exempt organizations, except for churches and certain other religious groups, are required to file annual reports, but these are rarely audited. Even if a report is audited, the IRS is interested only in the accuracy of the reported figures, not with the figures themselves. Therefore, a charity might report that it spends 90 percent of its income for salaries and the IRS would not be concerned. The U.S. Postal Service is concerned with charities only when they are involved in cases of reported mail fraud.

States do not regulate charities consistently, and some do not regulate them at all. About half the states put a limit on the amount of money that charities can spend on fund raising rather than on charitable endeavors. Other states have no percentage limitations and require only that charities file some type of report each year.

Only 33 states and the District of Columbia require charities to be licensed or registered. Those states are: Arkansas, California, Connecticut, Florida, Georgia, Hawaii, Illinois, Iowa, Kansas, Kentucky, Maine, Maryland, Massachusetts, Michigan, Minnesota, Nebraska, Nevada, New Hampshire, New Jersey, New York, North Carolina, North Dakota, Ohio, Oklahoma, Oregon, Pennsylvania, Rhode Island, South Carolina, South Dakota, Tennessee, Virginia, Washington, West Virginia and Wisconsin.

Of the 33 states and the District of Columbia listed above, only the following put any type of limitation of the percentage of contributions that can be used for administrative and fund-raising uses rather than for the actual charitable purpose involved: Arkansas, Connecticut, Florida, Georgia, Hawaii, Illinois, Kansas, Kentucky, Maryland, Massachusetts, Minnesota, New Hampshire, New Jersey, New York, North Carolina, North Dakota, Oklahoma, Oregon, Pennsylvania, Rhode Island, South Carolina, South Dakota, Tennessee, Virginia, Washington and West Virginia.

The agency regulating or registering charities in the above states also varies from state to state but is most frequently the secretary of state's office, the department of licensing or the state attorney general's office.

The Council of Better Business Bureaus Philanthropic Advisory Service provides information and advisory services about charities to corporations, foundations, soliciting organizations, chambers of commerce and the general public. The BBB sets voluntary standards for charitable solicitations, reports on organizations that solicit nationally or internationally and reports whether the organization meets BBB standards. It also counsels philanthropic organizations on how to meet BBB standards. Contact any of the three state offices mentioned above for the correct regulatory agency or the Council of Better Business Bureaus, Inc., Philanthropic Advisory Service, 1150 17th St. NW, Washington, D.C. 20036, Tel. 202-862-1200.

CHILD ABUSE

Instances of child abuse should be reported to the local office of the state protective service for children or the police. The name of anyone reporting in good faith is confidential. The agency will investigate the report. If possible the child will remain in the home while a professional helps to resolve the problem underlying the abuse. If the agency determines that the child is in danger, the child may be removed to a foster home. The agency will continue to work with the family so that the child can safely be returned home.

The National Center for Child Abuse and Neglect maintains a

clearinghouse of successful programs for prevention and treatment of abuse. For further information contact the Department of Health and Human Services, Office of Human Development Services, Administration for Children, Youth and Families, Children's Bureau, National Center for Child Abuse and Neglect, 400 6th St. S.W., Washington, D.C. 20013, Tel. 202-755-0587.

CHILD DAY CARE

There is no overall public system in the United States to provide free or low-cost day care for children. There are some publicly funded facilities, but not enough spaces for all who need them. Consult your local telephone directory under Day Care. Public day care centers may charge a fee on a sliding scale depending on family income, or may establish eligibility by income.

Private day care centers are available in most communities. Costs will vary. Churches and nonprofit organizations frequently offer day care at less cost than private centers. Large companies also may provide day care at low cost or free to children of employees.

Home day care also is available in most areas. Check your telephone directory or local newspaper.

Licensing requirements for day care facilities vary from state to state. Generally, they must comply with the local fire code, health de-

partment laws, and with regulations governing the number and training of employees and provision of programs, toys and bathrooms.

Licensing is required too for home day care, though it may be waived if fewer than six children are enrolled. Licensing of day care centers is usually administered by the state department of public welfare.

See also: DAY CARE: MEAL PROGRAMS

CHILD LABOR

The U.S. Department of Labor sets standards for workers under the age of 18. These standards are designed to protect the educational opportunities of minors and to prohibit their employment under conditions that might be detrimental to their health or well-being.

The Department of Labor issues lists of occupations considered too hazardous for children. Children 16 or 17 years old may work in any nonhazardous job for unlimited hours. Children 14 or 15 may work outside of school hours in nonhazardous jobs no more than three hours on a school day and 18 hours in a school week. Fourteen years is the minimum age for most nonfarm work, but children of any age may deliver newspapers, perform in radio, television, movie or theatrical productions or work for parents in a nonfarm business.

Regulations are somewhat different for children engaged in farm work. For youths 16 years of age and older, any farm job is permissible, whether hazardous or not, for unlimited hours. For 14- and 15-year-olds any nonhazardous farm job outside of school hours is permitted. For 12- and 13-year-olds, farm work outside of school hours on nonhazardous jobs is permitted on the same farm as the parents or with the parent's written consent. Children under 12 can work on farms owned or operated by parents or with the parent's consent, outside of school hours in non-hazardous jobs. Children 10 and 11 may work for no more than eight weeks between June 1 and October 15 for employers who receive approval from the Department of Labor. Children of any age may work for their parents on a farm owned or operated by the parents.

The department has the power to conduct investigations, to recommend changes in employment practices and to bring civil suit on behalf of workers. Violators of child labor provisions are subject to a civil penalty of up to $1,000 for each violation.

Lists of dangerous occupations and further regulations can be obtained from any Wage and Hour office listed in a local telephone directory, or contact: Department of Labor, Wage and Hour Division, the Office of Information and Consumer Affairs, Employment Standards Administration, Department of Labor, 200 Constitution Ave., NW, Washington, D.C. 20210. Tel.: 202-523-7316.

CHILDREN: ABANDONED

Abandoned children up to 18 years old should be reported to the local child welfare agency, children's protective service or the police. The children will generally be placed in foster homes while attempts are made to locate their parents. Abandonment of a child may result in the parent losing legal rights. Information about state programs for abandoned children may be obtained from the Child Welfare League of America, 67 Irving Place, New York, N.Y. 10003, Tel. 212-254-7410.

CHILDREN: AID TO FAMILIES WITH DEPENDENT CHILDREN

The federal government and the states cooperate in a program of financial assistance to families with limited income and to children who lack support of a parent because of death or continued absence, or because that parent is physically or mentally unable to care for dependents. The program is called Aid to Families with Dependent Children (AFDC). The cost is shared by the state and the federal government.

The child or children must be living with a close relative, or in an appropriate foster home if the court has found that living at home is contrary to a child's welfare. The child must generally be under 18 or 21 if attending school full-time.

The person or family must be in financial need to qualify for AFDC payments. He must be without sufficient money or resources to provide the essentials of living. State laws require that the income and resources of applicants be recorded and evaluated to determine the amount of assistance the child or family is to receive, but the necessary expenses of the individual are also considered. The amount of benefits varies from state to state, because the states bear part of the cost of the program, but all have a maximum benefit that can be paid to a family of any given size. Within the general guidelines provided by the federal government, states establish a minimum standard of living against which the individual's or family's available resources are measured.

The program is administered by the individual states through the state department of public welfare. The address of agency can be found in the telephone directory under the state listing.

Emergency assistance can sometimes be given through the AFDC program to a child under age 21 and his or her family even though they may not qualify for assistance under the regular program. Migrant workers, for example, who have dependent children might qualify for emergency assistance.

Any recipient of AFDC or applicant whose claim for aid is denied, delayed, reduced or discontinued may request and obtain a fair hearing with the state welfare agency.

In addition to the AFDC program states may have general assistance or general relief programs for needy individuals or families who do not qualify for aid under the AFDC program. States meet the cost of these programs out of their own funds. Applications can generally also be made at the state welfare office.

CHILDREN: SOCIAL SECURITY BENEFITS

Children who are under age 18 (or 22 if in school full-time) and are the survivor of a parent who qualified for Social Security are entitled to monthly benefits. Children over 18 who are severely disabled before age 22 and who continue to be disabled also qualify for benefits.

See also: CHILDREN: AID TO FAMILIES WITH DEPENDENT CHILDREN

CHILE

A valid passport is required for U.S. citizens traveling to Chile, but no visa is necessary for a stay of up to 90 days whether traveling on business or pleasure. All visitors must fill out a Tourist Card upon arrival which must be turned over to Chilean authorities when leaving the country. Proof of a smallpox vaccination is required for entry, and a typhoid shot is advised. Pets may be brought in provided they have a validated health certificate. There are no restrictions on currency, foreign or local (peso) but there may be difficulty in reconverting pesos into foreign currency. Tourists are advised, therefore, not to change more than they will need. Most of the people of Chile speak only Spanish; English is spoken in the larger hotels and shops. To rent a car an International Driving Licence is required. Flowers, fruits or vegetables cannot be brought into the country.

Chilean business, which had been under government control during the former Allende regime, has been gradually denationalized. The government encourages foreign investment. Trade with Chile is conducted through resident agents. All foreign exchange agreements must be approved by the Banco Central de Chile, whose approval is equivalent to the granting of an import licence.

The Embassy of Chile is located at 1732 Massachusetts Ave. NW., Washington, D.C. 20036, Tel. 202-785-1746. Consulates can be found in Arvada, Colo.; Boston; Chicago; Farmington Hills, Mich.; Galveston; Los Angeles; Miami; New Orleans; New York; Pearl City, Hawaii; and, San Francisco.

The American Embassy in Chile is located in Codina Building, 1343 Agustinas, Santiago, Chile, Tel. 710133/710326.

For further business information contact the Chilean Trading Corp., 1 World Trade Center, New York, N.Y. 10048, Tel. 212-938-0550.

CHINA

A valid passport and a visa are required for travel to China. To obtain a visa a traveler must apply by mail or in person to the Embassy of the People's Republic of China, 2300 Connecticut Ave. N.W., Washington, D.C. 20008, Tel. 202-328-2510. Two photos will be required plus a fee of $7. They will want to know the dates of the trip, the places to be visited and the planned entry and exit points. An entrance visa is good only at a pre-planned point of entry. They will also issue an exit visa which is good only at the pre-planned point of exit. Visas are good only for the prearranged length of stay and for prearranged places of visit. Most tourists to China travel in tour groups which are organized by the China International Travel Service (CITS). CITS arranges all aspects of group tours and is the organization that authorizes visas. Travelers are advised to plan well in advance as a visa may take a long time in coming. A business traveler must have an invitation from a Chinese company or trade organization. Individual trips can be arranged only by invitation from a native Chinese host or an official ministry in the country.

There are no health requirements if arriving from the United States. If are arriving from other parts of Asia or Hong Kong a cholera shot is needed. If arriving from Africa or Latin America or from an infected area, a traveller needs protection against yellow fever. The official currency of China is the renminbi. No renminbis may be imported or exported. Any amount of foreign currency may be brought into China, but it must be declared upon arrival. No more foreign currency is allowed out of the country than was brought in, so travelers are advised to save all conversion receipts for reconversion upon leaving. Mandarin is the official language of China, but many dialects are also spoken. Few people speak English except for official guides and interpreters. Travelers may not bring arms, pornography, narcotics or objectionable political literature into the country.

All trade with China is government controlled, and imports are handled by a government agency assigned to deal with a particular import. There are generally no restrictions on imports, but they are handled on a case by case basis. To find out which agency to contact or for further business information, call the Commercial Section of the Chinese Embassy at 202-328-2520.

Visitors to China should become familiar with the new transliteration system that was adopted in 1979. For example what was once Peking is now spelled Beijing and Szechwan is now Sichuan. The few transliterated street and shop signs that exist in China use this new system. Travelers should also be advised that evidence of a trip to Taiwan may prevent their entry into Communist China.

The American Embassy in China is located at Guang Hua Lu, Beijing, China.

CHIROPRACTORS

Chiropractic is the second largest of the healing arts professions with approximately 21,000 Doctors of Chiropractic (DC) practicing in every state and in many foreign countries. Chiropractic is licensed as a branch of generic medicine in all states, the District of Columbia and in Puerto Rico. The DC is licensed and regulated by a state board.

An individual must satisfy educational requirements of two years of preprofessional college and four years of professional chiropractic education, and must pass a state examination to be licensed as a Doctor of Chiropractic. Any complaints about Doctors of Chiropractic should be referred to the state licensing board, which has the power to revoke or suspend licenses.

The federal Medicare law and most state Medicaid acts include Doctors of Chiropractic as primary health providers, so Medicare and Medicade will in most instances pay bills for their services. Fees paid to chiropractors are allowable medical deductions for federal income tax purposes.

Chiropractic colleges are accredited by the Commission on Accreditation of the Council on Chiropractic Education (CCE). The CCE is recognized by the Secretary of the U.S. Department of Education and is included on the department's list of nationally recognized accrediting agencies and associations.

The largest national chiropractic organization is the American Chiropractic Association (ACA), with 16,000 members. The ACA has no regulatory powers, but it does have a code of ethics for chiropractors, and acts as the national voice for Doctors of Chiropractic.

Contact individual state entries for addresses of departments that administer the state chiropractic boards.

Contact the Council on Chiropractic Education, 3209 Ingersoll St., Suite 206, Des Moines, Iowa 50312, for accredited programs of study.

Contact the American Chiropractic Association, 2200 Grand Avenue, Des Moines, Iowa 50312, Tel.: 515-243-1121, for national policy and ethics questions.

CHURCH OF THE NAZARENE

The membership of the Church of the Nazarene is over 625,000, with over 8,000 ordained elders and 2,600 licensed ministers in the United States, Canada and Great Britain. Over 500 missionaries and 2,500 national ministers are active in other countries around the world. The International Headquarters of the Church of the Nazarene is in Kansas City, Missouri, along with a graduate theological seminary and a publishing house.

The quadrennial General Assembly of the Church is its law-making and elective authority. Its membership is elected by the district assemblies and representatives from the mission fields. The General Assembly elects a board of superintendents who supervise the worldwide church activities. It also selects a General Board, which conducts the business of the church between assemblies.

The Church of the Nazarene is divided into about 80 districts. Local churches elect delegates to the annual district assembly. Each district has a superintendent who plans for the work of the district, but each church has the right of independent action. Local churches must, however, have the agreement of the district superintendent in selecting a pastor and in purchasing property.

Contact the World Headquarters of the Church of the Nazarene 6401 Paseo St., Kansas City, Mo. 64131, Tel.: 816-333-7000.

CHURCHES OF CHRIST, SCIENTIST

There are more than 3,500 Christian Science churches, societies, and organizations in some 57 countries. The *Manual of the Mother Church* is considered the constitution of the Christ, Scientist movement. The provisions in the *Manual* are administered by the Board of Directors of the Church, which appoints the chief officers of the Mother Church located in Boston. Branch churches choose their own officers by election.

Christian Science practitioners are persons who work full time in the public practice of Christian Science healing. Patients pay the practitioner for their treatment. Practitioners who have qualified by church standards of character, experience and understanding are listed in the directory of practitioners in the official church organ, *The Christian Science Journal*.

The headquarters of the Churches of Christ Scientist is at The First Church of Christ, Scientist, Christian Science Center, Boston, Mass., 02115, Tel.: 607-262-2300.

CITIZENSHIP

All individuals born in the United States or its territories and any children of a U.S. citizen are citizens of the United States. Citizenship can be obtained by marrying a U.S. citizen or by naturalization.

See NATURALIZATION

CIVIL DEFENSE

The Defense Civil Preparedness Agency is responsible for preparing a viable Civil Defense program. It is also charged with providing local government with guidance and assistance in preparing their own programs. The Agency is responsible for an evacuation and shelter program, assessment of damage in the event of an attack and the protection and emergency operating capability of government agencies in keeping with the continuity of government. Contact the Defense Civil Preparedness Agency, The Pentagon, Washington, D.C. 20301, Tel. 202-697-4487 or the regional offices in Maynard, Mass.; New York City; Olney, Md.; Thomasville, Ga.; Battle Creek, Mich.; Denton, Tex.; Denver; Kansas City, Mo.; Santa Rosa, Calif.; and Bothell, Wash.

CLAIMS AGAINST THE GOVERNMENT

The General Accounting Office settles claims against the federal government by both individuals and businesses. Settlement of these claims by the GAO is binding upon executive branch agencies. However the Comptroller General may review these settlements. The claimant may also have recourse to Congress. For further information, contact the General Accounting Office, Claims Division, 411 G. St. N.W., Washington, D.C. 20548, Tel. 202-275-6202.

An individual may also sue the United States in the United States Court of Claims under certain circumstances. For further information contact the Clerk, United States Court of Claims, 717 Madison Place NW, Washington, D.C. 20005, Tel. 202-633-7257.

CLOTHING CARE LABELING

The Federal Trade Commission enforces the federal law that requires that all clothing manufactured in the United States except gloves, shoes and hats, must be labeled with instructions for proper care and cleaning. Suede, leather, fur and most vinyl garments are exempted.

Complaints about clothing not wearing properly when care instructions are followed can be reported to the store, the manufacturer or state or local consumer agency. (For state consumer agencies, see appendix.) Contact the Federal Trade Commission, Pennsylvania Ave. at Sixth St. NW, Washington, D.C. 20580, Tel. 202-523-3600.

COINS

The Bureau of the Mint produces coins and other numismatic items. It is also responsible for the custody of the government's silver and gold bullion. For further information contact the Department of the Treasury, Bureau of the Mint, 501 13th St. NW, Washington, D.C. 20220, Tel. 202-376-0872.

COLLEGE CREDIT BY EXAMINATION

Many colleges now offer college credit through life experience or examination. In addition, the College Level Examination Program offers a general examination and subject examinations in 47 categories for individuals who want to demonstrate mastery of a course sufficient to qualify for credit.

The New York State Regent's External Degree Program also sponsors a college proficiency examination program to evaluate the qualification of individuals for college credit through independent study or experience.

Colleges will not grant degrees based solely on examination for life experience credit, but many now will accept such credits as part of the requirements for a college degree.

Contact the College Level Examination Program, The College Board, Educational Testing Service, P.O. Box 1822, Princeton, N.J. 08541, Tel: 609-921-9000 or the New York State Regent's External Degree Program, Albany Cultural Education Center, Albany, N.Y. 12230, Tel: 518-474-2121.

COLLEGIATE ATHLETICS

The National Collegiate Athletic Association (NCAA) is a voluntary organization of more than 880 colleges, universities, conferences and organizations devoted to the administration of intercollegiate athletics. The NCAA serves as an overall national discussion, legislative and administrative body for the universities and colleges of the U.S. in matters of intercollegiate athletics. Through the NCAA, its members consider any athletic problem which has crossed regional or conference boundaries and has become national in scope. The NCAA also serves as the national athletic accrediting agency for colleges and universities. In addition it formulates rules for collegiate sports and serves as the clearinghouse for collegiate athletic records.

Any college or university may be

elected to active membership in the NCAA if it: 1) is accredited by the recognized academic accrediting agency of its region; 2) maintains a minimum of four intercollegiate sports, with one sport in each of the three traditional seasons of the academic year; 3) complies with all NCAA legislation dealing with financial aid, recruiting, playing and practice seasons, post-season competition and other areas of athletic administration; and, 4) agrees to cooperate fully with the NCAA enforcement program and to respect penalties imposed by that program.

The NCAA holds an annual convention, usually in the early part of January with each active and qualified allied member entitled to one vote on all issues before the convention.

As 18-member council is responsible for establishing and directing the general policy of the association between conventions. The council is composed of eight district vice presidents, eight vice presidents at large, the president and the secretary-treasurer. Members of the council are elected at the annual convention. An executive committee with 10-members including the president and secretary-treasurer is elected by the council to transact NCAA business and administer the events of the association.

The NCAA has established national championships in sports such as football, basketball, baseball, soccer, golf, swimming, outdoor track, cross country and tennis.

The NCAA has permanent offices at U.S. Highway 50 and Nall Avenue, P.O. Box 1906, Shawnee Mission, Kan. 66222. The telephone number is 913-384-3220.

COLOMBIA

A valid passport and a tourist card are required for travel to Colombia. A tourist card is obtainable by bringing a passport, two photographs and a return ticket to a Colombian diplomatic mission. The Embassy of Colombia is located at 2118 LeRoy Place NW, Washington, D.C. 20008, Tel. 202-387-8338. Consulates are located in Atlanta, Baltimore, Boston, Chicago, Detroit, Houston, Kansas City, Los Angeles, Miami, New Orleans, New York, Philadelphia, San Diego, San Francisco and Tampa. Those traveling on business will first have to visit the nearest Colombian consulate by appointment, where they will be informed of the necessary requirements. They should be prepared to provide Health and Marriage Certificates and a letter from their company detailing the nature of their business and accepting financial responsibility. Business travelers will probably have to wait up to two months for a response. Visitors will need proof of a smallpox vaccination. In addition, if they are coming from an infected area, proof of shots against cholera and yellow fever is required. Also advisable are shots against hepatitis and malaria. Pets are not allowed to be brought into the country.

The official language of Colombia is Spanish, but English is often spoken in larger hotels and shops. Colombian currency is the peso; only 500 pesos may be brought into or out of Colombia. Any amount of foreign currency may be imported or exported. A foreign driver's license or an International Driving License is necessary to rent a car.

Foreign trade with Colombia is usually handled through resident agents who can obtain the necessary licenses. Import licenses are needed for all goods. They are issued by the Instituto Colombiano de Comercio Exterior (INCOMEX). This agency also issues foreign exchange licenses, which are necessary for such transactions. The import of goods already available in Colombia may be restricted.

The U.S. Embassy in Colombia is located at Calle 37, 8-40, Tel. 285-1300, telex 44843. However, the mailing address for this Embassy is APO Miami 34038.

For further tourist information contact the Colombian Government Tourist Office, 140 East 57 St., New York, N.Y. 10022, Tel. 212-688-0151.

For additional business information contact the Colombian Government Trade Bureau at the above East 57 St. address, Tel. 212-758-4772.

COLORADO

The Consumer Protection Section of the Attorney General's of-
fice is responsible for consumer protection in Colorado. A consumer complaint is reviewed by a staff member to determine if the Section can help. If the complaint does not fall within the jurisdiction of the Section, the consumer is so notified. If the Section does handle the complaint, the business against whom the complaint is filed will be required to submit a written response, under oath, to the Office of Consumer Affairs. No further action will be taken by the Section unless the business has a pattern of violations of Colorado law.

The Section also has civil powers to file lawsuits where there is a pattern of consumer abuse and can obtain restitution or refunds for consumers. Court injunctions can be sought to restrain a business from illegal practices. Another alternative is an assurance of discontinuance where a confidential agreement between the business and the Attorney General's Office is obtained to discontinue certain business practices without the court's involvement.

Contact the Colorado Attorney General's Office, Consumer Protection Section, State Services Building, 1525 Sherman St., 3rd Floor, Denver, Colo. 80203, Tel. 303-866-3611.

Occupations and professions in Colorado are licensed through a number of licensing boards which set requirements for licensing, examine applicants' qualifications, issue licenses and accept complaints about licensees. These boards are administered by the Department of Regulatory Agencies. Send complaints about licensees or inquiries about licensing to the Department of Regulatory Agencies, 1525 Sherman St., Denver, Colo. 80203, Tel. 303-866-3304.

The Division of Commerce and Development offers help to businesses and industry interested in moving to or expanding in Colorado. Interested businesses should contact the Division of Commerce and Development, Business Development Section, Denver, Colo. 80203, Tel. 303-866-2205.

Colorado offers city or county revenue bond financing to industry.

The corporate income tax in Colorado is a flat 5%. The sales tax is 3%.

Individual income tax in Colorado ranges from 3% for income less than $1,134 to 8% for income in excess of $11,242.

For tourist information contact the Division of Commerce and Development, 500 State Centennial Building, Denver, Colo. 80203, Tel. 303-839-2350, or the Travel Marketing Section, Colorado Division of Commerce and Development, 602 State Capitol Annex, Denver, Colo. 80203, Tel. 303-839-3045.

COMMODITY MARKETS

Commodities are traded on commodity futures exchanges located in major U.S. cities and in foreign cities, such as London, Paris and Hong Kong. The largest of the United States commodity exchanges is the Chicago Board of Trade (CBOT). Other commodity exchanges around the country are: the Chicago Mercantile Exchange, the Commodity Exchange, Inc. of New York, the Kansas City Board of Trade (wheat), the Mid-American Commodity Exchange, the Minneapolis Grain Exchange, the New York Cocoa Exchange, the New York Coffee and Sugar Exchange, the New York Cotton Exchange and the New York Mercantile Exchange.

Commodity futures exchanges are membership organizations. Members produce, market or process commodities, or are brokers who principally execute orders for others. Individuals who are not members of an exchange can trade in commodity futures through brokerage firms that hold memberships in commodity markets through partners or officers.

Investment in commodity futures, is arranged through a futures contract bought through a brokerage house. The contracts offer standard terms of quantity, quality and location and require delivery of the commodity at a specified time in the future.

Most commodity futures contracts are not settled by actual delivery of the commodity, but are sold prior to their maturity.

Both full-service brokerage firms and firms that specialize in commodities futures offer trading. Brokerage houses generally require a minimum amount that they will accept to open a commodities account. The amount may be as little as several hundred dollars or as much as several thousand.

Trading in commodity futures is regulated in the United States both by the exchanges themselves and by the Commodity Futures Trading Commission (CFTC), an agency of the federal government.

Contact the Commodity Futures Trading Commission, 2033 K St. NW, Washington, D.C. 20581, Tel: 800-424-9838.

COMMUNIST PARTY

The national office of the Communist Party is located at 235 West 23rd Street, New York, N.Y. 10011, Tel. 212-989-4994. Communist Party candidates run for state and national office with assistance from the national party.

CANCER

The National Cancer Institute, in the Department of Health and Human Services, has a hotline that offers individuals information about the risks of cancer. The organization also provides material on the subject and gives emotional support where necessary. The hotline number is 800-638-6694 (800-638-6070 in Alaska and Hawaii and 800-492-6600 in Maryland). For further information on the Institute's programs contact the Department of Health and Human Services, National Institutes of Health, National Cancer Institute, 9000 Rockville Pike, Bethesda, Md. 20205, Tel. 301-496-5615.

The American Cancer Society is one of several groups that supports medical research and offers information on the disease. It also conducts programs designed to help people stop smoking. The Society can provide information on the many support groups which have been formed to aid cancer victims and their families. For further information contact the local branch of the Society of the headquarters at 777 Third Ave., New York, N.Y. 10017, Tel. 212-371-2900.

CONGRESS: MEMBERS OF

Members of Congress can be valuable in helping constituents who have problems with government bureaucracy. All Americans have three representatives: two senators and one member of the House. It is best to contact only one of these at a time, the one who is, in the individual's opinion, most likely to act. All contact should be made in writing. It is against the law for members of Congress to obtain information about an individual without his or her permission. Letters should be short and confined to one issue. They should include all background material on the problem. The congressman will probably give the problem to an aide for handling. The aide will initiate procedures quickly, but government bureaucracy is slow, and he or she will need time to solve the problem. If the individual does not receive a response to his complaint within a few weeks, he can then contact his other representatives.

Members of state senates and assemblies will handle disputes with the state bureaucracy in the same manner.

CONNECTICUT

The State of Connecticut Department of Consumer Protection is responsible for enforcing consumer protection legislation, and conducts regular inspections of wholesale and retail food establishments, drug-related establishments, bedding and upholstery dealers and manufacturers, and commercial establishments which use weighing and measuring devices.

The department also responds to consumer complaints, conducts investigations into alleged fraudulent activities and provides information and referral services. The Complaint Center in the Department of Consumer Protection processes consumer complaints, provides consumers with information regarding departmental jurisdiction, and refers the complaints to the proper division.

The Department of Consumer Protection will also mediate consumer complaints and has the authority to investigate and take action against businesses who have violated Connecticut law.

Contact the Department of Consumer Protection, 165 Capitol Ave., Hartford, Conn. 06115, Tel. 203-566-2822, Toll-free tel. 800-842-2649. Regional offices are located in Stamford and Norwich.

The Registration Division of the Department of Consumer Protection has the following licensing boards which regulate businesses or occupations: accountancy, architectural registration, landscape architects, occupational licensing boards, professional engineers and land surveyors, real estate, television and radio service, tree protection, veterinary registration, and well drilling. The Registration Division administers examinations and issues license and certificates and processes and investigates all complaints received by the boards. Complaints or requests for information about licensing should be directed to the Registration Division of the Department of Consumer Protection, at the address listed above.

The Department of Economic Development will provide a business ombudsman to assist businesses considering moving to or expanding in Connecticut. Request such assistance from the Department of Economic Development, 210 Washington St., Hartford, Conn. 06106, or call one of the toll-free numbers listed below, or call 203-566-7035.

Connecticut provides long-term industrial revenue bond financing to businesses to cover the purchase and development of land, construction, purchase of equipment and installation of pollution abatement equipment. State insurance coverage of first mortgage loans on business and industrial projects deemed beneficial to Connecticut is also provided by the state. Small contractor loans through the state provide working capital for small and minority contractors. These programs are offered through the Department of Economic Development at the above address.

There are no general, state or local personal income taxes in Connecticut and since there are no county governments, there are no county taxes. The state does not tax personal property and there is no sales tax.

Communities with voter approval can provide certain tax abatements for new industry and allow property tax exemptions for buildings equipped with solar energy systems.

The corporate business tax is a franchise type measured by corporate net income and generally follows the federal law. The statutory tax rate is 10%, but the effective rate amounts to 9% since the tax is itself deductible in computing tax liability. There is no corporate net worth tax, no state unincorporated business tax, and no DISC corporation business tax.

Connecticut has a 7.5% state sales and use tax which applies to most retail sales. A 3.5% state sales tax is assessed on certain business services.

Further information about the tax structure in Connecticut can be requested from the Department of Revenue Services, 92 Farmington Ave., Hartford, Conn. 06115, Tel. 203-566-8520. Offices are also located in Bridgeport, Hamden, Norwhich, and Waterbury.

Tourist information can be requested from the Department of Economic Development, Tourism Promotion Services, 210 Washington St., Hartford, Conn. 06106. A toll-free telephone is 800-243-2685 (for Maine through Virginia) or for Connecticut 800-243-1685, or call the regular number, 203-566-3385.

CONSERVATION
See FLOODING AND LAND DRAINAGE POLLUTION: WATER AND SOLID WASTE

CONSUMER COMPLAINTS
See BETTER BUSINESS BUREAU; CALL FOR ACTION; specific entries eg. FABRICS; and, state entries.

CONSUMER FRAUD
Suspected cases of consumer fraud should be reported to the state consumer protection office. See individual state entries. If the office does not have the power to investigate, and the case seems worthy of investigation, it will refer the complaint to the proper agency, which may be part of the attorney general's office.

Instances of consumer fraud in interstate commerce can be reported to the Federal Trade Commission (FTC), Sixth St. and Pennsylvania Ave. NW, Washington, D.C. 20580, Tel. 202-523-3711. The FTC cannot investigate every consumer complaint, but it maintains records of consumer complaints for use in future investigations.

See also entries on individual products or services.

CONSUMER INFORMATION: NATIONAL

The Consumer Information Center of the General Services Administration publishes a free *Consumer Information Catalog* that lists booklets of almost 30 agencies of the federal government. These booklets are available free or at low cost to the consumer.

Booklets are available on car repairs, on saving money on food, costs on health care, energy, household expenses, diet, exercise and on a wide variety of other topics. The center also welcomes suggestions from consumers for future booklets.

Contact the Consumer Information Center, General Services Administration, Pueblo, Colo. 81009, Tel: 303-544-5277, or the Consumer Information Center, General Services Administration Washington, D.C. 20405.

The Consumer Information Center also operates a media hotline for consumer information. Telephone 202-566-1794.

CONTRACEPTIVES: SAFETY

As prescription drugs or devices, contraceptives are regulated by the Food and Drug Administration (FDA). The FDA has published a detailed statement listing the relative health hazards and effectiveness of various contraceptive methods. The statement must be included with birth control pills. A similar package statement is required by the FDA to be given to all users of intrauterine devices.

CONTRACTS: GOVERNMENT

Each governmental agency and department has its own contracting office which deals with suppliers. The Commerce Department publishes the *Commerce Business Daily* giving all agency solicitations for bids. For further information contact the Commerce Department, International Trade Administration, U.S. Commercial Service, Main Commerce Building, Washington, D.C. 20230, Tel. 202-337-3094.

The Business Service Centers of the General Service Administration, located in Boston; New York; Washington, D.C.; Philadelphia; Atlanta; Chicago; Kansas City, Mo.; Fort Worth; Houston; Denver; San Francisco; Los Angeles; and Seattle offer advice to businessmen on how to obtain government contracts. For further information contact one of the above centers listed under U.S. Government in the telephone directory or the General Services Administration, Office of Industry and Customer Relations, 18th and F Sts. NW, Washington, D.C. 20405, Tel. 202-566-1043.

COPYRIGHT

An author can file for copyright when he or she has produced an original work in a tangible form. It is not necessary to publish a work to obtain a copyright. Nor is it always necessary to obtain a copyright for copyright protection. The law, however, is extremely confusing, and authors are urged to contact the copyright office. Copyright is registered at the Library of Congress, Copyright Office, Crystal Mall Annex, 1921 Jefferson Davis Highway, Arlington, Va. The mailing address is Library of Congress, Washington, D.C. 20559, Tel. 202-557-5800.

CORRESPONDENCE SCHOOLS
See HOME STUDY

COSMETICS
The Food and Drug Administration regulates the ingredients in cosmetics. It also regulates packaging and labeling to ensure that they provide: the identity of the product, the net contents, the name and the address of the distributor and any warnings that the FDA deems necessary. Ingredients must be listed in the order of amount contained, except for color ingredients which can be listed in any order. Fragrances and flavors do not have to be listed individually.

Cosmetic products generally do not have to be pre-tested before marketing as do products labeled drugs, although untested products may be required to carry a warning that the safety of the product has not been determined.

The FDA can use legal procedures to take the product off the market if it is shown to be a health hazard. The agency urges consumers who suffer adverse reactions to notify the manufacturer or the Food and Drug Administration, Cosmetics Technology, 200 C St. SW, Washington, D.C. 20204, Tel. 202-245-1057.

COSMETOLOGISTS
All states require cosmetologists to be licensed, but the qualifications for a license vary. In most cases an applicant must have completed the 10th grade, graduated from a state approved cosmetology school, passed a physical examination and celebrated her 16th birthday. The licensing examination includes a written and a practical test. Some states have a reciprocity agreement allowing licensed cosmetologists to practice in the other state without reexamination. Requirements and a list of approved training schools can be obtained from the state board of cosmetology or the Cosmetology Accrediting Commission, 1990 M St. NW, Washington, D.C. 20036, Tel. 202-331-9550.

See also individual state entries.

COUNSELORS: SCHOOL
Most states require school counselors to have teacher's certificate and experience as a teacher before they can qualify for a counselor's certificate. A few states certify counselors even if they have never taught school.

To qualify for a state certificate in counseling the applicant must generally have a master's degree in counseling and one to five years experience as a school counselor. Those who have completed their master's degree, including a supervised period of school counseling, are allowed to practice with a provisional certificate until they have met the experience requirements.

Specific certification requirements can be obtained from the state board of education, usually located in the state capital.

Contact the local school district office for the address of the state board.

COURT SYSTEMS: FEDERAL

The federal court system tries cases involving violations of federal criminal laws and civil cases in which the amount involved is more than $10,000 and the parties live in different states.

The lowest federal courts are the District Courts. There is a District Court in each state, in Washington, D.C. and in a number of U.S. territories. In addition to criminal and civil cases, these courts decide on maritime cases involving international waters, copyrights, trademarks, patents and bankruptcy. District courts are trial courts which have the power to determine the facts in a case and pass judgment.

On the same level as the District Courts are courts that specialize in certain types of federal cases.

These include the U.S. Customs Court, Tax Court and the Court of Claims, which tries cases against the federal government.

Above the District courts are the circuit courts, called the U.S. Courts of Appeals. These courts sit in 10 judicial circuits covering the United States and some of its territories. For example, the first district covers Maine, Massachusetts, New Hampshire, Rhode Island and Puerto Rico. The Courts of Appeals have the power to review decisions from the District Courts and the Tax Court and also review decisions of federal administrative agencies. The job of these Appellate courts is not to dispute the lower court's finding of fact, but to consider whether the judge has properly applied the law. The Courts of Appeal can either reverse the lower court's decision or send the case back to the lower court to be retried. Decisions of the Customs Court are reviewed by the U.S. Court of Customs and Patent Appeals.

The highest appeal court in the United States is the U.S. Supreme Court which reviews decisions from the Courts of Appeal and also from the U.S. Court of Claims. In addition, the Supreme Court decides disputes between states and reviews state supreme court decisions involving federal law or the constitution.

All federal judges are appointed by the President, subject to confirmation by the Senate, for life terms.

Federal legislation passed in 1978 created a separate bankruptcy court on the District Court level. These courts are to be fully operative by 1984. Appeals from the new bankruptcy courts will be heard by District Court judges unless a conflict of interest is involved, in which case appeals will be heard either by a panel of bankruptcy judges or by the higher Courts of Appeals. Judges for this court will be appointed for terms of 14 years.

COURT SYSTEMS: STATE

Under the Constitution, jurisdiction not vested in the federal court system rests with the state court systems. In addition, many cases within federal jurisdiction also may be tried in state courts, for example, suits involving citizens of different states. However, if a plantiff chooses to bring such an action in a state court, the case may be moved to a federal court by request of the defendant. Once a case has been ruled on by a state court, it can be appealed to the Supreme Court only if a federal question is involved. Otherwise, the decision of the state's supreme court is final.

The composition of a state's court system usually is outlined by the state's constitution, although some discretion is left to the state legislature. The legislature often has authority to determine the jurisdiction of the various levels of the courts.

Though the composition of state courts vary from state-to-state, it generally embraces five major levels: justice of the peace and other courts of lesser jurisdiction; courts of intermediate grade; courts of general trial jurisdiction; appellate courts and the state supreme court. Justices of the peace, courts of general trial jurisdiction and supreme courts exist in all states. Courts of intermediate grade and appellate courts are found in some states.

Justice of the peace sometimes are appointed by the governor but usually are elected by popular vote for a term of two to four years. The election district is most frequently a township or other county subdivision. No legal training is required to hold the position of justice of the peace. The justice of the peace presides over three types of cases: civil suits not involving more than a few hundred dollars; minor criminal cases such as traffic violations and misdemeanors; preliminary hearings in more serious crimes.

Courts of intermediate grade fall between the justice of the peace and general trial courts. They sometimes are established on the county level to deal with both civil and criminal matters. Intermediate courts frequently have authority to hear appeals from justice of the peace courts, and where probate courts do not exist, they have authority to hear probate questions. Judges of intermediate courts are usually elected on a county-wide basis.

General courts are authorized to handle civil cases with no dollar limit and criminal cases regardless of degree. They also hear appeals from justice of the peace courts. These courts usually are called circuit courts or district courts. The judges are elected by popular vote or appointed by the governor.

About a quarter of the states have established appellate courts. Appellate judges are elected by popular vote, or appointed by the governor. Most appellate courts consist of three or more judges who hear a case and render a verdict by majority vote. Since appellate courts primarily rule on matters of law and not on questions of fact, juries are not ordinarily used.

At the top of the state court system is the state supreme court with three to nine justices. Supreme court justices are elected by popular vote in many states— appointed by the governor or elected by the state legislature in other states. One justice is elected or named chief justice. The chief justice presides over the court's business and has some supervisory authority.

The jurisdiction of the state supreme court is principally that of an appellate body. In deciding cases, the state supreme courts rule by a majority vote, with one justice writing an opinion on behalf of the majority. Dissenting opinions are sometimes issued by those voting with the minority.

Majority opinions become legal precedents to be followed in subsequent cases, either civil or criminal.

CREDIT: BILLING PROBLEMS

The Federal Trade Commission regulates companies that are engaged in any form of interstate commerce and offer credit to their customers, such as department stores or credit card companies. The federal Fair Credit Billing Act requires creditors to correct billing errors promptly and without damage to the consumer's credit rating. Errors include being billed for merchandise either not ordered or not delivered, errors in arithmetic, failure to credit a payment and failure to mail the statement to the correct address provided that the creditor was notified of the address change at least 10 days before the end of the billing period.

In the case of a billing error, first notify the creditor in writing within 60 days after the bill was mailed. Include the account name and number and a description of the error. By law, the creditor must acknowledge the letter or correct the error within 30 days. Within two billing periods, or 90 days, the error must be corrected or an answer given in writing explaining why the creditor believes there is no error. If the consumer is not satisfied, he or she must notify the creditor within the time allowed to pay the bill, after receipt of the creditor's written explanation.

Once the consumer has written about a possible billing error, a creditor cannot give out information to other creditors or credit bureaus that would damage the consumer's credit rating. Nor can the creditor take any action to collect the disputed amount until the complaint is answered.

After the creditor has explained the bill, the consumer may be reported as delinquent on the amount in dispute, and the creditor may take action to collect the bill. If the creditor reports the delinquency to any other sources, the consumer must be notified. When the dispute is settled the creditor must report the outcome to each source that received information about the delinquency.

If dealing with the company directly cannot settle the dispute satisfactorily, the consumer may want to request help from the state consumer protection agency or Better Business Bureau, both of which can mediate the dispute or offer advice on other possible action.

The consumer can also report any suspected violations of law regarding credit to the Federal Trade Commission. The FTC cannot investigate individual complaints, but it maintains complaints on file for use in future investigations. Contact the State Consumer protection agency, Better Business Bureau or the Federal Trade Commission, Pennsylvania Ave. at Sixth St. NW, Washington, D.C. 20580, Tel. 202-523-3830.

See also: individual state entries, ADVERTISING: COMPLAINTS, BETTER BUSINESS BUREAU, CREDIT: CONSUMER APPLYING, CREDIT: RECORDS

CREDIT: CONSUMER

Each state has an agency that regulates credit offered to consumers by businesses operating in that state and subject to its laws. This office, often called the consumer credit commission, is usually located in the state capital. Types of consumer credit regulated include small loans, installment loans, secondary mortgage loans, retail installment sales and motor vehicle installment sales. The commissions issue licenses to those doing business under regulated loans not made by banks, savings and loan associations or credit unions.

Contact the state consumer credit commission for consumer complaints, or the state's consumer protection office (listed in the individual state entry), which will either mediate the complaint or refer it to the proper state agency for action.

CREDIT: CONSUMER, APPLYING

A great variety of sources issue credit: banks, savings and loan associations, credit unions, finance companies, credit card companies, department stores, etc. Creditor's decisions are based on applicant's capacity to repay a loan, the applicant's credit history, and the applicant's collateral. Creditors use different methods of looking at these factors. One lending institution might approve a loan when another would not.

An applicant for credit must be notified of approval or denial within 30 days of application. If credit is denied, the notice must be in writing and either state the reason or affirm the applicant's right to request an explanation.

The federal Equal Credit Opportunity Act states that race, color, age, sex, or marital status cannot be used against the applicant when applying for credit or in any part of the credit process. The act does not guarantee any applicant approval but does guarantee protection from disqualification on the abovementioned grounds.

Banks, savings and loan institutions and credit unions are required to make annual reports to their state or federal regulatory agency regarding their credit policies, and they are regularly inspected by these agencies. Refer credit problems unresolved by the bank, savings and loan institution or credit union to state or federal regulatory agency. A consumer specialist will respond to the complaint.

State consumer protection agencies will generally mediate complaints individually. (See individual state entries.) A federal agency like the FTC does not generally act on individual complaints but does investigate where there is a pattern of complaints against a particular company.

Contact the following federal agency that regulates the particular lending institution.

Banks in the Federal Reserve System

The Federal Reserve System
20th St. and Constitution Ave. NW
Washington, D.C. 20551
Tel. 202-452-3000

State-chartered banks not members of the Federal Reserve System

Federal Deposit Insurance Corporation
550 17th S. NW
Washington, D.C. 20429
Tel. toll free, 800-424-5488

National banks

Comptroller of the Currency
Consumers Affairs Division
Washington, D.C. 20219
Tel. 202-566-2000

Savings and Loan Institutions

Federal Home Loan Bank Board
Office of Communications
1700 G. St. NW
Washington, D.C. 20552
Tel. 202-377-6680

Credit Unions

National Credit Union Administration
Office of Public Information
2025 M St. NW
Washington, D.C. 20456
Tel. 202-357-1050

Retail department stores, consumer finance companies, all other creditors and all nonbank credit cards

Federal Trade Commission
Pennsylvania Ave. at Sixth St. NW
Washington, D.C. 20580
Tel. 202-523-3830.

CREDIT: INCIDENTAL

Doctors, lawyers, small retailers, and others often offer their customers the right to defer payments for goods or services. This credit is primarily for personal, family, or household purposes; not granted under terms of a credit card; not subject to any finance charges or interest; and is not granted under an agreement allowing the debtor to repay in more than four installments.

The Equal Credit Opportunity Act prohibits discrimination in incidental credit on the same basis as other credit. The law allows persons who have been discriminated against in connection with incidental credit to sue for actual damages and punitive damages.

Further information about incidental credit can be obtained from the board of governors of the Federal Reserve System, 20th St. and Constitution Ave. NW, Washington, D.C. 20551, Tel. 202-452-3201.

CREDIT: RECORDS

Credit bureaus, which maintain records on consumers' credit are under the jurisdiction of the Federal Trade Commission. These records may include information on the consumer's payment history, what credit cards or bank loans the consumer may have had, and other information such as employment that might reflect the individual's credit worthiness.

Under federal law creditors must also consider the credit history of accounts that women may have held jointly with their husbands. New credit information for joint accounts must be entered into credit records in the woman's name as well as in the man's.

If credit is refused, the creditor must supply the applicant with the name and address of the agency maintaining the report. The applicant can then request a credit report for examination. The bureau cannot charge a fee for the report if the request is within 30 days of the denial of credit. If the consumer finds an error in the agency's credit report, the bureau must investigate, and must remove from the credit file any errors that creditors admit are there. If the consumer disputes the creditor's report after the investigation, the consumer has the right to file a short statement stating his or her version. The statement must then be included in the credit file.

Complaints about credit bureaus can be directed to the Federal Trade Commission. The FTC cannot investigate individual consumer complaints, but does maintain a data bank of complaints that can be used in future investigations of the credit bureau industry or of specific credit bureaus.

Complaints about credit bureaus can be sent to the state consumer protection agency (see individual state entry), which will either mediate the complaint or forward it to another state agency for investigation.

Contact either a local FTC office, or the Federal Trade Commission, Pennsylvania Ave. at Sixth St. NW, Washington, D.C. 20580, Tel. 202-523-3830.

See also CREDIT: CONSUMER, APPLYING

CREDIT CARDS

Credit cards are issued by banks, retail department stores, gasoline and other companies. The Federal Trade Commission regulates all companies that issue credit cards to consumers. Credit cards issued by banks are regulated by the Federal Deposit Insurance Corporation (FDIC). Neither the FDIC nor the FTC can investigate every consumer complaint, but do regulate practices of credit card companies.

The federal Truth in Lending law protects users of credit cards. Credit card companies are required to specify the annual percentage rate and the finance charges (including service charges). The law also protects against unauthorized use of a credit card. The maximum the consumer is required to pay, for a lost or stolen credit card is $50. The unauthorized use of the credit card must have occurred before notification of loss to the card company. Otherwise the consumer is not even liable for that amount.

By law credit cards can be issued only to those who request them, but substitute or renewal cards can be issued without such request. Suspected violations of federal law should be reported to the FTC or FDIC (addresses in appendix), which will investigate if there are numerous or serious complaints.

See also: CREDIT: BILLING PROBLEMS, CREDIT: CONSUMER, APPLYING

CREDIT COUNSELING

A number of organizations offer consumer credit counseling. These include family service centers, credit unions, and religious organizations. The Consumer Credit Counselng Service (CCCS), sponsored by the National Foundation for Consumer Credit, Inc. (NFCC) is one of the major ones. The NFCC is supported by banks, credit card companies, finance companies, and other financial institutions. Services of CCCS are available at offices in all states except Alaska, Arkansas, Delaware and Mississippi.

There is often no charge for the CCCS counseling services such as the teaching of money-management techniques and help in the construction of debt payment plans.

CCCS offices are listed in the telephone directory as Consumer Credit Counseling Service or Credit Union League. Local credit unions also can refer you to the nearest CCCS office, or write

Credit Union National Association
P.O. Box 431, Madison, Wis. 53701,
Tel. 608-231-4000.

CREDIT UNIONS

Credit unions offer savings and loan services to members, often at lower rates than are available elsewhere. They are formed by a group of consumers sharing a common bond of occupation, association or residence in a well-defined neighborhood, urban community or rural area. Only members who have met the common criteria for joining are allowed to use the credit union services. After the expenses of the credit union are met, the earnings of the credit union are returned to its members in the form of dividends on shareholdings. Some credit unions also refund to borrowers a portion of the interest paid on loans.

Credit unions offer services similar to those of savings and loan institutions. These include savings accounts, loans and "money market" share certificates generally on the same terms as savings and loan institutions, although the interest rates on loans may be at lower rates than at non-member institutions. Credit unions do not offer checking accounts.

The National Credit Union Administration (NCUA), an independent government agency, regulates some 12,710 federal credit unions and also insures an additional 5,002 state-chartered credit unions. State-chartered credit unions are regulated by state agencies but insured by NCUA up to a maximum of $100,000, similiar to the Federal Deposit Insurance Corporation insurance on accounts in banks and savings and loan associations (see BANK ACCOUNTS: FEDERALLY INSURED).

Examiners from the NCUA periodically review credit unions both to assure that they provide services to members in accordance with regulations, and to provide advice on the overall soundness of the credit union operations. NCUA emphasizes the deregulation of credit unions as much as possible and the overall simplification of established regulations. The NCUA will assist groups who wish to start credit unions.

The NCUA accepts consumer complaints and initiates investigations. The complainant receives a letter of acknowledgement, and when the investigation is completed the complainant receives a written response from the investigating office. If the credit union if found to have violated federal regulations, the agency recommends that the credit union resolve the complaint and correct any deficiencies that led to it. NCUA will also refer complaints about state-chartered credit unions to the appropriate state agency.

NCUA maintains a toll-free telephone number that carries a daily update of agency activities and money market certificate and treasury bill rates as available each Tuesday. Contact the Office of Public Information, National Credit Union Administration, 2025 M St. NW, Washington, D.C. 20456, Tel.: 202-357-1050 or toll free 800-424-5531.

CRIB DEATH

The National Foundation for Sudden Infant Death, Inc. disseminates information about Sudden Infant Death Syndrome (crib death) and aids bereaved families who have lost a child. It also helps in caring for high risk infants. For further information contact the National Foundation for Sudden Infant Death, Inc., 310 South Michigan Ave., Chicago, Ill. 60604, Tel. 312-663-6050.

CRIME INSURANCE

See INSURANCE: CRIME (FEDERAL)

CRIME VICTIMS AND WITNESSES: AID TO

Many cities have special units in the district attorney's office or the police department to aid crime victims and witnesses of crimes. Probation departments and charitable organizations also may offer assistance. Most programs offer counseling by professionals or volunteers trained by professionals. Counseling includes information about the legal rights of the victim and the witness. Programs may also offer support services such as an escort through the police station, court or hospital if needed as well as referrals to rele-

vant social and health services.

In a few states victims of crimes can receive compensation depending on financial need. The victim-witness assistance program can provide information on this. For further information about programs in specific localities contact the National District Attorneys Association, 666 North Lake Shore Dr., Chicago, Ill. 60611, Tel. 312-944-2577.

See also: INSURANCE: CRIME (FEDERAL)

CRIMINAL JUSTICE: JUVENILES

In the United States, a child under the age of seven is presumed to be incapable of committing a crime. They are considered to be unable to distinguish between right and wrong or to understand the consequences of a particular act.

Children between age seven and 14 to 16, depending on the state, who commit serious crimes, are treated as juvenile delinquents. Juveniles are tried in juvenile courts which are separate from adult criminal courts. Courts offer guidance to convicted juveniles through the probation department; they may, in the case of repeated offenders or severe crimes, confine the juvenile in a reform school.

Recently, there has been a trend to treat juveniles who commit murder and other felonies as adults. It usually is necessary for the state to show the child knew the nature and consequences of his act before he or she can be tried as an adult in criminal court.

CRUISE SHIPS: RATES

The Federal Maritime Commission (FMC) regulates steamship lines to ensure that the rates charged the public are those on file with the Commission. It does not, however, have the power to regulate rates. If a voyage is canceled, the ship company must refund the fare. Should it refuse to do so, contact the FMC, which can deny a certificate of financial responsibility to the line for noncompliance. For further information contact the Federal Maritime Commission, 1100 L St. NW, Washington, D.C. 20573, Tel. 202-523-5800.

CRUISE SHIPS: SAFETY

See SHIPS: SAFETY

CRUISE SHIPS: SANITATION

Copies of the latest sanitation report for a cruise ship and monthly summaries of all sanitary inspections of cruise ships are available from the Public Health Service. Consumers can file complaints about sanitary conditions with this office, which will investigate them. They should be aware, however, that it is often hard to look into conditions that may have existed several weeks before the complaint was received. For further information contact the Public Health Service, Center for Disease Control, 1015 North

America Way, Miami, Fla. 33132, Tel. 305-350-4307.

CURRENCY: MUTILATED

Claims for the redemption of partially destroyed U.S. currency are handled by the Bureau of Government Financial Operations in the Treasury Department. For further information contact the Department of the Treasury, Bureau of Government Financial Operations, Pennsylvania Ave. and Madison Place NW, Washington, D.C. 20226, Tel. 566-2158.

CURRENCY: PRINTING

The Bureau of Engraving and Printing designs, engraves, and prints all major items of a financial character issued by the U.S. government. Included are paper currency; Treasury bonds, bills, notes, and certificates; postage, revenue, and certain customs stamps. For further information contact the Department of the Treasury, Management Services Division, Bureau of Engraving and Printing, 14th and C Sts. SW, Washington, D.C. 20228, Tel. 202-447-1391.

CURRENCY REPORTING

United States law requires that persons transporting or causing to be transported into or out of the United States more than $5000 must file a report (Customs Form 4790) with U.S. Customs. The $5000 or more may be in U.S. or foreign coin, currency, travelers checks, money orders, or negotiable instruments or investment securities in bearer form. Failure to comply with this portion of the Currency and Foreign Transactions Reporting Act of 1970 can result in civil and criminal penalties. For further information contact the nearest U.S. Customs office or the U.S. Customs Service, 1301 Constitution Ave. NW, Washington, D.C. 20229, Tel. 202-566-5607.

CUSTOMS: MAIL SHIPMENTS

The Postal Service sends all incoming foreign mail shipments, including parcel post and airmail, to the U.S. Customs Service for examination. Parcels that are free of duty, such as unsolicited gifts, are returned to the Postal Service for delivery without any additional charges. On other parcels the Customs Service attached a mail entry receipt showing the amount of duty to be paid and returns the parcel to the Postal Service which in turn charges a postal handling fee in addition to the duty.

Consumers disputing the amount of the duty should file a protest with the Customs Office that issued the mail entry receipt. Send a letter enclosing a copy of the mail entry receipt. If a consumer refuses to accept the package because of disagreement over the duty, he or she has 30 days to submit a written statement of objections to the postmaster at the post office where the parcel is being held. The statement will be forwarded to the Customs Office. The Customs Office will review the matter based on the information included in the letter or statement. For further information contact the local Customs Office listed under U.S. government in the telephone directory or the Treasury Department, Office of Assistant Secretary for Enforcement and Operations, U.S. Customs Service, 1301 Constitution Ave. NW, Washington D.C. 20229, Tel. 202-566-8195.

CUSTOMS: UNSOLICITED GIFTS

Duty free gifts may be sent to United States residents by the resident of a foreign country or a U.S. resident who is abroad if the gift meets several conditions. The fair retail value must be less than $25 (or $40 if sent from the U.S. Virgin Islands, American Samoa, or Guam) and the recipient must not receive more than $25 of gifts in the same day. The traveler cannot send a gift to himself duty free, and persons traveling together cannot send gifts to each other. The gift must have been ordered by a traveler in or resident of a foreign country, and not by mail order from the United States. Perfume containing alcohol, alcoholic beverages, and tobacco products do not qualify as duty free gifts.

Gifts which do qualify as duty free should be marked clearly "Unsolicited Gift," and have the name of the sender, nature of the gift, and the accurate fair retail value of the package clearly written on the outside.

Contact the nearest U.S. Customs office or the U.S. Customs Service, Department of the Treasury, Washington, D.C. 20229.

CUSTOMS CONTROLS: TRAVELERS

American citizens returning from abroad may make oral customs declarations if the value of articles purchased or received as gifts abroad for personal or household use does not exceed the personal exemption. This is presently $300 per individual or $1200 per family of four returning together. The personal exemption is $600 if returning directly or indirectly from the Virgin Islands of the United States, American Samoa or Guam, provided that not more than $300 of this exemption is applied to merchandise obtained outside those islands.

A written declaration is necessary when the total fair retail value of articles acquired abroad exceeds the personal exemption, or is more than one quart of alcoholic beverages, or is more than one carton of cigarettes or if a customs duty or internal revenue tax is collectible on any article. If the total fair retail value of articles exceeds the personal exemption, the next $600 worth will be assessed at a flat rate of 10 percent. The value of articles over this total will be subject to variable rates of duty depending on the types of articles included.

The United States Custom Service maintains customs inspection stations at all major ports of entry into the United States by car, airplane, train or boat. Customs declarations must be made at the customs stations at the port of entry.

Any complaints about customs controls can be made in writing to the Customs Service. Complaints will be answered individually by the Customs Service with investigations when appropriate.

Contact the United States Customs Service, 1301 Constitution Ave. NW, Washington, D.C. 20229, Tel.: 202-566-8195.

CYCLING

The governing body for both amateur and professional cycling is the United States Cycling Federation. The federation supervises all amateur and professional competitions and sponsors national cycling championships. Contact the federation at 1750 E. Boulder, Colorado Springs, Col. 80909, Tel.: 303-632-5551.

CZECHOSLOVAKIA

A valid passport and a visa are required for travel to Czechoslovakia. A visa may be obtained by a travel agent or by writing for an application to the Czech Tourist Bureau, 10 East 40 St., New York, N.Y. 10016, Tel. 212-689-9720, or to the Embassy of the Czechoslovak Socialist Republic, 3900 Linnean Ave. NW, Washington, D.C. 20008, Tel. 202-363-6315. Two passport-sized photos must accompany the application. It will take about 10 days for the application to be processed at the Washington Embassy. A visa costs $10. A visa is good only for the exact length of stay in the country. Business travelers will need a letter of invitation from a Czech Trade Corporation and proof of accommodation. There are no health requirements for entry into Czechoslovakia. A pet may be brought with a veterinarian's certificate of health. The two main languages spoken are Czech and Slovak. English, French and German are the most commonly spoken foreign languages. The monetary unit in Czechoslovakia is the Czechoslovak Crown. No Crowns may be taken into or out of Czechoslovakia. The U.S. Passport Office recommends that U.S. citizens purchase the currency of European Communist countries only in those countries; such currency should not be transported across international borders. Any amount of foreign currency may be brought in or out, but records of all exchange transactions should be kept to facilitate reconversion. To rent a car an International Driving License is necessary.

Czechoslovakia is a COMECON and Warsaw Pact country. All foreign trade is controlled by the state organization, the Ministry of Trade. Exporters to the country must deal through subdivisions of this organization called Foreign Trade Corporations. Some licencing of imports is required. All exchange transactions are handled through the Foreign Exchange division of the Ministry of Finance.

U.S. citizens are required to register in Eastern European countries. This is usually done by turning over the passport to the hotel, which then takes care of the registration. Travellers planning to stay more than a few days may wish to register at the American Embassy located at Trziste 15, 12548 Praha, Prague, Czechoslovakia, Tel. 536641/8.

For further tourist information contact the Czechoslovak Travel Bureau-CEDOK, 10 East 40 St., New York, N.Y. 10016, Tel. 212-689-9720.

For additional business information contact the Czechoslovak Commercial Attache Office, 292 Madison Ave., New York, N.Y. 10017, Tel. 212-532-2662.

D

DAY CARE: MEAL PROGRAMS

The Department of Agriculture provides funds to initiate, maintain, or expand nonprofit food service programs for children in day care facilities. Any licensed public or private day care center or school may be eligible for funds to assist a nonprofit meal program. Information is available from the Department of Agriculture, Food and Nutrition Service, 500 12th St. SW, Washington, D.C. 20250, Tel. 202-447-8211.

See CHILD DAY CARE

DEAFNESS

There are a number of organizations in the United States which offer assistance to people with impaired hearing. The National Association of the Deaf (NAD) protects the civil rights of deaf citizens in employment, promotes legislation to benefit the deaf and supports programs aimed at the vocational training, rehabilitation and education of the deaf. It also offers information on deafness. Contact the National Association of the Deaf, 814 Thayer Ave., Silver Spring, Md. 20910, Tel. 301-587-1788.

The International Parents' Organization (IPO) provides assistance to parents of children with hearing impairments. It is concerned with the educational, social, vocational and psychological needs of deaf children. For information contact the International Parents' Organization, c/o Alexander Graham Bell Association for the Deaf, 1537 35th St. NW, Washington, D.C. 20007, Tel. 202-337-5220.

Deafness may entitle the individual to benefits from various sources. For example deafness resulting from noise at work may entitle the worker for workman's compensation benefits. Other possible sources of benefits are social security and rehabilitation.
See also: WORKMAN'S COMPENSATION; DISABLEMENT: SOCIAL SECURITY BENEFITS; REHABILITATION; SOCIAL SERVICES

DEAFNESS: CHILDREN

The Health and Human Services Department requires that public schools in the United States provide services to deaf or hearing impaired children equal to that supplied to any other child in that school district. Most school districts have special classes for hearing impaired children. Contact the local school district central office, regional Health and Human Services Department office or the Department of Health and Human Services, 200 Independence Ave. SW, Washington, D.C. 20201, Tel. 202-245-6296.

DEATH CERTIFICATE

A death certificate may be obtained from the authority that registered the death, usually gratis or for a small fee. The federal government has published a pamphlet entitled "Where to Write for Birth & Death Records" that is designed to help the individual attempting to locate information. A copy can be obtained from the Superintendent of Documents, Government Printing Office, North Capitol and H Sts. NW, Washington D.C. 20401.

DEATH: SOCIAL SECURITY BENEFITS

The Social Security Administration will pay a lump-sum death benefit upon the death of any worker who is fully insured by Social Security or has social security credit for as little as a year and a half out of the three years just before death. The amount ($255 maximum) can be collected by the surviving spouse or other relative if the deceased is not married. It can be used to pay funeral expenses, but is still paid if there are no burial expenses. The payment is not made, however, if the deceased had insurance that would pay for burial expenses. The spouse or surviving relative must make application for the lump-sum benefit to the Social Security Administration through one of their local offices.

DEATH WITHOUT FUNDS FOR FUNERAL

If an individual dies without funds to pay for burial, the county or city will generally provide minimal expenses. Contact the city or county government for referral to the appropriate office to provide such funds.

DEBT COLLECTION

Under the Fair Debt Collection Practices Act, consumers have certain rights. Debt collectors are not allowed to harass the debtor. The consumer must receive written notice within five days of contact from a bill collector stating the amount of money owned and the name of the creditor. The collector must give instructions about what the consumer can do if he believes that the money is not owed. The consumer has the right to sue the bill collector in a state or federal court to receive damages, including court costs and attorney's fees if he believes his rights have been violated. Consumers can register complaints against member firms with the American Collectors Association, 4040 West 70th St., Box 35106, Minneapolis, Minn. 55435, Tel. 612-926-6547. The organization will mediate a dispute if requested by a member firm.

DELAWARE

The state agency responsible for consumer protection in Delaware is the Division of Consumer Affairs in the Department of Community Affairs and Economic Development. The Division seeks to promote equity in the marketplace through enforcement of the state consumer fraud laws, mediation of consumer complaints, and educational programs.

When a consumer complaint is received by the Division, a letter is sent to the business or individual named in the complaint requesting the party to respond. If the initial letter from the Division does not result in resolution of the complaint, the Division will offer mediation services. In the case of a pattern of complaints against a particular business, the Division has the authority to undertake an investigation and, if needed, issue Cease and Desist Orders. Cases may also be referred to the Attorney General's office for criminal investigation and prosecution.

Contact the Division of Consumer Affairs, 820 North French St., 4th floor, Wilmington, Del. 19801, Tel. 302-571-3250.

Occupations and professions in Delaware are licensed by individual boards which are administered by the Division of Business and Occupational Regulation, Department of Administrative Services, Dover, Del. 19901, Tel. 302-736-4525. The boards set requirements for licensing, license applicants, and accept complaints about licensees. Direct your inquiry to the Division, which will send it on to the proper licensing board.

Businesses interested in moving to or doing business in Delaware can request consulting services from the Department of Community Affairs and Economic Development, Dover, Del. 19901, Tel. 302-736-4456.

Delaware offers state sponsored revenue or general obligation bond financing to industry. It also offers state loans and loan guarantees for construction and equipment.

The corporate income tax in Delaware is 8.7%, and there is no sales tax.

The individual income tax rate ranges from 1.4% for income under $1,000 up to 13.5% for income in excess of $100,000.

For tourist information contact the Department of Community Affairs and Economic Development, 630 State College Rd., Dover, Del. 19901, Tel. 302-678-4354, or the Chamber of Commerce, Inc., 1102 West St., Wilmington, Del. 19801, Tel. 302-655-7221.

DEMOCRATIC PARTY

The 50 states have individual Democratic Party organizations with offices in the state capitals and major cities. The Democratic National Committee handles the national affairs of the Party: setting up conventions, coordinating the presidential election campaign and aiding state and local election efforts. The Committee is composed of three representatives from each state, the state chairmen, and a committeeman and committeewoman from each state. In the years when there is no Democratic President, the chairman of the Committee theoretically speaks for the Party. For further information contact the Democratic National Committee, 1625 Massachusetts Ave. NW, Washington, D.C. 20036, Tel. 202-797-5900.

See also ELECTION EXPENSES, ELECTION RESULTS, ELECTIONS: PRESIDENTIAL, REPUBLICAN PARTY

DEMONSTRATIONS

The right to demonstrate peacefully is protected by the Constitution. Local authorities may, however, require organizations or groups that wish to demonstrate at a particular time and place to notify them and often to obtain a license. Demonstrations at certain events may be restricted to certain areas. Demonstrators who trespass or who break city, state or federal laws are liable for arrest. For further information about specific requirements, contact the local police department.

DENMARK (including Greenland and the Faroe Islands)

A valid passport, but no visa, is required for travel to Denmark, Greenland and the Faroe Islands. Visas are necessary only for stays of longer than three months. There are no health requirements for entry unless arriving from an infected area. There are no limits on the amount of foreign or local currency that may be imported or exported. It is not advisable to bring a pet, they are subject to quarantine. The monetary unit of Denmark is the krone. Any amount of krones or of foreign currency may be taken in or out of the country. The krone is also the currency used in Greenland and the Faroe Islands. The official language of Denmark is Danish, but English is widely spoken. To rent a car, an American driver's license will suffice.

Copenhagen is a free port. Importing is usually handled through resident agents in Copenhagen and/or the Faroe Islands, but Danish importers can often deal directly with the foreign exporter. Trade with Greenland is handled through the Royal Greenland Trade Department in Copenhagen. Few licenses are required, and authorized banks are equipped to handle foreign exchange transactions.

The Embassy of Denmark is located at 3200 Whitehaven St. NW, Washington, D.C. 20008, Tel. 202-234-4300. There are consulates in Chicago, Los Angeles, New York and San Francisco. Further tourist information can be obtained from the Scandinavian National Tourist Office, 75 Rockefeller Plaza, New York, N.Y. 10019, Tel. 212-582-2802.

The U.S. Embassy in Denmark is located at Dag Hammarskjold Alle 24, Copenhagen, Denmark, Tel. 123144.

For further business information contact the Danish-American Chamber of Commerce, 75 Rockefeller Plaza, New York, N.Y. 10019, Tel. 212-245-0424.

DENTAL HYGIENISTS

Dental hygienists are qualified to provide patient care under the direction and supervision of a dentist. They are licensed by the state dental licensing boards. Licensed hygienists usually have completed a dental hygiene program at an institution accredited by the Commission on Accreditation of Dental and Dental Auxiliary Education Programs of the American Dental Association. The programs are a minimum of two years and are offered at both the associate and the baccalaureate levels. California and Kentucky will also accept applications for licensure from individuals who have successfully completed dental education in a foreign country. For further information contact the American Dental Association, 211 East Chicago Ave., Chicago, Ill. 60611, Tel. 312-664-3327. Complaints about dental hygienists should be directed to the supervising dentist or the state dental licensing board.

DENTISTS

In the United States dentists are licensed by the states in which they will practice, and a dentist can legally practice only in the state or states in which he or she is licensed. Licenses are usually issued by a state board of dental examiners.

Some states require that a candidate for licensing be a graduate of a dental school accredited by the Commission on Accreditation of Dental and Dental Auxiliary Education Programs of the American Dental Association. Only dental schools in the United States and Canada are eligible for accreditation by that commission.

All states require written and clinical examinations from any candidate for dental licensure. Check with the individual state licensing board for additional information or contact the American Dental Association

The following jurisdictions will accept graduates of foreign dental schools as candidates for licensing: Arizona, California, the District of Columbia, Florida, Illinois, Maryland, Massachusetts, Michigan, Minnesota, New York, Rhode Island, Tennessee, Texas, Utah, Washington, and Wisconsin. Check with the licensing boards in those states for specific requirements.

Complaints about dentists should be directed to the board of dental examiners in the state in which the dentist practices. Consult the individual state listings for the address of the state licensing agency which can make referrals to the state board of dental examiners or contact the American Dental Association, 211 East Chicago Ave., Chicago, Ill. 60611, Tel. 312-664-3327.

DEVELOPMENTAL TESTING: PRESCHOOL

Parents who suspect their preschool child may have developmental deficiencies or other learning disabilities should first discuss the problem with a physician who can make referrals to professionals for testing. They may also contact their state health department for the names of community organizations working on developmental deficiencies. Teaching hospitals can also refer parents to specialists.

DIETARY SUPPLEMENTS (VITAMINS AND MINERALS)

The Food and Drug Administration (FDA) is the regulating body for adult dietary supplements in the form of tablets, capsules, or drops and which otherwise do not resemble conventional food. There are, however, limits on FDA regulations. The FDA can set the minimum potency levels for vitamins and minerals in dietary supplements, thus preventing doses which are nutritionally insignificant. But it cannot require that dietary supplements be nutritionally useful. The FDA also cannot prohibit useless ingredients in dietary supplements, but it can restrict their composition for reasons of safety.

The FDA also has limited authority over the advertising of dietary supplements. The FDA is required to notify the Federal Trade Commission of a suspected advertising violation. If the FTC does not act within 90 days, the FDA may.

Questions or complaints about dietary supplements can be referred to the Food and Drug Administration, consumer communication management section, office of policy coordination, 5600 Fishers Lane, Rockville, Md. 20852, Tel. 301-443-3170.

DIRECT MAIL ADVERTISING

Those wishing to receive direct mail advertising in special areas should contact the Direct Mail Marketing Association, Inc., Consumer Relations Department, 6 East 43rd St., New York, N.Y. 10017, Tel. 212-689-4977.

DIRECT MAIL ADVERTISING: UNWANTED RECEIPT OF

To remove a name from a mailing list, contact the Direct Mail Marketing Association, Inc., Consumer Relations Department, 6

East 43rd St., New York, N.Y. 10017, Tel. 212-689-4977. To have a name removed from a specific advertiser's mailing list, file a Prohibitory Order, Postal Service form #2150, which is available at any post office.

DISABLED: BUSINESS LOANS

The Small Business Administration (SBA) will loan money to disabled persons who can demonstrate that they have the ability to own and operate a business successfully. In order to qualify for these low interest loans the applicants must have experienced difficulty getting financing from other sources. Contact the local SBA office or the SBA, 1441 L St. NW, Washington, D.C. 20416, Tel. 202-653-6605.

DISABLED: COLLEGE EDUCATION

Preadmission inquiries by colleges or universities as to whether an applicant is handicapped are barred by the Department of Health and Human Services. After admission, colleges or universities may request voluntary information about handicaps to allow for planning of necessary services. Quotas for admission of handicapped students are also ruled out by the Department of Health and Human Services. Standardized admission tests must be selected and administered so that the test results will measure aptitude or achievement and not the disability.

Universities and colleges are also required by the Department of Health and Human Services to make reasonable modifications in academic requirements when necessary to provide full educational opportunities for handicapped students.

Contact the Department of Health and Human Services' regional office, its main office in Washington, D.C., or the college or university to which one is applying for further information.

See also: REHABILITATION

DISABLED: CHILDREN, EDUCATION

The Department of Health and Human Services requires that no handicapped child be excluded from a public education because of disability. Handicapped children must be educated with non-handicapped students to the extent appropriate to their needs. Local and state educational agencies are responsible for locating and identifying unserved handicapped children.

See also: REHABILITATION

DISABLED: EMPLOYMENT

The U.S. Employment Service through the state employment agencies offers specialized employment counseling and placement assistance for the disabled. Contact the local state employment agency. The Civil Service Commission has selective placement programs designed to help disabled persons obtain employ-

ment with the U.S. government. For further information contact the local office of the Civil Service Commission or the coordinator of selective placement in any federal agency.

See also: REHABILITATION

DISABLED: HOUSING

The Department of Housing and Urban Development is responsible for developing housing programs for the disabled, including design, loan and rent subsidies. For further information contact the Department of Housing and Urban Development, Office of Independent Living for the Disabled, 7th and D Sts. SW, Washington, D.C. 20410, Tel. 202-755-5111.

DISABLED: SOCIAL SECURITY BENEFITS

Under Social Security Administration regulations a person is disabled if he or she has a mental or physical condition that prevents him from doing any substantial gainful work for a period that has lasted, or is expected to last for at least 12 months, or that is expected to result in death. Such disabled individuals may qualify for monthly cash payments.

Benefits can be paid to disabled workers under 65 and their families, and to disabled widows and widowers (age 50 and over). An unmarried child who became disabled before age 22 and is still disabled may receive benefits either when the parent starts getting social security retirement benefits or disability benefits, or on the parent's death if the parent qualified for social security payments to survivors.

To qualify, a person must have worked in employment covered by social security for a certain length of time, usually half of the years between age 21 and the time he was disabled for ages 24 to 30; and 5 to 10 years for workers 31 years or older at the time of disability. Five years of this time must have been in the last 10 years before becoming disabled.

Disability benefits begin after a waiting period of five full calendar months after the disability occurs, except for children disabled before age 22 who are entitled to benefits on a parent's work record. Payments continue as long as the person remains unable to work. If the disabled individual marries while receiving benefits as a person disabled in childhood or as a disabled widow or widower, the benefits will cease in most cases.

Persons who receive disability payments for 24 months are then eligible for Medicare. Medicare benefits may continue for an additional three years beyond the date a disabled person returns to work.

In 1980 disability benefits ranged from $139.50 to $647 per month for a single worker to as high as $970.50 per month for a worker with a family. The amount increases automatically with the cost of living. Retired people cannot collect both disability payments and social security retirement benefits. They are entitled to whichever is larger, usually the disability benefit.

Apply for disability benefits at the nearest social security office located in most cities. A physical and disability evaluation specialist will determine eligibility for payment. Application may be made by a spouse, parent or other relative or friend if the disabled person is unable to handle his or her affairs.

DISABLED: SPORTS FOR

See BLIND BOWLING, SPECIAL OLYMPICS, RIDING: DISABLED PERSONS

DISABLED: TOURIST INFORMATION

Federal agencies can offer information about government facilities that are accessible to the disabled as well as those designed specifically for them. For further information contact the Department of the Interior, National Park Service, Main Interior Bldg, Washington, D.C. 20240, Tel. 202-343-4621 or the Department of Agriculture, P.O. Box 3417, Washington, D.C. 20013, Tel. 202-447-3706. The individual park or forest can answer specific questions.

DISABLED: VOTING

Disabled persons can vote in person or cast an absentee ballot provided they are registered to vote.

See also DISCRIMINATION: VOTING

DISCRIMINATION: AGE

Federal law prohibits age discrimination by employers affecting interstate commerce and are engaged in an industry who have 20 or more employees by labor organizations with 25 or more members in an industry affecting interstate commerce, and by employment agencies serving these employers and employees. Age must be a bona fide occupational qualification for discrimination to be legal. Persons who feel that they have been a victim of age discrimination may request assistance from the local office of the Equal Employment Opportunity Commission listed in the local telephone directory under U.S. government. Persons may file a complaint or an anonymous charge which the EEOC will investigate. If discrimination is proved, the agency seeks conciliation. Should this prove impossible, the EEOC may sue, but it does not do so in all cases. It is most likely to take legal action if the case involves large groups or concerns a legal issue the Commission wishes to litigate. Persons who wish to take a case of discrimination to court must first file a claim with the EEOC. For further information contact the Equal Employment Opportunity Commission, 2401 E St. NW, Washington, D.C. 20210, Tel. 202-634-6930.

DISCRIMINATION: COMPLAINTS

The Commission on Civil Rights refers complaints about discrimination to specific agencies. For further information contact the United States Commission on Civil Rights, Complaint Referral, 1121 Vermont Ave. NW, Washington, D.C. 20425, Tel. 202-245-6758.

DISCRIMINATION: EDUCATION

Those who believe they have been the victim of discrimination in education should contact the Department of Education, Office of Civil Rights, 400 Maryland Ave. SW, Washington D.C. 20202, Tel. 202-245-6700.

DISCRIMINATION: EMPLOYMENT

Discrimination in employment, whether in hiring, promotion, salary or treatment, is unlawful on the basis of age, sex, marital status, race, color, religion or national origin.

Suspected incidents of discrimination both in hiring and in ongoing employment should be referred to the Equal Employment Opportunity Commission (EEOC).

When a complaint is received by EEOC it is evaluated to ensure that the complainant has a problem falling within the commission's jurisdiction. Investigation of the complaint may include a face-to-face conference in which information is exchanged and voluntary settlement is attempted. If the commission is unable to resolve

the complaint through conciliation, the complainant or the commission can pursue resolution of
the problem through the courts.

Contact the Equal Employment
Opportunity Commission, 2401 E
St. NW, Washington, D.C. 20506,
Tel.: 202-634-7040.

DISCRIMINATION:
FEDERAL EMPLOYMENT

Those federal employees who
feel they have suffered job discrimination should contact the
equal opportunity employment
section of the appropriate agency
or the Equal Employment Opportunity Commission.

See also: DISCRIMINATION:
EMPLOYMENT

DISCRIMINATION: HOUSING

Federal law prohibits discrimination in the sale or rental of residential property. For further information contact the Department of
Housing and Urban Development,
Office of the Assistant Secretary
for Fair Housing and Equal Opportunity, Office of Fair Housing Enforcement, HUD Building, Washington, D.C. 20410; Tel. 202-755-
5490. There is a toll-free number
outside Washington: 800-424-8590.

DISCRIMINATION:
PREGNANCY

While pregnant women who are
able to work must be permitted to
do so on the same conditions as
other employees, those unable to

work for medical reasons must be
given the same rights, leave privi-
leges and other benefits as disabled workers. Reduced coverage
in medical, sick leave or disability
benefit plans cannot be justified
because of pregnancy. Questions
on coverage and complaints of
discrimination in maternity leave
and pay should be directed to the
local office of the Equal Employment Opportunity Commission.
The Commission will investigate
complaints and seek reconcilia-
tion. It does not take all unresolved cases to court. Generally
the Commission takes legal action
only when a special issue or a
large group of people is involved.
Individuals must, however, file
with the EEOC before taking a
case to court. The EEOC has
stringent filing deadlines. For information on filing procedures
contact the local EEOC office or
the Equal Employment Opportunity Commission, 2401 E St. NW,
Washington, D.C. 20425, Tel. 202-
634-6930.

DISCRIMINATION: SEX

See DISCRIMINATION: EM-
PLOYMENT

DISCRIMINATION: VOTING

Those who believe they have
been denied the right to vote because of race, sex, religion or national origin should file a complaint with the Department of Justice, Criminal Division, Public In-
tegrity Section, Elections Unit, 315
9th St. NW, Washington, D.C., Tel.
202-724-7062.

DISCRIMINATION: WAGES

See DISCRIMINATION: EM-PLOYMENT

DISEASES

See specific disease

DISTRICT OF COLUMBIA

The District of Columbia Office of Consumer Protection is responsible for protecting the rights of consumers. Consumers can complain either by mail or in person to the Office of Consumer Protection, 1407 L St., N.W., Washington, D.C. 20005, Tel. 202-727-1308.

When a complaint is received by mail at the Office of Consumer Protection, the consumer is contacted within 72 hours by an investigator to confirm the complaint, make any additions, and request necessary documents. If the complaint is registered in person an investigator will meet with the complainant and attempt to resolve the complaint during the interview. An investigator assigned to each complaint reviews the facts, contacts the business involved, and acts as mediator.

If the Office is unable to resolve the problem after a thorough investigation, the case is transferred to the Legal Section for a formal settlement conference. Both the complainant and the business are invited to meet with the Legal Section in a settlement conference. The Office represents the complainant and the business can be represented by its attorney. If the complaint is not resolved at the settlement conference it is referred to an Administrative Law Judge who will hear both sides and render a decision which either party can appeal through the state court system.

The Licensing and Registration section of the Office of Consumer Protection licenses applicants for consumer goods repair licenses. Automotive and electronic repair shops in the District of Columbia must meet certain requirements to receive a license. The Licensing and Registration section will answer questions about the reputability of an automotive or electronic repair shop based on the record of consumer complaints. Actual consumer complaints about the businesses, however, should be directed simply to the Office of Consumer Protection as they are processed in the same manner as other consumer complaints.

The Department of Licenses, Investigations, and Inspections licenses the following occupations and professional categories: accountant, architect, barber, cosmetologist, dentist/dental hygienist, electrician, healing art, nursing home administrator, occupational therapist, optometrist, pharmacist, registered nurse, physical therapist, plumber, podiatrist, practical nurse, professional engineer, psychologist, real estate broker and sales person, refrigeration and air conditioning mechanic, steam and other operating engineer, undertaker and veterinarian.

Requirements for licensing are set and examinations administered by the individual boards for the above professions and occupations. All the boards may be contacted at the following address: 614 H St. N.W., Washington, D.C. 20001, Tel. 202-727-3673.

The Department does accept complaints about licensees. These complaints are investigated by the Office of Investigations and Enforcement, and a written report of the findings is submitted to the appropriate board. Action may include dismissal of the complaint, revoking of the license or something in between.

For business information about the District of Columbia contact the Metropolitan Washington Board of Trade, 1129 20th St. NW, Washington, D.C. 20036, Tel. 202-857-5900.

Tourist information can be requested from the Tourist Information Bureau, 1575 I St. NW, Washington, D.C. 20005, Tel. 202-789-7000.

DIVORCE

Each state sets its own requirements for obtaining a divorce such as the length of time one must live in a state in order to qualify as a resident of that state for a divorce. The court that grants divorces also varies from state to state. In some it is the Court of Domestic Relations, in others the Superior or State Supreme Court.

In recent years, the trend in the United States has been towards no-fault divorce proceedings, whereby the question of fault is reduced to minimal importance. Most states now have some form of no-fault divorce. No-fault divorce also tends to bar defense action, unless there is allegation of adultery. Where a defense is permitted, it sometimes can be used to prevent one spouse from claiming support from the other. In issuing a divorce decree, a court handles the distribution of property and determine the amount of alimony or child support that should be paid to either spouse.

While each state has its own laws concerning divorces and proper procedure must be followed, the general grounds for a no-fault divorce is the "breakdown of the marriage." A majority of the states use that term. Other states seek evidence of incompatibility or a period of living apart as evidence the marriage should be dissolved.

A conversion type divorce is permitted in several states under which a divorce is granted after a couple lives apart for a certain period of time.

If a divorce action is contested by one spouse, the action becomes more difficult. Adultery is grounds for divorce in nearly every state and desertion is also grounds in most states. Other common grounds for divorce in many states includes cruelty and impotence.

Alimony laws and awards vary greatly from state to state. In most states, the laws dealing with ali-

---

mony are flexible and is determined by the specifics in each case. Some states limit the amount of alimony that may be awarded is limited to a certain percentage of the husband's income. Some states permit lump sum settlements payable in installments. Some states now permit husbands to collect alimony from their wives. Some states permit alimony for the wife only if the husband is found guilty of some type of misconduct and they deny it to the wife if she is proved guilty of some form of misbehavior. Alimony for the wife normally ends when the woman remarries but continues if the husband remarries.

Child custody and support payments in divorce cases also vary greatly from state to state. Generally custody of younger children is awarded to the mother, although that is no longer exclusively true. Older children are usually permitted to choose which parent they wish to live with. Generally, if both spouses can agree on custody the court will go along with their wishes if there is no detriment to the child. Normally one parent is granted custody while the other is given visiting rights. The amount of child support differs from case to case but is generally based on the age of the child, the parent's income, past mode of living, the income of the spouse granted custody, etc. Persons contemplating divorce should secure legal advice.

See also SEPARATION

DOG LICENSES

In many states the state department of agriculture issues dog licenses. Many large cities also license dogs. For information about local compliance contact the nearest branch of the American Society for Prevention of Cruelty to Animals or Humane Society. A veterinarian, breeder or pet store owner will also have this information.

DOMINICAN REPUBLIC

A valid passport and a tourist card are required for travel to the Dominican Republic. A tourist card is obtainable either through a travel agent, through the airline upon leaving for the country or upon arrival in the Dominican Republic. Business travelers must apply for a visa at an Embassy or consulate with a valid passport, five photographs and a letter from their company detailing the nature of their business. There is a fee of $6.00. Proof of a smallpox vaccination is required for entry, and a TAB innoculation is advised. Travelers wishing to bring a pet, must bring a health and vaccination certificate signed by the county clerk to a diplomatic mission and pay a fee of $10 for a permit. The currency of the Dominican Republic is the peso. The import or export of the local currency is prohibited. However, any amount of foreign currency may be brought in or out of the country. Spanish is the official language of the country and English is occasionally spoken. To rent a car, an American license will suffice. Evidence of a visit to Cuba or another Communist country within two years may prevent entry into the Dominican Republic.

Trade with the Dominican Republic is handled through resident agents. There are restrictions on some imports and further restrictions on foreign exchange purchases which operate under a quota system. Importers must arrange for foreign exchange through local commercial banks.

The Embassy of the Dominican Republic is located at 1715 22 St. NW, Washington, D.C. 20008, Tel. 202-322-6280. Consulates are located in Denver, Galveston, Los Angeles, New York, New Orleans, Park Ridge (Ill.), Philadelphia and San Francisco.

The American Embassy in the Dominican Republic is located at Corner of Calle Cesar Nicolas Penson and Calle Leopoldo Navarro, Santo Domingo, Dominican Republic, Tel. 682-2171.

For further business information contact the Dominican Republic Export Promotions Center, 1 World Trade Center, New York, N.Y. 10048, Tel. 212-432-9498.

DRAFT REGISTRATION

See MILITARY DRAFT: REGISTRATION

DRAG RACING

The International Hot Rod Association sponsors drag racing competitions in the United States.

For further information contact the International Hot Rod Association, P.O. Box 3029, Bristol, Tenn. 37620, Tel. 615-764-1164.

DRIVERS LICENSES

The state department of motor vehicles issues motor vehicle licenses. To qualify for a license, the individual must generally pass a written test and a driving test. Requirements for eligibility to take the driving test vary from state to state. The applicant must generally supply his or her own vehicle for the test, and an officer of the licensing agency will ride with the applicant during the test, directing the applicant to perform turns, parking, etc. to determine the level of driving skill. If the applicant fails the test he or she can generally take the test again after a waiting period.

When a U.S. resident moves to a new state and applies for a license, a written test is generally required, but a new driving test may not be required if the applicant has a valid license from another state. For specific information contact the state motor vehicle bureau.

DROUGHT

In case of a drought the mayor or city council may order water conservation measures such as forbidding the washing of cars or the watering of lawns. In extreme cases civil or even criminal penalties may be imposed for violation of water conservation measures.

At the request of the state governor the President can declare a locality a disaster area because of drought. This entitles the residents and businesses to certain federal disaster assistance.

See also: DISASTER RELIEF, DISASTER LOANS.

DRUG CONTROL

The U.S. Department of Justice, Drug Enforcement Administration (DEA) is the federal agency responsible for controlling drugs and developing the overall federal drug enforcement strategy, programs and plans. The DEA conducts domestic and international investigations of major drug traffickers. It cooperates closely with other federal, state and local law enforcement agencies, as well as with appropriate foreign governments.

Local police departments generally have narcotics divisions that investigate and enforce drug control in each city. Information about drug dealing in a local area should generally be given to the local police narcotics division or to the Drug Enforcement Administration, Department of Justice, 1405 I St. NW, Washington, D.C. 20537, Tel. 202-633-1000.

DRUG DEPENDENCE

The Alcohol, Drug Abuse and Mental Health Administration provides funding for drug abuse research, treatment, training and prevention to state and local drug abuse programs. Many states and cities also provide financial assistance to qualified drug rehabilitation programs. In addition there are a number of private non-profit organizations which offer assistance to individuals who have drug-related problems. For information on programs and publications on drug abuse problems or programs contact the state or local department of health or the Department of Health and Human Services, Alcohol, Drug Abuse and Mental Health Administration, National Institute on Drug Abuse, 5600 Fishers Lane, Rockville, Md. 20857, Tel. 202-443-6500.

DRUGS: EXPERIMENTAL

Experimental drugs used in medical research with humans are regulated by the Food and Drug Administration (FDA). The FDA sets conditions that must be met in order for new drugs to be used on humans. These conditions include the results of animal tests that would justify clinical tests on humans and an outline of what is planned for the tests on humans. Law requires that doctors tell their patients about the experimental nature of the drugs except where the doctor thinks that this would be contrary to the best interests of the patient. Clinical testing of an experimental drug can be stopped at any time if the FDA determines that it would be unwise to continue with the testing. Questions or complaints about experimental drugs can be sent to the FDA.

Complaints about a specific doctor's use of experimental drugs can be sent to the state board of medical examiners, located in the state capital. The boards generally evaluate or investigate each complaint against a doctor. Allegations of malpractice can also be pursued through a civil suit. Consult a lawyer or contact the Food and Drug Administration, 5600 Fishers Lane, Rockville, Md. 20852, Tel. 301-443-3170.

DRUGS

The Food and Drug Administration (FDA) regulates both prescription and nonprescription drugs sold in the United States. New drugs must be submitted to the FDA for approval before marketing. Applicants must present documentation, based on testing by the manufacturer, that the drug is both effective and safe. FDA inspectors examine the entire manufacturing process and analyze samples of the drug. Each new drug is evaluated by a team of doctors, pharmacologists and chemists before approval. The FDA also ensures that labeling and advertising is truthful, fairly balanced and fully informative.

The Agency maintains surveillance of drugs after marketing. Previous approval of a drug can be suspended if it is determined that it is a health hazard. The manufacturer's rights are also protected by hearing procedures, and the FDA's actions may be subject to court review.

In the event of a reaction to any drug, consult a physician. If he or she believes the reaction to be unusual, the physician can report it to the FDA's Adverse Drug Experience Reporting System.

Consumers can also refer questions or complaints about drugs to the FDA. The agency cannot investigate every consumer complaint, but maintains a file of complaints for use in evaluating drugs. For further information contact the Food and Drug Administration, 5600 Fishers Lane, Rockville, Md. 20852, Tel. 301-443-3170.

DRY CLEANING

Complaints about damage to dry cleaning should be taken up with the drycleaner or launderer. The International Fabricare Institute will analyze a garment at the request of a member to see why it was damaged. This enables the parties concerned to see who was responsible.

For further information contact the International Fabricare Institute, 12251 Tech Rd. Silver Springs, Md. 20904, Tel. 301-622-2818.

DUMPING AT SEA

See POLLUTION: WATER AND SOLID WASTE

E

ECUADOR

A valid passport but no visa is required for travel to Ecuador for a stay of up to 90 days. Travelers must, however, have a return ticket. There are no health requirements for travelers arriving from the United States, but smallpox and hepatitis shots are advised. To bring a pet into the country, travelers must have a veterinarian's health certificate validated by a consulate before leaving the U.S. Any amount of foreign or local currency (the sucre) may be brought in or out of the country. Spanish is the official language of Ecuador. English is occasionally spoken. Visitors can drive either by using their American license to obtain a local permit or by presenting an International Driving License which does not require an additional permit.

All allowable imports to Ecuador are listed in one of two categories—either as essential goods or as luxury items. There are no restrictions for any item that is on the list. Any item not on the list is prohibited. Luxury goods are subject to a 30% surcharge over the usual duty. All importing is handled by resident agents, and all foreign exchange transactions are controlled by the Central Bank of Ecuador.

For additional information contact the Embassy of Ecuador, 25-25 15th St. NW, Washington, D.C. 20009, Tel. 202-234-7200. There are also consulates in Miami, Houston, Los Angeles, San Diego, Chicago, Seattle, El Paso, New Orleans and New York. The address of the U.S. Embassy in Ecuador is 120 Avenida Patria, Casilla 538, Quito, Ecuador, Tel. 548000.

For further travel information contact the Ecuador Travel Bureau, 167 West 72 St., New York, N.Y. 10023, Tel. 212-873-0600.

For additional business information contact the Ecuador-American Chamber of Commerce, 1 World Trade Center, New York, N.Y. 10048, Tel. 212-775-1180.

EDUCATION: FINANCIAL AID PROGRAMS

The federal government offers students three kinds of financial aid: grants, employment, and loans. The applicant must be a U.S. citizen, national, or permanent resident enrolled at least half-time in an eligible course of study at one of the 9,000 institutions participating in the programs (post-secondary college, university, vocational school, technical school, or hospital school of nursing).

— Basic Educational Opportunity Grants are awarded to undergraduate students with financial need.

— Supplemental Educational Opportunity Grants are available to students with exceptional financial need who would not be able to continue their educations without the grants.

— The College Work-Study Program provides jobs for students who need financial aid and must earn a part of their educational expenses.

— The National Direct Student

Loans are available to students who need a loan to help meet their educational expenses.
— The Guaranteed Student Loan Program enables students to borrow from eligible lenders (such as banks, credit unions, and savings and loan associations) at a low interest rate to meet educational expenses. In most states the loans are guaranteed by state or private nonprofit agencies.
— Health Education Assistance Loans are available to graduate students in the health professions. The loans are made by eligible lenders (such as banks, credit unions and savings and loan associations).

Many of these programs have been cut back extensively under the Reagan Administration. The various scholarship and loan programs funded by the federal government are administered by the Bureau of Student Financial Assistance, in the Department of Education. A toll-free number is available for questions: 800-638-6700 (800-492-6602 in Maryland). Contact by mail: Department of Education, Office of Public Affairs, 400 Maryland Ave. SW, Washington, D.C. 20202, Tel. 202-426-6573.

EGGS

The Food Safety and Quality Service of the Department of Agriculture provides mandatory inspection of all plants processing liquid, dried or frozen egg products. It also controls the disposi-
tion of all restricted shell eggs that might cause food illness. The service deals only with plants involved in interstate commerce. For further information contact the Department of Agriculture, Food Safety and Quality Service, 14th St. and Independence Ave. SW, Washington, D.C. 20250, Tel. 202-655-4000.

EGYPT

A valid passport and a visa are required for travel to Egypt. A visa may be obtained through a travel agent or by applying at an Egyptian diplomatic mission. Travelers need a passport, one picture and $3.00. The visa will be processed in about two days. It is good for a stay of up to three months. There are no additional requirements for business travelers. All visitors to Egypt must have at least $150 upon arrival, and their passports must be valid for at least six months after their departure date. Protection against cholera and yellow fever are required if coming from an infected area. TAB shots are advised. Pets may be brought in provided they have a veterinarian's health certificate. Any amount of foreign currency may be brought into the country but travelers may take out no more than they brought in. The import or export of Egyptian currency (Egyptian pound) is prohibited. Arabic is the official language of Egypt, and English and French are the most commonly spoken foreign languages. An International Driving

License is required to drive or rent a car. Egypt is one of more liberal Muslim countries, and the drinking of alcohol is legal. Evidence of a trip to Israel is no longer a problem for entry.

In spite of a relaxation on government control of business in the last decade, the major industries are still state controlled. Trading is usually handled through state trading organizations. However some trade is handled through resident agents. Certain imports require payments of taxes in addition to the usual import duty. Foreign exchange transactions are handled by the Central Exchange Control.

All visitors to Egypt are required to register with the authorities. This is usually handled by their hotel.

The Embassy of the Arab Republic of Egypt is located at 2310 Decatur Place NW, Washington, D.C. 20008, Tel. 202-232-5400. Consulates are located in New York and San Francisco.

The U.S. Embassy in Egypt is located at 5 Sharia Latin American, Garden City, P.O. Box 20, Cairo, Egypt, Tel. 28219.

For further travel information contact the Egypt Government Tourist Office, 630 Fifth Ave., New York, N.Y. Tel. 212-246-6960.

For additional business information contact the Egyptian Embassy Commercial Bureau, 20 East 46 St., New York, N.Y. 10017, Tel. 212-286-0060.

ELDERLY

See also FOOD PROGRAMS: MEALS ON WHEELS, NATIONAL PARKS: SENIOR CITIZEN PASSPORTS

ELDERLY: COMPANIONS

ACTION administers programs and distributes funds for the Senior Companion Program. This program provides low-income persons aged 60 and over with volunteer opportunities to aid other adults, especially senior citizens. However, due to federal budget cuts, the future of ACTION is in doubt. For information contact the local department of the aging or ACTION, Senior Companions, 806 Connecticut Ave. NW, Washington, D.C. 20525, Tel. 202-254-7310.

ELDERLY: EDUCATION

Many universities and high schools offer courses for the elderly at reduced rates or free. For information contact the local college or high school.

There is also a private organization called Elderhostel which offers reasonable one-week courses at over 400 colleges in the United States. Contact Elderhostel, 100 Boylston St., Boston, Mass., 02116, Tel. 617-426-7788.

ELDERLY: GOVERNMENT PROGRAMS FOR

The Administration on Aging is the principal federal agency with responsibility for federal programs aimed at identifying and serving the needs, concerns and interests of older persons. State agencies on the aging also serve as advocates at the community level. Many localities also have similar services. For further information contact the Health and Human Services Department, Office of Human Development Services, Administration on Aging, 330 Independence Ave. SW, Washington, D.C. 20201, Tel. 202-245-0669.

ELDERLY: HOME CARE

Under the Senior Companion Program the federal government provides support for those elderly unable to function at home. Senior companions are part-time volunteers, generally with low incomes, who spend 20 hours a week with other elderly persons. They receive a modest stipend to enable them to serve without cost to themselves. For further information contact the regional branch of ACTION or ACTION, Senior Companion Program, 806 Connecticut Ave. NW, Washington, D.C. 20525, Tel. 202-254-6560. See also: ELDERLY: HOME HEALTH CARE

ELDERLY: HOME HEALTH CARE

Home health aides are paraprofessionals who come into the home of a senior citizen to help in time of crisis. These services are available regardless of income, social status or other arbitrary limitation. Over 2,000 home health agencies participate in this Medicare program. For further information contact the local health department or Medicare office.

ELDERLY: HOUSING

The Department of Housing and Urban Development provides information about publically sponsored low and moderate cost housing for the elderly in various communities throughout the United States. For further information contact the Department of Housing and Urban Development, 451 Seventh St. SW, Washington, D.C. 20410, Tel. 202-755-5111.

ELDERLY: NUTRITION PROGRAMS

The federal government provides matching funds to states and localities that provide meals for elderly citizens who do not eat adequately because: they cannot afford to do so, they lack the skills to prepare their own nourishing meals, they have limited mobility, or they are not motivated to prepare and eat meals alone. The programs usually provide one meal a day, five days a week in central locations such as senior citizens centers, churches, or community centers. Up to 10% of the meals in any program can be delivered to the home. Participants pay only what they can afford.

For information about programs in a particular area or how to obtain funding for a nutritional program, contact the regional office of the Administration on Aging or the Department of Health and Human Services, Office of Human Development Services, Administration on Aging, National Clearinghouse on Aging, 330 Independence Ave. SW, Washington, D.C. 20201, Tel. 202-245-0669.

See also: FOOD PROGRAMS: MEALS ON WHEELS

ELDERLY: PUBLIC TRANSPORTATION (Half fares)

Public transportation systems receiving money from the Urban Mass Transportation Administration (UMTA) must charge senior citizens half fare or less during certain times of the day. For further information contact the Urban Mass Transportation Administration, Associate Administrator for Transit Assistance, 400 7th Street S.W., Washington, D.C. 20590, Tel. 202-426-4043.

ELDERLY: RETIRED SENIOR VOLUNTEER PROGRAM

ACTION administers and provides funds for the Retired Senior Volunteer Program (RSVP). This program develops volunteer service opportunities for people over 60 in places like hospitals, schools and courts. However, due to federal budget cuts, the future of this program is in doubt. For further information contact the local department of the aging or ACTION, Retired Senior Volunteer Program, 806 Connecticut Ave. NW, Washington, D.C. 20525, Tel. 202-254-7310.

ELECTION EXPENSES

Under federal law candidates for national office and their campaign committees must file periodic reports disclosing their campaign finance activities. These reports are available to the public.

Both individuals and political committees are restricted to a maximum contribution to each candidate or candidate's election committee for a given election. Individuals may give $1,000 to each candidate or candidate's election committee, $20,000 to national party's committee, $5,000 to any other political committee, or $25,000 total political contributions per calendar year for federal elections.

Multicandidate committees are limited to $5,000 to each candidate or candidate's election committee per election, $20,000 to a national party's committee and $5,000 to any other political committee. There is no combined limit on the total year's contributions in this case. Multicandidate committees are political committees registered for at least six months, with more than 50 contributors that—with the exception of state party committees—have made contributions to five or more federal candidates.

Other political committees have limits of $1,000 to each candidate or candidate's election committee per election, $20,000 to a national party's committee per calendar year and $5,000 to any other political committee per calendar year.

They also have no total spending limit.

There is no legal limit on campaign expenditures by individuals or committees that expressly advocate the election or defeat of a clearly identified candidate. These expenses cannot be made with any direct or indirect cooperation, consent, request or suggestion by a candidate or his authorized committee or agent. Each person or committee must report such expenditures when they exceed $250 per calendar year.

Political committees and political candidates must register and file periodic disclosure reports on their campaign finances with the Clerk of the House of Representatives, the Secretary of the Senate or the Federal Election Commission. They must also file with the secretary of state in the state or states where nomination is sought or where expenditures are made on the candidate's behalf.

Reports made by political committees are made public within 48 hours after they are filed. These reports contain detailed campaign finance information, including itemized accounts of expenses and contributions in excess of $200 and of any debts. Personal finance reports made by presidential and vice presidential candidates, except incumbents, are also made available. These reports can be copied at the Federal Election Commission (FEC) or at the particular secretary of state's office.

The Federal Election Commission has investigative and enforcement authority. Individuals or groups can file official complaints, which will be investigated by the FEC. If the FEC confirms that a violation of federal law has occurred, the commission will use methods such as civil penalties to ensure compliance. If those efforts fail, the FEC can file civil suit against the respondent in Federal District Court. In cases of alleged criminal violations, the FEC will refer the case to the Justice Department.

Contact the Federal Election Commission at their toll-free number, 800-424-9530, or write the Federal Election Commission, Public Communications Office, 1325 K St. NW, Washington, D.C. 20463, Tel. 202-523-4068.

ELECTION RESULTS

Election results in contests for the U.S. House of Representatives, the U.S. Senate, as well as for state contests such as state senate and governor are generally reported county by county or precinct by precinct according to state law. Results are reported to a board set up by the governor or secretary of state in each state. The board then declares the winner in each election.

In presidential elections the state has authority over procedures regulating the election of federal electors. The electors than meet at a date determined by law in the state capital to vote for president. The votes are sealed and forwarded to the Speaker of the House and the President of the Senate; the electors' votes are read in a joint session of Congress and the President-elect and Vice President-elect are declared.

ELECTIONS: CAMPAIGN CONTRIBUTIONS

Campaign contributions by any one individual are limited by law to a total of $1000 per candidate in the Presidential elections, and total political action committee donations to $5000. Corporations are not permitted to make campaign contributions, but political action committees (PACs) are sometimes formed by corporations, labor unions, and other organizations to receive voluntary contributions from their members or workers and distribute them to the candidate of their choice.

In the U.S. state primaries there is a system of partial public financing. Candidates must raise $5000 in each 20 states or more in individual contributions not exceeding $250 in order to qualify for matching federal funds. The candidates are limited to a spending ceiling of 14.7 million. There is full public financing from the federal Treasury in the general Presidential election, with both the Democratic and Republican nominees eligible to receive more than $29.4 million. Independent candidates are also eligible for federal funds, providing they achieve a minimum percentage of the popular vote in the November Presidential election, the exact percentage to be decided by the Federal Election Commission.

Contact the Federal Election Commission, Washington, D.C.

ELECTRIC AND GAS UTILITIES
See UTILITIES

EL SALVADOR

In December 1980 the U.S. State Department issued a travel warning to the effect that all travel to El Salvador, either as a tourist or on official business is extremely dangerous. However, U.S. citizens can still travel there if they so wish. A tourist requires only a valid passport to enter the country. For business travel, a letter from the traveler's company must be presented to a consular official stating the nature of his business and confirming financial responsibility. He can then obtain a visa good for 90 days. A smallpox vaccination is required for entry and protection against typhoid is advised. The monetary unit of El Salvador is the colon. There is a limit of 200 colones which may be transported in or out of the country, but there is no limit on the amount of foreign currency which may be imported or exported. The main language of El Salvador is Spanish, but English is often spoken in hotels and in business circles. To drive a car, an International Driving License plus a foreign license are required.

Trade with El Salvador is conducted usually through resident agents and occasionally directly by the companies involved. Import licenses are required for a few items such as arms, narcotics and certain foods, but usually none are needed. Foreign exchange is regulated by the Central Bank of El Salvador.

The Embassy of El Salvador is located at 2308 California Ave. NW, Washington, D.C. 20008, Tel. 202-265-3480. There are consulates in Houston, Los Angeles, Miami, New Orleans, New York and San Francisco.

The U.S. Embassy in El Salvador is at 25 Avenida Norte, San Salvador 1230, El Salvador, Tel. 257100.

EMERGENCY MEDICAL SERVICES

Emergency medical services are available at the emergency rooms of most hospitals. Many localities provide emergency ambulance service either through the police or fire departments or a special ambulance unit. In an emergency call the telephone operator to get the police emergency number.

EMERGENCY MEDICAL TECHNICIAN

The Department of Transportation designed a standard 81 hour training program for emergency medical technicians. It is given in all 50 states by police, fire, and health departments, in hospitals or as a course in medical schools, colleges and universities. An additional two day course is available for learning how to remove trapped victims. Admission to the EMT program is limited to those over 18 with a valid driver's license and a high school diploma or the equivalent.

Graduates of the EMI program who pass a written and practical examination administered by the National Registry of Emergency Medical Technicians earn the title of Registered EMT-Ambulance. They must register again every two years.

Information about EMT courses can be obtained from the emergency medical services department in the state health department. Information about registration of EMTs is available from the National Registry of Emergency Medical Technicians, 1395 East Dublin-Granville Rd, P.O. Box 29233, Columbus, Ohio 43229, Tel. 614-888-4484.

EMIGRATION

United States citizens who wish to emigrate should write the appropriate country's embassy or consulate in the United States. For the address of the embassy see individual country entries.

EMPLOYMENT ABROAD

Most countries require foreigners to have work permits for even temporary employment. Consult the embassy or a consulate of the country for specific requirements.

For the address of the embassy see the individual country entries.

EMPLOYMENT AGENCIES: GOVERNMENT

There are over 2400 local offices of the U.S. Employment Service and affiliated state agencies. Services include testing, counseling, placement and training. These agencies charge no fees. The locations of these agencies can be found in the telephone directory under U.S. government or the state government. Questions or complaints can be referred to the Labor Department, Employment and Training Administration, U.S. Employment Service, 6th and D Sts. NW, Washington, D.C. 20213, Tel. 202-376-6289.

EMPLOYMENT AGENCIES: PRIVATE

Private employment agencies generally charge fees either to the employer or the prospective employee. They sometimes offer counseling, resume preparation, and other sevices also on a fee basis. If the job offered by the agency is advertised as "fee paid" the fee is paid by the employer. Otherwise, the fee, which may amount to 10% of the first year's salary, may have to be paid by the hired employee. Inquiries or complaints about private employment agencies should be addressed to the National Association of Personnel Consultants, 1012 14th St. NW, Washington, D.C. 20005, Tel. 202-638-1721.

ENGINEERS

All states require licensing for engineers whose work may affect life, health or property, or who offer their services to the public. In most states an engineer's license requires graduation from an accredited engineering school, four years of relevant work experience and passing a state examination for engineers.

Contact the state licensing board listed in the individual state entry. There are a number of professional organizations for engineers, including the following:

Institute of Electrical and Electronic Engineers, 2029 K St. NW, Washington, D.C. 20006, Tel. 202-785-0017.

American Society of Civil Engineers, 345 East 47th St., New York, N.Y. 10017, Tel. 212-644-7496.

American Institute of Chemical Engineers, 345 East 47th St., New York, N.Y. 10017, Tel. 212-644-8025.

American Institute of Industrial Engineers, Inc., 25 Technology Park, Atlanta, Ga. 30092, Tel. 404-449-0460.

Society of Petroleum Engineers, 6200 North Central Expressway, Dallas, Texas 75206, Tel. 214-361-6601.

EPISCOPAL CHURCH

The Protestant Episcopal Church is part of the Anglican communion. Currently there are approximately 3 million members in the United States. The church is organized hierarchically into parishes, dioceses, provinces and the General Convention. The Convention is made up of two houses: the House of Bishops and the House of Deputies. The presiding bishop, elected by the Convention, is the head of the church. For further information contact the Episcopal Church Center, 815 Second Ave., New York, N.Y. 10017, Tel. 212-867-8400.

EQUESTRIAN SPORTS

The United States Equestrian Team Inc. (USET), is non-profit voluntary organization which represents the U.S. in international equestrian sports. USET has the sole responsibility for training, equipping and financing amateur teams to represent the United States in the Pan American and Olympic games, the World Championships and other international competitions. The USET is financed wholly through contributions from individual members and organizations. It also receives allocations from the U.S. Olympic Committee. The USET has offices at Gladstone, N.J., 07934, Tel. 201-234-1251, and South Hamilton, Mass., 01982, Tel. 617-468-7377.

See also: RIDING: DISABLED PERSONS

ESTATE ADMINISTRATION: OVERSEAS

The Department of State can give advice on the administration of the estates of deceased persons who owned property over-seas. Contact the Department of State Bureau of Consular Affairs, Office of Special Consular Services, 2201 C St. NW, Washington, D.C. 20520, Tel. 202-655-4000.

ESTONIA
See SOVIET UNION

EUTHANASIA

Euthanasia is illegal in the United States. The Euthanasia Educational Council, however, has been instrumental in the campaign to legalize living wills designed to prevent prolonged agony in the terminally ill. The will requests that if there is no reasonable expectation of recovery of physical or mental facilities that an individual be allowed to die and that a physician not keep him alive by artificial means or "heroic" measures. The wills are valid in 11 states: Alabama, Arkansas, California, Idaho, Kansas, Nevada, New Mexico, North Carolina, Oregon, Texas and Washington. For further information and a copy of the Council's "living will" contact the Euthanasia Educational Council, 250 W. 57th St., New York, N.Y. 10019, Tel. 212-246-6962.

EXCHANGE PROGRAMS

The American Field Service is a private non-profit educational organization that conducts exchange programs for 16 to 18 year old students. Students from 61 countries come to the United States to live with American families and study for one year. American teenagers live and study under the same conditions abroad. For further information contact American Field Service International Scholarships, 313 East 43rd St., New York, N.Y. 10017, Tel. 212-661-4550.

F

FAMILY PLANNING

Only licensed doctors can write prescriptions for contraceptives designated as prescription drugs by the Food and Drug Administration.

Information about, examinations for, and prescriptions of contraceptives can also be obtained from private doctors, municipal health clinics and clinics run by Planned Parenthood Federation, which has local offices throughout the country. If there is no listing in the local telephone director for Planned Parenthood Federation, write the national office: Planned Parenthood Federation, 810 Seventh Ave., New York, N.Y. 10019, Tel. 212-541-7800.

Planned Parenthood also makes available information and referral services on problem pregnancy, abortion, and male and female sterilization.

See also: ABORTION, GENETIC COUNSELING, INFERTILITY

FAROE ISLANDS
See DENMARK

FEDERAL BUREAU OF INVESTIGATION
See: LAW ENFORCEMENT

FEDERAL GOVERNMENT: EMPLOYMENT

The federal government has over 60 civil service area offices and operates over 100 Federal Job Information Centers which offer information about employment in all federal agencies. They also announce and conduct the examinations required for various federal jobs. The offices are listed in the telephone directory under U.S. government, office of personnel management. If there is no listing call 800-555-1212 for the nearest office. Information about employment in a particular agency is also available from that agency.

FENCING

The official governing body for amateur fencing in the United States is the Amateur Fencers League of America, Inc. (AFLA). The league organizes and conducts fencing competitions on local, sectional and national bases. Rules for the events are established by the AFLA.

AFLA selects and oversees the training of individual and teams that represent the United States in international fencing competitions such as the Olympics and the Pan American games. It also encourages fencing on the collegiate and high school levels by providing qualified officials for meets on those levels.

AFLA is a member of the International Fencing Federation (Fédération International d'Escrime-FIE) and the United States Olympic committee. Membership in AFLA is available to active fencers, coaches, officials and all others interested in the sport.

Contact the Amateur Fencers League of America, 601 Curtis St., Albany, Calif. 94706, Tel.: 415-525-8282.

FIGURE SKATING (ICE)

Amateur ice figure skating in the United States is governed by the United States Figure Skating Association (USFSA). Members of the USFSA include figure skating clubs, individual skaters and interested persons who belong to member clubs and are registered with the USFSA, and, individual skaters who do not belong to a member club. Associate members include individual schools, colleges and universities that recognize students participating in figure skating. Honorary members can be designated by the USFSA governing council.

The USFSA encourages figure skating skills and knowledge through a series of tests measuring the accomplishments of skaters in the four branches of figure skating. Those branches are: compulsory figures, free skating, pair skating and ice dancing. Through the tests skaters qualify for various levels of regional, sectional and national competition. The USFSA sends its national champions to the World Figure Skating Championships and the winter Olympic Games.

Contact USFSA at 20 First St., Colorado Springs, Colorado 80906, Tel.: 303-635-5200.

FINLAND

A valid passport but no visa is required for travel to Finland for a stay of up to three months. There are no health requirements for entry. Travelers are advised not to bring pets to Scandinavian countries because all animals are subject to a quarantine of from four to six months. Any amount of foreign or local currency (Finnish mark) may be brought into the country, but travelers may not take out more foreign currency than they brought in. The export of more than 3,000 marks is prohibited. Finnish is the official language, but English is widely spoken. An International Driving License is required to drive in the country.

Trade with Finland is usually handled by resident Finnish agents. Some licenses are required for imports of certain goods. There are no foreign exchange restrictions.

The address of the Embassy of Finland is 1900 24th St. NW, Washington, D.C. 20006, Tel. 202-462-0556. Consulates are located in Alexandria (Va.), Anchorage, Astoria (Oreg.), Atlanta, Baltimore, Berwyn (Ill.), Boston, Cleveland, Denver, Detroit, Duluth, Honolulu, Lake Worth (Fla.), Minneapolis, New Orleans, New York, Philadelphia, Portland, Salt Lake City, San Diego, San Francisco, Seattle, Tampa and Wilmington (N.C.).

The American Embassy in Finland is at Itainen Puistotle 14A, Helsinki, Finland, Tel. 171931.

For further information contact the Scandinavian National Tourist Office, 75 Rockefeller Plaza, New York, N.Y. 10019, Tel. 212-582-2802.

For additional business information contact the Finnish-American Chamber of Commerce, 540 Madison Ave., New York, N.Y. 10022, Tel. 212-832-2588.

FIREFIGHTERS

Firefighters are generally hired by local communities, which set the requirements for employment. Most demand that the applicant pass a written test, a medical examination, and tests of strength, physical stamina and agility. Most also require that the men or women be at least 18, meet specific height and weight standards and have a high school diploma. Some communities give extra credit for previous military service. Career information is available from the local fire department, community civil service commission or the International Association of Fire Chiefs, 1329 18th St. NW, Washington, D.C. 20036, Tel. 202-833-3420.

FIRE SAFETY

Buildings must be constructed and maintained to meet the local fire code. Consult the local fire department, city planning commis-

sion or city council for local fire code regulations.

FIREWORKS

The sale of fireworks is regulated by local ordinance. Many communities prohibit sale or use inside their city limits, except in public exhibitions with a permit. Consult the local police department for information.

FIRST AID COURSES

First aid courses are offered in almost every town and city. Sponsors are usually an adult education program or the local chapter of the American Red Cross. For information about local adult education courses, contact the local school district or church, college or university.

For information about American Red Cross first aid courses, contact the local chapter listed in the telephone directory, or one of the following:

Eastern area:
American Red Cross
615 N. St. Asaph St.
Alexandria, Va. 22314
Tel. 703-549-8300

Southeastern Area:
American Red Cross
1955 Monroe Drive, N.E.
Atlanta, Ga. 30324
Tel. 404-881-9800

Midwestern area:
American Red Cross
10195 Corporate Square
St. Louis, Mo. 63132
Tel. 314-658-2000

Western area:
American Red Cross
P.O. Box 3673
San Francisco, Calif. 94119
Tel. 415-776-1500

National Headquarters:
American Red Cross
17th St. and D St. NW
Washington, D.C. 20006
Tel. 202-737-8300

FISHING LICENSES
See: HUNTING AND FISHING LICENSES

FLORIDA
The state agency for consumer protection in Florida is the Division of Consumer Services in the Department of Agriculture and Consumer Services. The Division has statutory authority to serve as a statewide clearinghouse for consumer complaints. The Division is not allowed to act as a private attorney for individual consumers but will attempt to indicate other available remedies such as the small claims court. It will file a lawsuit where there is a pattern of provable illegal business conduct.

Contact the Department of Agriculture and Consumer Services, Division of Consumer Services, 110 Mayo Building, Tallahassee, Fla. 32304, Toll-free Telephone 800-343-2176.

The Department of Professional Regulation licenses and regulates occupations and professions through the following boards: accountancy, architecture, barbers, chiropractic, construction, cosmetology, dentistry, electrical contractors, funeral directors and embalmers, engineers, landscape architects, land surveyors, massage, medical examiners, naturopathy, nursing, nursing home administrators, optometry, osteopathic medical examiners, pharmacy, pilot commissioners, podiatry, real estate and veterinary medicine. The Department coordinates the activities of the boards, administers licensing examinations for the various boards, accepts and investigates complaints against licensees, prosecutes licensees who have allegedly broken Florida law regarding that occupation and revokes licenses of those found guilty of misconduct.

Questions about licensing in Florida or complaints about licensees should be referred to the Department of Professional Regulation, 130 North Monroe Street, Tallahassee, Fla. 32301.

Consultant services to businesses interested in moving to Florida are available from the Department of Commerce, Division of Economic Development, Collins Building, Tallahassee, Fla. 32301, Tel. 904-488-6300. Or contact the Chamber of Commerce, P.O. Box 5497, Tallahassee, Fla. 32301, Tel. 907-222-2831.

Florida has city or county sponsored revenue bond funding for businesses. Check with the Division of Economic Development for further information on business assistance.

There is no personal income tax in Florida. The sales tax is 4%, which is collected by the retailer at the time of sale.

The corporate income tax rate is 5% with an allowed exemption of $5,000.

For tourist information contact the Division of Economic Development, Department of Commerce, 107 West Gaines St., Tallahassee, Fla. 32304, Tel. 904-488-6300.

FOOD: ADDITIVES

The Food and Drug Administration (FDA) regulates the use of food additives. Food products may contain a variety of additives, which are generally designed to improve the marketability of products. Current federal laws dealing with food additives are based on the so-called Delancy Amendment, which prohibits any food additives that induce cancer in humans or animals.

New additives must be tested for safety by the manufacturer before they can be approved for marketing. The FDA also tests new and existing additives. Any that are found hazardous under FDA regulations are banned. The FDA also inspects factories and analyzes food products to ensure that they meet its standards.

Complaints or questions about food additives can be directed to the FDA, which cannot investigate individual complaints but does maintain them on file for use in evaluating food additives.

Contact the Food and Drug Ad-

ministration, 5600 Fishers Lane, Rockville, Md. 20862, Tel.: 301-443-2170.

FOOD: EMERGENCY

Numerous public and private groups provide food in the case of calamities which leave large numbers of people without food. The Department of Agriculture releases surplus food to relief agencies such as the Red Cross, the Salvation Army, and civil defense organizations. These agencies then administer the distribution of the food. For further information contact the American National Red Cross, 17th Street and D Street N.W., Washington, D.C. 20006, Tel., 202-737-8300; the Salvation Army Disaster Service, 503 E. St., N.W., Washington, D.C. 20001, Tel. 202-783-4050; and, the Department of Agriculture, Agriculture Stabilization and Conservation Service, Food and Materials Division, 14th St. and Independence Ave. SW Washington, D.C. 20250, Tel. 202-447-4428.

See also: DISASTER LOANS, DISASTER RELIEF

FOOD: FILTH LIMITS

The Food and Drug Administration sets the percentages of filth, such as excreta, hair, insect parts, rot, mold and dirt which food processors find difficult to remove and which is allowed to remain in food. The FDA assures consumers that most food items contain far less than the allowed percentage of filth. In addition, foods are usually cooked, killing any bacteria before consumption. The FDA can seize and destroy any food lots that contain more than the allowed limits of filth.

The FDA cannot investigate every consumer complaint, but maintains files on complaints for use in identifying particular companies or food products that are not meeting government standards.

Consumers can also contact city or state health departments about a particular store or food product. Depending on the circumstances, the health department will investigate and take appropriate action, such as declaring a food lot unfit for consumption or citing the store for negligence.

Consumers should also direct questions or complaints about filth in food to the Food and Drug Administration, 5600 Fishers Lane, Rockville, Md. 20862, Tel.: 301-443-2170.

FOOD: FISHERY PRODUCTS INSPECTION

The National Marine Fisheries Service supervises a voluntary inspection program for fish and fish products. The inspection is concerned with the cleanliness of the plant and the wholesomeness of the product. The processor can choose whether to have the government inspect a particular lot or have a federal inspector on the premises. Only in the latter case will the product be labeled USDC inspected. As in the case of fruits

and vegetable inspection, there is a "quality assurance" program in which the government evaluates the processing plant, the quality of the product and production practices. The producer can then label a product as packed under the "quality assurance" program.

For further information contact the National Oceanic and Atmospheric Administration, National Marine Fisheries Service, Seafood Quality and Inspection Division, 3300 Whitehaven St. NW 20235, Tel. 202-634-7458

FOOD: FRUIT AND VEGETABLE INSPECTION

The federal government inspects fruits and vegetables on a voluntary basis, primarily to grade the products. But the Food Safety and Quality Service also checks for filth limits. The inspection is provided to packers, processors and distributors that request it for a fee. The federal government has two inspection plans. In the first case the FSQS reviews random samples and grades the entire lot. In the second case, the agency evaluates the plant for cleanliness, quality control and production procedures. If the plant passes, the company can label a product as packed under the "quality assurance" program. The product itself does not have to be inspected. Questions and complaints can be referred to the regional office of the FSQS, located in New York, Atlanta, Chicago, Dallas and San Francisco. The address can be found in the telephone directory listed under U.S. Government. Or contact the U.S. Department of Agriculture, Food Safety and Quality Service, 14th Street and Indepencence Ave. SW, Washington, D.C. 20250, Tel. 202-655-4000.

FOOD: GRADING

The Food Safety and Quality Service of the Department Agriculture grades most foods intended for human consumption. Such grading is not required by law but rather is provided to packers, processors and distributors that request it for a fee. Foods graded include: beef, veal, lamb and mutton, pork, turkey, chicken, goose, squab, rabbit, eggs, butter, cheddar cheese, instant non-fat dry milk, fresh fruits and vegetables, nuts, canned, frozen and dried fruits and vegetables, rice, beans and peas. The National Marine Fisheries Service of the Department of Commerce grades fishery products.

Meat is graded for eating quality; poultry for edible portion of meat and appearance, eggs for appearance and size, butter and dairy products for flavor, texture and body and fruits and vegetables for color, size, and shape.

The grading system is somewhat confusing because of lack of uniformity in terms and because many packages do not bear a grade label. Grades for beef range from the top grade—prime—

through choice and good to standard. The grade range for poultry is acceptable and unacceptable. The range for fresh fruits and vegetables is: U.S. Fancy, U.S. No. 1, U.S. No. 2 and U.S. No. 3.

Consumers can address their complaints to the Department of Agriculture, Food Safety and Quality Service, 14th Street and Independence Ave. SW, Washington, D.C. 20250, Tel. 202-655-4000.

FOOD: LABELS

The U.S. Department of Agriculture (USDA) sets standards for the wording and illustration allowed on labels of food sold in the United States. Labels must contain a list of ingredients in that food, beginning with the item weighing the most and continuing to the item weighing the least. The net weight and the USDA mark of inspection must also be included. The name and address of the packer or distributor must appear on the label, and if the product is imported, the country of origin must also appear. Questions or complaints about food products and meat and poultry labeling can be sent to the Department of Agriculture, Food Safety and Quality Service, Food and Consumer Services, 14th St. and Independence Ave. SW, Washington, D.C. 20250, Tel. 202-655-4000.

FOOD: SUPPLEMENTAL PROGRAM

The federal government through the food and nutrition service of the Department of Agriculture makes available nutritious food to supplement the diets of pregnant and nursing women and children up to five years of age who otherwise would not have adequate diets.

The supplemental food is made available through cash grants to local agencies or through state health departments to Indian tribes. Local health officials such as doctors, nurses or nutritionists admit participants to the program. Food is distributed to the participants by the local or state agencies. Contact local health or social welfare agencies about the WIC (Women, Infants, and Children) Special Supplemental Food Program. Information about the national and state programs is available from the Department of Agriculture, information officer, food and nutrition service, 14th St. and Independence Ave. SW, Washington, D.C. 20250, Tel. 202-447-8206.

See also: SCHOOL LUNCH PROGRAM

FOOD CO-OPS

By pooling resources, time and money with others, consumers can buy food in bulk and thereby save money. Informal cooperatives are generally not regulated by any government body. For further information write the Cooperative League of the U.S.A., 1828 L St. NW, Washington, D.C. 20036, Tel. 202-872-0550.

FOOD PROGRAMS: MEALS ON WHEELS

Meals on Wheels provides a well balanced, nourishing noon meal to older, blind or disabled adults who are unable to prepare a balanced meal for themselves and have no one in the home to cook for them.

Individuals are charged a reasonable price for the meal if they can afford to pay, or they pay what they can afford. If the individual qualifies because of income or because he or she receives SSI federal funds pay for the meal.

Volunteers deliver meals five days a week except holidays. Special diets are served under supervision of a dietition. For further information contact the local Meals on Wheels program, usually listed in the telephone directory.

FOOD STAMPS

The Food and Nutrition Service of the Department of Agriculture supervises the program designed to provide food assistance for the poor. For current requirements for assistance, contact the Department of Agriculture, Food and Nutrition Service, 500 12th St. SW, Washington, D.C. 20250, Tel. 202-447-8138.

FOOTBALL: PROFESSIONAL

Professional football in the United States is controlled by the National Football League (NFL), although there are a number of minor league and semi-professional organizations. The NFL consists of 28 teams. Teams are operated by private, for-profit corporations. The league is governed by a commissioner chosen by a vote of the team owners. The current NFL commissioner is Alvin "Pete" Rozelle. The commissioner's office oversees the compilation of schedules and statistics, rules and regulations, and team rosters. The sale of a team to new ownership must be approved by the commissioner's office and a vote of the team owners.

The offices of the NFL are at 410 Park Ave., New York, N.Y. 10022, Tel. 212-758-1500.

FOREIGN CLAIMS SETTLEMENT

The Foreign Claims Settlement Commission has jurisdiction over claims of American citizens against foreign governments for losses and injuries sustained by them. Funds come from international settlements or liquidation of foreign assets in this country by the Departments of the Treasury or Justice, or from public funds provided by Congress.

Contact the Justice Department, Foreign Claims Settlement Commission, 1111 20th St. NW, Washington, D.C. 20579, Tel. 202-653-6152.

FOREIGN CURRENCY

United States citizens have no restrictions on buying foreign currency or on maintaining an account in a foreign bank.

Tourists or businesspeople traveling abroad can generally exchange dollars for foreign currency at major banks, but they will be charged a fee or percentage over the current exchange rate. The fee is generally lower at banks than at hotels or at other businesses offering to exchange currency. Contact a major commercial bank.

See also: BANKS: ACCOUNTS IN FOREIGN BANKS, SPECIFIC COUNTRY

FOREIGN CURRENCY EXCHANGE

Individuals in the United States can settle debts to foreign individuals or companies by buying bills of exchange in a foreign currency from a major bank in the United States. The foreign business or individual can then present the bill or exchange to a major bank in that country for payment or credit to an account.

Consult a bank with a foreign exchange department.

FOREIGN GOVERNMENT AGENTS

Agents or lobbyists for foreign governments, political parties, corporations or individuals are required to register with the Justice Department under the Foreign Agents Registration Act.

Contact the Department of Justice, Foreign Agent Registration, Constitution Ave. at Tenth St. NW, Washington, D.C. 20530, Tel. 202-724-6996.

See also LOBBYISTS: CONGRESSIONAL

FOSTER GRANDPARENT PROGRAM

Foster Grandparents are older persons who spend two hours a day giving personal care and emotional support to children in homes, institutions or temporary care centers. In return the grandparents get transportation to and from the institution and are reimbursed for whatever expenses they may incur on the job. Personal liability and accident insurance are provided along with hot meals and a modest stipend. To participate in the program, the individual must be in good health, 60 years of age or over and have an income at or below the poverty level defined in the state.

For further information call the ACTION toll-free number 800-424-8580, or write to ACTION, 806 Connecticut Ave., Washington, D.C. 20525. Due to federal budget cuts, however, the future of this program is in doubt.

FOSTER PARENTS

Foster parents are almost always needed by state welfare agencies and also private agencies (frequently church affiliated) who care for children from troubled homes. The children may have been removed from the home through the legal process because of abuse or neglect and placed in the custody of the state department of public welfare or department of child welfare. Private agencies frequently take children from voluntary placements by parents with personal problems that prevent an adequate home environment.

Prospective foster parents make application to the welfare department or private agency and are interviewed by the agency or department in a "foster parent study." Most agencies have requirements about space for the child in the home, length of marriage, etc. Single parents are also considered for foster parents.

When the applicants are approved as foster parents, they are generally placed on a list, and a child is placed with them when a home is needed. Children are usually placed on a temporary basis, although the time period may turn out to be days, weeks or months. Foster parents do not usually know in advance how long a child will be placed in the home. Infrequently a foster child becomes free for adoption, and the foster family can make application to adopt the child.

Contact a local state welfare office, or state child welfare office, or private child welfare agency for more specific information.

FRANCE

A valid passport but no visa is necessary for travel to France for a stay of up to three months. There are no health requirements for entry. Pets are allowed into the country, but the requirements are complicated and vary with different animals. For more information, contact the French Tourist Office, 628 Fifth Ave., New York, N.Y. 10020, Tel. 212-757-1125. There are no restrictions on foreign currency or francs (the French monetary unit) that can be brought into the country. But only 5,000 francs or the equivalent in foreign currency may be exported, in addition to any foreign currency travelers have declared on arrival. French is, of course, the official language, and English is spoken occasionally and reluctantly. Travelers may drive in France with an International Driving License.

Trade with France is conducted in various ways—directly with a French firm, through resident commission agents, through French importers. Foreign exchange transactions through authorized banks are usually paid after the imported goods have cleared French customs except for transactions involving less than 1,500 francs. For further information about trading with France contact the French Trade Information Service, 40 West 57 St., New York, N.Y. 10019, Tel. 212-541-6720 or the French desk at the U.S. Dept. of Commerce, Tel. 202-377-4941.

The Embassy of France is located at 2129 Wyoming Ave. NW, Washington, D.C. 20008, Tel. 202-322-8400. Consulates can be found in Boston, Chicago, Detroit, Houston, Los Angeles, New Orleans, New York, and San Francisco.

The U.S. Embassy in France is located at 2 Avenue Gabriel, 75382 Paris Cedex 08, France, Tel. 296-1202. There are U.S. Consulates in Bordeaux, Lyon, Marseille, Nice and Strasbourg.

For additional business information contact the France Trade Information Service, 40 West 57 St., New York, N.Y. 10019, Tel. 212-541-6720.

FREIGHT: PACKAGES

Private freight carriers file tariffs (statements of rates and conditions) either with the Civil Aeronautics Board, which is the regulatory agency for air freight carriers, or with the Interstate Commerce Commission, which regulates ground freight companies.

Rates for freight vary from one carrier to another and from city to city. One company might have the lowest rate on one route but not on others. Rates are also dependent on whether they include direct pickup and delivery or only depot-to-depot transportation, on the type of commodity and on the size and weight of the commodity.

The carrier's liability for loss or damage is limited to a specific amount per pound. Excess liability coverage can be purchased, however. Claims for damage or loss should be made in writing to the carrier as soon as the damage or loss is discovered.

Complaints about air freight service should first be made to the carrier involved. The two federal agencies named above usually cannot investigate individual complaints, but they keep records of complaints for use in future investigations.

Complaints about freight packages can also be referred to the state consumer protection agency (see individual state entry), which may be able to mediate a settlement.

Complaints about air freight can be sent to the Civil Aeronautics Board, Washington, D.C. 20428, Tel.: 202-673-5990, complaints about ground freight companies to the Interstate Commerce Commission, Washington, D.C. 20423, Tel.: 202-343-4761 or toll free: 800-424-9312.

FRENCH WEST INDIES (Including Martinique, Guadeloupe, St. Martin, St. Barthelemy, Marie-Galante, Les Saintes and La Desirade.)

These islands are considered to be two departments of France. No passport or visa is required for travel to these islands, but travelers must have identity papers containing a photograph for a stay of up to 21 days. There are no health requirements for entry. Pets may be brought to the islands provided they have a certificate of health from a veterinarian. Any amount of foreign currency may be taken in or out of the French West Indies, but it must be declared upon arrival. Only 500 francs (the local currency) may be taken out. To drive on the islands travelers need an International Driving Licence. French is the official language.

English is spoken at the major hotels and shops and in business circles.

Licenses are not required for most imported goods. Where they are needed application should be made to the local Prefecture. Imports may be restricted by what is available from the islands' mother country, France, but for allowable imports St. Martin is a free port. Foreign exchange transactions are subject to the same regulations as those in France.

For futher information contact the French Embassy or a consulate.

The U.S. Consulate in the French West Indies is located at 14 Rue Blenac, Boite Postale 561, Fort-de-France 97206, Martinique, Tel. 719301/03.

For further tourist information contact the French West Indies Tourist Board, 610 Fifth Ave., New York, N.Y. 10020, Tel. 212-757-1125.

See FRANCE

FRISBEE

The International Frisbee Disc Association regulates the sport and sponsors major tournaments around the world. For further information contact the International Frisbee Disc Association, P.O. Box 970, San Gabriel, Cal. 91766, Tel. 213-287-2257.

FUNERAL DIRECTORS AND EMBALMERS

A license is needed in all states to practice embalming. While state licensing standards vary, an applicant must usually be 21 years of age, have a high school diploma, be a graduate of a mortuary science school, serve an apprenticeship and pass a state board examination. About half the states require a year or more of college in addition to the training in mortuary science.

Most states also require funeral directors to be licensed. The qualifications are similar to those for embalmers. Information about both types of licenses is available from the state office of occupational licensing. Consult the individual state entry in this book for the name and address of the agency to contact.

Two professional organizations for funeral directors and embalmers are: the National Funeral Directors Association of the United States, 135 W. Wells St. Milwaukee, Wis. 53203, Tel. 414-276-2500 and the National Selected Morticians, 1616 Central St. Evanston, Ill. 60201, Tel. 312-475-3414.

See also: BURIAL

FUNERAL INDUSTRY

In the United States the funeral industry has traditionally been regulated by the states, and the regulation has sometimes been uneven and less than rigorous. The Federal Trade Commission has issued regulations for the funeral industry to encourage disclosure of prices, and lessening of misleading or false claims by funeral companies.

Complaints can be sent to the Federal Trade Commission (address in appendix) but individual complaints may or may not be investigated. All complaints are kept on file and frequent complaints about a particular company or exceptional complaints may be investigated.

Individual companies are more likely to be investigated by the state consumer agency (listed in the state entries), or the state licensing board. See also: FUNERAL DIRECTORS AND EMBALMERS

FURS

The Federal Trade Commission (FTC) enforces the Fur Labeling Act, which requires that a label be attached to furs stating in plain English the name of the animal producing the fur, the country or origin, whether the fur has been bleached, dyed or otherwise artificially colored, and whether it is composed of paws, bellies, pieces or waste furs. The label must also state the name of the firm responsible for the label either by name or by code registered with the FTC. These labels must accompany the fabric through all stages of the manufacture and distribution until the fabric reaches the consumer. Furs sold in the United States cannot be made from the fur of an animal on the endangered species list. (See also: ENDANGERED SPECIES.)

Complaints about fur labeling or quality should be referred to the

FTC. The commission cannot act on individual complaints because of limited agency resources, but does act when there is a pattern of abuse. Complaints can also be referred to the state consumer protection agency if bought from an in-state retailer.

Consult individual state entries or the Federal Trade Commission, Pennsylvania Ave. at Sixth St. NW, Washington, D.C. 20580, Tel. 202-523-3625.

G

GAMBLING

At present only two states, Nevada and New Jersey, have legalized casino gambling. Casinos are legal throughout Nevada but in New Jersey are confined to the municipality of Atlantic City. Both states have casino control commissions that license the operation of casinos and see that they are operated honestly.

A number of states have legalized parimutuel better on thoroughbred horse, trotter and dog races. States where such gambling exists generally have boards of governors that regulate the length of the racing season, license owners and jockeys and see that races are run honestly.

In all states but New York and Nevada, wagering on races is permitted only at the track site. In Nevada wagers may be made on races at casinos. New York State operates the Off Track Betting (OTB) system, a chain of betting parlours where bets may be made on horse races at selected tracks. A percentage of each wager placed at OTB goes into the state's revenue fund.

The State of California now has legalized card clubs for the playing of several types of poker. Players gamble among themselves while the card club owners charge a "chair rental"—a fee generally of a dollar per half-hour or more depending on the table stakes—thus removing the club owners from any direct interest in the games.

Many states now permit the playing of bingo for prizes or cash. In some states, bingo games may be operated only by nonprofit organizations such as churches, temples or schools.

Contact the state gambling authorities or the Public Gaming Research Institute, 51 Monroe St., Rockville, Md. 20850, Tel. 301-279-7000 for further information.

GAS AND HEATING OIL SUPPLY: COMPLAINTS

The Economic Regulatory Administration monitors complaints about the gasoline and heating oil supply in the United States.

Contact the Regulatory Administration at 2000 M St. NW, Washington, D.C. 20461, Tel. 202-254-5474, toll-free 800-424-9246.

GAS LEAKS

The local gas company will generally check for gas leaks free of charge. It will also repair free of charge any leak due to faulty equipment belonging to the gas company. Gas leaks in private equipment must be repaired by a qualified person. Outside gas leaks should also be reported to the local gas company.

GENEALOGICAL REPORTS

The following organizations offer help in researching early American records such as federal land records, passenger arrival lists, census records, church registers, obituaries, etc. that may help trace a family tree. Specific information requests should be in writing, although telephone requests are sometimes permitted.

The American Antiquarian Society
185 Salisbury St.
Worcester, Mass. 01609
Tel. 207-755-5221

The Genealogical Society
50 East North Temple
Salt Lake City, Utah 84111
Tel. 801-531-2331

The New York Public LIbrary
Fifth Avenue and 42nd St.
New York, N.Y. 10018
Tel. 212-340-0849

Newberry Library
60 W. Walton St.
Chicago, Ill. 60610
Tel. 312-943-9090

The National Archives
and Records Service
Eight St. and Pennsylvania Ave. NW
Washington, D.C. 20408
Tel. 202-523-3218

GENETIC COUNSELING

A doctor or obstetrician can refer a couple to a teaching hospital or medical hospital which does genetic counseling. The National Genetics Foundation, 250 W. 57th Street, New York, N.Y. 10019 212-586-5800 also gives information on genetic counseling services available throughout the country.

GEORGIA

The Governor's Office of Consumer Affairs (OCA) is Georgia's consumer protection agency. The Office has the power to conduct investigations, hold hearings, adopt rules and regulations, issue subpoenas through the Attorney General's Office, seek injunctions and accept assurances of voluntary compliance.

When the OCA receives a consumer complaint, an investigator is assigned to assist the consumer in settling the complaint. When business actions are determined to be unfair, but not unlawful, OCA offers mediation between the parties in dispute. OCA may also advise the consumer of alternative remedies available such as the small claims court. In cases where there are law violations, the complaint is referred to the legal section for possible action, although legal action is only taken if there have been numerous complaints about a particular business.

Contact the Office of Consumer Affairs, 225 Peachtree St. NE, Suite 400, Atlanta, Ga. 30303, Tel. 404-656-4900.

Georgia has 39 licensing boards which license occupations and professions: accountancy, architects, athletic trainers, auctioneers, barbers, chiropractic examiners, the construction industry, cosmetology, dentistry, professional engineers and land surveyors, foresters, funeral services, professional geologists, hearing aid dealers and dispensers, landscape architects, librarians, marriage and family counselors, medical examiners, nurses, nursing home administrators, occupational therapists, dispensing opticians, optometrists, pharmacists, physical therapists, podiatrists, polygraph examiners, private detectives and private security agencies, psychologists, recreational examiners, speech pathologists and audiologists, registered sanitarians, pest control, used car dealers, used motor vehicle parts sellers, veterinarians, water and wastewater treatment plants, and water well standards.

Information about licensing in the above occupations and professions can be requested from the Joint Secretary, State Examining Boards, State Capitol, Atlanta, Ga. 30334, Tel. 404-656-3900. Complaints about practitioners in the above fields should be made to the individual board in care of the above address.

The Department of Industry and Trade offers consulting services to businesses interested in moving to the state or doing business there. Contact the Department of Industry and Trade, 1400 N. Omni International, Atlanta, Ga. 30303, Tel. 404-656-3545. Also contact the Chamber of Commerce, 1200 Commerce Building, Atlanta, Ga. 30303, Tel. 404-524-8481.

Georgia offers state, city and county revenue bond financing to industry in the state.

The corporate income tax rate is 6%, and the sales tax 3%.

The individual income tax in Georgia ranges from 1% on the first $750 to 6% on income over $7,000.

For tourist information about Georgia contact the Tourist Division, Bureau of Industry and Trade, P.O. Box 1740, Atlanta, Ga. 30334, Tel. 404-521-0845.

GERMAN DEMOCRATIC REPUBLIC (GDR) AND EAST BERLIN (East Germany)

A valid passport and a visa are required for travel to East Germany. To obtain a visa a traveler must first get a Visa Entitlement Certificate through either a travel agent or by writing to the Reiseburo der GDR, 1026 Berlin, Alexanderplatz 5, Tel. 2150. He or she must have proof of accommodation at a hotel or at the home of family or friends. It will take several weeks to obtain the Visa Entitlement Certificate. After getting the certificate, present it to any GDR Embassy or border crossing point to obtain a GDR visa. Those traveling on business will need three photographs, an invitation from the East German organization to be visited and proof of accommodation. All visas are valid only for the predetermined length of stay. Exit permits are required; they are issued along with the visa. For a one-day visit to East Berlin from West Berlin (with return before midnight) a visa may be obtained from East German officials at the sector boundary (Checkpoint Charlie). A valid passport is required. All visitors to East Germany must register with East Germany police within 24 hours of arrival.

There are no health requirements for entry except if arriving from an infected country. The import or export of local currency (mark, also called ostmark) is strictly prohibited. Any amount of foreign currency may be brought into the country and must be declared on arrival. Receipts of all exchange transactions must be saved in order to reconvert marks on departure. The official language is, of course, German. English is not widely understood or spoken. To drive in East Germany an International Driving License will suffice.

All foreign trade with East Germany and all foreign exchange transactions are controlled by the state. Foreign companies are represented by state agencies. Licenses are required for all imports and are issued by the Ministry of Foreign Trade. For further business information contact the Chamber of Commerce (Kammer fur Aussenhandel) 108 Berlin, Schadowstrasse 1, Tel. 2202441.

The import of Western literature and some articles, like tape recorders, is prohibited.

The U.S. Passport Office cautions Americans to conduct themselves discretely in the GDR, since some Americans have been given lengthy prison sentences for acts which would be either minor offenses or even legitimate expression of views in the United States or Western Europe. It is also suggested that Americans leave a record of their travel plans (including addresses) with the U.S. Embassy in East Germany as well as one of the Consular offices in West Germany. The American Embassy in East Germany is located at 108 Berlin, Neustaedtische Kirchstrasse 4-5, Tel. 2202741. Consulates in West Germany are located in West Berlin, Bonn, Bremen, Dusseldorf, Frankfurt, Hamburg, Munich and Stuttgart.

The Embassy of the German Democratic Republic in the U.S. is at 1717 Massachusetts Ave. NW, Washington, D.C. 20036, Tel. 202-232-3134.

GERMANY, FEDERAL REPUBLIC OF (WEST GERMANY)

A valid passport is required for travel to West Germany, but a tourist or business visa is not necessary for a stay of up to three months. For longer stays, travelers must obtain a temporary residence permit from the local alien office in West Germany. Those coming from West Berlin to West

Germany need a transit visa which can be obtained at an East German diplomatic mission or at official border crossings. There are no health requirements for entry except if arriving from an infected area. To bring a pet into the country a traveler needs a certificate of vaccination against rabies. The Deutsche mark is the official currency of West Germany. There are no restrictions on the amount of marks or of foreign currency which may be brought in or out of the country. German is, of course, spoken throughout the country, but English and French are widely understood. To drive in West Germany obtain a International Driving License.

Trade with West Germany is comparatively unrestricted. It is often handled through resident agents based in commercial areas throughout the country, but also through German importers and distributors and branches of foreign companies in West Germany. There are few licenses required and there are no restrictions on foreign exchange.

The Embassy of the Federal Republic of West Germany is located at 4645 Reservoir Blvd. NW, Washington, D.C. 20007, Tel. 202-331-3000. Consulates are located in Atlanta, Boston, Chicago, Detroit, Houston, Los Angeles, New York, San Francisco and Seattle.

The U.S. Embassy in West Germany is at Deichmannsaue, D-5300 Bonn 2, Tel. (02221) 8955. American consulates can be found in Berlin, Bremen, Dusseldorf, Frank-

furt, Hamburg, Munich and Stuttgart.

For further travel information contact the German National Tourist Office, 630 Fifth Ave., New York, N.Y. 10111, Tel. 212-757-8570.

For additional business information contact the German-American Chamber of Commerce, 666 Fifth Ave., New York, N.Y. 10103, Tel. 212-974-8830.

GHANA

A valid passport and a visa are required for U.S. citizens traveling to Ghana for a stay of up to three months. To obtain a visa a traveler needs three photos, a return ticket; business travelers need a letter from their company detailing the nature of their business in Ghana. The fee is $8. A yellow fever shot is also needed to get a visa and protection against cholera, typhoid and malaria are advised. Pets can be brought into the country if accompanied by a veterinarian's certificate of good health. The local currency is the cedi. Cedis may not be imported or exported. There is no limit on the amount of foreign currency that can be taken into the country, but all money must be declared on arrival and all unused cedis reconverted before leaving departure. English is the official language, and Fanti, Ga, Ewe, Dagbeni and Hausa are among the local dialects spoken. Driving conditions are comparatively good for Africa and an International Driving License validated in Ghana is required.

Foreign trade is partially handled in the private sector and partially government controlled. Licenses are needed for most imports and exchange controls are strict.

The Embassy of Ghana is located at 2460 16th St. NW, Washington, D.C. 20009, Tel. 202-462-0761. There is a consulate in New York.

The U.S. Embassy in Ghana is located at Liberia and Kinbu Roads, P.O. Box 194, Accra, Ghana, Tel. 66881.

GIFTED CHILDREN

The Office of the Gifted and Talented in the Department of Education is a clearinghouse for information on programs for the gifted throughout the United States. Many local school districts and teachers can also provide information. Contact the Department of Education, Office of Special Education and Rehabilitative Service, Office of the Gifted and Talented, 400 6th St. NW, Washington, D.C. 20202, Tel. 202-245-2487.

GIRL SCOUTS

The Girl Scouts of the U.S.A. offers educational activities including leader training, international exchange programs and conferences and seminars on topics ranging from management to child development. It focuses on expanding personal interests, learning new skills, career exploration and community service. Member-ship is open to girls aged seven through eight (Brownie Girl Scouts) and girls aged nine through 17. The groups are lead by adult volunteers. Membership includes 2,400,000 girls and 571,000 adults. Contact the local Girl Scout organization or the Girl Scouts of the U.S.A., 830 Third Ave., New York, N.Y. 10022, Tel. 212-940-7500.

GLIDING

See SOARING

GOODS: UNORDERED

By federal law only merchandise mailed by a charitable organization in a request for a contribution or free samples clearly marked free samples may be sent through the mails without having been ordered. Any unordered merchandise may be considered a free gift, even if a bill is included and the item has been sent by mistake. Any difficulty should be reported to the Federal Trade Commission, Sixth St. and Pennsylvania Ave. NW, Washington, D.C. 20580, Tel. 202-523-3711, or the state consumer protection agency.

GOVERNMENT EMPLOYEES: RECRUITMENT AND EXAMINATIONS

The Civil Service Commission recruits and gives examinations to prospective federal employees. Information about federal jobs and civil service examinations may be obtained from a Federal Job Information Center located in major metropolitan areas. For the nearest information center call toll free 800-555-1212 or consult the local telephone directory under U.S. government, Civil Service Commission. Information can also be obtained from the Civil Service Commission, Office of Personnel Management, 1900 E. St. NW, Washington, D.C. 20415, Tel. 202-632-6101.

GOVERNMENT INFORMATION CENTERS

See INFORMATION CENTERS: FEDERAL

GOVERNMENT PROPERTY: SURPLUS

The General Services Administration (GSA) has responsibility for selling the federal government's surplus real and personal property. Surplus real property is first offered to public agencies for sale. Businesses and individuals have a better chance of buying surplus personal property, such as used government automobiles, typewriters, plumbing and heating equipment and hardware.

The GSA maintains mailing lists of persons and businesses interested in particular types of property. Contact the regional office of the GSA to be placed on its mailing list. The addresses of the 10 regional offices are listed in the appendix. Or write the General Services Administration, 18th and F Sts. NW, Washington D.C. 20405, Tel. 202-566-1231.

Surplus property of the Department of Defense is sold separately. Contact the Defense Logistics Services Center, Federal Center Building, Battle Creek, Mich. 49016, Tel. 616-962-6511.

GOVERNMENT PUBLICATIONS

The U.S. Government Printing Office (GPO) prints and sells through mail orders and government bookstores over 25,000 different publications that originated in various government agencies. Books, Pamphlets and other publications are available on almost every government program, the activities of the U.S. Senate and House of Representatives, as well as other topics of general interest, such as the environment or food additives. Selected government publications, including annual reports of government agencies are available in depository libraries throughout the country. A list of libraries where GPO materials are deposited is also available from the Washington, D.C. office.

Some publications are free and others must be purchased. If the material requested is not available free, or if the request is not clear, the GPO will send a list of publications to facilitate the order.

For a list of addresses of U.S. Government Printing Bookstores see the appendix. Or contact the Superintendent of Documents, Government Printing Office, North Carolina at H. St. NW, Washington, D.C. 20402, Tel. 202-783-3238.

GREECE

U.S. citizens need a valid passport, but no visa to visit Greece for a stay of up to three months. Travelers who stay longer must obtain a residence permit from the alien police. This is valid for six months from the date of entry into Greece. There are no health requirements, but if travelers are coming from an infected area, smallpox and/or yellow fever shots are required. Pets are allowed in with a certificate of vaccination. The Greek monetary unit is the drachma. Travelers may bring 1,500 drachmae in or out of Greece. Any amount of foreign currency may be imported, but any money in excess of $500 must be declared in order to take it out of the country. Greek is the official language; English and French are generally spoken in major hotels and shops. Travelers can drive in Greece with an International Driving License.

Trade with Greece is usually handled through resident agents or local distributors. Some imports are restricted and all are subject to government approval and/or licensing. Approval or licensing of imports implies approval of foreign exchange through authorized banks. Greece became a Common Market member in January, 1981.

The Embassy of Greece is located at 2221 Massachusetts Ave. NW, Washington, D.C. 20008, Tel. 202-667-3168. There are Greek consulates in New York, Chicago, Boston, San Francisco and New Orleans.

The American Embassy in Greece is at 91 Vassilissis Sophias Blvd., Athens 140, Greece, Tel. 712951 or 718401. There is an American consulate in Thessaloniki.

For further tourist information can contact the Greek Tourist Agency, 565 Fifth Ave., New York, N.Y. 10017, Tel. 212-682-3520.

For further business information contact the Greek Trade Center, 150 East 58 St., New York, N.Y. 10022, Tel. 212-751-2404.

GREENLAND
See DENMARK

GRENADA

Proof of citizenship is required for travel to Grenada as well as a return ticket and sufficient funds. Neither a passport nor a visa is necessary. There are no health requirements if arriving from the United States or neighboring islands, but smallpox vaccinations are needed if coming from another area and yellow fever innoculations if traveling from an infected area. To bring a pet get permission from the Superintendent of Agriculture in Grenada. For more information, contact the Grenada Tourist Information Office, 141 East 44 St., New York, N.Y. 10017, Tel. 212-599-0301. The monetary unit used in Grenada is the East Caribbean dollar. There are no restrictions on currency allowed in or out of the island, but business travelers must declare all money upon arrival. English is the official language. Travelers can drive in Grenada with an International Driving License.

Trade with Grenada is conducted under a general import license covering most imports. There are no foreign exchange restrictions.

The Embassy of Grenada is located at 927 Vermont Ave. NW, Washington, D.C. 20005, Tel. 202-347-3198. There is a consulate in New York.

GREYHOUND RACING

Rules for the sport of greyhound racing are made by state legislatures in the United States. Although the rules are fairly uniform throughout the country, there may be slight variances among states.

Information about greyhound racetracks can be obtained from the American Greyhound Track Operators, 139 S.E. 14th Lane, Miami, Fla., 33131, Tel. 305-893-2103.

Another organization which promotes the sport of greyhound racing is the National Greyhound Association, P.O. Box 543, Abilene, Kan. 67410, Tel. 913-263-4660.

GUADELOUPE

See FRENCH WEST INDIES

GUATEMALA

A tourist card is required to travel to Guatemala for a stay to be determined by the Guatemalan immigration authorities. To obtain a tourist card you must apply in person to an embassy, consulate or an airline serving Guatemala with some identification (passport or birth certificate). A certificate of vaccination against smallpox is required for entry. Precautions against yellow fever are advised. Pets may be brought in provided they have a certificate of vaccination against rabies from a veterinarian. There is no limit to the amount of foreign currency that can be taken in or out of the country. The local currency is the quetzal. Quetzals may be brought into Guatemala in any amount, but only Q100 per day may be taken out. Spanish is the official language and various local Indian dialects are also used. English is not widely spoken. Travelers can drive there with an International Driving License.

Trade with Guatemala is usually conducted through local agents and import distributors. Most imports require no licensing, but they are subject to rather high import duties. There are no restrictions on foreign exchange.

The Embassy of Guatemala is located at 2220 R St. NW, Washington, D.C. 20008, Tel. 202-332-2865. There are consulates in Chicago, Houston, Los Angeles, Miami, New Orleans, New York and San Francisco.

The United States Embassy in Guatemala is at 7-10 Avenida de la Reforma, Zona 10, Guatemala City, Guatemala, Tel. 31-15-41.

GYMNASTICS

The Amateur Athletic Union is the governing body for amateur gymnastics in the United States. It sponsors developmental programs and national competitions, including the Olympic trials. Collegiate gymnastics are regulated by the National Collegiate Athletic Association. The AAUC can be reached at 3400 West 86th St., Indianapolis, Ind. 46268, Tel. 317-297-2900. The NCAA is located at U.S. Highway 50 and Nall Ave., P.O. Box 1906, Shawnee Mission, Kan. 66222, Tel. 913-384-3220.

H

HAITI

Proof of citizenship and a return ticket are required for U.S. citizens traveling to Haiti for a stay of up to 30 days. There are no health requirements if arriving from the United States, but typhoid shots are recommended. Pets are allowed into Haiti with a veterinarian's certificate of good health. The local currency is the gourde. There are no limits on the amounts of local or foreign currency that may be taken in or out of the country. French is the official language of Haiti, and most of the population also speaks Creole. Some English is also spoken. To drive a car, an International Driving License is required.

Trade with Haiti is handled through local agents. Some goods require licenses and there are no exchange controls.

The Embassy of Haiti is located at 2311 Massachusetts Ave. NW, Washington, D.C. 20008, Tel. 202-332-4090. There are consulates in New York, Dallas and Miami.

The U.S. Embassy in Haiti is located at Harry Truman Boulevard, Port-au-Prince, Haiti, Tel. 20200.

For further information contact the Haiti Government Tourist Bureau, 1270 Avenue of the Americas, New York, N.Y. 10020, Tel. 212-757-3517.

HANDBALL

The International Handball Federation is the world governing body for handball. The U.S. Handball Association regulates and promotes the sport of handball in the United States. It also holds regional and national tournaments. Membership in the association is a requirement for entry into major competition. The organization gives financial assistance to players depending on ranking. For information on International Handball Federation programs contact the Amateur Athletic Union, 3400 West 86th St., Indianapolis, Ind. 46268, Tel. 913-384-3200. Also contact the U.S. Handball Association at 4101 Dempster St., Skokie, Ill., Tel. 312-673-4000.

HANG GLIDING

The United States Hang Gliding Association is the sole national organization responsible for the development, promotion and protection of hang gliding activities in the U.S. It sanctions, supervises and documents official hang gliding competitions and maintains U.S. hang gliding records. The association is governed by a board of 20 regional directors elected by association members and five directors-at-large elected by the regional directors. It is responsible for designating the U.S. team for the world hang gliding championships, which are held every two years.

Contact the U.S. Hang Gliding Association, P.O. Box 66306, Los Angeles, Calif., 90066, Tel.: 213-390-3065.

As aircraft, gliders are regulated by the Federal Aviation Administration. For further information contact the Department of Transportation, Federal Aviation Administration, 800 Independence Ave. SW, Washington, D.C. 20591, Tel. 202-426-1960.

HAWAII

The Office of Consumer Protection (OCP) is the state agency in Hawaii responsible for protecting the interests of consumers and legitimate business enterprises. OCP will handle complaints involving: retail installment sales, unfair competition and endless sales schemes, landlord/tenant disputes, mail order purchases, door-to-door sales, unfair and deceptive business practices and unlicensed contractors. All complaints first undergo a fact finding and mediation stage. If there is no violation of law and the parties re-

fuse compromise, the OCP cannot force compliance. If the investigator believes there has been a violation of law, the case is referred to the legal section for further review and possible action.

OCP also maintains files of consumer complaints which are public record and may be reviewed at the OCP office upon request.

Contact the Office of Consumer Protection, 250 South King Street P.O. Box 3767, Honolulu, Hawaii 96812, Tel. 808-548-2540. Offices are also located in Liheu, Kauai; Wiluku, Maui; Hilo, Hawaii.

The Department of Regulatory Agencies licenses and regulates the following occupations and businesses: accountancy, acupuncture, architects, banks, barbers, boxing, cable T.V., cemetary, chiropractic, collection agencies, contractors, cosmetology, dental, dispensing opticians, electricians, elevator mechanics, engineers, fair housing, hearing aid dealers, insurance, landscape architects, massage, medical doctors, mortgage brokers, motor vehicle industry, motor vehicle insurance, motor vehicle repair, naturopathy, nursing, nursing home administrators, optometry, osteopathy, pest control, pharmacy, plumbers, port pilots, private detectives and guards, psychologists, real estate, rental agencies, speech pathology and audiology, subdivision registration, surveyors, travel agencies, and veterinarians. Information about licenses or complaints about individuals in the above types of occupations or businesses can be directed to the Department of Regulatory Agencies, 250 King Street, P.O. Box 3767, Honolulu, Hawaii 96812, Tel. 808-548-2560 or 548-2540.

The Department of Planning and Economic Development strives to attract quality business to Hawaii. Interested businessmen may request assistance from the Department of Planning and Economic Development, Kamamalu Building, 250 South King Street, Honolulu, Hawaii, mailing address: P.O. Box 2359.

The Capitol Loan Program, administered by the Department of Planning and Economic Development, assists small businesses unable to obtain adequate financing.

The Department's Industry Development and Product Promotion program is a multi-phased effort aimed at increasing Hawaii's self-sufficiency. It promotes both agricultural and manufactured products and stimulates industrial development by providing assistance to industry groups.

The income tax in Hawaii allows personal exemption of $750 (double exemption for those over 65, and larger exemptions for disabled). Tax rates for individuals are 2.25% on the first $500 and increasing to 11% over $30,000. Tax rates for the head of household are 2.25% on first $500 and increasing to 11% for over $60,000.

The tax rate on corporations in Hawaii is 5.85% up to $25,000 and 6.435% over $25,000. A general excise tax on businesses is ½ of 1% on wholeselling and intermediary services, producing and manufacturing. All other business activities such as retailing business and professional services, amusement, commissions, rentals, etc., are taxed at 4%. A use tax of ½ of 1% is charged if for resale at retail and 4% is charged for use of consumption on the purchase price or value of tangible personal property not taxable under the general excise tax.

For tourist information contact the Hawaii Visitors Bureau, P.O. Box 2274, Honolulu, Hi. 96804, Tel. (808) 923-1811.

HAZARDOUS MATERIALS: ACCIDENTS AND SPILLS

The Chemical Transportation Emergency Center (CHEMTREC), part of the U.S. Department of Transportation, provides technical information on the evaluation and analysis of 18,000 or more chemicals, substances and tradename products. CHEMTREC can describe possible effects on the environment and suggested methods for control and/or containment in the event of an accident or spill. The center also maintains a directory of experts and industry cooperatives that can be contacted to provide additional advice or on-scene assistance.

Contact the CHEMTREC toll-free number: 800-424-9300 only for emergency reporting of chemical accidents and spills. Other inquiries should be directed to CHEMTREC, National Response Center, Washington, D.C. 20593, Tel.: 202-426-1105.

See also: TOXIC SUBSTANCES CONTROL, PESTICIDES: SAFE USE

HEALTH MAINTENANCE ORGANIZATIONS

As an alternative to traditional group health insurance many employers are now offering health maintenance organization (HMO) membership to their employees. HMO's provide a complete range of health benefits, including preventive care, regular checkups, office visits, and full hospitalization.

The Department of Health and Human Services has regulatory powers over HMOs through the Office of Health Maintenance Organizations, 12420 Parklawn Dr., Rockville, Maryland 20857. Toll free telephone 800-638-6686, Tel. 301-433-2300.

HEARING AIDS

Food and Drug Administration regulations permit hearing aids to be sold only to people who have had a medical evaluation of their hearing loss. This is done to prevent people from buying hearing aids that will not help them. The medical evaluation requirement can be waived if the purchaser signs a statement saying that he or she knows a medical examination is advisable. Manufacturers of hear-

ing aids must provide customers with a detailed brochure explaining what hearing aids can do, how they work and how to use them. For further information, or to register complaints, contact the Department of Health and Human Services, Food and Drug Administration, 5600 Fishers Lane, Rockville, Md. 20857, Tel. 301-443-2894.

Persons looking for a medical specialist qualified to evaluate a hearing problem should contact a physician, who can refer them to a specialist, or the county medical society or local medical school. The American Speech-Language-Hearing Association can supply a list of certified audiologists or local centers performing examinations. For further information contact the American Speech-Language-Hearing Association, 10801 Rockville Pike, Rockville, Md. 20852, Tel. 301-897-5700.

The Better Hearing Institute, a nonprofit educational organization, provides information about hearing loss, hearing aids and assistance available to the hearing-impaired. It also handles consumer complaints about hearing aids. For further information contact the Better Hearing Institute, 1430 K St. NW, Washington, D.C. 20005, Tel. 202-638-7577.

See also: HEARING LOSS: TESTING

HEARING LOSS: TESTING

Several organization can refer individuals to hearing and speech centers for testing. Contact the National Association for Hearing and Speech, 6110 Executive Blvd, Rockville Md. 20852, Tel. 301-897-8682 and the Alexander Graham Bell Association at 3417 Volta Place NW, Washington, D.C. 20007, Tel. 202-337-5220.

See also: LIP READING

HEART DISEASE: AMERICAN HEART ASSOCIATION

The American Heart Association is one of the major groups involved in research into heart disease. It also sponsors annual scientific meetings and teaching institutes, funds teaching scholarships and provides public information materials.

With assistance from the American Heart Association, local communities sponsor programs to screen the public for heart disease, provide training in cardiopulmonary resuscitation, and offer public education programs designed to emphasize prevention and identification of heart disease.

Contact the local heart association or the American Heart Association, National Center, 7320 Greenville Ave., Dallas, Tex. 75231, Tel. 214-750-5300.

HEMOPHILIA

The National Hemophilia Foundation supports research into the disease and provides interested parties with information on it. The organization also helps blood recruitment drives and advises individuals on where they can obtain treatment. For further information contact the National Hemophilia Foundation, 19 W. 34th St, New York, N.Y. 10001, Tel. 212-563-0211.

HIGH SCHOOL: EQUIVALENCY EXAMINATION

By passing a high school equivalency examination called the General Education Development tests (GED), an individual can get a certificate accredited by his or her state department of education and accepted on the same basis as a high school diploma.

The GED examination is in five parts: English, social studies, natural sciences, literature and mathematics. Any adult can take the test at approximately 2,000 centers throughout the country. For information about the test contact the local superintendent of schools or school adult education supervisor. Or write to the Adult Education Association of the U.S.A., 810 18th St. NW, Washington, D.C. 20006, Tel. 202-347-9574.

Although an individual may take the examination without any preparation, many school districts or communities offer a course to help them prepare for the test.

See also: HOME STUDY

HIKING

The National Campers and Hikers Association has regional information centers to give hikers and campers reports on local roads, trails, campsites and game laws. Contact the National Campers and Hikers Association, 7172 Transit Road, Buffalo, N.Y. 14221, Tel. 716-634-5433.

The National Park Service offers information and hiking trails and camping in the national parks. Contact the National Park Service, 18th and C Sts. NW, Washington, D.C. 20240, Tel. 202-343-7394.

HOCKEY: PROFESSIONAL

The National Hockey League (NHL) controls the sport of professional hockey in the United States and Canada. The league consists of 21 teams in 21 cities, 14 in the United States and 7 in Canada. It is affiliated with two minor hockey leagues, the American Hockey League and the Central Hockey League, which function as farm systems from which players are recruited. Recruitments are also made from the Canadian Junior Hockey League, from Europe and from colleges in the U.S. and Canada. The league administers all areas of the sport, from scheduling games and making rules to handling public relations, marketing, legal problems and security. The President of the league is John A. Ziegler who is elected by the Board of Governors which consists of the 21 team owners. The sale of a team must be approved by the Board of Governors.

The office of the National Hockey League is located at 1221 Avenue of the Americas, Suite 1444, New York, N.Y. 10020, Tel. 212-398-1100.

HOCKEY: AMATEUR

Amateur ice hockey in the United States ranges from the squirt league for nine-year-olds to the U.S. Olympic team. All levels are governed by the Amateur Hockey Association of the United States (AHHAUS).

AHHAUS directs amateur hockey competition on several league levels: squirt league for nine- and 10-year-olds, peewee league for 11- and 12-year-olds, bantam league for 13- and 14-year-olds, midget league for 15- and 16-year-olds and junior league for 17- to 19-year-olds. The association conducts local, regional and national championships at the various league levels and makes player awards.

The AHHAUS also provides training for coaches and referees and promotes uniformity in playing rules and interpretations. It is also a clearinghouse for information to assist local organizations in solving problems.

The association is a member of the U.S. Olympic Committee and and the International Ice Hockey Federation. As a member of those organizations, AHHAUS is responsible for organizing and training the U.S. national, national junior and Olympic teams for world and Olympic competition. It also works with the professional National Hockey League on matters of mutual interest.

Contact the association's permanent office at 2997 Broadmoor Valley Road, Colorado Springs,

Colo. 80906, Tel.: 303-576-4990.

HOME FIXTURES: COMPLAINTS

Complaints about home fixtures such as windows and tiles may be made to the National Association of Home Manufacturers which will attempt to mediate the dispute. For further information contact the National Association of Home Manufacturers, 6521 Arlington Blvd., Falls Church, Va. 22042, Tel. 703-533-9696.

HOME LOANS: FARMS AND RURAL AREAS

See AGRICULTURAL LOANS

HOME RENOVATION ASSISTANCE

The Department of Housing and Urban Development (HUD) has programs that offer loans for rehabilitation of residential properties in conjunction with other neighborhood revitalization projects. For further information contact the nearest HUD office or the Department of Housing and Urban Development, HUD Bldg, 451 7th St. SW, Washington D.C. 20410, Tel. 202-755-6420.

HOMES: CONSTRUCTION COMPLAINTS (NEW HOMES)

Consumers who have complaints about the quality of workmanship and material in new homes should refer them to the National Association of Home Builders, Consumer Affairs Department, 15th and N Sts. NW,

Washington D.C. 202-452-0404.
See also: HOME WARRANTIES (New Homes)

HOME IMPROVEMENT: CONTRACTORS

Home improvements may require approval by the city or county building code office. Since regulations vary greatly from location to location, check with local government offices before starting work.

Home improvement contractors are unevenly regulated. Electricians generally have to be licensed by the state licensing board. Other contractors are frequently monitored through the state consumer protection agency, which may investigate companies that have a high rate of complaints. The reputation of home improvement contractors can be checked through the Better Business Bureau (see entry) before a contractor is chosen.

Complaints about the actual work of home improvement contractors can be made through the Better Business Bureau, state consumer protection office (see individual state entry), small claims court or, if the contractor is licensed, through the state licensing board for the particular trade. See individual state entries for addresses of the proper licensing agencies.

HOME STUDY

Home study consists of enrollment and study with an educational institution that provides lesson materials prepared in a sequential order for the student to study independently. The student mails completed assignments to the school for correction, grading, comment and guidance by qualified teachers. Courses vary from only a few to hundreds of assignments.

An estimated 500 institutions offer home study programs in the United States.

One way to tell the quality of the home study school is by learning which are accredited by the National Home Study Council. The Council is recognized by the National Commission on Accrediting as the accrediting body for home study schools.

Home study school accreditation certifies that a school has voluntarily undergone a comprehensive study and examination that demonstrates that the school performs the functions that it claims, that the school sets educational objectives for students and that it furnishes materials and services that enable students to meet the educational objectives set.

Accredited home study schools include degree, nondegree, vocational and avocational programs. Program offerings are wide ranging. They include high school diploma programs, art, computer, drafting, electronics engineering and photography courses, courses for the blind, diesel truck driving, paralegal skills, and yacht design; and full college curricula offered by several colleges.

In most cases individuals who want to take courses for college credit must have a high school diploma. High school diplomas can also be obtained through home study courses. Other vocational or avocational courses do not require high school diplomas.

A full list of accredited home study schools can be requested from the National Home Study Council, 1601 18th St., NW, Washington, D.C. 20009, Tel. 202-234-5100.

HOME WARRANTY (NEW HOMES)

Some new homes are now protected by warranties offered by the Home Owners Warranty Corporation (HOW). The Corporation is made up of 116 councils, each of which is composed of builders who have met criteria set up by the corporation. Builders may offer the home warranty if they use HOW's dispute resolution procedure, comply with HOW's building standards and enroll all their homes in the program.

As backing for the home warranties, the builders pay an insurance premium and a service charge for each house they build, both of which are passed on to the buyer of the home. The premium varies from $2.60 to $3.90 for each $1000 of the selling price of the house, depending on the region of the country; and the service fee ranges from $10 to $50 per house.

HOW warranties on new homes last for 10 years. The items covered by the warranty become more restrictive each year. In the first year the builder must repair any defects that appear that do not conform to either local building codes or HOW's standards. In the second year the warranty continues to cover structural defects, but not appliances. Wiring and ductwork are covered for the second year; but for the remaining eight years only structural defects are covered.

Disputes between the home owner and the builder are settled through HOW's conciliation or arbitration. Conciliation is tried first and if an agreement cannot be reached, the case is presented to an arbitrator from the American Arbitration Association. If an arbitrator determines that a builder should make repairs and the builder refuses, HOW will make the repairs. Builders are dropped from the program when they fail to meet HOW standards, but the homes they build under the HOW program are still covered.

New Jersey is the only state that requires home builders to offer warranties. In that state every builder must register with the state and must offer a 10-year warranty. Builders who do not comply with the dispute settlement portion of New Jersey law lose their right to build houses in New Jersey. Information about home warranties in New Jersey can be obtained from the New Jersey Department of Community Affairs, Home Warranties, Trenton, New Jersey 08625, Tel. 609-292-3794.

Information about HOW home warranties can be requested from the National Association of Home Builders, Fifteenth St. at M St. NW, Washington, D.C. 20005, Tel. 202-452-0200.

HOME WARRANTY (USED HOMES)

Several companies offer warranties on existing homes. Those companies approved by the National Association of Realtors inspect the home for major aspects of structural soundness, which are then covered in the warranty. The cost of inspection and protection varies from company to company.

Contact the local board of realtors or the National Association of Realtors, 430 N. Michigan Ave., Chicago, Ill. 60511, Tel.: 312-440-8000.

HONG KONG

A valid passport but no visa is required for U.S. citizens traveling to Hong Kong for a stay of up to one month. Business travelers need no special papers. There are no health requirements for entry except cholera shots if coming from an infected area. Pets are subject to a three month quarantine in Hong Kong. The local currency is the Hong Kong dollar. There are no restrictions on the amount of local or foreign currency that can be taken in or out of Hong Kong. The languages most commonly spoken there are English and Chinese. To drive a car, an International Driving License or an American license is required. There is a departure tax of HK$15.

Trading with Hong Kong is generally handled through agents or importing companies. Licenses are not required for most goods and there are no exchange controls.

Consular affairs of Hong Kong are handled by British consulates.

The U.S. Consulate General in Hong Kong is located at 26 Garden Rd., Hong Kong, Tel. 5239011.

For further tourist information contact the Hong Kong Tourist Association, 548 Fifth Ave., New York, N.Y. 10036, Tel. 212-947-5008.

Additional business information can be obtained by contacting the Hong Kong Trade Development Council at the same address, Tel. 212-582-6610.

HOSPITAL: PATIENT'S RIGHTS

The American Hospital Association has adopted a Patient's Bill of Rights, to which it encourages hospitals to comply. Many hospitals now post the Patient's Bill of Rights and some distribute it to patients.

Although the Patient's Bill of Rights is not spelled out in any law, the American Hospital Association's backing does give it some weight. A patient has every right to insist on certain basic considerations while hospitalized. According to the American Hospital Association these include the right:

1) To considerate and respectful care.
2) To complete information from physicians concerning diagnosis, treatment, and prognosis in understandable terms.
3) To receive whatever information necessary to give informed, advance consent to any procedure and/or treatment.
4) To every consideration for privacy concerning a medical care program.
5) To refuse treatment to the extent permitted by law, and to be informed of the medical consequences of such action. (This would mean that an adult has the right to die from a hopeless condition).
6) To expect that all communications and records pertaining to care will be treated as confidential.
7) To expect a hospital to respond, within reason, to requests for services.
8) To get information about any relationship between a hospital and other health care and educational institutions treating the patient, and to get information (including names) on the existence of any professional relationship between individuals treating a patient. (This means that the patient has the right to know whether treatment is by a member of a university hospital or by a physician's student.)
9) To be advised if the hospital proposes to perform human experimentation in the course of a patient's care or treatment.

10) To expect reasonable continuity of care.
11) To examine and receive an explanation of bills, regardless of the source of payment.
12) To know what hospital rules and regulations apply to a patient's conduct.

About 20 percent of all hospitals now employ a type of consumer representative frequently called a patient advocate. These advocates help patients resolve complaints and recommend changes in hospital policy or procedure that will benefit patients.

For a copy of the Patient's Bill of Rights contact the American Hospital Association, 840 North Lake Shore Dr., Chicago, Ill. 60611, Tel. 312-280-6000.

HOSPITALS: BILLING COMPLAINTS

Complaints about hospital billing may be made to the local consumer protection office or the state or local office of Blue Cross/Blue Shield. Those problems not resolved by the local office may be referred to the national organization at 1700 Pennsylvania Ave. NW, Washington, D.C. 20006; 202-785-7932.

HOUSEBOATS

The Houseboat Association of America offers services to those interested in houseboating, including chart services, a special buying service, an insurance program and discounts on houseboat rentals and purchases. Contact the Houseboat Association of America, 4251 Spruill Ave., Charleston, S.C. 29406, Tel: 803-554-0200.

HOUSING FEDERAL SUBSIDIES

The Department of Housing and Urban Development offers subsidies to make home ownership more available to lower income families. The subsidies go to the lenders of FHA (Federal Housing Authority) insured mortgages and are used to reduce the interest rate and therefore the monthly mortgage payments.

Families are generally eligible if their income is 80% or less of the median income for the area in which they live. The purchaser of the home is required to recertify his income and family status annually.

Rent subsidies are also available to low income families. The subsidies are not made directly to the families but are made to the owners of approved multifamily rental housing projects to supplement the partial rental payments of eligible tenants. The subsidy cannot exceed 70% of the market rental rate. To qualify for a subsidy, families must have an income that is not more than 80% of the median income in their area. They must also meet other criteria.

Applicants seeking subsidies for home ownership should contact FHA approved mortgage lenders. Applications for rent subsidy are submitted through the owners or sponsors of multifamily housing projects. General information about these programs can be obtained from the local HUD office or the Department of Housing and Urban Development, 451 Seventh St., SW, Washington, D.C. 20410, Tel. 202-755-5111.

HOUSING: PRIVATE RENTED HOUSES OR APARTMENTS

Laws affecting tenants and landlords vary from state to state, but some 30 states have a "warranty of hability" clause which requires that if the landlord does not maintain an apartment properly, the tenant does not have to pay the rent. The landlord also has the right to take the tenant to court or start eviction proceedings if the tenant does not pay rent. The court, usually city or county, exercises the legal authority over tenant-landlord disputes.

Contact the local housing authority for information about the laws affecting rental apartments and houses in the area (the mayor's office may direct tenants to the right agency).
See also DISABLED: HOUSING

HUMAN BODY: DONATION TO MEDICAL SCHOOL AT DEATH

A person's body can be donated to a medical school at death for use in training future doctors. A relative can make a telephone call to a nearby medical school to arrange for the donation, and the medical school will usually arrange for transportation. A death certificate is required. It must be made out by the attending physician and be taken to the city or county health department. Embalming is not usually necessary unless the body is to be transported by a common carrier, such as an airline or trucking company.
See also: DEATH CERTIFICATE

HUNGARY

A valid passport and a visa are required for travel to Hungary. To obtain a visa apply in person or by mail to a Hungarian diplomatic mission. Travelers will need a valid passport and two photographs. There is a fee of $6. Visas can also be obtained upon arrival at the airport in Budapest or at a frontier border crossing if arriving by car. However, they cannot get a visa if they arrive at the border by train. The visa is valid for six months. The requirements are the same for business travelers. There are no health requirements for entry unless coming from an infected area. Pets may be brought in with a health certificate from a veterinarian. The Hungarian currency is the forint. there is a limit of 100 forints which may be taken in or out of the country. But there is no limit on the amount of foreign currency which may be imported or exported. Hungarian is the national language but some German, English, French and Russian are also spoken. To drive in Hungary obtain an International Driving License.

All foreign trade with Hungary is government controlled. Licenses are required for all imports and are issued by the Ministry of Foreign Trade. Exchange transactions are authorized by the Hungarian National Bank.

The Embassy of Hungary is located at 3910 Shoemaker St. NW, Washington, D.C. 20008, Tel. 202-362-6730. There is a consulate in New York City.

The address of the American Embassy in Hungary is V. Szabadsag ter 12, Budapest, Hungary, Tel. 329-375.

HUNTING AND FISHING LICENSES

All fishers, hunters and trappers are required to purchase licenses issued by individual state fish and game departments or commissions. Fees from the licenses are generally used for fish and game management. Licenses are usually sold through local vendors including grocers, liquor stores and sporting good stores. The fees for the licenses vary from state to state, and are generally higher for nonresidents. Most states also have game wardens responsible for patrolling fields, woods and waterways to enforce fish and game laws. Contact the state department of environment or Conservation for information.

I

ICELAND

A valid passport but no visa is required for travel to Iceland for a stay of up to three months. There are no health requirements for entry. Pets should not be brought because they are subject to quarantine. There is no limit to the amount of foreign currency that can be taken in or out of the country, but no more may be exported than was originally brought in. A limit of 20,000 krona (the local currency) may be imported or exported. The official language of the country is Icelandic but English, Danish and German are also spoken. An International Driving License is required for driving.

Foreign trade with Iceland is often done through resident agents, but goods can also be ordered directly from foreign companies. Few import licenses are needed, and there are few restrictions on foreign exchange.

The Embassy of Iceland is located at 2022 Connecticut Ave. NW, Washington, D.C. 20008, Tel. 202-265-6653. There are many consulates in the U.S.—Los Angeles; San Francisco; Seattle; Portland, Ore.; Minneapolis; Atlanta; Boca Raton, Fl.; Tallahassee; Boston; Boulder, Colo.; Harrisburg, Pa.; Chicago; Dallas; Detroit; Houston; New York; Norfolk, Va.; Philadelphia and Hollywood, Fla.

The American Embassy in Iceland is at Laufasvegur 21, Reykjavik, Iceland, Tel. 29100.

For further tourist information contact the Scandinavian Tourist Office, 75 Rockefeller Plaza, New York, N.Y. 10019, Tel. 212-582-2802.

IDAHO

The Consumer Protection Agency in Idaho is a division of the Attorney General's Office. Unfortunately, due to the lack of funding by the state legislature, the office is no longer actively engaged in enforcing the Idaho Consumer Protection Act or in resolving individual complaints by consumers.

Under Idaho law consumers have the right to sue in court to recover losses resulting from business practices in violation of the Idaho Consumer Protection Act. The consumer can sue for actual damages or $500, whichever is greater. The law also provides for punitive damages and recovery of court costs and attorney's fees.

The Better Business Bureau in Boise does offer mediation services to consumers who have complaints though they have no legal authority. Direct complaints to the Boise Better Business Bureau, 216 N. 8th Street, Boise, Id. 83702.

The Bureau of Occupational Licenses issues licenses for the following professions: architects, barbers, cosmetologists, nursing home administrators, optometrists, podiatrists, psychologists, health specialists, hearing aid fitters, landscape architects, social workers, veterinarians and morticians. Information about licenses in these professions can be obtained from the Bureau of Occupational Licenses, 2404 Bank Drive #312, Boise, Idaho 83705,

Tel. 208-334-3233. Complaints about licensees can also be sent to the Bureau which has the power to revoke licenses.

The Division of Economic and Community Affairs provides assistance to businesses interested in moving to Idaho. Direct incentives to new businesses such as tax credits, tax increment financing or industrial development bonds are not available. Interested businessmen should contact the Division of Economic and Community Affairs, State Capitol Building, Boise, Idaho 83720, Tel. 208-334-3416.

Personal income tax in Idaho is 7.5% on income over $5,000. Corporate taxes are 6.5% and the sales tax, 3%.

For tourist information contact the Division of Tourism and Industrial Development, State Capitol Building, Boise, Id. 83720, Tel. (208) 384-2470.

ILLEGITIMATE CHILDREN

Although laws regarding legitimacy vary from state to state, a child is generally considered legitimate if the parents marry either before or after his or her birth. Divorce or annulment of the parents' marriage does not affect legitimacy.

Child support from the father can be obtained through the courts for an illegitimate child, but paternity must be proven. Proof of paternity or the granting of child support make the child legitimate.

A father must still pay child support even if the mother remarries, unless the child is adopted.

The illegitimate child usually inherits from the mother and her family as though the child were legitimate. In some cases the courts have awarded part of the father's estate to his illegitimate child, but usually only after protracted court proceedings.

It is not possible to tell from the birth certificate whether or not a child is legitimate.

See also: BIRTH REGISTRATION

ILLINOIS

The state agency with responsibility for consumer protection in Illinois is the Consumer Protection Division of the Attorney General's Office. Consumer complaints received by the Attorney General's office are evaluated by an attorney to determine if fraud is involved. In many cases consumer complaints can be resolved through mediation at an informal hearing where both parties have an opportunity to discuss their different positions.

The Attorney General's Office is the enforcement agency for the Consumer Fraud and Deceptive Business Practices Act. Businesses which are the subject of numerous or serious consumer complaints may be investigated by the Attorney General's Office. The Office has the authority to subpoena persons and relevant documents, get a court order to enjoin a business from operating in the state of Illinois and obtain civil penalties of up to $50,000.

Contact the Consumer Protection Division, Attorney General's Office, 500 South Second St., Springfield, Ill. 62706.

The Department of Registration and Education issues 100 different licenses which fall into 32 professional and occupational groups: architects, athletic exhibitions, barbers, beauty culturists, chiropractors, collection agencies, dental practice, detection of deception examiners, detectives, doctors (osteopaths, physicians and physicians' assistants), embalmers, funeral directors, horseshoers, land sales, land surveyors, nurses, nursing home administrators, optometrists, pharmacists, physical therapists, podiatrists, professional engineers, psychologists, public accountants, real estate brokers and salesmen, sanitarians, shorthand reporters, social wokers, structural engineers, tree experts, veterinarians, and weather modification. Also within the Department's jurisdiction are professional service corporations and the issuing of licenses to manufacture, dispense and distribute controlled substances.

The Department licenses or registers qualified applicants and then inspects and investigates to be certain that the licensing laws are obeyed. Complaints from consumers are referred to the investigation section which determines if the allegation is a violation of the law or the Department's rules and regulations. If a charge against a licensee is legally provable, a formal complaint is drawn up by the Department with specific charges and a hearing is held. A recommendation is made to the Director of the Department of Registration and Education. If the Director approves a recommendation of discipline or revoking of a license, the licensee can appeal the decision to the Illinois Circuit Court.

For information about licensing requirements contact the Department of Registration and Education, 55 East Jackson Blvd., Chicago, Ill. 60604, Tel. 312-793-8544. An office is also located in Springfield at 320 West Washington, Springfield, Ill. 62786, Tel. 217-785-0800.

The Department of Commerce and Community Affairs promotes the growth of business and industry in Illinois. The Department's Division of Commercial and Industrial Development promotes the establishment of new business and industry in the state and helps existing firms expand. Interested firms should contact the Department of Commerce and Community Affairs, 222 South College St., Springfield, Il. 62706, Toll-free in Illinois 800-252-2923, or Tel. 217-782-3891.

There is no personal property tax in Illinois. Corporate income tax was increased in 1979 to replace the revenue lost by the abolition of the personal property tax.

The basic corporate income tax is a flat 4%, and a replacement tax of 2.85% is legally a separate tax from the basic corporation tax. The replacement tax is not subject to increase and is sheduled to fall to 2.5% in 1981.

The personal income tax in Illinois is 2½% in 1981. The Illinois Constitution specifies that the basic corporate income tax rate be linked to the personal income tax rate in an 8:5 ratio.

The state sales tax in Illinois is 4.0% with a maximum of 2.0% optional local sales tax.

The effective property tax rate in Illinois is 2.4%.

Further information about the tax structure in Illinois can be obtained from the Department of Commerce and Community Affairs at the address listed.

For tourist information about Illinois contact the Office of Tourism, Illinois Department of Business and Economic Development, 205 W. Wacker Dr., Room 100, Chicago, Ill. 60606, Tel. 312-793-4732.

IMPEACHMENT OF FEDERAL OFFICERS

The U.S. House of Representatives has the power to impeach federal officials it believes guilty of treason, bribery or high crimes and misdemeanors. Usually the House Judiciary Committee draws up an impeachment resolution. If the resolution is adopted by the House of Representatives, a trial is held by the Senate with members of the House acting as the prosecutors, except when a president is impeached, in which case the Chief Justice presides at the Senate trial. Conviction of treason, or high crimes and misdemeanors requires two thirds approval of the senators present, and there is no appeal. Punishment of those convicted is limited to removal from office and disqualification from further federal office.

IMPORTS

The U.S. Customs Service of the Department of the Treasury has responsibility for collecting the revenue from imports, including custom duties, excise taxes, fees and penalties due on imported merchandise. It also seizes contraband, including illegal narcotics and drugs.

Freight shipments entering the country must clear customs at the first port of arrival. The merchandise can also be forwarded while in customs custody from the port of arrival to another port of entry closer to the destination.

Private custom house brokers are available at each port of entry. They can be designated to act as an importer's agent or representative in entering a shipment through customs. Licensed customhouse brokers charge a fee for effecting entry, clearance and release of goods through customs. This is not a U.S. Customs charge.

U.S. law prohibits the importing of certain items, including: lottery tickets, narcotics and dangerous drugs, obscene articles and publi-cations, seditious and treasonable materials, hazardous articles and products made by convicts or by forced labor.

Automobiles can be imported only if they meet U.S. standards for safety and pollution control. Firearms and ammunition are subject to restrictions by the Bureau of Alcohol, Tobacco, and Firearms. Applications to import firearms and ammunition may be made only through a licensed importer, dealer or manufacturer.

Fruits and vegetables, as well as plants, cuttings, seeds and certain endangered plant species are either prohibited from entering the country or require an import permit. Meats, livestock and poultry are subject to regulations similar to those for fruits and agricultural products. See: PEST CONTROL.

Merchandise from certain countries is not allowed to be imported into the U.S. without license from the U.S. Department of the Treasury. The countries are: Cambodia, Cuba, North Korea and Vietnam.

For general information and information on import restrictions contact the Department of the Treasury, U.S. Customs Service, Foreign Assets Control Division, 1301 Constitution Ave. NW, Washington, D.C. 20220, Tel. 202-566-5286.

For auto import requirements check with the Environmental Protection Agency, 401 M St. SW, Washington, D.C. 20406, Tel. 202-755-2673 and the Department of

Transportation, 400 Seventh St. SW, Washington, D.C. 20590, Tel. 202-426-4000.

Obtain requirements for firearm and ammunition imports from the Bureau of Alcohol, Tobacco, and Firearms, Department of the Treasury, 1200 Pennsylvania Ave. NW, Washington D.C. 20226, Tel. 202-566-7511.

Requests for plant, fruit and vegetable permits should .be directed to USDA, Information Division of the Animal and Plant Inspection Service, 14th St. and Independence Ave. SW, Washington, D.C. 20250, Tel. 202-447-3977, or contact the USDA Plant Protection and Quarantine, Bettsville, Md. 20705 Tel. 301-344-2577 and Springfield, Md., Tel. 301-451-9464.

INDIA

U.S. citizens entering India by sea or air for purposes of tourism and planning to stay less than 30 days require a valid passport and proof of onward transportation but no visa. This no-visa facility is good only if there have been no visits to India during the previous six months. Travelers entering overland, for any reason other than tourism, or for a planned stay of more than 30 days require one of the following types of visas:

1) Tourist visa—valid for three months and three entries. The requirements are a valid passport, one passport size photograph signed on the back and a return ticket.

2) Entry visa—valid for three months and one entry. The requirements are a valid passport and one passport photograph signed on the back.

3) Business visa—valid for three months and one entry. The requirements are a valid passport, one photograph signed on the back and a letter from their company detailing the nature of their business and confirming financial responsibility.

4) Student visa—validity dependent on duration of studies. The requirements are a valid passport, one photograph signed on the back, a letter from a recognized Indian institution confirming the admission of the applicant and evidence of financial arrangements made for the stay.

5) Visa for research scholars—valid for one year and one entry, this visa can be extended if necessary. The requirements are four applications with four photographs signed on the back, a detailed outline for the proposed research project, countersigned by the sponsoring institution in India to be submitted in quadruplicate, and evidence of financial responsibility.

Students and researchers should allow three months for the processing of their visas. The above requirements are to be submitted with a visa application to an Indian diplomatic mission. The

Embassy of India is located at 2107 Massachusetts Ave. NW, Washington, D.C. 20008, Tel. 202-265-5050. There are consulates in Chicago, New York and San Francisco. The fee for any of the above visas is $2.00.

Upon arrival in India, visitors who have a visa other than the tourist visa must register with Indian authorities within seven days and report any changes of address.

If arriving from Africa or Latin America, evidence of a yellow fever shot is required. Otherwise, there are no particular health requirements, although smallpox and cholera innoculations are advised. Pets can be brought into the country provided they have a health certificate from a veterinarian. An International Driving License is necessary for driving in India.

The Indian monetary unit is the rupee. No rupees may be taken in or out of the country. Any amount of foreign currency may be brought in but must be declared on arrival, and no more may be taken out than brought in. The main language of India is Hindi, although many other local dialects are spoken. English is widely spoken as a second language.

Trade with India is in the hands of both the government and the private sector. Allowable imports vary depending on the Indian government's current economic plans. There is a list of banned imports. Some imports are covered by an Open General License and others are licensed on a case by case basis. Exchange controls are in effect except for those imports which come under of open license. Foreign exchange is authorized by the Reserve Bank of India.

The U.S. Embassy in India is located at Shanti Path, Chanakyapuri 21, New Delhi, India, Tel. 690351.

For additional tourist information contact the India Government Tourist Office, 30 Rockefeller Plaza, New York, N.Y. 10112, Tel. 212-586-4901.

For further business information contact the Trade Development Authority of India, 445 Park Ave., New York, N.Y. 10022, Tel. 212-753-6655.

INDIANA

The agency with responsibility for consumer protection in Indiana is the Consumer Protection Division of the Attoreny General's Office. The Attorney General of Indiana cannot represent an individual citizen in a private legal proceeding against a particular business, but the Consumer Protection Division does have the power to act if it appears that a merchant is engaging in a pattern of deceptive consumer sales activity.

The Division will write to the individual or company named in the complaint and invite the party to respond. If the initial letter from the Consumer Protection Division does not produce a resolution, the office will assume the role of mediator and attempt to bring about a settlement. If those efforts are not successful, the complainant must contact a private attorney or file a suit in the local small claims court.

Contact the State of Indiana Office of the Attorney General, Consumer Protection Division, 219 State House, Indianapolis, Ind. 46204, Tel. 317-232-6330, Toll-free in Indiana 800-382-5516.

There is no central administrative agency which coordinates licensing of occupations and professions in Indiana. Individual boards set requirements for licensing, review applicants and accept complaints about licensees. Inquiries about occupational or professional licensing in Indiana should be sent to the Consumer Protection Division which will send them on to the proper licensing board.

The Department of Commerce offers consulting services to businesses and industry. Contact the Department of Commerce, State House, Indianapolis, Ind. 46204, Tel. 317-232-8800.

Indiana offers state, city or county revenue bond financing for industry and city or county general obligation bond financing. It also offers state loan guarantees for construction and purchase of equipment.

The corporate income tax rate in Indiana is 6%, and the state sales tax 4%.

The individual income tax rate in Indiana is 1.9% flat rate.

For tourist information contact the Tourism Development Division, Department of Commerce, State House, Room 336, Indianapolis, Ind. 46204, Tel. 317-633-5423.

INDIAN CLAIMS

The Indian Claims Commission hears and determines any claims against the United States on behalf of any Indian tribe, band or other identifiable groups of American Indians residing within the United States. For further information contact the Indian Claims Commission, 1730 K St. NW, Washington, D.C., Tel. 202-653-6184.

INDIAN JEWELRY AND CRAFTS

The Indian Arts and Crafts Board Act, as well as laws in Alaska, Arizona, California, Minnesota, Montana, Nevada, New Mexico and South Dakota make it illegal to misrepresent Indian products such as jewelry and other crafts. For help in determining the authenticity of Indian jewelry and crafts, contact the Indian Arts and Crafts Association, 2401 12th St. NW, Albuquerque, N.M. 87102, Tel. 505-242-1385.

151

INDIANS: GOVERNMENT SERVICES

The Bureau of Indian Affairs administers several government programs for American Indians. Included are programs for education, housing, loans for business purposes, general assistance for needy Indians on reservations, and social services. Contact the Department of the Interior, Bureau of Indian Affairs, C. St., between 18th and 19th Sts. NW, Washington, D.C. 20240, Tel. 202-343-1100, or the nearest field office of the Bureau of Indian Affairs.

INDONESIA

Indonesia consists of over 13,000 islands including Sumatra, Java, Bali, Kalimantan, Sulawesi (Celebes) and West Irian. U.S. citizens traveling to Indonesia require a valid passport and a visa. Tourists can get either a tourist visa, good for a stay of up to two weeks with a two-week extension available, or a visitors visa, good for a stay of up to one month which may be extended for up to three months. Visa applications must be accompanied by a valid passport, two photographs, a round trip ticket and a fee of $3. Business travelers need, in addition, a letter from their company detailing the nature of business to be conducted and confirming financial responsibility for the applicant. The fee for a business visa is $5.50. Visas must be used within three months of date of issue. There are no health requirements for entry except a yellow fever shot if coming from an infected area. However, it is advisable to be protected against cholera, typhoid, paratyphoid and malaria. Pets may be brought into the country with a veterinarian's certificate of good health. The local currency is the rupiah. Rupiahs may not be imported and their export is limited to 25,000. There is no limit to the amount of foreign currency which may be brought in or out of the country. The official language of the country is Bahasa Indonesia but many other regional languages are spoken including Javanese and Balinese. English, Dutch and Chinese are the most commonly spoken foreign languages. There are practically no cars for rent on the islands.

Foreign trade is handled both by government agencies and by private agents. A large number of imports are handled by various state trading companies. Import licenses are not required and imports controlled by the private sector must be handled by Indonesian-owned companies only.

The Embassy of Indonesia is located at 2020 Massachusetts Ave. NW, Washington, D.C. 20036, Tel. 202-293-1745. There are consulates in New York and San Francisco.

The U.S. Embassy in Indonesia is located at Jalan Merdeka Selatan 5, Jakarta, Indonesia, Tel. 340001.

For additonal business information contact the American Indonesian Chamber of Commerce, 2 Park Ave., New York, N.Y. 10017, Tel. 212-683-6170.

INDUSTRIAL INJURY AND DISEASE
See WORKER'S COMPENSATION

INFANT CARE
See PARENTING

INFANT DEATH SYNDROME
See CRIB DEATH

INFERTILITY
The American Fertility Society can refer couples with fertility problems to a clinic in their area. For further information contact the American Fertility Society, 1801 Ninth Ave. S. Birmingham, Ala. 35205, Tel. 205-933-77222.

INFORMATION CENTERS: FEDERAL
Federal Information Centers (FIC) are operated by the federal government in major metropolitan areas. Staff members are prepared to help consumers find the right federal or state agency or locate information. FICs are designed to be contacted by telephone for easy and immediate access. An FIC staff member will provide an appropriate agency address and telephone number if the question raised cannot be answered immediately.

INFORMATION: FREEDOM OF
Any person has access to information in federal government files without having to say why it is needed or how it will be used. Under to the 1976 Freedom of Information Act, the government must show why the information cannot be released if the request is denied. This Act applies to federal information collected on all types of subjects, from civil rights compliance to government product testing. To make a request contact the Freedom of Information Unit of the appropriate government agency. For more information write the Freedom of Information Clearinghouse, 2000 P St. NW, Washington, D.C. 20036 or call Tel. 202-785-3704.

INFORMATION REFERRALS
The National Referral Center, which is part of the Library of Congress, is a free service that directs those who have questions concerning any subject to organizations that can provide the answer. The center does not generally provide the names of individual experts on a particular subject, however, nor does it provide the information directly. It makes referrals to organizations that have specialized knowledge and are willing to share it with others. Some of these organizations charge for their services. The Center includes these terms in their referral information.

The National Referral Center uses a subject-indexed, computerized file of 13,000 organizations. A description of each resource is entered in the file, including its special fields of interest and the types of information service it is willing to provide. Included are not only technical libraries, information and documentation centers, and abstracting and indexing services, but also professional societies, university research bureaus and institutes, federal and state agencies, industrial laboratories, museums, testing stations, hobby groups and grass-roots citizens' organizations.

The center will accept requests on any subject. Telephone requests are encouraged because they allow discussion and refinement of specific requests. When the topic is not covered in the file, the center will attempt to locate new information resources. In response to a referral request the center will provide the names, addresses, telephone numbers and brief description of appropriate information resources, usually in the form of a computer printout. Requests for referral should include the information required and information sources already contacted and the qualifications of the individual requesting assistance, such as participation in a government contract, membership in a professional society, etc.

The file is accessible to readers at the Library of Congress through computer terminals located in several reading rooms, and to many federal agencies nationwide through the RECON computer network operated by the Department of Energy. It is also accessible to private citizens by visiting the fifth floor of the Library of Congress, Thomas Jefferson Building, Second St. and Independence Ave. SE, Washington, D.C. 20450. Individual users can contact the Library of Congress, National Referral Center, Washington, D.C. 20540, Tel. 202-287-5670. Organizations that would like to be included in the file can also call 202-287-5680.

INSURANCE AGENTS AND BROKERS

Every state requires that insurance agents and brokers be licensed in the state in which they sell insurance. To qualify for a license an applicant must pass a written examination covering insurance fundamentals and the state insurance laws and must be 21 years of age.

For information about licensing consult the individual state entry for the address of the state licensing agency, which can make referrals to the state board licensing insurance agents and brokers.

INSURANCE CLAIM REPRESENTATIVES

Insurance claim representatives investigate claims, negotiate settlements with policy holders and authorize payment from the insurance company to the policy holder or other claimant. They are sometimes called claim adjusters or claim examiners.

Insurance companies generally prefer representatives to have a college degree, although some may have some type of special knowledge that enables them to evaluate claims. Experience in auto repair, for example, could serve as a qualification for adjusting claims on damage in car wrecks.

About three-quarters of the states require claim representatives to be licensed. Consult the individual state entry for the address of the state licensing agency. This can make referrals to the state board that licenses claims representatives.

To qualify for a license an applicant must usualy pass a written examination on the fundamentals of adjusting, be 21 years of age, have completed an approved course in insurance or loss adjusting and have filed a surety bond. Some insurance companies offer educational programs to their employees to help them qualify for licensing as claim representatives.

Information about such educational programs can be obtained from the Insurance Information Institute, 110 William St. New York, N.Y. 10038, Tel. 212-669-9200.

INSURANCE COMPANIES: REGULATION

The insurance industry is one of the few large American industries that is not regulated by the federal government, primarily because pressure from the industry has prevented passage of the needed legislation. Insurance companies are regulated by individual state insurance commissions. There

are, however, laws requiring companies to outline consumer rights regarding the sale of insurance to prospective customers. Consumers with complaints about the industry should report them to the municipal or state consumer office. They can also file complaints with the state insurance commission. However, only a few states act on individual complaints. Most do not have the staff necessary to adequately deal with them. And, in a few states, the commission does not have the will to act.

INSURANCE: CRIME (FEDERAL)

The federal government offers low-cost crime insurance to residents or businesses in states with high crime rates and no commercially available, low cost crime insurance. Legislation requires that the program be made available in any state in which the Federal Insurance Administration (FIA) concludes that there exists a critical problem of crime insurance availability and/or affordability. Surveys are made by the FIA to determine area eligibility. Evidence is received from local officials, consumer groups or private citizens.

Currently included in the program are: Alabama, Arkansas, California, Colorado, Connecticut, Delaware, the District of Columbia, Florida, Georgia, Illinois, Iowa, Kansas, Maryland, Massachusetts, Minnesota, Missouri, New Jersey, New York, North Carolina, Ohio, Pennsylvania, Puerto Rico, Rhode Island, Tennessee, Virginia,

155

New Mexico, the Virgin Islands, Washington and Wisconsin. Applications for Federal Crime Insurance can be obtained from any licensed property insurance agent or broker in the covered states or directly from the Federal Insurance Administration.

Contact Federal Crime Insurance, 1725 Eye St. NW, Washington, D.C. 20472, Tel. (toll free) 800-638-8780 (Maryland call collect: 301-652-2637).

INSURANCE: FIRE

The insurance industry operates the government subsidized FAIR Plan for those who cannot obtain insurance for fire, riot or vandalism at reasonable cost. Plans are available in the following states: California, Connecticut, Delaware, Georgia, Illinois, Indiana, Iowa, Kansas, Kentucky, Louisiana, Maryland, Massachusetts, Michigan, Minnesota, Missouri, New Jersey, New Mexico, New York, North Carolina, Ohio, Oregon, Pennsylvania, Rhode Island, Virginia, Wisconsin and Washington. They are also available in Puerto Rico and the District of Columbia. For further information contact the Federal Insurance Administration, Federal Emergency Management Agency, Washington, D.C. 20472, Tel. 202-634-6772.

INSURANCE: FLOOD

The National Flood Insurance Program provides federally subsidized flood insurance to property owners in flood, mudslide or flood-related erosion prone areas, where the community has adopted acceptable flood management regulations. For further information contact the local insurance company, the local office of the Department of Housing and Urban Development, or the Federal Emergency Management Agency, Federal Insurance Administration, HUD Building, 1725 Eye St. NW, Washington, D.C. 20472, Tel. 202-755-9096, or toll free 800-638-6620.

IOWA

The consumer protection agency for the state of Iowa is the Consumer Protection Division of the Department of Justice. Consumer complaints can be made either by mail, telephone or in person. The Division will contact the person or company being charged and mediate an agreeable resolution for both parties, or will inform the complainant that they are unable to help them. The Division also has the authority to bring lawsuits against businesses which have a pattern of consumer abuse.

Contact the Consumer Protection Division, 1209 E. Court, Des Moines, Iowa 50319, Tel. 515-281-5926.

The State Department of Health licenses occupations and professions through the following boards: barber, chiropractic, cosmetology, dental examiners, mortuary science, nursing home administrators, optometry, physical therapy, podiatry, psychology, speech pathology and audiology and hearing aid dealers. Information about requirements for licensing in these occupations can be obtained from the State Department of Health, Lucas State Office Building, Des Moines, Iowa 50319, Tel. 515-281-4401. The Department will receive complaints on licenses. Complaints are investigated by the Department, and appropriate action is taken including the revoking of licenses.

The Development Commission, Industrial Development Staff offers assistance to businesses building or expanding in Iowa. The Commission administers the industrial revenue bond program and other programs to help businesses that settle in Iowa. Contact the Industrial Development Division, 250 Jewett Building, Des Moines, Iowa 50309, Tel. 515-281-3251.

Iowa, according to the Development Commission, is the only state with a single factor corporate income tax, which means that only products sold for delivery in the state are taxed in Iowa. The tax rates are 6% on the first $25,000 of net taxable income, 8% on the next $75,000 and 10% on all over $100,000. Net income for Iowa tax purposes is determined after 50% of federal income tax is deducted.

Personal income tax is based on the adjusted gross income as reported on the federal income tax return. There is an option of either an itemized form or a standard deduction. Tax rates range from 1.25% plus $5.12 for income less than $2,046 to 13% plus $7,590 for income in excess of $76,725.

A sales tax of 3% is imposed on transactions involving the transfer, exchange, or barter of tangible personal property for a consideration; on rental of rooms, apartments, etc., for less than 31 days; receipts of amusement devices and games of skill and commercial recreational activities. Exemptions include purchase for resale, sales of food and prescription drugs.

For tourist information contact the Iowa Development Commission, 250 Jewett Building, Des Moines, Iowa 50309, Tel. 515-201-3619 or 281-3401.

IRELAND

A valid passport and a return ticket are required for U.S. citizens traveling to Ireland. The length of stay will be determined by Irish immigration authorities upon arrival. There are no further requirements for business travelers. There are no health requirements. Pets brought to the country are subject to a six month quarantine. There is no limit to the amount of foreign or local currency (Irish pound) which may be brought in or out of the country. The two official languages of Ireland are Irish, also called Gaelic, and English. English is the most commonly used. To drive in Ireland, an International Driving License is required.

Local agents handle most importing, and most goods do not

need licensing. Exchange transactions are subject to Irish law. Prospective foreign investors in Ireland should contact the Industrial Development Authority, Lansdowne House, Ballsbridge, Dublin 4, Ireland, Tel. 686633.

The Embassy of Ireland is located at 2234 Massachusetts Ave. NW, Washington, D.C. 20008, Tel. 202-483-7639. There are Irish consulates in Boston, Chicago, New York and San Francisco.

The U.S. Embassy in Ireland is at 42 Elgin Road, Ballsbridge, Dublin 4, Ireland, Tel. 688777.

For further information contact the Irish Tourist Board, 590 Fifth Ave., New York, N.Y. 10036, Tel. 212-246-7400.

For additional business information contact the Ireland-U.S. Council for Commerce & Industry, 460 Park Ave., New York, N.Y. 10022, Tel. 212-751-2660.

IRONWORKERS

Structural ironworkers, riggers and machine movers, ornamental ironworkers, and reinforcing ironworkers may learn their trades informally on the job, but most learn through a three year apprenticeship program sponsored by the local union. The program combines on the job training with 144 hours of classroom instruction each year. Consult the state apprenticeship agency or the local branch of the International Association of Bridge, Structure and Ornamental Iron Workers.

ISRAEL

A valid passport but no visa is required for U.S. citizens traveling to Israel on either business or pleasure for a stay of up to three months. There are no health requirements for entry except if coming from an infected area. Pets may be brought into the country with a veterinarian's certificate of good health. The Israeli pound is the local currency, and up to 1,000 pounds may be exported. There are no limits on the amount of foreign currency that can be taken in or out of the country. Foreign currency is also accepted. A traveler paying bills in American dollars, for example, can avoid paying local taxes. Hebrew is the national language of Israel. Arabic, English and German are the most commonly spoken foreign languages. To drive a car, an International Driving License is required.

Trade with Israel is generally handled through local agents, but some items may be handled by government agencies. There are no controls on foreign exchange and few import licenses are required.

Persons traveling to Israel should be advised that evidence of a visit there may prevent entry into Arab countries and, conversely, evidence of visits to Muslim countries may preclude entry into Israel.

The Embassy of Israel is located at 1621 22 St. NW, Washington,

D.C. 20008, Tel. 202-483-4100. There are consulates in Atlanta, Boston, Chicago, Houston, Los Angeles and New York.

The American Embassy in Israel is located at 71 Hayarkon St., Tel Aviv, Israel, Tel. 54338.

For additional business information contact the Israel Trade Center, 350 Fifth Ave., New York, N.Y. 10118, Tel. 212-560-0660.

ITALY

Whether traveling on business or pleasure, U.S. citizens need only a valid passport to travel to Italy for a stay of up to three months. There are no health requirements except if arriving from an infected area. Pets may be taken into the country, but regulations vary for different types of animals. It is best, therefore, to check with an Italian consular office for specifics. The Italian currency is the lira. 100,000 lire may be transported in or out of Italy. Any amount of foreign currency may be brought in, but it must be declared. Travelers cannot take out more than they brought in. Italian is the official language, some English and French is also spoken. To drive a car, an International Driving License is required.

Trade with Italy is conducted either through resident agents or through import distributors. Few imports require licenses. Foreign exchange is controlled by the Italian Exchange Control Authorities.

The Italian Embassy is located at 1601 Fuller St. NW, Washington, D.C. 20009, Tel. 202-234-1935. There are consulates in Boston, Chicago, Cleveland, Detroit, Los Angeles, New Orleans, New York, Philadelphia and San Francisco.

The American Embassy in Italy is at Via Vittorio Veneto 119A, 00187 Rome, Italy, Tel. 4674. There are consulates in Genoa, Milan, Naples and Turin.

For further information contact the Italian Government Tourist Office at 630 Fifth Avenue, New York, N.Y. 10111, Tel. 212-245-4822.

For additional business information contact the Italian Trade Commission, 499 Park Ave., New York, N.Y. 10022, Tel. 212-980-1500.

J

JAI-ALAI

World Jai-alai, Inc. trains prospective professional players and sponsors tournaments. The U.S. Amateur Jai-alai Association is the ruling body for amateurs. For further information contact World Jai-alai, Inc., 3500 Northwest 37th Ave., Miami, Fla. 33142, Tel. 305-633-6400 and the U.S. Amateur Jai-alai Association, 100 Southeast Second Ave. Miami, Fla. 33131, Tel. 305-377-3333.

JAMAICA

U.S. citicens arriving directly from the United States, Puerto

Rico or the American Virgin Islands need only proof of citizenship, sufficient funds and a return ticket to enter Jamaica for a stay of up to six months. Business travelers must apply for a work permit by sending a letter to the Ministry of National Security, 12 Ocean Blvd., Kingston Mall, Jamaica, detailing the nature of their business. Cholera and yellow fever innoculations are required only if arriving from an infected area. Pets are not allowed into Jamaica. The local currency is the Jamaican dollar; its import or export is prohibited. There is no limit to the amount of foreign currency that can be taken in but all money must be declared upon arrival and more cannot be taken out than was brought in. English is the official language of the island. For driving, an International Driving License is required.

Trade with Jamaica is conducted either through local resident agents or personal visits by foreign company representatives to Jamaican importers or exporters. The State Trading Corporation controls the import of certain items. Licenses are required for more imported goods.

The Embassy of Jamaica is located at 1850 K Street NW, Washington, D.C. 20006, Tel. 202-452-0660. There are consulates in New York and Miami.

The American Embassy in Jamaica is located at the Jamaica Mutual Life Center, 2 Oxford Road, 3rd floor, Kingston, Jamaica, Tel.

809-929-4850.

For further travel information contact the Jamaica Tourist Board, 2 Dag Hammarskjold Plaza, New York, N.Y. 10017, Tel. 212-688-7650.

For additional business information contact the Jamaica Trade Commission, 866 Second Ave., 10th floor, New York, N.Y. 10017, Tel. 212-866-7650.

JAPAN

A valid passport and a visa are required for U.S. citizens traveling to Japan. To obtain a visa present a valid passport, a round trip ticket and/or a letter from a travel agent confirming travel plans to a Japanese diplomatic mission. A tourist visa is valid for four months. Business travelers must present two photographs, a valid passport and a letter from their company detailing the nature of their business and confirming financial responsibility. The length of a business visa is variable, but it is usually good for re-entries during a four year period. There are no health requirements except if arriving from an infected area. The regulations concerning the import of pets vary from animal to animal. For example, Japan has no requirements for cats entering the country, but has stringent rules about dogs, depending on the breed of the animal and what part of the United States the animal is from. It would be best to check specifically with a Japanese diplomatic mission for information on a particular animal.

Any amount of yen (the local currency) or foreign currency may be brought into Japan. Any amount of foreign currency may be reconverted, but exchange receipts must be shown. There is a limit of three million yen that may be taken out of Japan. The language of the country is, of course, Japanese, but some English is spoken, especially at the popular tourist attractions. To drive in Japan, an International Driving License is required. There is a departure tax of 1,500 yen.

Foreign trade with Japan is conducted either through agents, trading companies or directly through personal visits. Licenses are not required except for restricted imports, mostly agricultural products, and there are no exchange controls in effect.

The Embassy of Japan is located at 600 New Hampshire Ave., NW, Washington, D.C. 20037, Tel. 202-234-2266. There are consulates in Anchorage, Atlanta, Chicago, Honolulu, Houston, Los Angeles, New Orleans, New York, Portland, San Francisco and Seattle.

The U.S. Embassy in Japan is located at 10-1 Akaska 1-chome, Minato-ku (107), Tokyo, Japan, Tel. 5837141.

For additonal tourist information contact the Japan National Tourist Organization, 630 Rockefeller Plaza, New York, N.Y. 10020, Tel. 212-757-5640.

For further business information contact the Japan Trade Center, 1221 Avenue of the Americas, New York, N.Y. 10020, Tel. 212-997-0400.

JEHOVAH'S WITNESSES

The Jehovah's Witnesses are evangelicals who believe in the theocratic rule of God, the sinfulness of organized religion and an imminent millennium. The overall direction of the Jehovah's Witnesses comes from the Governing Body at the world headquarters in New York City.

Representatives are sent out each year to confer with the branch representatives in 15 or more zones in the more than 200 countries where the church is active. The branch offices have committees of three to seven members to oversee the work in the country or area of the branch office. The area is further divided into districts, and the districts into circuits. Each circuit has about 20 congregations. a district overseer assists congregations in each circuit.

The local congregation meets in its "Kingdom Hall." Areas of local communities are mapped out in small territories, which are assigned to individual Jevohah's Witnesses who attempt to call on the people in each home in their territory to distribute and discuss their missionary literature.

Contact the Jehovah's Witnesses at the local congregation or at the world headquarters 25 Columbia Heights, Brooklyn, N.Y. 11201, Tel. 212-625-3600.

JEWS: CONSERVATIVE

The organizations that speaks for Conservative Jews in the United States is the United Synagogues of America, 155 Fifth Ave., New York, N.Y. 10010, Tel. 212-533-7800.

The Synagogue Council of America represents all branches of the Jewish faith. It is located at 10 East 40 St., New York, N.Y. 10016, Tel. 212-686-8670.

JEWS: ORTHODOX

The national organization representing Orthodox Jews is the Union of Orthodox Jewish Organizations of America, located at 45 West 36 St., New York, N.Y. 10018, Tel. 212-563-4000.

A coordinating organization for all branches of Judiasm is the Synagogue Council of America located at 10 East 40 St., New York, N.Y. 10016, Tel. 212-686-8670.

JEWS: REFORMED

The organization representing Reformed Jews in the United States is the Union of American Hebrew Congregations located at 838 Fifth Ave., New York, N.Y. 10021, Tel. 212-249-0100.

A coordinating organization for all branches of Judaism is the Synagogue Council of American located at 10 East 40 St., New York, N.Y. 10016, Tel. 212-686-8670.

JOB SAFETY

See SAFETY: AT WORK, WORKER'S COMPENSATION

JORDAN

A valid passport and a visa are required for U.S. citizens traveling to Jordan. A visa may be obtained by presenting a passport valid for at least three months from the date of application and one photograph to a Jordanian consular official. Business travelers also require a letter from their company detailing the nature of their business and confirming financial responsibility for the applicant. All visas are good for 12 months and one entry into the country. There are no health requirements except if arriving from an infected area, but TAB shots are advised. Pets brought into the country require a health certificate from a veterinarian. The local currency of Jordan is the Jordanian dinar. Up to JD100 may be taken in or out of the country, but there is no limit on the amount of foreign currency which may be imported or exported. Arabic is the official language of Jordan, but there is some English and French spoken. To drive a car, an International Driving License plus a U.S. license are required.

Jordan is one of the more liberal of the Moslem countries. Alcohol is not prohibited and women are becoming integrated into social and business life.

Trade with Jordan is conducted through resident agents. All imports require licenses; and there are prohibitions on certain items. The issue of an import license guarantees the necessary foreign exchange.

The Embassy of the Hashemite Kingdom of Jordan is located at 2319 Wyoming Ave. NW, Washington, D.C. 20008, Tel. 202-265-1606. There are consulates in Houston, Los Angeles, New York, Chicago, Palm Beach (Fla.) and Detroit.

The U.S. Embassy in Jordan is located at Jebel Amman, P.O. Box 354, Amman, Jordan, Tel. 44371/6.

Travelers to Jordan should be advised that evidence of a past or planned trip to Israel may prevent their entry into the country.

JUDICIARY

See COURT SYSTEMS: STATE, COURT SYSTEMS: FEDERAL

JUDO

The Amateur Athletic Union (AAU) conducts training programs and competitions in judo in the United States, including the Olympic trials. The AAU is located at 3400 West 86th St. Indianapolis, Ind. 46268, Tel. 317-872-2900.

K

KANSAS

Consumers can report instances of consumer fraud to the Consumer Protection Division if the Attorney General's office through the Consumer Hotline 800-432-2310, or 913-296-3751, or by writing the Consumer Protection Division, Office of the Attorney General, 2nd floor, Kansas Judicial Center, Topeka, Kan. 66612.

Kansas law protects consumers from deception or misrepresentation in connection with the sales of merchandise and services. Consumers in Kansas can request the Consumer Protection Division to mediate their complaints or prosecute if the Division decides to do so. Consumers can also bring private suits against businesses or individuals allegedly engaged in consumer fraud.

Many occupations and professions in Kansas are licensed through the State Board of Technical Professions, 11th floor, 535 Kansas Avenue, Topeka, Kan. 66603, Tel. 913-296-3053. Contact the board with requests about requirements for licensing or complaints about licensees.

Kansas grants qualified businesses tax credits for a period of up to ten years. To qualify a new business must be a taxpayer in the state, a revenue producing enterprise, and must establish a new business facility. New business is allowed an income tax credit of $50 per each new employee plus $50 for each $100,000 of new capital investment. This tax liability cannot exceed more than 50% of the total income tax liability for the year the credit is taken. Tax credit opportunities are also available to certain expanding businesses.

For corporations whose facilities are within the state boundaries, corporate income tax is computed at a rate of 4½% of net income derived before the deduction of Federal income tax. Net income in excess of $25,000 is subject to a 2¼% surtax. For corporations with facilities outside the state as well as inside, the net income taxed is a proportion based upon the percentage of the corporation's business located in Kansas.

For business information contact: Kansas Department of Economic Development, 503 Kansas Avenue, Topeka, Ks. 66604, Tel. (913) 296-3841, Kansas Association of Commerce and industry, 500 First National Tower, One Townsite Plaza, Topeka, Kan. 66603, Tel. 913-357-6321.

For tourist information call or write the Economic Development Department, Tourism Division, 503 Kansas Ave. Topeka, Kan. 66604, Tel. 913-296-3487.

KENTUCKY

The Consumer Protection Division of the Attorney General's Office handles consumer complaints in Kentucky. The Division advises and educates consumers and mediates consumer complaints. After a written complaint is received by the Division, the consumer is notified of what action the Division will be able to take. Contact the Consumer Protection Division, 209 St. Clair St., Frankfort, Ky. 40601, Tel. 502-564-6607.

The Division cannot act as a private attorney on an isolated complaint. Complainants who need immediate legal action are referred to the Small Claims Court or to an attorney. The Kentucky Bar Association will provide names of attorneys to those who need them. Call the Kentucky Bar Association 800-372-2999, or in Louisville 583-1801.

Licensing of occupations and professions in Kentucky is done by individual licensing boards which are administered by the Division of Occupations and Professions, Bureau of Administrative Services, Department of Finance, Twilight Trail, Building A, Frankfort, Ky. 40601, Tel. 502-564-3296. Inquiries about licensing or complaints about licensees can be sent to this address and the letter will be sent on to the proper licensing board for action.

Kentucky offers tax incentives for businesses. Exempt from all local property taxes are new businesses manufacturing machinery and equipment, inventories of raw materials and goods in the process of manufacture, and pollution control equipment.

Cities may, by local option, exempt the property of a new manufacturing facility from city taxes for up to five years.

Residents of Kentucky pay a state income tax on their net income of 6% on income in excess of $8,000 and lesser percentage on amounts under that figure.

Corporate income taxes in Kentucky are 6% for amounts over $100,000 and lesser percentages for corporate income under that amount. Small corporations with taxable income under $25,000 are usually exempt from corporate income taxes. Corporations having taxable income both in and outside Kentucky pay state income tax only on the portion of the income earned in Kentucky.

The state sales tax is 5% of the gross receipts for the sales of taxable goods and services. Exempt from the sales tax are items purchased for resale, machinery for new and expanded industry, raw materials, supplies and tools used in manufacturing and pollution control materials.

Businesses interested in expanding or in moving to Kentucky are offered planning assistance by the Department of Commerce, Capital Plaza Tower, Frankfort, Ky. 40601, Tel. 502-564-2064.

For tourist information about Kentucky contact the Division of Advertising and Travel Promotion, Capitol Annex, Frankfort, Ky. 40601.

KENYA

A valid passport and a visa are required for U.S. citizens traveling to Kenya. To obtain a visa travelers need proof of onward transportation and, if traveling on business, a letter from their company detailing the nature of their business in Kenya. The fee is $6.10 and the visa is valid for three months with a variable length of stay. Smallpox and yellow fever shots are required and protection against cholera and typhoid if coming from an infected area. The importation of pets requires a permit from authorities in Kenya. An application for a permit can be obtained from the Kenyan Embassy or a tourist office. The local currency is the Kenya shilling. Its import or export is not allowed. Any amount of foreign currency may be taken in but must be declared on arrival and not more taken out than was brought into the country. The official language is Swahili, but English is spoken extensively. In addition, many tribal languages such as Luo and Kamba are used. To drive a car an American license endorsed by the Kenyan police is required.

Foreign trade is generally handled by local agents. Prior authorization is required for most imports and goods that compete with local products are restricted. Foreign exchange is authorized by the Central Bank.

The Embassy of Kenya is located at 2249 R St. NW, Washington, D.C. 20008, Tel. 202-387-6101. Visas may also be obtained from tourist offices in New York and Los Angeles.

The U.S. Embassy in Kenya is located at Cotts House, Wabera St., P.O. Box 30137, Nairobi, Kenya, Tel. 334141.

KIDNEY DISEASE

For general information about kidney disease contact the National Kidney Foundation, 2 Park Ave., New York, N.Y. 10016, Tel. 212-889-2210. Most people who have permanent kidney failure and need regular kidney dialysis treatment or a kidney transplant are now covered by Medicare. Applications should be made at any social security office. For further information contact the Department of Health and Human Services, Social Security Administration, 6401 Security Blvd., Baltimore, Md. 21235, Tel. 301-245-7175.

L

LABOR MEDIATION
See MEDIATORS: LABOR

LANDSCAPE ARCHITECTS
A bachelor's degree in landscape architecture is usually the minimum qualification for landscape architects. More than half of the states require a license for landscape architects who practice independently. Applicants must pass a uniform national examination. To qualify to take the examination, the applicant must have a college degree in landscape architecture. Sometimes lengthy experience in the field can be substituted. Contact the state licensing board for information or the American Society of Landscape Architects, 1750 Old Meadow Rd. McLean, Va. 22101, Tel. 703-466-7730.

LATVIA
See SOVIET UNION

LAW ENFORCEMENT
Law enforcement in United States is delegated by the governors to localities, cities and towns. Cities and towns usually have their own police forces, while the state police handle law enforcement in areas outside the jurisdiction of city or town police, in rural areas or along highways.

Local police departments handle violations against property or persons such as burglary or assault. Many cities have emergency telephone numbers to report serious injuries or crimes in progress.

The Federal Bureau of Investigation (FBI) of the U.S. Department of Justice investigates violations of federal law. It is a fact-finding organization rather than a police force, although its officers do have the authority to make arrests where there is suspicion that an individual has broken federal law.

The FBI has jurisdiction over all robberies of financial institutions that are members of the Federal Reserve System, insured by the Federal Deposit Insurance Corporation or by the Federal Savings and Loan Insurance Corporation, are federally-insured credit unions or are organized under the Federal laws of the United States. The FBI also has jurisdiction over kidnapping cases, unless the victim has been located or released within 24 hours, and over cases where stolen goods have been transported over state lines.

The FBI maintains fingerprint records of some 64 million persons. These prints are from arrested persons, aliens, government job applicants, military personnel and citizens who have voluntarily submitted their fingerprints for personal identification reasons. Under a Department of Justice order an individual can obtain a copy of his or her arrest record by submitting a written request directly to the FBI Identification Division together with a set of fingerprints, name and birth date. There is a fee of $5.

The FBI maintains a National Crime Information Center, which is a computerized information system containing information on missing persons, a stolen property bearing serial numbers, persons on whom an arrest warrant is outstanding, and records on individuals arrested and fingerprinted for serious crimes. Criminal justice agencies in numerous locations in the United States have access to the information, although it is not available to the general public.

The FBI Laboratory offers its facilities and scientific expertise to all law enforcement agencies in the United States. The experts from the laboratory will also appear in court to testify to the results of their examinations.

Citizens may report suspected federal crimes to the local branch of the FBI, by the telephone number in the front pages of most telephone directories.

City, state and federal law enforcement organizations work in close cooperation. Suspected crimes reported to the inappropriate agency are noted, and the proper law enforcement agency informed. Law enforcement agencies also share information, records and results of investigations, since individuals may be under investigation by more than one agency or have records in several agency files.

Interpol is the international police organization used by member nations to investigate crimes that extend over international borders. Interpol is normally contacted only through another law enforecement organization.

For information about local police departments call or write the public information officer at local precincts or police headquarters. State police can be reached by the telephone number or address listed in the telephone directory under the state government listing. For Federal information contact a Field Division Office of the FBI or the Federal Bureau of Investigation, United States Department of Justice, Washington, D.C. 20535, Tel. 202-324-3000. Information requests can also be sent to Interpol, Secretariat General, 26, rue Armengaud, 92210 Saint Cloud, Paris, France.

LAWYERS

An individual must be admitted to the state bar in order to practice law in that state. In most states an applicant must pass a written bar examination, but four states waive this requirement for graduates of their own law schools: Montana,

South Dakota, West Virginia and Wisconsin. In addition, most states require an applicant to have completed three years of college and have graduated from a law school approved by the American Bar Association (ABA) or by the proper state authority. Law schools that do not meet the ABA requirements qualify the graduate to take the bar examination only in the state where the school is located.

California is the only state that will accept the study of law totally by correspondance as a qualification for taking the bar examination. California also accepts four years in a law office or judge's office as preparation for the test. Other states that accept a combination of experience in a law office or judge's office and years in law school as qualifications for the bar examination are Alaska, Maine, New York, Vermont, Virginia, Washington and Wyoming. States allowing individuals to take the examination based totally on their own study or experience in a law office are Vermont, Virginia and Washington.

Admission to law school depends on performance in college, usually in a four year program. Some law schools will accept students after three years, however. Most schools also consider the student's aptitude for the study of law as reflected in the Law School Admissions Test (LSAT), which is administered by the Educational Testing Service.

State bar associations have the power to remove a lawyer from legal practice within that state if professional misconduct is proven. Complaints should be lodged with the bar association of the state in which the lawyer practices and is a member of the bar.

Questions about the study or practice of law can be referred to the state bar association or the American Bar Association, 1155 East 60th St., Chicago, Ill. 60637, Tel. 312-947-4000.

LAYAWAY PURCHASES

On a layaway purchase a customer pays a part of the purchase price down, and the purchase remains in the store until the customer pays for it in full. The use of the lawaway system is regulated mainly by the states. Most states have laws that require retailers to give full refunds of the purchase price if the layaway goods are no longer available in the same condition as they were at the time of purchase. The retailer is usually required to give the customer a written statement of the terms of the layaway agreement at the time of the initial payment. The agreement must include the amount of the deposit received, the length of time the goods will be held on layaway, a description of the goods and the total purchase price of the goods, including the interest, finance or special handling charges.

Complaints about lawaway purchases should be referred to the

state consumer protection office.
See: individual state entry

LEARNING DISABILITIES

Parents who suspect that their child has a learning disability should ask the teacher about the testing and therapy the school district offers, or contact the office of the superintendent of schools in the district. The local university may have a learning disorder center that can test and help the child. For further help in locating programs contact the Association for Children with Learning Disabilities, 4156 Library Rd., Pittsburgh, Pa. 15234, Tel. 412-341-1515.

LEGAL PROBLEMS OVERSEAS

United States consulates located in capital cities and large cities throughout the world generally will not offer legal advice, but can help individuals find an attorney to help with legal problems overseas. See individual country entry for addresses of embassies or consulates in foreign countries.

LIBERAL PARTY

The national office for the Liberal Party is 165 West 46th St., Suite 1400, New York, N.Y. 10036, Tel. 212-582-1100.

LIBERIA

A valid passport and a visa are required for U.S. citizens traveling to Liberia. Two photos, $2, a letter from a doctor stating that the traveler is in good health and a return ticket are necessary with the passport application. Business travelers need a letter from their company detailing the nature of their business. The permitted length of stay is variable. Yellow fever and cholera shots are required for entry, and protection against malaria is advised. Medical facilities in Liberia are generally adequate. Pets can be brought in with a veterinarian's certificate of good health. The local currency is the Liberian dollar. There are no limits on amounts of local or foreign currency that can be taken in or out of the country. English is the official language. Among the many African languages also spoken are Vai, Bassa, Kru and Kpelle. To drive a car, an International Driving License will suffice plus registration with the local police.

There is a large U.S. investment in Liberia as a result of the encouragement of the Liberian government. Importing is done directly by local wholesalers and distributors or by branches of foreign companies located in the country. Licenses are not required for imports and there are no exchange controls in effect.

It is prohibited to take certain items into Liberia. Among them are sugar, frozen chicken, candles and matches.

The Embassy of Liberia is located at 5201 16th St. NW, Washington, D.C., Tel. 202-723-0437. There are consulates in Chicago,

Detroit, Houston, Los Angeles, New Orleans, New York, Philadelphia and Port Arthur.

The U.S. Embassy in Liberia is located at United Nations Drive, P.O. Box 98, Monrovia, Liberia, Tel. 22991.

For further business information contact the Liberian Commercial Consulate, 150 East 56 St., New York, N.Y. 10022, Tel 212-826-0798.

LIBERTARIAN PARTY

The national office for the Libertarian Party is 1516 P St. NW, Washington, D.C. 20005, Tel. 202-232-2003.

LIBRARIES: LIBRARY OF CONGRESS

Although the primary purpose of the Library of Congress is to serve Congress, the library offers its extensive collections in Washington for public use. The library is probably the world's largest, with almost 76 million items in its collections. In addition to 19 million books and pamplets, the library has more than 33 million manuscripts, including the papers of 23 American presidents; 3.6 million maps and atlases; 4 million pieces of music from classical to rock; 9 million prints and photographs; more than a quarter of a million reels of motion pictures and half a million sound recordings of American folklore and music.

Admission to the research facilities of the Library of Congress is free. Anyone over high school age can use the general reading rooms, but a few rare collections can be used only by those with a serious purpose for doing so, most often a specialized research project.

In addition to the mail catalog, which holds author, title and subject cards interfiled, there is a computer catalog center that provides on-line information on English language books cataloged from 1968 to the present. Special catalogs in various reading rooms index manuscripts, films, maps, microforms, musical scores, tapes and technical reports.

The National Union Catalog offers a separate index to the holdings of the Library of Congress and 1100 cooperating libraries, which may have books not available from the Library of Congress. A Resource Guidance Office helps readers not familiar with the library in planning their research and with information about special collections open for research purposes only.

Researchers who have exhausted library resources in their area and are not able to travel to the library may direct reference requests, in writing, to the Library of Congress. Research Services Department, General Reading Room Division, Washington, D.C. 20504.

See also: INFORMATION REFERRALS: GENERAL

LIBRARIES: NATIONAL ARCHIVES

The National Archives and Records Service of the General Services Administration preserves and makes available for research use the nation's records of enduring value, both textual and audiovisual. On display in the Nation Archives Building are the Declaration of Independence, the Constitution and the Bill of Rights, as well as other exhibits depicting the history of the country.

The materials in the archives cover more than two centuries and total billions of pages of textual material, 6 million photographs, 5 million maps and charts, 100,000 films and 80,000 sound recordings. Pension and census records are available for genealogical research. Immigration, capital and labor, westward expansion of the country, public health, agriculture, history of various industries and federal fiscal policy administration are among the many subjects extensively documented.

In many cases, however, the records are arranged, not by subject matter, but in the order in which they were arranged in the federal agency, bureau or department that produced them. For example, all records of the Department of Agriculture are kept together as a record group.

Anyone over age 16 may obtain a researcher identification card to use the collections at the National Archives. A researcher under age 16 can use the records when accompanied by an adult with a valid card. Consultants at the archives will help researchers clarify the objectives of the research, suggest research approaches and order the necessary records from the stacks. The National Archives staff does not do detailed research for inquirers by mail but will answer concise, specific requests.

Contact the Central Reference Division, General Services Administration, Washington, D.C. 20408.

LIBRARIES: PRESIDENTIAL

Seven presidential libraries are administered by the National Archives and Records Service (NARS) of the General Services Administration, including the Gerald R. Ford Library, dedicated in April 1981.

The libraries preserve and make available to the public the presidential papers and collections, prepare documentary and descriptive publications and exhibit historic documents and musuem items. The following are the addresses of the seven existing presidential libraries:

Dwight D. Eisenhower Library
Southeast 4th Street
Abilene, Kansas 67410
Tel. 913-263-4751

Gerald R. Ford Library
1000 Beal Ave.
Ann Arbor, Mich. 48109
Tel. 313-668-2218

Herbert Hoover Presidential
Library
South Downey Street
West Branch, Iowa 52358
Tel. 319-643-5301

Lyndon B. Johnson Library
2313 Red River Street
Austin, Texas 78705
Tel. 512-397-5137

John F. Kennedy Library
Federal Archives and Records
Center
380 Trapelo Road
Waltham, Massachusetts 02154
Tel. 617-223-7250

Franklin D. Roosevelt Library
Old Albany Post Road
Route 9
Hyde Park, New York 12538
Tel. 914-229-8114

Harry S. Truman Library
Highway 24 at Delaware Street
Independence, Missouri 64050
Tel. 816-833-1400

LIBRARIES: PUBLIC

City and county libraries in the United States are open for use by anyone. The issue of library cards for the borrowing of books may be reserved for residents of the locality, but in most cases anyone can use the books on the open stacks. Most public libraries are owned and run by the city or county.

Most libraries offer lending services for books, records, tape cassettes, pictures and other special materials. Many also offer reference services, often over the telephone for easily obtainable information. Libraries also usually offer special services for children, such as story reading at special times or crafts programs.

Books not included in the local library's collection can frequently be obtained by the library through interlibrary loan. Consult the local library for information. Consult the library or local government for

further information on the operation of the library. For further information on library services and policies contact the American Library Association, 50 East Huron St., Chicago, Ill. 60611, Tel. 312-944-6780.

LIBRARY OF CONGRESS CATALOG CARD NUMBERS

The Library of Congress, through its Cataloging Distribution Service, makes available to libraries throughout the world its preprinted library catalog cards for books printed or distributed in the United States. Library of Congress catalog card numbers are assigned to books likely to be added to the library's collection or for which the library anticipates demand for the printed catalog cards. The Library of Congress catalog card numbers appear on the copyright page in books. They are used by librarians and others who want to order catalog cards, by those who want to identify catalog records in automated data bases or by those who wish to catalog books using the Library of Congress system.

To obtain Library of Congress catalog cards or information about number assignments contact the Library of Congress, Cataloging-in-Publication Office, Washington, D.C. 20540, Tel. 202-287-6372.

LICENSE PLATES: SPECIAL

All states allow motorists to request special numbers or letters on their license plates for an additional fee. The highest fee is in South Dakota—$100. Motorists can have any number or letters they want provided they have not be issued to someone else or are not on a list of non-issuable letters or numbers (LBJ, JFK, expletives etc.). Generally the plate can have no more than seven letters or letters and digits. For further information contact the state motor vehicle bureau.

LICENSES: OCCUPATIONS AND PROFESSIONS

See specific occupations or professions and individual state entries.

LIP READING

The U.S. Department of Education requires all schools receiving federal aid to provide educational services to deaf or hearing impaired children. Many, therefore, have special classes in lipreading. Consult your local school board for specific information.

The National Association for Hearing and Speach and the Alexander Graham Bell Association for the Deaf both have many local chapters that offer lipreading instruction. Contact their national offices at 6110 Executive Blvd. Rockville Md. 20852, Tel. 301-897-8682 and 3417 Volta Place NW, Washington, D.C. 20007, Tel. 202-337-5220 respectively for the nearest chapter.

LIQUOR: LICENSES

All states license the manufact-
ure and sale of some type of alcoholic beverages, and all receive some revenue from liquor taxes. State liquor licenses generally cost the most for manufacturers, followed by wholesalers and retailers. In the manufacturing area, distilleries, breweries and wineries are charged for licenses on a descending scale in that order. License fees are usually less for wholesalers of beer than of distilled spirits or wine. On the retail level, the license fee varies according to whether the liquor is sold for on-premises or off premises consumption. The amounts of the license fee vary widely from $25 for some retail licenses to $1000 or more for distillery licenses. The rate of the excise tax also varies greatly from state to state: from about $1.50 to $2.50 per gallon on distilled spirits, 15 to 60 cents per gallon on wine and five to 15 cents per gallon on beer.

In addition to state licenses, many states permit localities, usually counties and municipalities, to license retail liquor establishments. Some states also permit local licensing of manufacturers and wholesalers. Most states have what are known as ABC boards (alcoholic beverage control boards) that deal with the licensing of liquor establishments. Contact the state alcoholic beverage control board for laws, regulations and further information.

LITHUANIA
See SOVIET UNION

LOBBYISTS: CONGRESSIONAL

The constitutional protections of free speech, press, assembly and petition have resulted in a relative lack of restriction on lobbying.

The Federal Regulation of Lobbying Act of 1946 requires that paid lobbyists to the U.S. Congress register with the House and the Senate and file quarterly reports with the House of Representatives. Many interest groups, however, are not required to register.

See also: FOREIGN GOVERNMENT AGENTS

LOST OR FOUND PROPERTY

In most cities valuable lost or found property is reported to the local police station. Property lost or found on public transportation is reported to the management.

LOUISIANA

The Department of Urban and Community Affairs, Office of Consumer Protection serves as a liaison between business and the consumer in Louisiana. Its primary functions are the dissemination of consumer information, education of consumers, mediation of complaints and prevention of consumer fraud.

Complaints are received by the Office of Consumer Protection through the public assistant line, telephone calls, walk-ins, and the mail. Complaints are reviewed by the section head, and assigned to a mediator who writes the business advising it of the complaint and requesting its position. If there is no indication of illegal trade practice, the mediator attempts to arrange an amicable settlement. If fraud or unfair or deceptive trade practice is suspected, an investigation is made and the information is forwarded to the proper legal authorities, such as the Attorney General's office or the local District Attorney.

Contact the Department of Urban and Community Affairs, Office of Consumer Protection, 1885 Wooddale Blvd. Suite 1218, P.O. Box 44091, Capitol Station, Baton Rouge, La. 70804, Toll-free in Louisiana 800-272-9868.

Licensing of occupations and professions in Louisiana is handled by individual boards for each profession or occupation, rather than through a central licensing agency. Inquiries about licensing or complaints about licensees can be sent to the Office of Consumer Protection, which will send it on to the proper licensing board.

Louisiana has been actively trying to attract business. Its ten year tax exemption law provides that any manufacturing establishment entering Louisiana, or any manufacturing establishment expanding its Louisiana facilities is eligible to receive exemption on buildings and equipment from state, parish (county) and local property taxes for a period of ten years. The Board of Commerce and Industry stresses that manufacturers using this tax advantage have a moral obligation to favor, where competitive, Louisiana manufacturers and suppliers of goods and services and to use Louisiana labor. Interested manufacturers can obtain information on this and other programs from the Office of Commerce and Industry, P.O. Box 44185, Baton Rouge, La. 70804, Tel. 504-342-5359.

Tourist information about Louisiana is available from the Louisiana Tourist Development Commission, P.O. Box 44291, Capitol Station, Baton Rouge, La. 70804, Tel. 504-342-4889.

LUTHERAN CHURCHES

Lutherans follow the teachings of Martin Luther, one of the great Protestant reformers. Currently there are over 8 million adherents in the United States found largely in four major branches. The branches are generally organized into geographic districts or synods. While these local groups remain the most important structures in church polity, there is a tendency toward centralization in national conferences. For further information contact the American Lutheran Church, 422 South Fifth St., Minneapolis, Minn. 54415, Tel. 612-388-3821; the Lutheran Church in America, 231 Madison Ave., New York, N.Y. 10016, Tel. 212-696-6700; the Lutheran Church—Missouri Synod 500 North Broadway, St. Louis, Mo. 63102, Tel. 314-231-

6969, and the Wisconsin Evangelical Lutheran Synod, 3512 West North Ave., Milwaukee, Wisc. 53208; Tel. 414-786-7839.

M

MADEIRA ISLANDS
See PORTUGAL

MAIL ADVERTISING: UNWANTED RECEIPT OF

To have a name removed from mailing lists or to receive more direct mail advertising or mail in a special interest area a person should contact the Direct Mail Marketing Association, Inc., Consumer Relations Department, 6 East 43rd St., New York, N.Y. 10017, Tel. 212-689-4977. To have a name removed from a specific advertiser's mailing list file a Prohibitory Order, Postal Service Form #2150, which is available at any post office.

MAIL FRAUD

Suspected mail fraud should be reported to the postmaster or the chief postal inspector who will investigate the complaint and, if warranted, refer it to the U.S. Attorney's office in the area. For further information contact the U.S. Postal Service, Chief Postal Inspector, 475 L'Enfant Plaza SW, Washington, D.C. 20260, Tel. 202-245-5445.

MAIL ORDER MERCHANDISE

Mail order merchandise is regulated by the Federal Trade Commission and by the U.S. Postal Service. It must be mailed within 30 days of order unless another period is specified in the advertisement. If the order is not shipped within that time, the consumer has the right to cancel the order and get a refund. Certain items, such as magazines and items ordered through book or record clubs are not covered by this rule.

A consumer is not required to pay for unordered merchandise, and it is unlawful for a firm to require payment. In fact, the only legally sent unordered merchandise is free samples and materials sent by charitable organizations soliciting contributions. Unordered merchandise can be disposed of as the consumer wishes.

If a company sends a bill for unordered merchandise or if it fails to send ordered merchandise that has been billed, or for any other problems with mail order merchandise, contact the Federal Trade Commission or the U.S. Postal Service. The Postal Service will send an individual reply and will help solve the problem with the resources it has available. The Federal Trade Commission cannot act on individual complaints. Both agencies will keep complaints on file and will initiate investigations of companies that have numerous complaints against them.

Consumers can also file complaints with the state consumer protection agency (see individual state entry) or the Better Business Bureau, which will attempt to mediate a settlement.

Contact the state consumer protection agency (see state listings) the Better Business Bureaus (see listing), the Federal Trade Commission, Pennsylvania Ave. at Sixth St. NW, Washington, D.C. 20580, Tel. 202-523-3625, or the U.S. Postal Service, 475 L'Enfant Plaza West SW, Washington, D.C. 20260, Tel. 202-245-4000 or contact its region divisional offices.

MAIL: PORNOGRAPHY

By law no sexually oriented advertisements may be mailed to anyone who does not wish to receive them. Consumers who have received such mail and wish to prevent receiving any more should fill out and return Form PS 220 "Application for Listing" from the Postal Service. If they are still receiving material 30 days after they have returned the form, they should notify the post office or the Chief Postal Inspector, U.S. Postal Service, 475 L'Enfant Plaza West SW, Washington, D.C. 20260, Tel. 202-245-4534.

MAIL: PROTECTION

From the time an item of mail is placed in a post office recepticle until the addressee has removed it from the mail box, the mail is protected by the U.S. Postal Service. Theft, tampering or other crimes against the Postal Service are federal offenses. Suspected crimes should be reported to the chief postal Inspector who will investigate them. If warranted he may refer criminal violations to the U.S. Attorney and civil violations to the Postal Service Law Department. For further information contact the U.S. Postal Service, Inspection Service 475 L'Enfant Plaza West SW, Washington, D.C. 20260, Tel. 202-245-5445.

MAIL ORDER TRANSACTIONS: COMPLAINTS

The Consumer Protection Program of the Postal Inspection Service helps resolve problems with mail order transactions even if fraud is not involved. For further information about the program contact the U.S. Postal Service, Inspection Service, 475 L'Enfant Plaza West SW, Washington, D.C. 20260, Tel. 202-245-5445.

MAINE

The Attorney General's Office, Consumer and Antitrust Section is responsible for administering the state's unfair trade practices and antitrust laws. The Section accepts consumer complaints and seeks amicable resolutions of consumer complaints against businesses. It also initiates consumer fraud investigations and secures restitution of money or goods as a result of those investigations, where possible. All complaints received from consumers receive a reply and the Section attempts resolution by contacting the business involved. Complaints are maintained on file for use in determining which businesses or trade practices should be investigated in the future. Send complaints to the Department of the Attorney General, Consumer and Antitrust Section, Statehouse Station 46, Augusta, Maine 04333, Tel. 207-289-3731.

The Bureau of Consumer Protection is responsible for protecting the citizens of Maine against unfair and deceptive business practices in consumer credit, home repair financing, collection agencies and insurance premium finance companies. Direct consumer complaints for businesses in the above areas to the Bureau of Consumer Protection, Statehouse Station #35, Augusta, Maine 04333, Tel. 207-289-3731.

The majority of occupations and professions licensed in Maine come under the jurisdiction of the Department of Busines Regulation, which is an administrative arm of the licensing boards. Professions and occupations licensed in Maine include the following: accountant (certified public), ambulance services, architect, assessor (certified), attorney, auctioneer, audiologist, automobile inspection mechanic, barber, beekeeper, blood banking specialist, boxer (professional), bus operator, chemist, chiropractor, collection agent, commercial fisherman, counselor, cytotechnologist, dental hygenist, dentist, dietitian, driver education instructor, electrician, elevator inspector, engineer, forester, funeral service, guide (fishing and hunting), hairdresser, harness racing, hearing aid dealer and fitter, home repair contractor, insurance agent and broker, land surveyor, medical laboratory technician, medical technologist, minister, nurse, occupational therapist, optometrist, osteopathic physician, pharmacist, physical therapist, physician, plumber, podiatrist, private detective, psychologist, real estate broker and agent, securities salesmen or broker, speech pathologist, teacher, truck driver and veterinarian.

Information about specific requirements for licensing in these professions and occupations can be obtained from the Department of Business Regulation, State House Station 35, Augusta, Maine 04333, Tel. 207-289-3916.

Complaints about licensed individuals are handled by the individual licensing boards, which can be contacted through the Department of Business Regulation at the above address. Revocation of licenses can only be done through a process involving an administrative court and judge.

The Guarantee Authority makes direct loans to qualifying local non-profit corporations for construction of buildings. It also provides loan guarantees to businesses and individuals with plans for establishing new, or expanding existing industrial, manufacturing, agricultural, fishing or recreational ventures within Maine. Municipalities also issue bonds for financing construction, expanding of local industry, recreational facilities, and pollution control equipment. The Small Business Loan Authority also provides loan guarantees to small business of up to $30,000. Contact the State Development office for information about these incentive programs for businesses. (See address below.) Also contact the Chamber of Commerce, 477 Congress St., Portland, Maine 04111, Tel. 207-774-9871.

Corporate income tax is 4.% on the first $25,000, plus 6.93% on all income above $25,000, based upon federal taxable income.

The tax rate for unincorporated businesses and individuals is 1% on income under $2000 increasing to 10% on income over $25,000. The tax rate for married taxpayers and widows and widowers filing joint federal returns is 1% on income of less than $4,000 increasing to 10% on income over $50,000.

The sales tax is 5% on gross retail sales receipts made within the state, with exemptions on new machinery and equipment used for production or research; water and air pollution facilities; food items for home consumption; fuel for domestic heating; medicines, and depreciable machinery and equipment for use by commercial farmers and fishermen.

Contact the State Development Office, State House, Augusta, Maine 04333, Tel. 207-289-2656.

For tourist information contact the Maine Publicity Bureau, 97 Winthrop St. Hallowell, Maine 04347, Tel. 207-289-2423.

MAPS: FEDERAL

The Geological Survey of the Department of the Interior offers topographic survey maps and atlases for most regions of the United States. In order to purchase them the consumer should circle the section desired on a road map and request the quandrant names and numbers from the Survey. The consumer can then buy the maps desired. Publications and maps can be purchased from the Geological Survey, Branch of Distribution, 1200 South Eads St. Arlington, Va. 22202. For further information call 703-860-7181.

MARINE WEATHER CHARTS

See WEATHER CHARTS: MARINE

MARRIAGE

Broadly defined, marriage is the voluntary social and legal union of a man and woman contracted through a civil and/or religious ceremony before legal witnesses usually for the founding and maintaining of a family. Each state has its own requirements for marriage licenses, ages of consent, medical examinations, etc. Some states require a certain period of time between the issuance of the license and the marriage ceremony. Other states require that the marriage

ceremony either take place within a certain period after the issuance of the license or the license becomes invalid. About a dozen states recognize common law marriage, whereby the two parties cohabit without benefit of a legal ceremony. Some states recognize common law marriages established before a certain date, while others recognize common law marriages established in states that do themselves recognize such marriages.

Most states bar marriages where one party is under the legal minimum age. The age varies from state to state but is generally 17 or 21 years old without parental consent, and usually younger with parental consent. Most states also prohibit marriages when one partner has been judged insane or when the partners are closely related by blood, as in the case of first cousins. Interracial marriages cannot be barred.

Marriage licenses are generally issued by a city or county clerk or marriage license bureau.

Most religious denominations have their own theology and ceremonial of marriage and impose various requirements for marriages under their auspices. Consult local pastors for further information.

See also: DIVORCE SEPARATION

MARRIAGES ABROAD

Marriages abroad between United States citizens have only the validity given them by the local law of the country.

American Foreign Services officers are not authorized to perform marriages abroad in which one or both of the parties are American citizens, but they may act as witnesses and are authorized to issue a certificate to that effect.

The presence of an American Foreign Service officer as witness does not give any special sanction to a marriage.

Consult the American Embassy or Consulate in the country in which the ceremony is to take place for further details.

MARRIAGE AND FAMILY COUNSELING

The American Association for Marriage and Family Therapy (AAMFT) is the professional association for the field of marital and family therapy. It is recognized in the field as the main certifying organization. Credentials from AAMFT serves as certification in states that do not yet have licensure or registration laws for marriage and family counselors. AAMFT currently admits individuals to clinical membership on the basis of certain criteria including graduate study and supervised clinical experience. The graduate study requirements are a master's or doctoral degree in marriage and family therapy or a closely allied professional field. The experience requirement is a minimum of 200 hours of supervised practice in marriage and family therapy, 1500 hours of clinical experience in the practice of marriage and family therapy, two calendar years of experience after the awarding of the master's degree while receiving ongoing supervision by an AAMFT approved supervisor. Marriage and family counselors are usually psychologists or social workers, and should be licensed or registered in states that require it. (See PSYCHOLOGISTS, SOCIAL WORKERS for a list of such states.)

Local agencies that offer marriage and family counseling are listed in the yellow pages of the telephone directory under Marriage and Family Counselors, Psychologists, Social Workers or Counseling. Some social welfare agencies also offer marriage and family counseling. State mental health agencies (see MENTAL HEALTH) also make referrals to reputable agencies.

Family Service Centers are located in major cities and offer marriage and family counseling on a sliding fee scale based on family income. Standards are set for Family Service Centers by the national office, The Family Service Association of America, at 44 East 23rd St., New York, N.Y. 10010, Tel. 212-674-6100.

For further information about AAMFT contact the American Association for Marriage and Family Therapy, 924 West Ninth St., Upland, Calif. 91786, Tel. 714-981-0888.

MARTINIQUE
See: FRENCH WEST INDIES

MARYLAND

The Consumer Protection Division of the Maryland Attorney General's Office is responsible for enforcing the various state consumer protection statutes dealing with unfair and deceptive trade practices. Statutes govern such areas as: automobile repair, credit card usage, door-to-door sales, the unsolicited sending of merchandise, sales promotion, deceptive advertising, unit pricing, multi-level distribution companies, consumer debt collection, home appliance repair, telephone solicitations and mobile home parks.

The Consumer Protection Division will accept consumer complaints, negotiate settlements when possible and file legal action suits when a pattern of law violations exist as indicated by numerous complaints against one business. Volunteers review complaints lodged with the Division, forward it to another agency if the Division does not have jurisdiction, or attempt to mediate the dispute and reach a solution that is fair and satisfactory to both parties. If the mediation fails, both sides will be offered the opportunity to submit the dispute to binding arbitration. If the volunteer finds after consulting the Division records that the complaint is part of a widespread and illegal practice that affects a large number of consumers, he may refer it to the Division's legal staff for more investigation and possible court action. Instead of lawsuits, however, in many cases the Legal staff will issue Cease and Desist Notices. A hearing is held within 60 to 90 days of the Cease and Desist notification. At the hearing the Division has the authority to issue an order requiring the business or individual to cease the improper trade practice and pay restitution to the consumer who complained. Civil penalties can, however, be obtained only through the civil court system.

Contact the Consumer Protection Division, Office of the Attorney General, 26 South Calvert St. Baltimore, Md. 21202, Tel. 301-659-4250. Branch offices are located in College Park, Hagerstown, and Salisbury.

The Department of Licensing and Regulation licenses the following businesses and occupations: Architects, banks and credit unions, barbers, boxers, wrestlers, managers and promoters, consumers loan companies, cosmetologists, employment agencies and employment counselors, electricians, foresters, harbor pilots, hearing aid dealers, home improvement contractors and salesmen, horse riding stables, insurance agents and brokers, landscape architects, moving picture machine operators, plumbers, professioanl engineers, professional land surveyors, public accountants, race track employees, real estate brokers and agents, savings and loan associations and stationary engineers.

Information about licensing requirements can be obtained from the Department of Licensing and Regulation, Office of the Secretary, One South Calvert St. Baltimore, Md. 21202, or requested through the Maryland toll-free telephone, 800-492-7521 (regular phone 301-659-6200).

Complaints about licensed practitioners in any of the above fields can be sent to the Department of Licensing and Regulation at the above address. Complaints are received by the administrative staff, analyzed by an independent group of investigators and adjudicated by a full time staff of hearing officers.

The Department of Health and Mental Hygiene licenses the following health related occupations: audiologists and speech pathologists, chiropractors, dentists and dental hygienists, funeral directors and embalmers, nurses, nursing home administrators, optometrists, osteopaths, pharmacists, physical therapists, physicians, podiatrists, psychologists, and sanitarians. Questions about licensing in one of the above occupations or complaints about practitioners should be referred to the Department of Health and Mental Hygiene, 201 Preston Street, Baltimore, Md. 21201. Complaints are handled in the same manner as described above for the Department of Licensing and Regulation.

The Department of Economic and Community Development offers consulting services to businesses interested in moving to Maryland. Businesses requesting services should contact the Department of Economic and Community Development, 2525 Riva Rd., Annapolis, Md. 21401, Tel. 301-269-2120 or contact the Chamber of Commerce, 60 West Street, Annapolis, Md. 21401, Tel, 301-269-0642.

Maryland offers city or county revenue bond financing to businesses moving to or expanding in Maryland and state loan guarantees for construction or equipment. Incentives are offered for locating industrial plants in areas of high unemployment.

The state corporate income tax rate is 7% and the sales tax 5%.

Individual income tax rate ranges from 2% for amounts under $1,000 to 5% for income over $5000.

For tourist information about Maryland contact the Division of Tourist Development, Department of Economic and Community Development, 1748 Forest Dr. Annapolis, Md. 21401, Tel. 301-269-2686.

MASSACHUSETTS

In Massachusetts consumers are protected by the Executive Office of Consumer Affairs, which is a cabinet level office. The primary emphasis in consumer affairs in Massachusetts is one of self-help. Individuals who write or call to complain are given guidance in taking corrective action on their own. Consumer inquiries can be directed to the Executive Office of Consumer Affairs, One Ashburton Pl., Room 1411, Boston, Mass. 02108, Tel. 617-727-7755.

Massachusetts licenses professions and occupations through twenty-eight individual boards, each of which examines and licenses applicants, holds disciplinary hearings, and establishes standards for professional conduct. The following boards can be contacted through one address, Division of Registration, 100 Cambridge Street, Room 1520, Boston, Ma. 02202, Tel. 617-727-3076: accountants, barbers, dentists, doctors, drinking water operators, embalmers and funeral directors, electricians, engineers, health officers, land surveyors, nursing home administrators, opticians, pharmacists, plumbers and gasfitters, psychologists, real estate brokers and salesmen, sanitarians, veterinarians, waste water treatment operators, architects, chiropractors, dental hygienists, electrologists, hairdressers, landscape architects, nurses, optometrists, physical therapists, podiatrists, radio and T.V. technicians and social workers.

The Department of Commerce and Development offers assistance to businesses interested in moving to or expanding in Massachusetts. Interested businesses should contact the Department of Commerce and Development, Executive Office of Economic Affairs, 100 Cambridge St., Boston, Mass. 02202, Tel. 617-727-3221.

Massachusetts offers state, city or county revenue bond financing for industry, as well as city or county general obligation bond financing. The state also offers loan guarantees for construction and machinery for industry. Incentives are given by the state, city or county for establishing industrial plants in areas of high unemployment.

The corporate income tax in Massachusetts is 9.4962%, which includes a 14% surtax plus a tax of $2.60 per $1,000 on taxable property. Corporations which are engaged exclusively in interstate or foreign commerce are taxed at 5% of net income and are not subject to surtax. Banks and trust companies are subject to 12.54% corporate income tax, which also includes the surtax.

Massachusetts has a 5% sales tax. The personal income tax is a flat rate of 5.375%.

Request tourist information from the Department of Commerce and Development, Division of Tourism, 100 Cambridge St., Boston, Mass. 02202, Tel. 617-727-3221.

MEDIATORS: LABOR

The Federal Mediation and Conciliation Service helps prevent disruptions in the flow of interstate commerce by providing mediators to assist in labor-management disputes. Either side in a dispute can invite the Service to intervene, or it can do so by its own decision. The federal mediators must rely solely on persuasive techniqus in resolving disputes; the agency has no law enforcement authority.

The facilities of the Service are available to any industry affecting interstate commerce as a last resort or in exceptional cases. Employers and unions are required to register with the Service in the event of a dispute affecting commerce not settled within 30 days, if there is prior service of a notice to terminate or modify an existing contract. For further information contact the Office of Information, Federal Mediation and Conciliation Service, 2100 K St. NW, Washington, D.C. 20427, Tel. 202-653-5290.

MEDICAID

Medicaid is a program funded by the federal government and administered by the state through their state public welfare offices. It provides for payment of medical care for recipients of Aid to Families with Dependent Children (AFDC) and Supplementary Security Income (SSI). (Medicaid should not be confused with Medicare which is a Social Security Administration program for medical care for retired persons and senior citizens.)

Payment for medical expenses is made directly to the suppliers of medical care and services, such as doctors and hospitals. Medicaid

pays expenses for inpatient hospital services, outpatient hospital services, other laboratory and X-ray services, skilled nursing home services and home health care services for individuals 21 and over. It also pays for early and periodic screening, diagnosis, and treatment for individuals under 21, as well as for family planning services, and physicians' services. Other items are optional. Policy is set by individual states.

Some persons who do not qualify for cash assistance under AFDC or SSI may qualify for medical benefits under Medicaid. These individuals have sufficient income and resources for the essentials of life, according to standards decided by that state, but cannot meet the cost of medical expenses.

Applicants for Medicaid coverage should apply to the nearest state public welfare office.

MEDICAL DEVICES

The federal agency responsible for the safety, efficiency and labeling of medical devices is the Bureau of Medical Devices in the U.S. Food and Drug Administration. The bureau evaluates devices before they are allowed on the market, and will take steps to prevent the marketing of devices found to be dangerous to the public. It also develops standards for the manufacture of devices, and conducts research into the possible health hazards caused by their use.

Complaints and questions

about medical devices can be sent to the Bureau of Medical Devices. The bureau cannot investigate every complaint, but it maintains files and investigates instances of numerous complaints against a manufacturer or product.

Consumer complaints can also be pursued through the state consumer protection agencies listed in the individual state entry, or by filing a civil suit through a private attorney. Contact the Bureau of Medical Devices, Food and Drug Administration, 5600 Fishers Lane, Rockville, Md. 20857, Tel.: 301-443-3380.

MEDICAL DOCTORS

All states require that a physician be licensed in order to practice medicine. Applicants for licenses must be graduates of an accredited medical school. They must also have completed one to two years in an accredited graduate medical education program (residency), as well as pass a licensing examination.

Most medical schools admit students with a minimum of three years of college, with course work in particular areas such as biology and chemistry, but most students accepted to medical school have bachelor's degrees. Medical school usually requires four years of study for the M.D. degree. Information about medical schools can be obtained from the Council on Medical Education, American Medical Association, a professional society for the promotion of medical doctors' interests, which also sets standards for the profession.

All states have some type of licensing reciprocity, but the acceptance of licensing in one state by another state is decided on the individual physician's credentials.

For specific state licensing requirements, consult the state listings for the address of the state licensing agency. This will have the address of the state board of medical examiners.

Complaints about doctors can be referred to the state board of medical examiners.

For further information contact the American Medical Association, 535 N. Dearborn St., Chicago, Ill. 60610, Tel. 312-751-6000.

MEDICAL IDENTIFICATION BRACELETS OR NECKLACES

Medic Alert, a non-profit organization, provides necklaces and bracelets with a Medic Alert emblem on one side. On the reverse side is engraved the medical problem, the file number of the wearer and the telephone number of Medic Alert's central file. Anyone giving medical aid to the wearer is immediately aware if the person has a medical problem and can obtain further information by calling the Medic Alert central file.

Medic Alert charges a one time joining fee of about seven dollars, which entitles the member to an emblem bracelet and the services of the foundation. Write Medic Alert Foundation International,

Turlock, Calif. 95380, Tel. 209-668-3333.

MEDICAL RECORDS ADMINISTRATORS

The American Medical Record Association (AMRA) offers national registration to medical records administrators. Many hospitals and other institutions who hire medical records administrators prefer applicants who are registered.

Applicants for registration must have graduated from an approved school in medical record administration and must have passed an examination given by the AMRA. Those who qualify are given professional recognition as Registered Record Administrators (RRA).

Programs in medical records administration in colleges and universities lead to the B.A. degree. One year certification programs are also available to those who have a B.A. degree in another field. Programs are approved by the American Medical Association and the American Medical Record Association.

Contact the AMRA at the John Hancock Center, 875 North Michigan Ave., Chicago, Ill. 60611, Tel. 312-787-2672 for further information.

MEDICAL TECHNOLOGISTS AND TECHNICIANS

Several states—Alabama, California, Georgia, Florida, Hawaii, Illinois, Nevada, Pennsylvania and Tennessee require that medical technologists and technicians be licensed. Requirements usually include passing a written examination. Consult the state board of medical examiners for specifics.

Certification is offered for medical technologists and technicians by several organizations upon the passing of an examination. The Board of Registry of the American Society of Clinical Pathologists, P.O. Box 4872, Chicago, Ill. 60680, Tel. 312-738-1336, offers certification as a medical technologist (MT) (ASCP). The International Society of Clinical Laboratory Technology offers certification as Registered Medical Technologists (RMT). The ISCLT can be reached at 818 Olive, Suite 918, St. Louis, Mo., Tel. 314-241-1445. Both organizations also offer certification as a technician.

Medical technicians are trained in various ways. Many are enrolled in vocational or technical school programs that are usually two years in length. Some are trained in the armed forces.

The minimum educational requirement as a medical technologist is generally a B.A. degree plus completion of a specialized training program. Many colleges and universities offer such training programs, which are accredited by the American Medical Association. For information about accredited programs contact the American Medical Association, 535 N. Dearborn St., Chicago, Ill. 60610, Tel. 312-751-6000.

MEDICARE

Medicare is a medical insurance program set up under the Social Security system. Its main purpose is to help people 65 and over to pay their medical bills, but in some cases people under 65 are eligible. Medicare is divided into two parts. Part A covers hospital and/or nursing home costs; Part B covers medical costs including doctors' fees and other costs not covered by Part A.

Anyone over the age of 65 who is eligible for Social Security retirement benefits can get Medicare Part A free of charge. A disabled person under 65, who has been collecting disability benefits for two years is eligible as are disabled widows or widowers between the ages of 50 and 65. A person or his dependent requiring kidney dialysis or transplant is eligible provided that he or the head of his household has worked in a job covered by Social Security. This exception aside, dependents of Medicare members are not eligible until they too meet one of the above requirements. Aliens, convicted criminals and some federal employees covered by other health plans are not eligible for Medicare.

Anyone eligible for Part A of Medicare can elect to take Part B for a charge of $11 per month. A person not eligible for Social Security can still get Medicare but has to pay for it. The charges are $78 per month for Part A and $11 per month for Part B. However, it is necessary to take both Parts A and B.

A person automatically becomes enrolled in Medicare when he or she applies for Social Security retirement benefits at age 65. However, people who do not want to elect Part B must notify the Social Security office. Otherwise, $11 per month will be deducted from their Social Security check. A person not planning to retire at age 65 can still get Medicare by applying at the Social Security office.

The year is divided into four benefit periods of three months each. For each benefit period the payment cycle repeats. Under the coverage in Part A a person hospitalized from one to 90 days pays the first $204 of the bill. After that Medicare pays all expenses for the next 60 days and for the next 30 days, the patient pays $51 per day. After 90 days the benefit period runs out. In order to start coverage after 90 days, there must be a 60-day hiatus between hospital visits.

In Part B, after a yearly deductable of $60, Medicare pays 80% of all "reasonable" costs. Reasonable costs are fees that Medicare has deemed average costs for a particular service. If a doctor charges very high fees, Medicare insurance may not necessarily cover 80% of the bills.

Medicare coverage is limited to the United States and its territories. However, in some cases it may pay for some costs accrued in foreign countries.

For further information or to apply for Medicare contact the nearest Social Security office.
See also: MEDICAID

MEMORIAL SOCIETIES

Memorial Societies are associations formed to permit members to receive inexpensive funerals and burial or cremation. This is generally done by contracting with a single funeral home for all services. For further information contact the Continental Association of Funeral and Memorial Societies, 1828 L St. NW, Washington, D.C. 20036, Tel. 202-293-4821.

MENTAL DISABILITY: CHILDREN

See MENTAL RETARDATION, CHILDREN: SOCIAL SECURITY BENEFITS, CHILDREN: AID TO FAMILIES WITH DEPENDENT CHILDREN, REHABILITATION.

MENTAL HEALTH: STATE SERVICES

All states offer programs for mental health through a state agency such as the department of Mental Health and Mental Retardation.

Services may include diagnosis and evaluation, inpatient and outpatient treatment, day care and partial care, special education, halfway houses, specialized programs for children, alcoholics, and drug abusers, and follow-up care for patients returning to the community after hospitalization. State mental health agencies coordinate efforts with other state agencies such as the state rehabilitation commission.

MENTAL RETARDATION

All states offer some services to the mentally handicapped or mentally retarded. Such programs are usually under the jurisdiction of the state Department of Mental Health and Mental Retardation.

States also offer special education to the mentally handicapped through the public schools. Policies vary from state to state, but generally each school system must offer appropriate education to all children of school age or contract for services with outside agencies.

See also: DISABLED: CHILDREN, EDUCATION

METHODIST CHURCHES

Methodists adhere to the teachings of John Wesley, an Anglican minister who emphasized conversion and personal holiness. There are currently about 13 million members of the denomination in the United States. The movement is divided into many branches, among them the African Methodist Episcopal Church and the United Methodist Church. The latter is the largest branch with almost 10 million members. The churches are generally organized in geographical jurisdictions headed by a bishop. National policy is in the hands of a council of bishops and a general conference composed of delegates from the various local groups. For further information contact the United

Methodist Communications Office, 100 Maryland Ave., NE, Washington, D.C. 20002, Tel. 202-488-5633 or the African Methodist Episcopal Church, 951 Old Grove Manor, Jacksonville, Fla. 32207, Tel. 904-355-8262.

METRIC SYSTEM: EDUCATION

The Metric Education Program of the Office of Educational Research and Improvement, Department of Education, offers grants for teaching students, parents and other adults to use the revised Metric System of Measurement. Assistance is available to educational institutions, public and private nonprofit organizations. For further information contact the Metric Education Program, Office of Educational Research and Improvement, Department of Education, 400 Maryland Ave. SW, Washington, D.C. 20202, Tel. 202-653-5920.

MEXICO

U.S. citizens traveling to Mexico solely for purposes of tourism need no passports or visas, but require a tourist card. These cards are available from Mexican consulates or tourist offices, Mexican immigration offices at ports of entry and at airlines serving Mexico. It is granted upon presentation of proof of citizenship (birth certificate, passport, etc), and is good for a stay of up to 90 days. Business travelers must have a business card which is good for up to

six months. They must apply in person to a Mexican consulate with their passport, three photographs, a letter from their company detailing the nature of their business in Mexico and $44. Mexico also issues technicians cards which are valid for 30 days. Technicians must apply in person with a letter from the Mexican company requiring their services, six full-face and three profile photographs and $88.

There are no health requirements for entry into Mexico unless arriving from an infected area. However, smallpox, typhoid, paratyphoid and polio shots are advised, especially if travelers are planning to visit the more tropical areas of the country. Pets are allowed but a veterinarian's certificate of good health is required. There are no limits on the amounts of foreign or local currency (peso) that can be imported or exported from Mexico, but the export of gold coins is prohibited. The official language of the country is Spanish, but there is some English spoken particularly in the areas of Mexico bordering on the United States. To drive a car, an International Driving License is required.

Trade with Mexico is done either by establishing a branch of the business in the country or through local agents. Import licenses are required for many imports, but there are no exchange controls.

Visitors should be advised that evidence of a previous visit to Cuba will probably void their travel cards. There is an airport departure tax of $5 when leaving the country.

The Embassy of Mexico is located at 2829 16th St. NW, Washington, D.C. 20009, Tel. 202-234-6000. There are consulates in Albuquerque, Atlanta, Austin, Boston, Brownsville, Calexico, Chicago, Corpus Christi, Dallas, Del Rio, Denver, Detroit, Douglas, Eagles Pass (Tex.), El Paso, Fort Worth, Fresno, Houston, Kansas City, Laredo, Los Angeles, Lubbock (Tex.), McAllen, Miami, New Orleans, New York, Nogales, Philadelphia, Phoenix, Presidio, Sacramento, St. Louis, San Antonio, San Bernardino, San Diego, San Francisco, San Jose and Seattle.

The U.S. Embassy in Mexico is located at Paseo de la Reforma 305, Mexico City, Mexico 5, D.F., Tel. 553-3333. There are U.S. consulates in Guadalajara, Hermosillo, Monterey, Tijuana, Ciudad Juarez, Matamoros, Mazatan, Merida and Nuevo Laredo.

For further tourist information contact the Mexican National Tourist Council, 405 Park Ave., New York, N.Y. 10022, Tel. 212-755-7212.

For additional business information contact the Mexico Permanent Trade Center, 115 East 57 St., New York, N.Y. 10022, Tel. 212-371-3823.

MICHIGAN

The Department of the Attorney General, Consumer Protection Division is the agency in Michigan with responsibility for consumer protection. The Division's primary function is to offer needed government protection to consumers in their day-to-day activities in the marketplace. An extensive computerized file of consumer complaints and current consumer fraud practices is maintained by the Division, and consumers can contact the Division requesting the complaint record of a particular business.

The Division does take action to investigate and mediate consumer complaints, where appropriate, or refers the consumer to another agency which has jurisdiction. The Division will also prosecute businesses which have violated the state consumer code.

Contact the Department of the Attorney General, Consumer Protection Division, Law Building, Lansing, Mich. 48913, Tel. 517-373-3500.

The Department of Licensing and Regulation licenses businesses and occupations through the following boards: accountancy, athletic board of control, barbers, collection agencies, cosmetology, hearing aid dealers, horologists, private employment agencies, chiropractors, dentists, marriage counselors, medical doctors, morticians, myomassologists, nurses, nursing home administrator, optometrists, osteopathic physicians, pharmacists, physical therapists, podiatry, psychologists, sanitarians, social workers, veterinarians, health occupations council, architects, builders, community planners, engineers, foresters, land sales, landscape architects, land surveyors, real estate brokers.

For most occupations licensed by the Department of Licensing and Regulation, applicants must not only present evidence of good character such as financial stability, references, absence of a criminal record, but must also pass an examination in the field. Some occupations require extensive education, experience, or both for an individual to qualify for a license. Specific requirements for each license can be obtained from the specific board through the Department of Licensing and Regulation, 320 North Washington Square, P.O. Box 30018, Lansing, Mich. 48909, Tel. 517-373-1870.

The Department of Licensing and Regulation also has complaint and enforcement units to assist consumers and to take disciplinary action against those who demonstrate incompetence or who deceive or injure the public. After a complaint is received it is assigned to an investigator who will contact both the complainant and licensee. If it appears that the licensee has violated the law, a formal public hearing before a department hearing examiner will be held. The licensee can be disciplined or can lose the license. Criminal or civil penalties cannot be assessed by the Department, but must be pursued through the courts.

The Office of Economic Development in the Department of Commerce actively pursues attracting new business to Michigan. Tax incentives are offered to businesses moving to or expanding in Michigan. Local communities have the option of exempting new industrial plants and new commercial projects from 50% of all property taxes, except on land, or freezing the assessments of rehabilitated plants for up to 12 years.

The single business tax is the only business tax levied in Michigan, a 2.35% value-added tax with deductions and exemptions for newly acquired buildings, machinery, and equipment, labor costs of over 63% of the gross tax base, and for small, low profit or unincorporated businesses.

Interested businesses may contact the Office of Economic Development, Box 30225, Lansing, Mich. 48909, Tel. 517-373-3550, Toll-free 800-292-9544 in Michigan.

The personal income tax is 4.6% based on the federal adjusted gross income of individuals with a $1,500 personal and dependency exemption (and an additional $1,500 exemption for taxpayers over 65 years or certain disabled individuals).

The state sales tax is 4% based on the gross proceeds from retail sale of tangible personal property for use or consumption. Exempt are foods not for immediate consumption and prescription drugs for resale.

Tourist information can be obtained from the Michigan Travel Commission, 300 S. Capitol, Suite 102, Lansing, Mich. 48926, Tel. 517-373-2090.

MIDWIVES

The nurse-midwife provides prenatal care and care at birth. She also continues to see the mother and child after birth. Midwives work under the supervision of doctors in hospitals, medical centers, clinics etc. Licensing requirements vary from state to state. For further information contact the state licensing board.

The American College of Nurse-Midwives recognizes programs of organized training and clinical experience. For information of these programs contact the association at 1012 14th St. NW, Washington, D.C. 20005, Tel. 202-347-5445.

MILITARY DRAFT: REGISTRATION

Registration and any possible draft is administered by the Selective Service System, an independent, civilian-staffed agency of the federal government.

Beginning in 1981 all 18-year-old-men must register for the draft within 30 days of their 18th birthday. Only nonimmigrant aliens, certain dual nationals and treaty aliens, members of the active armed forces and cadets or midshipmen at the service academies are not required to register. Any man who is not able to register during the period specified due to circumstances beyond his control,

such as being in the hospital or in a correctional facility, must register within 30 days from the time that it is possible for him to do so.

Registration can take place at any post office where the man will fill out a form asking for: name, address, telephone number and date of birth. The Selective Service System is also asking registrants for their social security number. If he is outside the United States, he can register at the nearest U.S. Embassy or consular office. The registrant can also check a special box if he wants armed forces recruiters to call or visit.

No draft cards are now being issued. Within 90 days of registration, an acknowledgement letter is mailed to the registrant with a form to report any change of address and to verify information on the registration form. The penalty for failing to register is the same as for evading the draft, up to five years in prison and/or a fine of up to $10,000.

There is currently no draft for the armed forces in the United States. The Selective Service System has recently moved to new, larger headquarters and is in the process of picking local draft boards nationwide. In the event of a return of the draft, draftees will be selected by a lottery to determine random sequence of birth dates. Each birthday will be assigned a number of 1 to 365 picked randomly to determine the order in which registrants would be inducted. All registrants are currently classified 1-H, a general holding category.

If an individual is ordered to report for service in the event of a draft, he will be given instructions on how to file a claim for reclassification if he believes that he should or cannot report for service within the time scheduled (10 days as of this writing). The following are some proposed reasons for exemptions or deferments:

Conscientious objector—can, but is not required to serve in the military as a noncombatant, if not must give a period of civilian service (two years) in the national interest.

College students—can request a postponement until the end of the semester, or until the end of the year if a senior.

Ministers—required to register but not required to serve in the armed services. Students in a recognized theological or divinity school or undergraduates preparing full-time for such study may be deferred.

Hardship—deferment for those whose induction would result in severe hardship to persons who depend solely on them for financial, physical or psychological support, at the discretion of the local draft board.

Medical specialists—subject to procedures different from those of individuals in other professions. May be drafted to age 35, but students preparing for medical careers may be deferred.

Reservists—receive a separate classification.

Not qualified for service—Armed Forces set the standards used by the Selective Service System for acceptability for military service and conducts the examinations for medical, mental and moral disqualification.

Sole surviving son—those whose father, brother or sister died in line of duty and who are sole surviving son.

Surviving son—those whose father or brother or sister was killed in line of duty after December 31, 1959 or died subsequent to that due to injuries sustained in service, those whose father, brother or sister is in a captured or missing-in-action status.

Many classification decisions of the local boards are subject to appeal to higher boards. Consult a counselor.

An individual would be most likely to be drafted during the calendar year in which he turns 20. The next year, if there is a draft, he drops into a lower priority group, and continues to drop into lower priority groups until his 26th birthday, when he is over the age of liability for the draft.

Further information about the military draft or registration process is available from the Selective Service System, National Headquarters, 1023 31st St. NW, Washington, D.C. 20435, Tel. 202-724-0424.

The following private, civilian

groups—many church sponsored—also offer free and qualified counseling on classifications and deferments, application procedures, legal rights, responsibilities and alternatives:

American Friends Service
Committee
1501 Cherry St.
Philadelphia, Pa. 19102
Tel.: 215-241-7000.

Central Committee for
Conscientious Objectors (CCCO)
2208 South St.
Philadelphia, Pa. 19146
Tel.: 215-545-4626

National Interreligious Service
Board for Conscientious
Objectors (NISBCO)
550 Washington Building
Fifteenth St. at New York Ave. NW
Washington, D.C. 20005
Tel.: 212-393-4868.

Selective Service Law Panel of Los
Angeles
1911 Wilshire Blvd.
Los Angeles, Calif. 90057
Tel.: 213-413-4430.
    See also: ARMED FORCES

MINIMUM WAGE
See WAGES: MINIMUM

MINNESOTA
The Office of Consumer Services in the Department of Commerce is responsible for representing and furthering the interests of consumers in Minnesota. The Office offers a voluntary complaint mediation service for individuals having a problem in the marketplace or with other government agencies. It also offers consumer information, referral services for other government agencies and enforces Minnesota's Consumer Fraud Statute.

A large number of written consumer complaints are resolved to the complainant's satisfaction through the Office of Consumer Services mediation services. The Office also advises consumers not satisfied with the result other options such as conciliation court or private legal counsel.

In the case of potential violations of Minnesota statute, the office tries to resolve the problems of the individual consumer and to eliminate fraudulent or deceptive business practices which affect the public in general. The office uses a variety of means beyond the initial letter: a telephone conversation, an informal meeting, an Assurance of Discontinuance, or the filing of a lawsuit. An Assurance of Discontinuance is a legal document filed with the court which is not an admission of guilt but is an agreement that in the future, the business will refrain from engaging in certain specified practices.

Contact the Minnesota Office of Consumer Services, 128 Metro Square Building, 7th and Robert St., St. Paul, Minn. 55101, 612-296-2331.

Minnesota licenses the following occupations and professions through a number of boards administered by the Department of Economic Development: abstractors, accountants, adjusters, architects, assessors, attorneys, auctioneers, barbers, beauticians, boiler operators, chiropractors, cosmetologists, dentists and dental hygienists, detectives, electricians, embalmers, engineers, insurance brokers and salespersons, midwives, morticians, nursing home administrators, optometrists, osteopathic physicians, pharmacists, physical therapists, physicians and surgeons, plumbers, podiatrists, practical nurses, psychologists, real estate brokers and salespersons, registered nurses, securities brokers and agents, steamfitters, teachers, veterinarians, watchmakers, water conditioning contractors and installers, water well contractors and water and waste treatment operators.

This Department also licenses non-occupational businesses.

Information about licenses or complaints about licensing can be requested from the Department of Economic Development, Bureau of Business Licenses, 480 Cedar St., St. Paul, Minn. 55101, Tel. 612-296-0617.

The Department of Economic Development provides a variety of services to businesses interested in moving to Minnesota, including assistance with site selection, and in the case of small businesses, development financing. Interested firms should contact the Office of the Commissioner, Department of Economic Development, 480 Cedar St., St. Paul, Minn. 55102, Tel. 612-296-2755, or The Association of Commerce and Industry, 200 Hanover Building, 480 Cedar St., St. Paul, Minn. 55101, Tel. 612-227-9591.

Minnesota offers state, city and/or country revenue bond financing to aid business development. It also makes state loans for construction, equipment and machinery. Incentives are offered for establishing industry in areas of high unemployment.

The state corporate income tax rate is 12%. The sales tax is 4%.

Individual income tax rates vary from 1.6% for amounts up to $600 to 16% for income in excess of $32,800.

For tourist information contact the Tourism Division, Minnesota Department of Economic Development, 480 Cedar St., Hanover Building, St. Paul, Minn. 55101, Tel. 612-296-5027.

MISSING PERSONS

Missing persons should be reported to the local police. Be prepared to describe where the person was last seen and to give a good description, including the clothes that the person was probably wearing. The police will initiate a search if the age, length of absence of other factors indicated that the person may be in danger.

MISSING PERSONS: ABROAD

To inquire about citizens missing abroad contact the Depart-

ment of State, 2201 C St. N.W.,
Washington, D.C. 20520, Tel. 202-
655-4000.

MISSISSIPPI

The consumer protection agency in Mississippi is the Consumer
Protection Division of the Attorney
General's Office. The Division accepts consumer complaints, investigates them when appropriate
and attempts satisfactory resolution. It has the power to obtain restraining orders to prevent unfair
or deceptive business practices
form continuing.

Occupations and professions
are licensed by individual licensing boards which evaluate applicants, issue licenses and review
any complaints about licensees.
Inquiries about licensing or complaints about licensees can be
sent to the above Consumer Protection Division which will send
them on to the proper licensing
board.

Corporations and businesses
can request assistance from the
Department of Agriculture and
Commerce, Jackson, Miss. 39205,
Tel. 601-354-6563. Also contact the
Chamber of Commerce, P.O. Box
1849, Standard Life Building, Jackson, Miss. 39205, Tel. 601-969-
0022.

Mississippi offers city or county
revenue bond financing as well as
general obligation bond financing.
Cities or counties in the state also
offer incentives for establishment
of industrial plants in areas of high
unemployment.

The corporate income tax rate is
3% for income under $5,000 and
4% for income over that amount.
The sales tax is 5%.

The individual income tax is 3%
for income under $5,000 and 4%
for income over that amount.

For tourist information contact
the Tourism Department, State
Economic Department, Jackson,
Mississippi 39205, Tel. 601-354-
6715.

MISSOURI

Missouri's Department of Consumer Affairs assists consumers
in actual grievance procedures
against a company when a complaint does not involve fraudulent
activities. The department also
refers problems and inquiries to
the agency best suited and most
likely to give a prompt response
and resolution to a consumer
problem. When a consumer sends
a complaint to the Department, a
consumer complaint specialist
reviews the complaint and determines which agency is most appropriate. The specialist then contacts the complainant with a copy
of the referral letter and a letter explaining their action. If the Department can handle the complaint,
the complainant is provided with a
complaint form to fill out and return. Upon receipt of the complaint form the firm involved is
contacted.

The Department of Consumer
Affairs cannot take legal action on
a consumer complaint, but some
of the divisions do have statutory

authority in their particular area. See below.

The Department of Consumer Affairs does monitor complaints noting recurrent problem areas. They notify other agencies and also aid in preparation of legislation to remedy such problem areas.

Contact the Department of Consumer Affairs, P.O. Box 1157, Jefferson City, Mo. 65102, Tel 314-751-4962.

The Attorney General's office, Consumer Protection Division does have the authority to take legal action in cases of consumer fraud. At the direction of the Department of Consumer Affairs, or in obvious cases of consumer fraud, contact the Attorney General-Consumer Protection Division, P.O. Box 899, Jefferson City, Mo. 65102, Tel. Toll-free in Missouri 800-392-8222.

Contained in the Department of Consumer Affairs are several divisions that regulate and license specific businesses and professions. These are:

The Missouri Division of Insurance, 515 East High St., Jefferson City, Mo. 65101 314-751-2650 (handles complaints against insurance companies, agents and brokers).

Missouri Division of Professional Registration, 3523 North Ten Mile Dr., Jefferson City, 65101 314-751-2334. (The various licensing boards within the Division of Professional Registration review complaints against licensed professionals. Boards in Missouri license: Accountants, architects, professional engineers, land surveyors, barbers, chiropractors, beauticians (board of cosmetology), dentists, embalmers and funeral directors, professional speech pathologists, clinical audiologists, hearing aid dealers and fitters, nurses, optometrists, pharmacists, podiatrists, real estate agents and brokers, and veterinarians.)

Missouri Public Service Commission, P.O. Box 360, Jefferson State Office Building, Jefferson City, Mo. 65102, 314-751-4308 (consumer services section) Toll-free 800-392-4211 (Regulates all privately owned utilities in the state such as gas, electric, water, sewer and telephone companies. The Mobile Homes Division handles complaints about mobile homes manufactured after Jan. 1974 and oversees construction standards for mobile homes.)

Missouri Division of Finance, 515 East High St., Jefferson City, Mo. 65101 314-751-3463 (Regulates state banks and small loan companies; enforces Missouri's usury laws.)

Missouri Division of Credit Unions, 911-B Leslie Blvd., Jefferson City, Mo. 65101, 314-751-3419 (Regulates state credit unions.)

Missouri Division of Savings and Loan Supervision, 308 East High St., Jefferson City, Mo. 65101, 314-751-4243 (Regulates state savings and loan associations.)

Missouri Human Rights Commission, P.O. Box 1129, Jefferson, City, Mo. 65101, 314-751-3597 (Handles complaints concerning discrimination.)

The Division of Commerce and Industrial Development has the prime objectives of attracting capital investment to the state. Staff members prepare custom-made in-depth research presentations for both domestic and foreign business prospects. Interested businesses should contact the Division at Box 118, Jefferson City, Mo. 65102, Tel. 314-751-4241. The Chamber of Commerce can be contacted at P.O. Box 149, Jefferson City, Mo. 65101.

The corporate income tax rate is 5% in Missouri, and federal income tax payments can be deducted before state corporate income tax liability is computed.

In communities with populations of 4,000 or more, private developers may establish a redevelopment corporation which can purchase land, buildings and equipment but incur property tax liability on just the land for the first ten years of ownership. In such corporations, for the first 15 years, the real property owned is assessed for property tax purposes at only 50% of the normally assessed valuation.

The state sales/use tax rate is 3.125% with the exemptions of the following: manufacturing machinery and equipment, air pollution control equipment, water pollution control equipment and electrical energy used to manufacture when its costs exceed 10% of all other production costs. Municipalities have local option to impose a sales tax of up to 1%.

For tourist information contact the Division of Tourism, P.O. Box 1055, Jefferson City, Mo. 65101, Tel. 314-751-4133.

MOBILE HOMES

The Department of Housing and Urban Development (HUD) sets minimum standards for construction and safety of mobile homes. Homes manufactured after 1974 are required to meet the standards in order to be legally sold.

Mobile homes sold new come with some kind of warranty of the quality and workmanship of the home for a specified time. The dealer is generally the one that honors the warranty. If trouble arises in getting a warranty honored, first contact the dealer, and then the manufacturer.

If a consumer suspects that a mobile home manufactured after 1974 does not meet minimal standards, he or she can complain to HUD. Complaints about dealer practices can be sent to the Federal Trade Commission. Neither federal agency can respond to every consumer complaint, but they do keep complaints on file for use in their investigations. Complaints can also be made to a state consumer protection agency, listed in the individual state entry, which will mediate complaints.

Many mobile homes are financed by personal loans rather than by mortages as are conventional homes. Arrangements for financing can usually be made through the mobile home dealer. A bank or credit union may also be willing to provide the financing, either by a personal loan or mortgage, at a lower rate of interest. It is also possible to obtain a Federal Housing Administration or a Veterans Administration-insured loan for a mobile home, usually at lower interest rates, lower down payments and with a longer time to pay off the loan. Check with a bank, credit union, or the local FHA office.

For information or complaints on warranties contact the Department Housing and Urban Development, 451 Seventh St. SW, Washington, D.C. 20410, Tel. 202-755-5111 or a regional office. For complaints on dealer practices contact the Federal Trade Commission, Pennsylvania Ave. at Sixth St. NW, Washington, D.C. 20580, Tel. 202-523-3625.

MONTANA

The state agency in Montana which handles consumer complaints is the Department of Business Regulation, Consumer Affairs Division, 805 North Main, Helena, Mont. 59601, Toll-free Tel. (800)332-2272 in Montana. Local county attorneys also have authority to handle consumer fraud concerning the sale or offer of sale, lease, rental or loan of a product or service.

The Consumer Affairs Division or county attorneys will attempt to resolve a consumer complaint informally, if possible, by contacting the business involved and requesting a response. Both also have the legal authority to petition the state court for an injunction to prevent the use of unfair or deceptive business practices, but they will generally only use that authority when there have been numerous complaints against a business or company.

State boards license the following occupations or professions in Montana: Abstractors, architects, barbers, chiropractors, cosmetologists, dentists, electricians, hearing aid dispensers, massage therapists, medical doctors, morticians, nurses, nursing home administrators, optometrists, osteopathic physicians, pharmacists, plumbers, professional engineers and land surveyors, psychologists, public accountants, real estate brokers or agents, and veterinarians. Contact the individual boards in the state capital for information on requirements. See also individual entries on these professions and occupations.

Information about business and industry should be requested from the State Chamber of Commerce, Box 1730, Helena, Mont. 59601, Tel. 406-442-2405.

The Department of Commerce, Division of Economic Development assists in-state and out of state manufacturing businesses on matters pertaining to financing, markets, transportation, taxes, etc. Interested businesses should contact the Division at Capitol Station, Helena, Mont. 59620, Tel. 406-449-3494.

Industrial tax incentives are available in Montana. Firms qualifying as new industry are eligible for a 73% reduction of property taxes during the first three years of operation. Firms granted this incentive are usually those which mine, process, or manufacture new products.

Cities of populations greater than 5,000 have the local option to grant a property tax reduction of up to 50% during the first 10 years following new construction or expansion. The same property cannot qualify for both of the above exemptions.

A 1% corporate license (income) tax credit is provided for the first three years to new and expanding industries engaged in the mechanical or chemical transformation of materials or substances into new products. To qualify, an expanding business must increase total permanent jobs by 30%.

Individuals and corporations which qualify as small business corporations may use 20% of their federal investment tax credit as a credit against state income tax liability or corporate license tax liability.

Air and water pollution control equipment is taxed at 3% of market value for property tax purposes.

The corporate income tax, or license tax as It Is called in Montana, is 6¾% of the corporation's net income from sources within the state for the period covered. A corporation is generally allowed the same deductions from its Montana gross income as are allowed under the federal internal revenue code. The federal income tax is not allowed as a deduction in computing net income. All corporations subject to the license tax must pay a minimum of $50 tax.

Montana taxpayers may elect to take a standard 15% of their adjusted gross income (subject to a limitation to a maximum of $1,000 on a separate return and $2,000 on a joint return) for their state income tax or they can itemize deductions from adjusted gross income in a manner similar to those on federal income tax returns. There is a 10% surtax added to the Montana individual income tax that is scheduled to be eliminated on Jan. 1, 1982.

Montana does not have a general sales tax. Selective sales taxes are levied upon certain items such as motor fuels, tobacco, and alcoholic beverages.

Tourist information should be requested from the Travel Promotion unit, Department of Highways, Helena, Mont. 59601, Tel. 406-449-2654.

MONTESSORI SCHOOLS

Teachers in Montessori nursery schools are professionally trained and certified by the American

Montessori Society. Write the Society for a list of Montessori schools or teacher training centers at 150 Fifth Ave., New York, N.Y. 10010, Tel. 212-924-3209.

MOROCCO

A valid passport but no visa is required for U.S. citizens traveling to Morocco for a stay of up to three months. Smallpox, cholera and yellow fever vaccinations are required if arriving from an infected area. Typhoid, paratyphoid and smallpox protection is advised. Pets are allowed into the country with a notarized certificate of good health. The local currency is the dirham; its import or export is prohibited. There are no limits on the amount of foreign currency that may be taken in or out of the country. The official language is Arabic; some Berber dialects are also spoken. French is the most commonly spoken foreign language. To drive a car, an International Driving License is required.

Trade with Morocco is handled through resident agents. The government, in trying to lessen the trade deficit, is currently limiting some imports. Licenses are required for some goods.

Although Morocco is a Muslim country, the former French presence has left the Moroccans tolerant of Western ways. Alcohol is not prohibited. Evidence of a previous or planned trip to Israel may prevent entry.

The U.S. Passport Office recommends that Americans traveling in Morocco safeguard their passports at all times, as police reports regarding lost or stolen passports will not be issued until after a full investigation which normally takes one month. Loss or theft of a passport should be reported immediately to the American Embassy in Rabat or the Consulate in Casablanca or Tangier.

The Embassy of Morocco is located at 1601 21st St., NW, Washington, D.C. 20009, Tel. 202-462-7979. There is a consulate in New York.

The American Embassy in Morocco is located at 2 Avenue de Marrakech, Rabat, Morocco, Tel. 30361/2; the American Consulate in Casablanca at 8 Boulevard Moulay Youssef, Tel. 60521/2; the Consulate in Tangier at Chemin des Amoureux, Tel. 35904/5.

For further tourist information contact the Moroccan National Tourist Office, 521 Fifth Ave., New York, N.Y. 10017, Tel. 212-421-5771.

MORTGAGES: HOME, FEDERALLY INSURED

The federal government does not lend money for home mortgages, but it does provide mortgage insurance to assist home buyers in purchasing new and existing one-to-four-family dwellings. The home buyer makes a down payment and obtains a mortgage for the rest of the purchase price through a Federal Housing Administration (FHA)-approved lender such as a bank, savings and loan association, mortgage company or insurance company.

Although the mortgage loans are commonly called FHA loans, the federal government does not provide the loan. The loan is merely insured through the Federal Housing Administration (FHA), so that the bank is protected against loss on the mortgage. Lenders will thus allow more liberal mortgage terms than the home buyer might otherwise be able to afford.

In order to qualify for an FHA insured loan a home buyer must have a good credit record, the cash needed at closing of the mortgage and enough steady income to make monthly mortgage payments without difficulty. The property to be bought must meet FHA minimum standards, which require that the home be liveable, soundly built and suitably located for site and neighborhood. FHA appraises the home to determine the maximum amount of mortgage it is willing to insure.

Apply for an FHA-insured loan through any FHA-approved lender. General information about FHA programs may be obtained from the local FHA office, or the Department of Housing and Urban Development, 451 Seventh St. SW, Washington, D.C. 20410, Tel. 202-755-5111.

MOTOR VEHICLE LICENSES
See DRIVERS LICENSES

MOUNTAINEERING
There are a number of organizations around the United States for those interested in exploring the mountains, forests and water courses of the country.

The Sierra Club, which has branches all over the United States, promotes mountaineering among its other efforts. The headquarters of the Sierra Club is located at 530 Bush St., San Francisco, CA 94108, Tel. 415-981-8634.

The Appalachian Mountain Club offers information on exploring the Appalachian mountains. It is located at 5 Joy St., Boston, Mass. 02108, Tel. 617-523-0636.

The Mountaineers promotes the sport of climbing in the mountains of the Northwest. The Mountaineers is located at 719 Pike St., Seattle, Wash. 98101, Tel. 206-623-2314.

Information on climbing within national parks can be obtained from the National Park Service, 18th and C Sts. NW, Washington, D.C. 20240, Tel. 202-343-7394.

MOVERS: COMPLAINTS
Complaints about interstate movers may be made to local consumer agencies or to a consumer action panel of the American Movers Conference. For further information contact the American Movers Conference, 111 North 19th St., Arlington, Va. 22209, Tel. 703-524-7659.

MOVIE THEATERS
Movie theaters or cinemas are generally subject to local regulations. Most cities require movie theaters to have food handlers licenses for their refreshment bar. Contact the city or county health department.

Movie theaters are also subject to the local fire code regulations and must be able to pass a fire inspection according to local regulations. Contact the local fire department.

MULTIPLE SCLEROSIS

The National Multiple Sclerosis Society, established in 1946, supports research to find effective means to prevent and arrest the disease. The national office of Society administers research, medical, educational and other programs. The national office will provide the address of the nearest local chapter.

Services to individuals with MS and their families are the direct responsibility of the 142 chapters and branches in the United States. All chapters conduct active programs, including information, counseling and referral services, the lending of medical equipment, the training and placement of volunteers, group activities and recreation programs. The 78 multiple sclerosis clinical centers are supported by the local chapters.

Contact the National Multiple Sclerosis Society, 205 East 42nd St., New York, N.Y. 10017, Tel. 212-986-3240.

MUTUAL FUNDS

Mutual Funds are regulated by the Securities and Exchange Commission which requires the disclosure of financial information and other data on securities sold publicly. The composition of the board of directors, the capital structure, mergers and the sales and management fees are all covered by regulations. The commission may take court action when plans for reorganization of an investment company are believed by the commission to be unfair to security holders. For further information contact The Securities and Exchange Commission, 500 North Capitol St. NW, Washington, D.C. 20549, Tel. 202-523-3952.

N

NAMES

Statutes in the United States generally recognize only one name for a person. An individual, however, can adopt and use any name he chooses unless he does so to escape punishment or defraud others. This adopted name is said to become his real name by reputation.

Names can be changed legally by a court proceeding which usually requires general notice to be given of the change, as in a newspaper announcement.

Consult a lawyer for legal change of a name.

See also BIRTH REGISTRATION.

NATIONAL ARCHIVES

The National Archives and Records Service of the General Services Administration preserves and makes available for research use the nation's records of enduring value, both textual and audio-visual.

The Declaration of Independence, the Constitution and the Bill of Rights are on display at the National Archives building.

The National Archives Building is located at Eighth St. and Pennsylvania Ave. NW, Washington, D.C. 20408, or contact the General Services Administration, National Archives and Records Service, Eighth St. and Pennsylvania Ave. NW, Washington, D.C. 20408, Washington, D.C. 20408, Tel. 202-523-3134.

NATIONAL PARKS: SENIOR CITIZEN PASSPORTS

The National Park Service offers an entry passport free to those sixty-two years of age or older. The "Golden Age Passport" is valid for the entire lifetime of the individual, covers entrance fees charged by the National Park Service facilities and entitles the individual to a 50 percent discount on recreational use fees, including camping fees administered by seven federal agencies.

"Golden Age Passport" is valid for the entire lifetime of the in-Service and the U.S. Forest Service, and at areas of the National Park System where entrance fees are charged.

Contact the National Park Service, Department of the Interior, Washington, D.C. 20240, Tel. 202-343-7394.

NATURALIZATION

Naturalization is the process for a foreign national to become a United States citizen. The applicant must satisfy several requirements in order to qualify for naturalization: (a) be at least 18 years of age (b) have been lawfully admitted to this country for permanent residence (c) reside in the United States continuously for at least half of a five year period just before filling the petition for naturalization, and must be outside the country no more than six months at a time during this period. (d) be a person of good moral character who believes in the principles of the Constitution of the United States. (e) be able to speak, understand and write simple English unless physically unable to do so. (f) have a knowledge of the government and history of the United States (g) never have been a member of a subversive organization such as the Communist Party. Children under 18 of parents being naturalized automatically become citizens if they become naturalized at the same time as their parents, or if one parent is already a citizen. Children under 18 entering without naturalized parents must file a Form 604 with the Naturalization Service.

To be naturalized, the individual files an application, a fingerprint card and a biographic information form obtained from the nearest office of the Immigration and

Naturalization Service or from the clerk of a naturalization court. The forms are filed at the nearest Naturalization Service office. After notification by letter, the applicant must appear before a naturalization examiner with two character witnesses. After a 30-day waiting period the applicant will have a final hearing where the judge will pronounce him or her a citizen.

A booklet, *Naturalization Requirements and General Information,* available from the Government Printing Office or the Immigration and Naturalization Service explains the requirements and process fully. There is a fee of twenty-five dollars upon filing an application.

A person whose certificate of naturalization or citizenship has been lost or destroyed can obtain a copy by filing a form for that purpose obtained from the Immigration and Naturalization Service.

For further information about naturalization contact the nearest Immigration and Naturalization office or the Immigration and Naturalization Service, 425 I St. NW, Washington, D.C. 20536, Tel. 202-655-4000.

See also: ALIENS

NAUTICAL CHARTS

Nautical charts, pilot books to supplement the charts, and tables of tides and currents are available from the Commerce Department, National Oceanic and Atmospheric Administration, National Ocean Survey, Distribution Division, 6501 Lafayette Ave., Riverdale, Md. 20854, Tel. 202-443-8243. They are also frequently available at local marinas and marine chart dealers.

NEBRASKA

In Nebraska consumer complaints are referred to the Department of Justice, Consumer Protection Division, Lincoln, Neb. 68508, Tel. 402-471-2682. Once a written complaint is received, the Division will send a letter with a copy of the complaint to the business involved and request that the company respond with their side of the story. The Division has the right to compel the business to comply with an investigation, and will do so if the business does not respond within a reasonable period. The Division makes investigations of businesses that do not respond to complaints and are the subject of numerous complaints, and takes court action when warranted.

The Consumer Protection Division in Nebraska has jurisdiction over almost any type of consumer purchase including real estate, insurance, or any type of service.

Occupations and professions in Nebraska are licensed through a number of individual licensing boards, rather than through a central licensing authority. Inquiries about licensing or complaints about licensees can be sent to the Consumer Protection

Division listed above, which will send the letter on to the proper licensing board.

The state of Nebraska carries out an extensive business and industrial recruitment program through the Department of Economic Development. Businesses considering locating or expanding in Nebraska have access to statewide and community information through the Department of Economic Development, Box 94666, Lincoln, Neb. 68509, Tel. 402-471-3111, street address 301 Centennial Mall South. The Chamber of Commerce and Industry can be contacted at P.O. Box 81556, Lincoln, Neb. 68501, Tel. 402-432-4273.

As tax incentives for businesses, business inventories are exempt from personal property taxation. The corporate and personal income tax rates are among the lowest in the nation and have been lowered two years in a row.

Nebraska's corporate income tax rate is 3.75% on the first $25,000 and 4.125% over $25,000, based on federal taxable income attributable to Nebraska operations.

The personal income tax rate is 15% of adjusted federal income tax liability.

The state sales tax is 3%, and several communities levy an additional sales tax. Manufacturing equipment purchased by new or expanding industry is exempt from this tax.

There is no state property tax in Nebraska. Cities, counties, school districts and other subdivisions levy real and personal property taxes. Their tax rates are according to the needs of the subdivision.

For tourist information, contact the Division of Travel and Tourism, Nebraska Department of Economic Development, P.O. Box 04666. State Capitol, Lincoln, Neb. 68509, Tel. 402-471-3111.

NETHERLANDS

A valid passport, but no visa is required for U.S. citizens traveling to the Netherlands for a stay of up to three months. There are no health requirements unless coming from an infected area. Pets may be brought into the country with a veterinarian's certificate of health and proof of a rabies shot; this certificate must be validated by the Animal and Plant Health Inspection Service of the United States. The local currency is the guilder. There are no limits on the amount of guilders or of foreign currency which may be brought in or out of the country. The official language is Dutch, but English, French and German are also spoken with some frequency. An International Driving License is required.

Trade with the Netherlands is usually conducted through resident agents, but an exporter can also deal directly with a Dutch importer or distributor. Import licenses are generally not needed and there are few exchange controls.

The Embassy of the Netherlands is located at 4200 Linnean Ave. NW, Washington, D.C. 20008, Tel. 202-244-5300. There are consulates in Chicago, Houston, Los Angeles, New York and San Francisco.

The American Embassy in the Netherlands is located at Lange Voorhout 102, The Hague, Netherlands, Tel. 624-4911. There are U.S. consulates in Amsterdam and Rotterdam.

For further tourist information contact the Netherlands National Tourist Office, 576 Fifth Ave., New York, N.Y. 10036, Tel. 212-245-5320. For business information contact the Netherlands Industrial Commissioner, 1 Rockefeller Plaza, New York, N.Y. 10020, Tel. 212-246-1434.

NETHERLANDS ANTILLES (Aruba, Bonaire, St. Maarten, St. Eustatius, Saba, Curacao)

The Netherlands Antilles is part of the Netherlands; its affairs are handled by the Netherlands Embassy. Proof of citizenship (passport, birth cirtificate) is needed for U.S. citizens traveling to the Netherlands Antilles for a stay of up to six months. Tourists may be asked to show a return or onward ticket and proof of sufficient funds for their stay. There are no health requirements for entry if arriving from the United States. Pets may be brought to the islands with a veterinarian's certificate of health and proof of a rabies shot; this certificate must be validated by the U.S. Animal and Plant Health Inspection Service. The local currency is the Netherlands Antilles guilder, also called the florin. There are no limits on the amount of local or foreign currency that may be brought in or out of the country, but visitors are advised to change all their guilders when leaving since it is difficult to change them outside of the islands. U.S. currency is also accepted on the islands. The requirements for driving vary from island to island; for example, Aruba, Bonaire and St. Maarten require only an American license but Curacao an International Driving License. The official language is Dutch but English, Spanish and a local dialect called Papiamento are also spoken. French is also spoken on the French side of the island of St. Maarten.

Although there are a few imports that are restricted, there are few licenses required for the rest, and few exchange controls.

The Embassy of the Netherlands is located at 4200 Linnean Ave. NW, Washington, D.C. 20008, Tel. 202-244-5300. There are consulates in Chicago, Houston, Los Angeles, New York and San Francisco.

There is an American consulate in Curacao located at St. Anna Blvd. 19, P.O. Box 158, Willemstad, Curacao, Tel. 13066.

For further tourist information contact the Caribbean Tourism Association, 20 East 46 St., New York, NY 10017, Tel. 212-682-0435.

For further business information contact the Netherlands Antilles Economic Mission, 30

Rockefeller Plaza, New York, N.Y. 10112, Tel. 212-765-3737.

NEVADA

The Nevada Department of Commerce, Consumer Affairs Division is responsible for consumer protection. The Division enforces Nevada's Deceptive Trade Practices, Automotive Repair, and Door-to-Door Sales Statutes. Complaints about firms doing business in Nevada are submitted in writing to the Department of Commerce, Consumer Affairs Division, State Capitol Complex, Carson City, Nev. 89710, or branch offices in Las Vegas and Reno. The Division also maintains a Toll-free telephone line in Nevada, 800-992-0900, for consumer questions.

The Consumer Affairs Division has administrative authority to subpoena, hold hearings and obtain assurances of discontinuance of business practices which violate Nevada law. If consumer complaints warrant it, litigation is pursued through District Court.

The Division provides a referral list of state regulatory agencies in Nevada and what businesses, professions, or area it regulates. Contact the Division at the above address for referral help.

The Department of Commerce in Nevada licenses the following businesses: real estate, insurance, mobile home sales and service, banking and savings and loan institutions.

Other occupations and professions are licensed in Nevada by in-dependent licensing boards. Direct inquiries about licensing or complaints about licensees to the Department of Commerce at the above address, which will send it on to the proper licensing board.

The Department of Economic Development assists businesses who want to relocate in Nevada. As a business incentive, Nevada has one of the lowest tax rates in the United States. There are no other special tax incentives available. Businesses requiring assistance should contact the Department of Economic Development, Capitol Complex, Carson City, Nev. 89710, Tel. 702-885-4322 or contact the Chamber of Commerce Association, P.O. Box 3499, Reno, Nev., Tel. 702-323-1877.

Nevada does offer city or county revenue bond financing to businesses, and city, county, and state incentives for the establishment of industrial plants in areas of high unemployment.

Nevada has no state corporate or individual income taxes.

The sales tax in Nevada is 3%, which includes a mandatory 1% county sales tax.

Tourist information can be obtained from the Department of Economic Development, Division of Travel and Tourism, Carson City, Nev. 89710, Tel. 702-885-4322.

NEW HAMPSHIRE

The consumer protection agency in New Hampshire is the Attorney General, Consumer Protection and Antitrust Division. The

Division receives and mediates consumer complaints. It cannot investigate every consumer complaint but initiates investigations when there is a pattern of complaints on a particular business or trade practice.

The Consumer Protection and Antitrust Division has the power to hold hearings, subpoena witnesses and records, seek court orders for restitution, and obtain restraining orders.

Consumer complaints may be sent to the Attorney General, Consumer Protection and Antitrust Division, State House Annex, 25 Capitol St., Concord, N.H. 03301, Tel. 603-271-3641.

There is no central licensing agency in New Hampshire for occupations and professions. Inquiries about licenses or complaints about licensees can be sent to the above Consumer Protection Division, which will refer the letter to the proper state board.

Businesses interested in moving to New Hampshire may request consulting services from the Division of Industrial Development, State House Annex, Concord, NH 03301, Tel. 603-271-1110.

New Hampshire offers state authority revenue bond financing, state loan and loan guarantees for industrial construction and equipment or machinery, and state financing aid for existing plant expansions.

The corporate income tax in New Hampshire is 8% with business and unincorporated businesses. There is no state sales tax.

There is no personal income tax in New Hampshire.

For tourist information contact the Office of Vacation Travel, Division of Economic Development, P.O. Box 856, Concord, N.H. 03301, Tel. 603-271-2343.

NEW JERSEY

The Office of Consumer Protection, in the Division of Consumer Affairs is the main investigative and complaint processing unit in New Jersey. Consumer complaints can be lodged in person or by writing the Office of Consumer Protection, Room 1100, Raymond Building, Newark, N.J. 07102, or the branch office in Camden. Consumer complaints cannot be taken over the telephone, but assistance and advice is provided by the Newark office at 201-648-3622 and the Camden office at 609-757-2840. Complaints are investigated and mediated by the staff when appropriate. The Office of Consumer Protection also functions as an enforcement agency for New Jersey fraud regulations concerning auto sales, auto advertisements and repairs, home improvements, advertising, mail order sales, appliance sales and services, sale of home furnishings, dog and cat sales, banned hazardous products and unit pricing in the food market.

The Division of Consumer Affairs in New Jersey also licenses businesses and occupations through the following boards: architects, barbers, beauty culture, certified public accountants, examiners of electrical contractors, marriage counselors, mortuary science, nursing, examiners of ophthalmic dispensers and ophthalmic technicians, optometrists, pharmacy, professional engineers and land surveyors, professional planners, psychological examiners, veterinary medical examiners, dentistry, medical examiners, master plumbers, shorthand reporters. Information about licensing by these boards can be obtained from that specific board through the Division of Consumer Affairs at the above address.

Complaints about the above businesses or professions should be referred to the executive secretary of the board, though assistance with problems can also be obtained from the deputy director of the Division of Consumer Affairs. The Enforcement Bureau of the Division conducts all investigations and inspections for the regulatory boards. Contact the Chief of the Enforcement Bureau, Division of Consumer Affairs at the above address regarding any investigations or inspections of the above types of businesses or professions.

The Department of Labor and Industry offers assistance to businesses interested in New Jersey, either for expansion or in moving to the state. Contact the Department of Labor and Industry, Division of Economic Development, Labor and Industry Building,

Trenton, N.J. 08625, Tel. 609-292-2121, or the Chamber of Commerce, 5 Commerce St., Newark, N.J. 07102, Tel. 201-624-6888.

New Jersey offers state sponsored revenue bond or general obligation bond financing for industry, as well as state loans and loan guarantees for construction and purchase of equipment. The state, as well as cities, offer incentives for the establishment of industrial plants in areas of high unemployment.

The corporate income tax rate in New Jersey is 7.5%, and the sales tax 5%.

The individual income tax rate ranges from 2% for income less than $20,000 to 2.5% for income in excess of $20,000.

Request tourist information from the Office of Tourism and Promotion, Department of Labor and Industry, P.O. Box 400, Trenton, N.J. 08625. Tel. 609-292-2470.

NEW MEXICO

In New Mexico the Attorney General's Office, Consumer Division is responsible for protecting consumers from fraudulent business practices by enforcing consumer protection laws and education of the public. The jurisdiction is, however, limited to primarily combating unfair, deceptive, and unconscionable trade practices through investigation, negotiation, and, if necessary, civil or criminal enforcement actions in state and federal courts.

The Consumer Advocates Unit

in the Consumer Division of the Attorney General's office receives and processes consumer complaints. Consumer advocates who are paralegals trained in consumer law review personally the consumer complaints made in writing or in person to the Consumer Division. The advocates represent the consumer's interest in resolving the complaint through mediation or negotiation with the businesses.

In cases where the complaint involves violations of law and cannot be resolved or is part of a pattern of conduct affecting more than one individual, the consumer advocate refers the case to the attorneys in the Consumer Division for possible enforcement actions in court.

Contact the Deputy Attorney General, Consumer Division, P.O. Drawer 1508, Sante Fe, N.M. 87501, Tel. 505-827-5521, or contact the branch office in Albuquerque.

Occupations and professions in New Mexico are licensed by individual boards who set licensing requirements, license applicants, and review complaints about licensees. Inquires about licensing or complaints about licensees can be sent to the Consumer Division listed above, which will send the letter on to the proper licensing board.

The Commerce and Industry Department offers assistance to businesses in New Mexico or those interested in moving to the state.

Contact the Commerce and Industry Department, Bataan Memorial Building, Santa Fe, N.M. 87503, Tel. 505-827-5571.

Request tourist information from the Tourism and Travel Division, Commerce and Industry Department, Bataan Memorial Building, Santa Fe, N.M. 87503, Tel. 505-827-5571.

NEW YORK

The Consumer Protection Board in New York State has the power to conduct investigations and studies of consumer problems and make recommendations to the Attorney General's office for judicial action when appropriate. The Board is not a complaint resolution agency, but each year channels thousands of consumer complaints to local, state, and federal agencies that do have the authority to help resolve individual consumer problems. Many counties and cities in New York State have their own consumer protection Bureaus that mediate consumer complaints. If there is not one in your area, contact the Consumer Protection Board which will refer your complaint to the appropriate agency. Their address is 99 Washington Avenue, Albany, N.Y. 12210, Tel. 518-474-8583.

The licensing of occupations and professions in New York State is made through a number of licensing boards which are administered by the Division of Professional Licensing Services. Inquiries about licensing or complaints about licensees can be directed to the New York Division of Professional Licensing Services, Cultural Education Center, Albany, N.Y. 12230, Tel. 518-474-3817.

The Department of Commerce offers consulting services to companies who are considering moving or expanding to New York State. Contact the Department of Commerce, Room 905, 99 Washington Avenue, Albany, N.Y. 12245.

New York State provides tax incentives to companies moving or expanding in New York State such as: selling tax free revenue bonds to make low cost, long term mortgage loans for construction, acquisition, or renovation of commercial building; loans to small, undercapitalized firms when funding is not available from the usual lending sources; issuing tax-exempt revenue bonds to assist companies in solving pollution problems; on the job assistance training. A company creating new jobs in the state may qualify for tax incentives such as business tax credits that may approach 100% of the corporate franchise tax liability for as long as ten years.

By the beginning of 1982 there will be no unincorporated business tax.

The corporate income tax rate in New York is 10% for business corporations and 12% for banking and financial corporations.

New York State personal income tax on amounts over $15,000 is 10%. State law prohibits the taxation of personal property both at the state and local level. Some cities do impose a seperate income tax.

Request tourist information the New York State Department of Commerce, 99 Washington Ave., Albany, N.Y. 12245, Tel. 518-474-2121.

NEW ZEALAND

A valid passport and proof of onward transportation are needed for U.S. citizens traveling to New Zealand for a stay of up to 30 days. In addition, the passport must be valid for at least six months beyond the scheduled departure date. There are no health requirements for entry except a smallpox vaccination if arriving from an infected area. Pets are subject to quarantine in the country. The local currency is the New Zealand dollar. There are no restrictions on the amount of local or foreign currency that may be taken in or out of the country. The official language of New Zealand is English; Maori is also spoken. To drive an American driving license will suffice.

Import licenses are required for all imports; they are difficult to obtain. They are applied for, usually by local importers and are decided on by the government of New Zealand on a case by case basis.

The Embassy of New Zealand is located at 37 Observatory Circle NW, Washington, D.C. 20008, Tel.

202-328-4800. There are consulates in New York, Los Angeles and San Francisco.

The U.S. Embassy in New Zealand is located at 29 Fitzherbert Terrace, Thorndon, New Zealand, Tel. 722068. Their mailing address is SPO San Francisco 96690.

NICARAGUA

A valid passport and a visa are required for U.S. citizens traveling to Nicaragua. For a tourist visa a round trip ticket and two photographs must accompany the visa application; for a business visa, two photographs and a letter from the company detailing the nature of the business and assuming financial responsibility are needed. Both types of visa are good for a stay of up to 30 days. There are no health requirements for travelers arriving from the United States, but typhoid, paratyphoid and polio shots are advised. It is also advisable to carry malaria pills. The U.S. State Department warns visitors to watch out for street crime in the capital city of Managua. Pets require a veterinarian's certificate of good health. The local currency in Nicaragua is the cordoba, which is also locally called the peso. There are no restrictions on the import or export of local or foreign currency. Spanish is the official language. Although some English is spoken, a working knowledge of Spanish is advisable. To drive a car an American license or International Driving License is required.

Trade with Nicaragua is govern-
ment controlled. Persons wishing to do business within the country must contact the Instituto Nacional de Comercio Exterior e Interior. Foreign exchange transactions are controlled by the Central Bank of Nicaragua.

The Embassy of Nicaragua is located at 1627 New Hampshire Ave. NW, Washington, D.C. 20009, Tel. 202-387-4371. There are consulates located in Chicago, Miami, New Orleans, New York, Pearl City (Hawaii), San Francisco and Seattle.

The U.S. Embassy in Nicaragua is located at Km 4½ Carretera Sur, Managua, Nicaragua, Tel. 23061/8 or 23881/7.

NIGERIA

A valid passport and a visa are required for U.S. citizens traveling to Nigeria. To obtain a visa the applicant needs one photograph, and a return ticket. The fee is $2.85. Business travelers need a letter from their company detailing the nature of their business in Nigeria. The visa is good for three months, and the length of stay is variable. A yellow fever shot is required for entry; protection against cholera, typhoid and malaria is advisable. Pets are not allowed into the country. The local currency is the naira. Up to 50 nairas may be taken in or out of the country. There is no limit on the amount of foreign currency that may be taken in or unused foreign currency that can be taken out of the country, but it may be difficult to reconvert nairas before leaving. English is the official language of the country; other languages spoken include Hausa, Ibo, Edo, Yorubu and Fulani. To drive a car an International Driving License or an American license is required. Evidence of a proposed or previous visit to South Africa may prevent the issuing of a visa.

Trade with Nigeria is handled both by private agents and government agencies. Most imports are covered by an open license but some require specific import licenses. Exchange controls are in effect.

Nigeria has a large Muslim population, and visitors should observe the Muslim laws against alcohol when among Muslims. Weapons and narcotics cannot be imported into the country.

The Embassy of Nigeria is located at 2201 R St. NW, Washington, D.C. 20037, Tel 202-822-1600. There are consulates in New York and San Francisco.

The U.S. Embassy in Nigeria is located at 2 Eleke Crescent, P.O. Box 554, Lagos, Nigeria, Tel. 610097. There is an American consulate in Kaduna.

NOISE ABATEMENT

Noise abatement is generally left to local city governments. It is the responsibility of local police to enforce the local noise abatement ordinance, if there is one. The Environmental Protection Agency (EPA) offers assistance to states and communities for noise pollu-

tion or noise abatement projects.

Contact the EPA at its regional office located in most major cities or at 401 M St. SW, Washington, D.C. 20460, Tel. 202-755-2673.

NOISE: AIRCRAFT

The Aircraft Noise Abatement Act of May 1979 requires airlines to order quieter aircraft by 1985 but allows the older aircraft to be flown for up to three years after the deadline if the replacements have been ordered. The Environmental Protection Agency (EPA) regulates airline compliance with federal guidelines on noise. It will not deal with individual complaints, but will keep them on file for reference. If a number of complaints are received about a particular airline, it may act. For further information contact the EPA at its regional offices located in most major cities or the main office at 401 M St. SW, Washington, D.C. 20460, Tel. 202-755-2673.

NOISE: CONSTRUCTION SITES

Local city governments may have ordinances regulating noise at construction sites, such as the hours that heavy construction may take place if it is in an area where it may annoy residents.

The Environmental Protection Agency is beginning to issue recommendations about noise reduction on construction equipment, but it does not at present have regulations about maximum noise levels at construction sites.

NOISE: WORK
See SAFETY: AT WORK

NORTH CAROLINA

The agency responsible for consumer protection in North Carolina is the Department of Justice, P.O. Box 629, Raleigh, N.C. 27611, Tel. 919-733-7741. The agency receives consumer complaints and mediates complaints through contact with the business concerned. It cannot investigate every consumer complaint but maintains a file for use in future investigations. The Department has the power to subpoena witnesses or records, issue cease and desist orders, and prosecute cases against businesses on behalf of consumers.

North Carolina has 35 examining and licensing boards, starting from the board of architecture to the veterinary medical board. There is no central administrative office for the boards, but inquiries can be addressed to the individual board in Raleigh, North Carolina. The consumer protection office in the Department of Justice will also forward any inquiries about licensing to the proper state board. The boards have the power to set licensing requirements, accept complaints, and investigate allegations of misconduct.

The Department of Commerce offers consultant services to businesses considering a move to North Carolina. Interested businesses should write or call the Department of Commerce, 430 N. Salisbury Street, Raleigh, N.C. 27611, Tel. 919-733-7980.

Corporate income taxes in North Carolina is 6% of net income.

Individual income tax is 3% on the first $2,000 and increasing to 7% on income over $10,000.

Tourist information can be requested from the Travel Development Section, Department of Natural and Economic Resources, P.O. Box 27687, Raleigh, N.C. 27611, Tel. 919-733-4171.

NORTH DAKOTA

The State Laboratories Department is the principal consumer protection agency for North Dakota. The Department is responsible for administering laws relating to food, drugs, beverages, cosmetics, controlled substances, hazardous substances, poisons, livestock medicines, commercial feeds, fertilizers, pesticides, paints, petroleum products and antifreeze. It also performs sanitary inspections of motels, hotels, camping facilities, restaurants, etc.

The State Lab has a Consumer Affairs Office which serves as a clearinghouse for consumer complaints and inquiries. The Office will, upon receipt of a written consumer complaint, contact the business and try to bring about a fair resolution of the problem.

Contact the State Laboratories Department at Box 937, Bismark, N.D. 58505, Toll-free Tel. 1-800-472-2927, or 701-224-2485. The office is located at 2635 East Main Ave.

The Attorney General's Office has a consumer fraud Division which will also accept and investigate consumer complaints. Contact the office toll free in North Dakota, 800-472-2600, or write The North Dakota Attorney General, Consumer Fraud Division, 1st floor, Capitol Building, Bismarck, N.D. 58505.

The Attorney General's Office, Regulatory Licensing Division also licenses businesses and organizations such as the following: alcoholic beverages, tobacco, coin operated amusement devices, private detectives, hearing aid examiners and fitters, gambling.

The Business and Industrial Development Department offers consulting services to businesses moving or expanding in North Dakota. Contact the Business and Industrial Development Department, 513 E. Bismarck Ave., Bismarck, N.D. 58505.

In an effort to attract new industry to North Dakota, the state has authorized certain tax exemptions for businesses which bring new jobs to the state. Businesses which are encouraged to apply for tax exemptions include those engaged in: assembling, fabricating, manufacturing, mixing, processing, storing, warehousing, or distributing, any agricultural, mining, or manufacturing products. Retail and service oriented industries are not eligible. A city or county can grant an exemption from the ad valorem tax on real property for a maximum of five years. The income from any such project may also be excluded from state income tax for the same period if the municipality requests the exemption from the State Board of Equalization.

Business income tax rate increases from 3% for amounts under $3,000 to 8.5% for corporate income of excess of $15,000. Banks and financial corporations pay 5% of any corporate income.

The personal income tax rate in North Dakota ranges from 1% for income under $3,000 to 7.5% for income in excess of $30,000.

Request tourist information from the North Dakota Travel Division, State Highway Department, Capitol Grounds, Bismark, N.D. 58505, Tel. 701-224-2525.

NORTHERN IRELAND
See UNITED KINGDOM

NORWAY
A valid passport but no visa is required for U.S. citizens traveling to Norway for a stay of up to three months. For longer stays a visa is needed. There are no health requirements for entry unless arriving from an infected area. Pets brought into the country are subject to quarantine. The local currency is the krone. There are no limits on amounts of local or foreign currency which may be brought into the country, but only 800 kroner may be exported. Tourists may take out no more foreign currency than they brought in.

Norwegian is the official language but Finnish and Lappish are spoken in certain areas of the country. To drive a car an International Driving License is required.

Trade with Norway is usually handled through appointed local agents. Only a few items require licensing. Foreign exchange transactions are handled through authorized banks.

The Embassy of Norway is located at 4200 Wisconsin Ave. NW, Washington, D.C. 20016, Tel. 202-966-9550. There are consulates in Chicago, Houston, Los Angeles, Minneapolis, New Orleans, New and San Francisco.

The American Embassy in Norway is located at Drammensveien 18, Oslo 1, Norway, Tel. 566880. For further tourist information contact the Scandinavian National Tourist Office, 75 Rockefeller Plaza, New York, N.Y. 10019, Tel. 212-582-2802.

For additional business information contact the Norwegian-American Chamber of Commerce Inc., 800 Third Ave., New York, N.Y. 10022, Tel. 212-421-9210.

NUCLEAR ENERGY

The Nuclear Regulatory Commission oversees the non-military uses of nuclear energy including the construction and utilization of nuclear-powered generating plants. Complaints on related topics should be addressed to the Nuclear Regulatory Commission 1717 H St. NW, Washington, D.C. 20555, Tel. 202-492-7715.

NURSERY SCHOOLS

Nursery schools generally accept only children from age three to five who they believe will benefit from a group experience. Therefore children must be able to function effectively away from their mothers or fathers. Classes meet regularly usually two, three or five mornings or afternoons during the week depending on the age level.

Nursery schools are usually licensed by the state public welfare department, as are day care centers. To qualify for a license a center must have adequate facilities, and at least a minimum child-teacher ratio. The school must also be able to pass health and fire inspections.

NURSES

All states require a license to practice professional nursing. To qualify a nurse must be a graduate of a school for nursing approved by the state board of nursing and must pass a written state competency examination.

Approved nursing schools may be of three types: diploma, baccalaureate, and associate degree. Diploma programs usually require three years of training and are conducted by hospitals and independent schools. Associate degree programs require two years of nursing education in junior and community colleges. Baccalaureate programs (B.S. or B.A.) require four years of study in a college or university. B.A. or B.S. programs are preferable for those who want to continue their education to the master's degree or who want to go into administrative or management positions. A high school diploma is required for admission into any school of nursing.

State licensing is on levels depending on the educational qualifications of the applicant. Those with associate degrees may be designated licensed vocational nurses in most states, while those with diplomas and degrees are designated as registered nurses. A few states make a special designation for those with master's degrees with the lesser designation for nurses without master's degrees. Contact the state board of nursing, located in the state capitol, for specific requirements.

Information about education and career opportunities for nurses is available from the American Nurse's Association, 2420 Pershing Rd., Kansas City, Mo. 64108. The telephone number is 816-474-5720.

See also: MIDWIVES

NURSES: (LICENSED VOCATIONAL NURSES) LICENSED PRACTICAL

Licensed practical nurses or vocational nurses, under the direction of physical and registered nurses, provide nursing care that requires technical knowledge but not the professional training and education of registered nurses. Admission to an approved school of practical nursing does not require a high school diploma, but preference is sometimes given to high school graduates. Programs are offered by junior colleges, trade and technical schools. They are usually one year in length.

All states in the United States require the licensing of practical or vocational nurses. To qualify for licensure the nurse must complete a course in practical or vocational nursing that has been approved by the state board of nursing and must pass a written examination. Personnel trained in Military programs similar to practical nursing programs may also be eligible for licensure.

For information about licensing contact the state board of nursing examiners, located in the state capital, or write to the state licensing department listed in the individual state entry.

Information about practical nurse training can be requested from the National Association for Practical Nurse Education and Service, 254 West 31st St., New York, N.Y. 10017, Tel. 212-736-4540.

See also: MIDWIVES

NURSING HOMES

Although the Department of Health and Human Services has set some minimum standards for nursing homes, they are licensed by the states and supervised by state officials. The Federal Housing Administration sets criteria that a proposed nursing home must meet in order for the home to be eligible for FHA mortgage insurance.

Information about homes can be obtained from local and state health care associations. The Health Care Financing Administration, Chief Production & Distribution Branch, 577 East High Rise Bldg., 6325 Security Blvd., Baltimore, Md. 21207, Tel. 301-594-4659 publishes a national directory of nursing homes. The regional offices of the Federal Administration on Aging can also give information about nursing homes.

The American Health Care Association, 1200 15th St. NW, Washington, D.C. 20005, Tel. 202-833-2050 is the largest federation of nursing homes.

Complaints about local nursing homes should be made to the state agency licensing nursing homes.

O

OHIO

Ohio's consumer protection agency is in the Attorney General's Office. The Office accepts consumer complaints and attempts to mediate with the business concerned. It has the power to hold hearings and investigate violations of the state's unfair and deceptive trade practice law. The Office cannot investigate every consumer complaint, but maintains records on all complaints and initiates investigations where

patterns of complaints exist. Send complaints to the Attorney General's Office, 30 East Broad St., State Office Tower, 17th floor, Columbus, Oh. 43215. Tel. 614-466-4320.

Occupations and professions in Ohio are licensed by individual boards which determine qualifications for licensing, license applicants, and review complaints against licensees. Inquiries about licensing or complaints about licensees can be sent to the Attorney General's Office listed above, which will send the letter on to the proper licensing board.

The Department of Commerce offers assistance to businesses in Ohio or those which are interested in moving to the state. Contact the Department of Commerce, 180 E. Broad St., Columbus, Ohio 43215, Tel. 614-466-3636. Also contact the Chamber of Commerce, 17 South High St., 8th Floor, Columbus, Ohio 43215, Tel. 614-228-4201.

Ohio offers state, city, or county revenue bond financing for industry, as well as state loans and loan guarantees for construction and purchase of machinery for industry. Incentives are also offered for establishing industrial plants in areas of high unemployment.

The corporate income tax rate is 4% for amounts up to $25,000 and 8% for corporate income over that amount. The state sales tax is 4%.

The individual income tax ranges from .5% for income under $5,000 to 3.5% for income in excess of $40,000.

Request tourist information from the Travel Bureau, Ohio Department of Economic and Community Development, 30 East Broad St., Columbus, Ohio 43215, Tel. 614-466-8844.

OIL AND HAZARDOUS MATERIAL SPILLS

The Office of Water Operations at the Environmental Protection Agency implements programs designed to prevent and clean up oil spills. The clean up is conducted by the Coast Guard. The Federal Maritime Commission, Office of Water Pollution requires that all ships using U.S. waters register financial responsibility to repay clean up costs.

For further information contact the local Coast Guard office or the United States Coast Guard, Department of Transportation, 2100 2nd St. SW, Washington, D.C. 20593, Tel. 202-426-1587.

Discharges of oil or hazardous materials from transportation spills or accidents must be reported to the National Response Center (NRC), of the U.S. Department of Transportation by the person in charge of the vessel, facility or vehicle from which the discharge occurred. The oil or hazardous material discharge may be into U.S. waters or onto dry land.

Anyone observing an environmental emergency caused by oil or hazardous material discharge should call the NRC.

The NRC rapidly notifies other federal and state agencies of environmental emergencies and provides advice and assistance on procedures for cleanup.

NRC's toll-free line is 800-424-8802. Other inquiries should be referred to the National Response Center Staff, Department of Transportation, Washington, D.C. 20593, Tel. 202-426-1105.

See also: HAZARDOUS MATERIALS: ACCIDENTS AND SPILLS.

OKLAHOMA

The consumer protection agency in Oklahoma is the Department of Consumer Affairs, which is responsible for enforcing the Consumer Protection Act. The Department accepts consumer complaints and attempts mediation. It also has the authority to investigate complaints, though staff limitations prevent investigating every complaint. Where patterns of complaints exist against one business or a business practice, the Department initiates an investigation. It has power to issue subpoenas, hold hearings, and sue in court on behalf of consumers to collect expenses for consumers and civil penalties which are used to further the activities of the Department of Consumer Affairs.

Consumer complaints are sent to the Department of Consumer Affairs, 460 Jim Thorpe Building, Oklahoma City, Okla. 73105, Tel. 405-521-3653.

Licensing of occupations and

professions is not centralized in one agency in Oklahoma, but is handled individually by the following boards: accountants, architects, barbers, podiatrists, chiropractors, cosmetologists, dentists, druggists and pharmacists, embalmers and funeral directors, engineers, medicine, nurses, optometrists, osteopaths, veterinarians, healing arts, cleaners, electrologists, real estate brokers and salesmen, physical therapists, sanitarians, optical goods and devices, public auctioneers, plumbers and plumbing contractors, water and sewage works operators, foresters, social workers, bail bondsmen and runners, psychologists, junk dealers and fitters, speech pathologists and audiologists.

Information requests about licensing in the above occupations and professions should be directed to the individual board, Oklahoma City, Okla. The Department of Consumer Affairs, listed above, will also refer inquiries to the proper state board.

Complaints about licensees in Oklahoma can be sent to the individual boards, which have the power to investigate and revoke licenses, when appropriate.

Businesses interested in relocating in Oklahoma or expanding their facilities in Oklahoma can obtain consultant services through the Economic and Community Affairs Department, Oklahoma City, Okla. 73105, Tel. 405-840-2811.

Nearly 100 Oklahoma communities have established public trusts to issue revenue bonds for industrial projects without public voting on each project. These funds may be used for purchase and improvement of industrial sites, construction of buildings and financing of equipment. In addition, a majority of Oklahoma counties have voted approval of general obligation tax-supported bonds for industrial development which may be used to finance industrial projects.

The Oklahoma Industrial Finance Authority will loan up to 25% of the cost of land and buildings which may be secured by a first or second mortgage.

For more information about Oklahoma's financing possibilities, contact the Economic and Community Affairs Department mentioned above.

The corporate income tax is 4% on the net income derived from Oklahoma property and business applicable to business corporations.

The personal income tax is on net income from property owned and business done in Oklahoma. The rate ranges from ½% on the first $1,000 to 6% on amounts over $7,500.

The Oklahoma sales tax is 2% on gross proceeds from all sales of tangible personal property. Most Oklahoma cities have an additional sales tax of 1%.

Request tourist information from the Tourism Promotion Division, Tourism and Recreation Department, 500 Will Rogers Building, Oklahoma City, Okla. 73105, Tel. 405-521-2406.

OLYMPICS

United states participation in the Olympic Games is governed by the United States Olympic Committee (USOC) in Colorado Springs, Colorado. The individuals and teams selected to represent the United States in the Olympics are chosen by tryouts or competitions directed by individual sports organizations under the direction of the U.S. Olympic Committee. The tryouts are open only to U.S. citizens who are amateur athletes, who are eligible under the regulations of the International Olympic Committee and who have won the right to compete in the Olympics trials according to the rules of the individual sport concerned.

Those organizations recognized by the USOC as the National Sports Governing Bodies with the right to select the Olympic competitors in that sports are:

Aquatics: Acquatics Division of the Amateur Athletic Union (AAU)

Archery: National Archery Association

Athletics (track and field): track and field division of the AAU

Basketball: Amateur Basketball Association of the U.S.A.

Biathlon and Modern Pentathlon: U.S. Modern Pentathlon and Biathlon Association

Bobsledding: Bobsledding Division of the AAU

Boxing: Boxing Division of the AAU

Canoeing and Kayaking: American Canoe Association

Cycling: U.S. Cycling Federation

Equestrian Sports: American Horse Shows Association

Fencing: Amateur Fencers' League of America

Field Hockey: Field Hockey Association of America (men) or U.S. Field Hockey Association, Inc. (women)

Figure Skating: U.S. Figure Skating Association

Gymnastics: U.S. Gymnastics Federation

Ice Hockey: Amateur Hockey Association of the U.S.

Judo: Judo Division of the AAU

Luge: Luge Division of the AAU

Rowing: National Association of Amateur Oarsmen

Shooting: National Rifle Association of America

Skiing: U.S. Ski Association

Soccer Football: U.S. Soccer Federation

Speed Skating: U.S. International Speed Skating Association

Team Handball: U.S. Team Handball Federation

Volleyball: U.S. Volleyball Association

Weightlifting: Weightlifting Division of the AAU

Wrestling: Wrestling Division of the AAU

Yachting: U.S. Yacht Racing Union

Information about tryouts in each sport can be obtained from the governing association mentioned above, or from the U.S. Olympic Committee, 1750 East Boulder St. Colorado Springs, Colo. 80909, Tel. unlisted; or the U.S. Olympic Training Center, 1776 East Boulder St., Colorado Springs, Colo. 80909, Tel. 303-475-8820.

See also: SPECIAL OLYMPICS

OPTICIANS

Dispensing opticians dispense eyeglasses and contact lenses from prescriptions written by optometrists or ophthalmologists. The following states require licenses: Alaska, Arizona, California, Connecticut, Florida, Georgia, Hawaii, Kentucky, Massachusetts, Nevada, New Jersey, New York, North Carolina, Rhode Island, South Carolina, Tennessee, Vermont, Virginia and Washington.

Requirements for licensing vary from state to state but generally stipulate a minimum amount of education or training and both a written and practical examination. Consult the state licensing board, listed under the state entry, for specific licensing requirements.

The professional organization for opticians is the Opticians Association of America at 1250 Connecticut Ave. NW Washington, D.C. 20036. Tel. 202-659-3620.

See also: OPTOMETRISTS.

OPTOMETRISTS

Optometrists examine eyes for structural and visual defects and prescribe correctional lenses, exercises, or other nonsurgical or drug remedies.

Optometry schools admit students with a minimum of two years of college study at an accredited college or university. Schools of optometry consist of a four-year professional program. Optometrists may also continue their study for a master's or doctorate degree in physiological optics, neurophysiology, public health administration or health administration. Schools of Optometry are accredited by the Council on Optometric Education of the American Optometric Association.

All states require optometrists to be licensed. Applicants must have a Doctor of Optometry degree from an accredited optometric school and pass a written examination. For applications and specific requirements for licensing, contact the state licensing board listed in the state entry for the licensing board for optometrists. Reciprocity for an optometrist's licenses between states is decided on the basis of the individual's credentials. Consult the state licensing board.

Complaints about optometrists can be made to the state licensing board, which has the power to revoke licenses.

OREGON

The state agency with responsibility for consumer protection in Oregon is the Consumer Services

Division of the Oregon Department of Commerce. The Division will process and mediate consumer complaints about products and services, answer inquiries and furnish consumer information such as the complaint record of a particular business or product, refer the consumer to appropriate agencies, and issue warnings to businesses engaging in consumer abuse. It cannot give legal advice or assistance, recommend brands, bring suit on behalf of consumers, or regulate businesses.

Upon receipt of a consumer complaint the Division will contact the business and ask for a brief statement about the complaint. The Consumer Services Division will also mediate a dispute. The consumer is so informed, if the Division determines that the consumer complaint has no merit. If the firm refuses to make any adjustments on a complaint the Division thinks is valid, the complainant is referred to small claims court, to a private attorney, or to the Oregon State Bar Lawyer Referral Service if the complainant does not know a competent attorney.

Contact the Consumer Services Division, Labor and Industries Building, Salem, Ore. 97310, Tel. 503-378-4320, Toll-free 800-452-7813.

The Department of Justice also has a consumer protection division whose responsibility is to prevent and prosecute violations of the Unlawful Trade Practices Act which prohibits certain practices by businesses who advertise or sell goods or services to consumers. These prohibited practices include: false price advertising misrepresentations of the characteristics of goods and services, pyramid sales schemes, performance of unauthorized services, and failure to give personal name, company name, and purpose of call within 30 seconds of beginning a telephone or door-to door solicitation. Consumers who believe that they have been the victim of one of these kinds of misrepresentation can file a complaint with the Department of Justice, Consumer Protection Division, 500 Pacific Building, 520 SW Yamhill, Portland Ore. 97204, Tel. 503-229-5548 or Toll-free in Oregon 800-452-7813.

The Department of Justice cannot take formal action on every complaint received from consumers, since it is primarily a law enforcement agency and some complaints fall outside its authority or may be such that sufficient evidence is not available. The Department does, however, welcome consumer complaints, because they initiate many cases within the Department against businesses engaging in unlawful practices.

The Department of Commerce is also responsible for most of the licensing and regulatory functions in the State of Oregon.

Occupations or professions licensed by the Department of Commerce are: architects, barbers, billing adjusters, boiler/pressure inspectors, boilermaker/steamfitters, builders, certified public accountants, collection agency operators and solicitors, contractors, debt consolidators, electricians, engineers, escrow agents, factoring adjustors, factoring agency managers, geologists, hairdressers, insurance agents, insurance adjustors, land surveyors, landscape contractors, liquified petroleum gas dealer/installers, manicurists, municipal auditors, personal income tax preparer/consultants, pilot (river), plumbers, public accountants, radio and TV Service Dealer/technicians, real estate brokers, real estate appraisers, real estate salespersons, securities broker/dealers, securities investment advisor/salesmen and welders.

The boards in the Department of Commerce have the authority to set the qualifications for persons licensed in that occupation or profession, conduct examinations, and issue certificates or licenses. It also has the authority to accept complaints from the public, investigate complaints, and take appropriate action such as dismissing the complaint or revoking the license of the licensee involved.

Direct inquiries about licensing or complaints about licensees to the Department of Commerce,

Labor and Industries Building, Salem, Ore. 97310, Tel. 503-378-4320.

Consulting services about business in Oregon can be requested from the Department of Commerce, Salem, Ore. 97310, Tel. 503-378-4100.

Oregon offers state, city, or county revenue bond financing to industry, as well as state incentives for establishing industrial plants in areas of high unemployment.

Additional information about business and industry in Oregon can be obtained from the Department of Economic Development, 317 South Alder Street, Portland, Ore. 97204, Tel. 503-229-5535, or the Associated Oregon Industries, Inc., 1149 Court St., N.E., P.O. Box 12519, Salem, Ore. 97309, Tel. 503-588-0050.

Oregon is one of only five states that does not have a general sales tax. Individuals pay personal income tax from 4% on the first $500 to 10% on income over $5,000. Couples filing joint returns pay 4% on the first $1,000 with increasing percentages up to 10% on amounts over $10,000.

Any corporation doing business or producing income in Oregon pays corporate excise and income tax of 7.5% of Oregon net income.

Further information about taxes in Oregon is available from the Department of Revenue, State Office Building, Salem, Ore. 97310, Tel. 503-378-3745.

Tourist information can be requested from the Travel Information Section, 101 Highway Building, Salem, Ore. 97310, Tel. 503-378-3438.

ORGAN DONATION

Parts of a person's body can be donated after death by relatives or through a will made by that individual. Body parts such as kidneys, eyes or skin tissue will be used for transplants or research. A family doctor, local hospital or nearby medical school can help to arrange donations of body parts at death.

Two nonprofit organizations provide assistance in making plans to donate body parts at death. They provide a free, wallet-sized donor card that is recognized as a legal document in most states and in Canada.

Contact Living Bank, P.O. Box 6725, Houston, Texas 77025, Tel. 713-528-2971 and Medic Alert, Turlock, Calif 95380, Tel. 209-668-3333. Also contact the American Medical Association, 535 North Dearborn, Chicago, Ill. 60605, Tel. 312-675-6000, for further information and donor cards.

OSTEOPATHIC PHYSICANS

Doctors of Osteopathic Medicine (D.O.) are one of two types of physicians licensed in the United States. The other is the medical doctor (M.D.)

D.O.s emphasize the musculoskeletal system (muscles, bones and joints) and the interrelationship of body structure and organic functioning that medical doctors do not. D.O.s use structural diagnosis and manipulative therapy along with more traditional forms of diagnosis and treatment.

Educational requirements for D.O.s are basically the same as for medical doctors. A D.O. has had the prescribed amount of premedical training, has graduated from an undergraduate college, has received four years of training in a medical school and has served a one-year internship with an approved intern training program. A number of medical specialties are open to D.O.s through a three-to-four-year residency program. D.O.s use all the scientifically accepted methods of diagnosis and treatment, including drugs and surgery. In most state D.O.s are examined by the same state licensing boards as M.D.s.

All states require osteopathic physicians to be licensed. A candidate must be a graduate of an approved school of osteopathic medicine and pass an examination given by the state licensing board for D.O.s. Some states require candidates to pass an examination in the basic sciences before being qualified to take the test in osteopathic medicine. Most states require one year of internship in an approved hospital after graduation from osteopathic school. The states that do not require such internships are: Indiana, Louisiana, Massachusetts, Missouri, New Hampshire, New York, Tennessee, Texas and Wyoming. States requiring two year internships are: Connecticut, Hawaii and New Hampshire. All states except Alaska have license reciprocity with other states, but reciprocity is at the discretion of the state board and is often decided on the qualification of the individual applicant.

For specific information about licensing consult the state licensing board, generally the board of medical examiners or board of osteopathic examiners, located in the state capital. The licensing boards can be contacted through the state occupational licensing department, listed in the individual state entries.

The professional organization of osteopathic physicians is the American Osteopathic Association. The AOA is recognized as the official accrediting body for osteopathic hospitals and colleges by the United States Department of Education, and serves as the main lobbying body for the profession. It has limited power to discipline members but grants membership only to those who observe its bylaws. Contact the AOA at 212 East Ohio St., Chicago, Ill. 60611, Tel. 312-280-5800.

See also: MEDICAL DOCTORS

OVERSEAS BUSINESS: GOVERNMENT AID

See BUSINESS: OVERSEAS

P

PAKISTAN

A valid passport but no visa is necessary for U.S. citizens traveling to Pakistan for tourist purposes for a stay of up to 30 days. For business travel, a visa is required. Applications should be accompanied by a letter from your company detailing the nature of the business and assuming financial responsibility. Types of visas available include a multiple visa good for six re-entries within a year and stays of up to three months on each visit. Visitors planning to stay longer than one month must register with the immigration authorities within 30 days of arrival.

Cholera, yellow fever and smallpox vaccinations are required only if arriving from an infected area. Malaria tablets are recommended. Pets are allowed into the country but a veterinarian's certificate of vaccination and good health is required to obtain a permit from Pakistani authorities upon arrival in Pakistan. The monetary unit in Pakistan is the Panistani rupee. Its import is limited to 100 and export to 20. There is no limit, however, to amounts of foreign currency that can be taken in or out of the country. To drive a car an International Driving License is required. The most commonly spoken language in Pakistan is Urdu; English is usually spoken in business and tourist circles. Importing liquor is prohibited. Alcoholic beverages are sold only to tourists in the hotels.

Trading with Pakistan is mostly government controlled; the government is the major importer. The government publishes a list of allowable imports by the private sector. Exchange controls are in effect.

The Embassy of Pakistan is located at 2315 Massachusetts Ave. NW, Washington, D.C. 20008, Tel. 202-332-8330.

The U.S. Embassy in Pakistan is located at Diplomatic Enclave Ramma 4, Islamabad, Pakistan, Tel. 26161.

PANAMA

Evidence of U.S. citizenship (passport, birth certificate) is necessary for travel to Panama for a stay of up to 30 days for purposes of tourism or business. There are no health requirements for entry except cholera shots if coming from an infected area. However, malaria pills and yellow fever shots are advised. Pets require a certificate of vaccination and good health from a veterinarian validated by a consular official in the United States and even with that are subject to quarantine in Panama for a length of time to be decided by Panamanian authorities. The currency in Panama is the balboa. There is no limit on amounts of local or foreign currency that can be brought in or taken out of the country. U.S.

dollars are generally accepted throughout Panama. Spanish is the official language; English is widely spoken. To drive a car an International Driving License is required.

Trade with Panama is usually handled through resident agents. Such licenses as are required are issued and approved by the Ministry of Commerce. The government offers tax advantages for foreign investors, and the Colon free zone allows exemptions from customs and other charges for firms importing goods for re-export in their original or in altered form.

The Embassy of Panama is located at 2862 McGill Terrace NW, Washington, D.C. 20008, Tel. 202-483-1407. There are consulates in Baltimore, Dallas, Houston, Los Angeles, Miami, New Orleans, New York, Philadelphia, Portland, San Antonio and San Francisco.

The U.S. Embassy in Panama is located at Avenida Balboa y Calle 38, Apartado 6959, Panama City, Panama, Tel. 253600.

For further travel information contact the Panama Government Tourist Bureau, 630 Fifth Ave., New York, N.Y. 10111, Tel. 212-246-5841.

For additional information on the Colon free zone or other business contact the Panama Trade Center, 219 East 44 St., New York, N.Y. 10017, Tel. 212-286-0742.

PAN AMERICAN GAMES

The Pan American Games is a competition, held every four years, among amateur athletes representing countries in the Western Hemisphere. It is modeled after the Olympic Games, and most Olympic rules and regulations apply. The governing organization, the Pan American Sports Organization, is made up of the representatives of the Olympic committees of the Americas as recognized by the International Olympic Committee. For further information contact the International Olympic Committee at 1750 East Boulder St., Colorado Springs, Colo. 80909, Tel. 303-632-5551.

PARACHUTING AND SKYDIVING

The United States Parachute Association (U.S.P.A.) sanctions parachute competitions including national championships and national collegiate parachuting championships. It also selects the U.S. team for international competitions and maintains statistics on parachute competitions. The association sponsors a rating program to certify parachute jumping instructors.

The U.S.P.A. is the only national organization representing skydivers in the United States. The association establishes safety standards and recommends procedures for safe jumping, sanctions competitive sport parachuting and establishes standards for competition and cooperates with other sporting aviation groups in promoting sporting and general aviation within the United States. Membership in the association is open to anyone interested in parachuting or skydiving.

For a listing of approved clubs and centers or for further information contact the United States Parachute Association, 806 15th St. NW, Suite 444, Washington, D.C. 20005, Tel.: 202-347-5773.

PARENTING

The American Red Cross gives courses taught by registered nurses designed to help expectant parents cope with new parenthood. The Mother and Baby Care is usually offered free by the local branch of the Red Cross. For information about courses contact the local branch of the American Red Cross or the American National Red Cross, 17th and D St. NW, Washington, D.C. 20006. Tel. 202-737-8300.

PARKING TICKETS

Parking tickets are generally issued by local municipal police. However, they may also be issued by the state police, highway patrol or sheriff's department. The amount of parking ticket fines varies from community to community. Some municipalities have boxes attached to parking meters where violators may pay their meter fines by depositing the ticket and the required amount in the box. Generally violations may be paid by mail or in person at the local police station and city or county offices. Those wishing to plead innocent can have a trial before a judge or, in some instances, a jury trial. Normal appeal procedures apply to court hearings on parking violations.

Information on how and where to pay fines, and how to plead innocent and have a hearing is generally printed on all parking tickets.

PARKINSON'S DISEASE

The National Parkinson Foundation, in association with the School of Medicine of the University of Miami treats men and women from all over the world on an outpatient basis. Treatment includes: psychological counseling and physical, speech, and occupational therapies. The Foundation also conducts research into the treatment and cure of the disease.

Inquiries about the National Parkinson Foundation can be sent to the National Parkinson Institute, 1501 N.W. 9th Ave., Miami, Florida 33136. The telephone number is 305-547-6666.

PAROLE OR PARDON

Each state has a board that administers its parole system. Inmates of state prisons are eligible for parole after serving a set portion of the maximum sentence ordered by the court. Generally inmates are reviewed whenever they become eligible for parole whether or not application for parole was made. The board must

determine whether or not the inmate is to be paroled when eligible based upon the inmate's crime, behavior in prison and any other applicable factors.

The governor of each state has the authority to pardon an inmate of a state prison or a person convicted in state courts. The state board of pardons and paroles may make recommendations regarding the pardon of such persons. The governor's executive clemency may be either a lessening or a suspension of punishments determined by the state courts.

For further information contact the state parole board or division.

PASSENGER SHIPS: SANITATION

See CRUISE SHIPS: SANITATION

PASSPORTS

U.S. passports document the citizenship of Americans traveling in foreign countries. They are issued by the U.S. Department of State. The applicant who has never before been issued a passport must apply in person at one of the U.S. Department of State Passport Agencies, a federal or state courthouse or a designated class 1 post office.

If the applicant was issued a passport in his or her own name within the last 8 years and was at least 18 years old when it was issued, the passport can be renewed by mail or in person with an application obtained at a location listed below. Proof of citizenship must be displayed upon application. A previously issued passport is proof of citizenship. If the applicant does not have a passport, a birth certificate is the usual proof (see also: BIRTH CERTIFICATE). If no birth record exists, a letter of no record from the state or local department of vital statistics may be submitted with the best obtainable documentary evidence of citizenship such as a baptismal certificate. Naturalized citizens must present a naturalization certificate, a consular record of birth, a certificate of birth or a certificate of citizenship.

The applicant must establish his or her identity to the satisfaction of the person executing the application. A driver's license, a previously issued passport, or other identity document with signature and picture or physical description is acceptable. A passport applicant must supply two identical photographs, either color or black and white. They must be full face, printed on thin, non-glossy paper with a plain, light background and be no smaller than 2½ × 2½ inches and no larger than 3 × 3 inches.

The passport fee is $10. A fee of $3 is also charged for execution of the passport except when application is by mail. Passports are valid for five years unless otherwise limited. Loss of a valid passport should be reported in writing immediately to the Passport Services office, Washington, D.C. or to the nearest U.S. consular office when in a foreign country.

For applications contact passport services field offices located in Boston, Chicago, Honolulu, Los Angeles, Miami, New Orleans, New York, Philadelphia, San Francisco, Seattle, Detroit, Houston and Stamford or contact the Passport Services, Bureau of Consular Affairs, Room G-62, 1425 K St. NW, Washington, D.C. 20524, Tel. 202-783-8170.

See also: individual country entry

PEACE CORPS

The Peace Corps is a federally sponsored project that sends volunteer corps of volunteers overseas in countries whose needs are critical and who request volunteers to aid in their economic and social development. The volunteers serve for two years working in the communities to which they are sent and living among the people. For further information contact Action/Peace Corps, 806 Connecticut Ave. NW, Washington, D.C. 20525, Tel. 202-254-7346.

PENNSYLVANIA

In Pennsylvania the state department which will help consumers with complaints against businesses is the Bureau of Consumer Protection, Office of the Attorney General, Strawberry Square, 15th floor, Harrisburg, Pa. Complainants should contact the nearest bureau office in writing. When the bureau receives a complaint it assigns an investigator who then contacts the company to obtain their side of the story. If the officials of the company refuse to reply to the Bureau's inquiry, they can be forced to do so by the issuance of a subpoena.

The Pennsylvania Bureau of Consumer Protection cannot act as the attorney for an individual complainant, but if it discovers that the trade practices of a business violate the law, the Bureau has the authority to go to court and order a halt to such practices. In such cases the Bureau can also ask the court to require that guilty businesses repay consumers who have been defrauded.

Branch offices of the Bureau of Consumer Protection are located in Erie, Harrisburg, Allentown, Philadelphia, Pittsburgh, and Scranton.

Twenty-two professions and occupations are licensed in Pennsylvania: architects, auctioneers, barbers, chiropractors, cosmetologists, dentists, funeral directors, landscape architects, medical doctors, motor vehicle sales, nurses, nursing home administrators, optometrists, osteopaths, pharmacists, physical therapists, podiatrists, professional engineers, psychologists, public accountants, real estate brokers, and veterinarians. Each profession or occupation listed has a separate board which may license several related job titles under that occupation or profession, such as real estate broker and out of state developer.

The twenty-two licensing boards are administered by the Bureau of Professional and Occupational Affairs, Harrisburg, Pa. 17120, 717-783-3650. The boards can be contacted through the Bureau, but the individual boards have the power to discipline their licensees including the revocation of licenses. The Bureau of Professional and Occupational Affairs maintains a comprehensive complaints handling process which involves review of each complaint by an attorney. If the complaint seems substantive, it could proceed through a formal hearing and ultimately result in the suspension or revocation action.

Pennsylvania offers the services of a business ombudsman to businesses and industries to provide help with any problem concerning state government. The Business Ombudsman can be contacted at the Pennsylvania Department of Commerce, 400 South Office Building, Harrisburg, Pa. 17120, Toll-free 800-932-0664.

The Pennsylvania Department of Commerce says that it is committed to offering a financing package to new or expanding businesses that is competitive with any state in the nation. They offer up to 100% financing for the acquisition of land, building, and equipment through methods such as the low interest industrial revenue bonds and mortgage program. Air and pollution control facilities and equipment can also be financed through this program. The bond and mortgage terms are extended to 20 years at rates lower than conventional financing. For information about these programs contact the Director of Economic Development, Department of Commerce, Room 425, South Office Building, Harrisburg, Pa. 17120, Tel. 717-787-6500.

The corporate net tax in Pennsylvania is assessed at 10.5% on net income reported to the federal government. Corporations with interests in other states pay only a portion based on the percentage of their property, payroll, and sales values in Pennsylvania. The capital stock tax is imposed at a 10 mill rate, with key exceptions for manufacturers whose facilities are subject to little or no capital stock tax.

The Pennsylvania state personal income tax is 2.2% across the board. The sales tax 6%, with exceptions for some items such as materials, machinery and supplies used in manufacturing.

For further information about financing and taxation for businesses in Pennsylvania, contact the Department of Commerce at the above address.

Request tourist information from the Bureau of Travel Development, Pennsylvania Department of Commerce, 431 South Office Building, Harrisburg, Pa. 17120, Tel. 717-787-5453.

PENSIONS

The Pension Benefit Guaranty Corp. guarantees basic pension benefits in covered private pension plans if they terminate with insufficient assets. Mandatory coverage is provided for most plans. For information about plans or about Individual Retirement Accounts for those not covered by pension plans, contact the Pension Benefit Guaranty Corp, 2020 K St. NW, Washington, D.C. 202-254-4880.

PEN PALS

Several organizations help elementary and high school students to establish communication with overseas students in letters or tapes. For further information contact Letters Abroad, 209 East 56 St., New York, N.Y. 10022, Tel. 212-752-4290; World Pen Pals, 1694 Como Ave., St. Paul, Minn., 55108, Tel. 612-647-0191; or the International Friendship League, 22 Batterymarch St., Boston, Mass. 02109, Tel. 617-523-4273.

PENTATHLON

Pentathlon sport competitions involve five events, one a day, over five days: horseback riding, fencing, pistol shooting, swimming and cross-country running.

The United States Modern Pentathlon and Biathlon Association trains and selects U.S. teams to represent the United States in the Olympic Games, Pan American Games, World Championships and other international competitions. It also conducts developmental clinics for potential team members.

Contact the association at 707 E. Broad St., Falls Church, Va. 22046, Tel. 202-693-7755.

PERU

A valid passport and a round trip ticket are required for U.S. citizens traveling to Peru for a stay of up to 90 days. Business travelers need a visa which costs $10. A letter from the company confirming financial responsibility should be presented with the visa application. There are no health requirements for entry if arriving from the United States. Pets may be brought in, but rules vary with each animal. For example, a dog requires a veterinarian's certificate of good health which is validated by a Peruvian consulate and which costs $5. For regulations covering other animals it is best to check with the nearest Peruvian consulate. The local currency is the sol. There is a limit of 5,000 soles which may be imported or exported from Peru. There is no limit, however, on the amount of foreign currency which may be taken in or out. The official languages of Peru are Spanish and Quechua, which is an Indian language. Some English is also spoken. To drive a car an International Driving License is required.

Trade with Peru is conducted either through appointed local agents or directly with importers or wholesalers. The government has a list of permitted imports and only the items listed may be imported into the country. Licenses, issued by the Ministry of Commerce, are required for all imports. Travelers should be advised that if they bring radios, record players or tape recorders into the country, they will have to declare them for personal use or they may be confiscated. There are also restrictions on the export of archaeological artifacts.

The Embassy of Peru is located at 1700 Massachusetts Ave. NW, Washington, D.C. 20036, Tel. 202-833-9860. There are consulates in Chicago, Houston, Los Angeles, Miami, New Orleans, New York and San Francisco.

The U.S. Embassy in Peru is located at Corner Avenidas Inca Garcilaso de la Vega and Espana, Casilla 1995, Lima, Peru, Tel. 286000.

PEST CONTROL

The U.S. Department of Agriculture, Animal and Plant Health Inspection Service is responsible for programs to control or eradicate plant pests and diseases. The USDA cooperates with state agencies, farmers and private organizations in these pest control efforts. When significant amounts of pesticides are used in the control programs, it also monitors the effects upon fish, wildlife, beneficial insects, water and public health.

Agriculture quarantine inspection officers inspect, restrict or quarantine foreign plants entering the United States.

Inspection permits must be issued for all imported plant material including fruits and vegetables, and plants or plant parts intended for growing. Inspection services are maintained at all major entry points.

Contact the local USDA office, Department of Agriculture, Animal and Plant Health Inspection Service, Information Division, 14 St. and Independence Ave. SW, Washington, D.C., 20250, Tel. 202-447-3977, or contact, USDA, Plant Protection and Quarantine, Bettsville, Md., Tel. 301-344-2577 and Springfield, Md., Tel. 301-451-9464.

PESTICIDES

The Department of Agriculture monitors the use of pesticides in its pest control and eradication programs. It studies the effects of any significant amounts of pesticides on fish, wildlife, beneficial insects, water and public health.

The Environmental Protection Agency (EPA) Office of Pesticide Programs regulates pesticides and attempts to reduce their use to ensure human safety and protection of environmental quality. Through research and study, the EPA establishes tolerance levels for pesticides that occur in or on food, and also monitors the residue levels of pesticides in food, humans, nontarget fish and wildlife and their environments. The agency also investigates pesticide accients.

For further information contact the Department of Agriculture, Office of Assistant Secretary for Natural Resources and Environment, Office of Coordinator for Environmental Quality, 14th St. and Independence Ave. SW, Washington, D.C. 20250, Tel. 202-447-3965 and the EPA, Office of the Assistant

Administrator for Toxic Substances, Office of Pesticide Programs, 410 M St. SW, Washington, D.C. 20460, Tel. 202-755-0707.

See also: PEST CONTROL, TOXIC SUBSTANCE CONTROL

PET LICENSING AND RABIES VACCINATIONS

State laws require rabies vaccinations for dogs and authorize local communities to set up their own licensing and vaccination programs and requirements. States such as Texas and New York are also beginning to require vaccination of cats.

Information about dog and cat licensing and vaccination can be obtained from the local city authority or the state veterinarian's office, generally located in the state capital.

PET SHOPS

In most areas pet shops are not required to be licensed. They are, however, subject to state and local laws or regulations for humane treatment of animals, including cleanliness of cages and other areas where animals are housed. The state health department generally has the authority to close a shop if cleanliness standards are not met.

Complaints about animal treatments can be made to the local animal protective organization, the local police or the state health department.

See also: ANIMAL WELFARE, ANIMALS: CRUELTY TO

PHARMACISTS

All states require pharmacists to be licensed. To qualify for a license the applicant must be a graduate of an accredited college of pharmacy, must have passed a state board examination and must have completed a specified amount of practical experience or an internship under the supervision of a licensed pharmacist.

Degree programs accredited by the American Council on Pharmaceutical Education require at least five years of study beyond high school. Graduates usually receive a B.S. or a Bachelor of Pharmacy degree. Graduate programs are also available leading to the Doctor of Pharmacy degree. Admission requirements vary, but many colleges of pharmacy require one or two years of prepharmacy education in an accredited college or university.

The American Pharmaceutical Association (APA), serves as a clearinghouse of information for pharmacists, promotes the safe and effective use of drugs by members and maintains a code of ethics for the profession. Contact the APA at 2215 Constitution Ave. NW, Washington, D.C. 20037, Tel. 202-628-4410. Contact the state licensing board for information and applications. See individual state entry for information about state boards.

Complaints about pharmacists can also be made to the state licensing board, which has the authority to investigate complaints, to take disciplinary action, or to revoke a license. If a pharmacist has broken state law, civil or criminal penalties may also be pursued through the courts.

PHILIPPINES

A valid passport and a round trip ticket are required for U.S. citizens traveling to the Philippines for a stay of up to 21 days. For a longer stay, a visa good for 59 days can be obtained by presenting one photograph, a round trip ticket and a passport at a Philippine consulate. Business travelers need a visa good for one or two days. Their visa application must be accompanied by a letter from their company detailing the nature of their business and confirming financial responsibility for the applicant, plus one photograph and a passport. There are no health requirements for entry. Yellow fever shots are required if arriving from an infected area. To bring a pet into the country permission must first be sought from the Bureau of Animal Industry, Pet Division, Metro Manila, Republic of the Philippines. That permit plus a veterinarian's certificate of good health must be validated at a Philippine consulate in the United States before departure. The monetary unit of the islands is the peso. There is a 550 limit on their import or export. There is no limit on foreign currency brought in or out, but all money must be declared on arrival. Cars may be temporarily imported to the islands if covered by a Carnet de Passages en Douanes obtained in the United States and a letter from the Philippine Motor Association guaranteeing re-export within one year. All cars must be registered with the Land Transportation Commission upon arrival. An International Driving License is also required. The import of weapons, pornography, anti-Philippine literature and gambling devices are prohibited. The official languages of the Islands are Philopino (also called Tagalog), English and Spanish. Many local dialects are also spoken.

Trading with the Philippines is done either through agents or with trading companies. No licenses are generally required although some consumer goods are restricted. Foreign exchange is arranged through letters of credit.

The Embassy of the Philippines is located at 1617 Massachusetts Ave. NW, Washington, D.C. 20036, Tel. 202-483-1414. There are consulates in Chicago, Honolulu, Los Angeles, New Orleans, New York, San Francisco and Seattle.

The U.S. Embassy in the Philippines is located at 1201 Roxas Blvd., Manila, The Philippines, Tel. 598011.

For additional tourist information contact the Philippine American Travel Service, 535 Fifth Ave., New York, N.Y. 10017, Tel. 212-687-6333.

For business information contact the Philippine Chamber of Commerce at the same address,

Tel. 212-972-9326.

PHYSICAL THERAPISTS

Physical therapists treat diseases by mechanical means such as massage, regulated exercise and the application of water, light, heat or electricity. A license is required in all states to practice physical therapy. Applicants for a license must have a degree or certificate from an accredited physical therapy program. They must also pass a state board examination. For specific licensing requirements, contact the state licensing board.

Physical therapy programs are offered on both the bachelor's and master's degree level. Programs are accredited by the American Medical Association and the American Physical Therapy Association, a professional organization for the promotion and continuing education of physical therapists.

Contact the American Physical Therapy Association, 1156 Fifteenth St. NW, Washington, D.C. 20005, Tel. 202-466-2070.

PHYSICIANS
See MEDICAL DOCTORS

PLANTS: IMPORTING
See PEST CONTROL

PODIATRISTS

Podiatrists are health professionals who treat the human foot. Podiatrists are educated at colleges of podiatric medicine located in Chicago, Cleveland, New York City, Philadelphia and San Francisco. The minimum college requirement for applicants to a college of podiatry is two years with course work in areas such as biology and mathematics, but 90 percent of all entering students have baccalaureate degrees. Upon graduation from a college of podiatry, the degree of Doctor of Podiatric Medicine (D.P.M.) is awarded. Individual state boards license podiatrists according to their own regulations. Generally, an applicant for a license must have graduated from an accredited college of podiatric medicine and must have passed a written and oral state proficiency examination. Georgia, Michigan, New Jersey and Rhode Island require an additional one-year residency in a hospital or clinic for licensure. Consult the state board for the exact licensing requirements.

The American Podiatry Association is an association of 8,000 members. The association establishes the code of ethics for podiatrists and promotes the interests of podiatrists in the United States.

Any complaints about podiatrists should be sent to the licensing board in the state concerned. The board will investigate the complaint and, if necessary, discipline the podiatrist or revoke the license. Malpractice suits, however, should be pursued through civil courts with the assistance of a lawyer.

For information about colleges of podiatric medicine contact the American Association of Colleges of Podiatric Medicine, 20 Chevy Chase Circle, NW, Washington, D.C. 20015, Tel. 202-537-4950.

For general information on podiatry and licensing contact the American Podiatry Association, Department of Public Affairs, at the same address, Tel. 202-537-4900.

POISON PREVENTION PACKAGING

A federal law administered by the U.S. Consumer Product Safety Commission requires that certain hazardous household products must be sold in packaging that most children under five cannot open. The purpose of the law is to reduce poisonings among small children. Drugs currently required to be in safety packaging include human prescription drugs in oral dosage forms, all controlled drugs in dosage forms intended for oral administration, aspirin products, methyl salicylate, iron-containing preparations, such as dietary supplements, and aspirin substitutes.

A purchaser can request that prescription medicines be packaged in easy-to-open containers. Manufacturers can also market easy-to-open packaging for a non-prescription drug if they offer a popular size of the same medication in the safety packaging, but the label must clearly state: "This package for households without young children."

Contact the Consumer Product Safety Commission at 1111 Eighteenth St. NW, Washington, D.C. 20207, Tel. 202-634-7700.

POISONS

In the case of poison ingestion, contact your doctor, hospital, poison control center immediately.

Some 560 poison control centers throughout the U.S. offer help 24 hours a day. These centers, which are usually part of a hospital maintain a file that lists information on the toxicity, ingredients, and symptoms of poisons, as well as recommended treatment. The Government Bureau of Product Safety each year puts out a directory of all the poison control centers in the country which is available from the U.S. Government Printing Office, Washington, D.C. 20402. Check the local telephone directory for the location of the regional poison control center or ask a doctor or local hospital.

See also: POISON PREVENTION PACKAGING

POLAND

U.S. citizens traveling to Poland must first obtain a money voucher from a Polish diplomatic mission or tourist office. They must previously exchange $15 a day for every day of their proposed visit. Then a visa may be applied for with a valid passport and two photos. The visa is usually good for six months and the length of stay is variable. Business travelers must also have a money voucher as well as an invitation from the Polish company or government agency they will be dealing with. Foreign visitors planning to stay more than 30 days must register at the Foreign Visitors Registration Office. There are no health requirements necessary for entry, but yellow fever and smallpox vaccinations are needed if arriving from an infected area. Pets require a veterinarians certificate of good health. The local currency of Poland is the zloty and their import or export is strictly prohibited. Foreign currency may be brought in any amounts but it must be declared and exchange receipts retained for reconversion when leaving the country. The official language is, of course, Polish and Russian and German are widely understood. Some French and English are also spoken.

All foreign trade is government controlled through the State Foreign Trade Enterprises who deal directly with foreign companies and who also issue the licenses needed for all imports. The issuance of an import licenses automatically makes foreign exchange available from the Foreign Trade Bank.

The Embassy of the Polish People's Republic is located at 2224 Wyoming Ave. NW, Washington, D.C. 20008, Tel. 202-234-3800. There are consulates in Chicago and New York.

The U.S. Embassy in Poland is located at Aleje Ujazdowskie 29-

31, 00-540 Warsaw, Poland, Tel. 283041. There is a U.S. consulate in Krakow.

For further information contact the Polish National Tourist Office, 500 Fifth Ave., New York, N.Y. 10036, Tel. 212-354-1487.

For additional business information contact the Polish Commercial Counselors Office, 1 Dag Hammarskjold Plaza, New York, N.Y. 10017, Tel. 212-486-3150.

POLICE OFFICERS: COMPLAINTS AGAINST

Most police departments have an inspector's office responsible for dealing with citizen complaints about police officers. The inspector's office generally investigates the complaints, determines whether they are justified and then takes appropriate disciplinary action against the police officer or officers. Such action can include reassignment, suspension, dismissal or criminal charges through the appropriate local prosecuting agency. If the complaint proves unfounded, the complaining citizen is notified and no further action is taken against the accused officer.

A citizen who feels that he or she has been the victim of criminal action by a police officer may also go to the local prosecuting agency or bring civil action against the officer or officers, against the police department, or the local government. In addition, alleged civil rights violations by local police agencies may be reported to the Federal Bureau of Investigation.

Contact the city or state police inspector's office or police department civilian review board; the U.S. Department of Justice, Civil Rights Division, Constitution Ave. at Tenth St. NW, Washington, D.C. 20530, Tel.: 202-633-2000; or the FBI, Ninth St. and Pennsylvania Ave. NW, Washington, D.C. 20535, Tel. 202-324-3000.

POLICE OFFICERS: RECRUITMENT

Police officers in the United States are generally employed by local police departments, each with its own civil service regulations for hiring. Most cities require that applicants be 21 years of age and meet specific height and weight standards. Hiring of the particular applicant depends also on his or her performance on competitive examinations, including written tests and tests of strength and agility. Candidates are usually also interviewed, and are given personality tests by some police departments. Large police departments may want some college credits, although a degree is not usually required.

Obtain information about entrance requirements from the local police department or civil service commission. Information is also available from the International Association of Chiefs of Police, 11 Firstfield Road, Gaithersburg, Md. 20760, Tel. 301-948-0922.

POLICE OFFICERS: STATE

Each state has civil service regulations which govern the appointment of state police officers. Most require that applicants have a high school education or some college and be at least 21 years of age. Applicants must pass examinations, both written and tests of strength and agility. Both men and women must meet physical requirements of weight, height and eyesight. An applicant's character and background are also usually investigated.

For information about specific entrance requirements in a particular state, contact the state's civil service commission or state police headquarters, which are usually located in the state capital.

POLITICAL PARTIES

See individual political party entries

POLLUTION: AIR

The Environmental Protection Agency is responsible for policies and regulations on air pollution control. The agency develops national standards for air quality and hazardous emission standards for airplanes, automobiles and industry. It is also responsible for enforcement of its standards and regulations. For information contact the Environmental Protection Agency, Public Information Center, 401 M. St. SW, Washington, D.C. 20460, Tel. 202-755-0707.

POLLUTION: WATER AND SOLID WASTE

The Environmental Protection Agency develops national programs, technical policies and regulations for water and solid waste pollution control. The agency also provides technical assistance for regional programs. The enforcement office of the EPA plans and coordinates public hearings and other legal proceedings. Contact the Environmental Protection Agency, Public Information Center, 401 M St. SW, Washington, D.C. 20460, Tel. 202-755-0707.

The Land and Natural Resources Division of the U.S. Department of Justice is responsible for conducting law suits in both federal and state courts relating to protection of water purity in this country. Law suits may involve any water supply in the country. The Justice Department works closely with the EPA on decisions about any legal action. For further information contact the Department of Justice, Land and Natural Resources Division, Constitution Ave. and 10th St. NW, Washington, D.C. 20530, Tel. 202-633-2000.

See also: CONSERVATION, RESOURCES DAMAGED LAND AND WATER, HAZARDOUS MATERIALS: ACCIDENTS AND SPILLS

POPULATION

See CENSUS: POPULATION

PORTUGAL

A valid passport is required for travel to Portugal (which includes the Azores and the Madeira Islands). No visa is needed for a stay of up to 60 days. Those who plan to stay longer than 60 days must apply at the Portuguese Embassy or a consulate for a visa. The Embassy of Portugal is located at 2125 Kalorama Road NW, Washington, D.C. 20008, Tel. 202-265-1643. Consulates are located in Boston, New Bedford, New York, Newark, Philadelphia, Providence, and San Francisco. There are no vaccination certificates necessary for entry, but visitors are advised to get shots against cholera, typhoid and poliomyelitis. Those planning to bring a pet must apply before leaving at a Portuguese consulate with proof of required shots.

The monetary unit of Portugal is the escudo. Travelers may take up to 5,000 escudos in or out of the country along with any amount of foreign currency. This must be declared upon arrival. Portuguese is the official language, but English and French are often spoken in the major hotels and shops. For car rentals an International Driving License is required.

Trading with Portugal is usually handled through local agents who work on commission. The Bank of Portugal must authorize all exchange transactions. Import licenses are needed for goods costing over 5,000 escudos. These are issued by the Director General of Commerce. The Portuguese government has placed some restrictions on imports, usually luxury items.

The American Embassy in Portugal is located at Avenida Duque de Loule No. 39, 1098 Lisboa Codex, Lisbon, Tel. 570102, Telex 12528.

For further information contact the Portuguese National Tourist Office, 548 Fifth Avenue, New York, N.Y. 10036, Tel. 212-354-4403.

For additional business information contact the Portugal-U.S. Chamber of Commerce, 5 West 45 St., New York, N.Y. 10036, Tel. 212-354-4627.

POSTAGE METERS

Postage meters can be leased from government approved suppliers. Postage is then bought from the U.S. Postal Service at a local Post Office, where the meter is set to dispense the amount of postage purchased. For further information consult the local post office.

POSTAL RATES

The Postal Rate Commission makes recommendations to the U.S. Postal Service on postage rates and fees. It also notifies the Postal Service of complaints about postage rates, postal classifications, and other postal services. For further information and to register a complaint, contact the Postal Rate Commission, Officer of the Commission, 2000 L Street NW, Washington, D.C. 20268, Tel. 202-254-3800.

POSTAL SERVICE: COMPLAINTS AND SUGGESTIONS

Complaints and suggestions about local Post Office service can be referred to the main Post Office in a particular town. Other complaints and suggestions can be referred to the United States Postal Service, Consumer Advocate, 475 L'Enfant Plaza West SW, Washington, D.C. 20260, Tel. 202-245-4514.

POSTAL SERVICE: GUIDE

Postal regulations are contained in the Postal Service Manual and other publications of the Postal Service which are available from the Superintendent of Documents, Government Printing Office, Washington, D.C. 20402; Tel. 202-783-3238. Pamphlets on many post office services are offered free of charge at the local post offices.

POST OFFICE BOXES

Individuals and businesses can rent post office boxes at most U.S. Post Offices. Generally the renter receives a key or combination for the lock to the box. For further information consumers should contact the local post office where they wish to rent a box.

POST OFFICES

The U.S. Postal Service provides mail processing and delivery services for businesses and individuals in the United States, re-

ceives mail from abroad, and forwards mail from the United States to foreign countries. The Postal Service is also responsible for protecting the mails from loss or theft and for apprehending individuals who violate postal laws.

A consumer with a problem with mail service should complete a Consumer Service Card, which is available from letter carriers and post offices. The local postmaster or a designated assistant will contact the consumer upon receipt of the completed card.

If the problem cannot be resolved locally contact the Consumer Advocate, U.S. Postal Service, Washington, D.C. 20260, Tel. 202-245-4514.

POWER BOAT RACING

The American Power Boat Association is the governing body for the sport in the United States. It formulates rules, conducts regattas and certifies records. For further information contact the Association at 17640 Nine Mile Rd. East Detroit, Mich. 48021, Tel. 313-773-9700.

PRESBYTERIAN CHURCHES

Presbyterian churches follow the doctrines of John Calvin, one of the leading reformers of the Reformation. The Church is organized on a pyramidal hierarchy of courts composed of both ministers and laity. There are currently nine branches of the denomination with over 4 million members. For information on the church contact the United Presbyterian Church in the U.S.A., 475 Riverside Dr., New York, N.Y. 10115, Tel. 212-870-2515 or the Presbyterian Church in the United States, 341 Ponce de Leon Ave., NE Atlanta, Ga. 30308, Tel. 404-873-1531.

PRISONS: FEDERAL

The Bureau of Prisons operates a system of prisons for the custody and care of persons convicted of federal crimes and sentenced by the federal courts to serve time. The system has prisons varying from maximum to minimum security depending on the nature of the offense.

It also operates a series of community programs, runs medical, planning and development services and coordinates state and local correctional networks through staff development, the collection and dissemination of correctional information, technical assistance and policy formulation and coordination. For further information contact a regional office or the Bureau of Prisons, 320 First St. NW, Washington, D.C. 20534, Tel. 202-724-3198.

See also: PAROLE OR PARDON

PROBATE

When a person dies leaving a will, the will must be proven valid in court before its provisions can be carried out. This process is called probate. This first requires the notification of all persons who may inherit the deceased's property. Laws governing probate are

state laws, and the court that handles the process in each state varies. For example, in Texas it is the County Court, in New York State it is the Surrogate Court and in Massachusetts, the District Court. Generally, the court sits in the county in which the deceased resided. The procedure only moves to a higher state or federal court if there is evidence of fraud, a dispute between people residing in different states or various claims being made for taxes by different states. Once the will is certified in court and the necessary papers provided, the court then authorizes the executor of the will to carry out its provisions.

Wills that have been lost or wills that were made orally can be probated in some states if proof that the will was executed is provided.

Persons wishing to probate a will are advised to consult an attorney.

PRODUCT SAFETY: RETAILERS' RESPONSIBILITY

By federal law a retailer must report orally to the Consumer Product Safety Commission (CPSC) within 24 hours if he or she has reason to believe that a product being sold is in violation of an existing product safety rule or could pose a substantial risk of injury to the public. The oral report should be followed quickly by a written report. Manufacturers, importers, distributors and retailers must report unless they have actual knowledge that the CPSC has already been notified of the potential problem. Criminal penalties are not assessed against manufacturers, distributors and/or retailers unless it can be proved that a law or regulation was willfully violated after notification.

The CPSC may ask the retailer to identify purchasers of the product and tell them how they may return the item or have it fixed. Retailers can contact the Consumer Product Safety Commission through the Division of Product Defect Correction, Washington, D.C. 20234, Tel. 301-492-6608 or the Commission's Toll-free number, 800-683-2666 (in Maryland 800-492-2937).

See also: SAFETY: CONSUMER PRODUCTS

PROTESTANT EPISCOPAL CHURCH
See EPISCOPAL CHURCH

PSYCHOLOGISTS (IN PRIVATE PRACTICE)
The use of the title "psychologist in private practice" is restricted by all states to individuals who have been licensed or certified. Requirements include a doctoral degree in psychology, in counseling or in a closely related field, and a certain number of courses taken under licensed psychologists. Applicants for licensure also must have professional experience supervised by a licensed psychologist.

The American Board of Professional Psychology awards diplomas to indicate professional experience, merit and competence. Such a diploma is an option of the individual psychologist. Those with doctorates in clinical, counseling, industrial, organizational and school psychology, who have five years of experience and professional endorsements, and who pass an examination can qualify.

Individuals with a doctoral degree in psychology or in a closely allied field can be employed by organizations and institutions as psychologists even though they are not certified. Those with a master's degree in psychology can qualify as psychological assistants, administering and interpreting some kinds of psychological tests and performing counseling, usually under the supervision of a psychologist. If they have teaching experience they may also be hired as school counselors.

For specific state licensing requirements, contact the appropriate state agency listed under the state entry below.

A professional organization that sets professional standards and promotes psychologists' interests is the American Psychological Association, 1200 Seventeenth St. NW, Washington, D.C. 20036, Tel. 202-833-7600.

PUBLIC LANDS: PURCHASE BY PRIVATE CITIZENS
The Bureau of Land Management administers any sale of federally-owned public land. Relatively small parcels of land for

which there are not anticipated federal, state, local government or public needs are sold at auction by BLM. Auctions are announced in advance in area newspapers. Listings of public lands to be sold in the near future are carried in the Bureau of Land Management's quarterly *Our Public Lands.* Auctions are held at regional sites, not in Washington. The field office will have information about the auction sites.

Each parcel of land offered for sale is appraised by the government. It cannot be bought for less than the appraised price. By law, adjoining landowners can acquire a parcel offered for sale by either matching the highest bid or by paying three times the appraised price, whichever is less. All parcels of public lands sold by the bureau must be paid for in full at the time of sale.

Contact the regional office of the Bureau of Land Management located in Anchorage, Phoenix, Sacramento, Denver, Alexandria, Boise, Billings, Reno, Santa Fe, Portland, Salt Lake City and Cheyenne; or the Bureau of Land Management, Department of the Interior, Washington, D.C. 20240, Tel. 202-373-5717. Further information about specific parcels and a form for bidding are available from the field office for the state where the parcel is located. *Our Public Lands* can be ordered from the Government Printing Office, North Capitol and H St. NW, Washington, D.C. 20401, Tel. 202-275-2051.

Q

QUARANTINE: HUMAN

The U.S. Public Health Service administers a system of worldwide epidemic inspection of arriving persons, animals, and shipments at ports and airports having international traffic.

For more information contact a regional office of the Public Health Service in New York, Washington, Chicago, Atlanta, Kansas City, Dallas, Denver, or San Francisco. The regional offices are listed in the telephone directory under U.S. Government.

Or, contact the Center for Disease Control, U.S. Public Health Service 1600 Clifton Rd. NE, Atlanta, Ga. 30333, Tel. 404-283-3286

QUARANTINE: PLANT AND ANIMAL

See IMPORTS: PEST CONTROL

R

RADIATION

The Bureau of Radiological Health is the federal agency responsible for programs designed to reduce the exposure of man to hazardous ionizing and non-ionizing radiation. It develops standards for safe limits of radiation exposure and methodology for controlling radiation exposures.

In addition the agency conducts research on the health effects of radiation exposure. The Bureau is also concerned with emissions of radiation from electronic products and conducts an electronic product radiation control program. For further information contact the Food and Drug Administration, Bureau of Radiological Health, 5600 Fishers Lane, Rockville, Md. 20857, Tel. 301-443-3380.

RAILROAD ACCIDENTS

All railroad accidents in which there is a fatality or substantial property damage, or which involve a passenger train are investigated by the National Transportation Safety Board. The purpose of the investigation is to determine the probable cause of the accident so that transportation safety may be improved. The board publishes reports made to Congress on railroad accidents with recommendations for changes in equipment or practice. It has no enforcement powers.

During the investigation the board may hold a public hearing at which parties associated with the accident or the investigation are invited to testify. The board maintains a public docket in its headquarters, which contains all records of accident investigations. The docket is open to the public. The U.S. Department of Transportation may take action on the board's recommendations, such as issuing new guidelines for transportation safety or revoking licenses or certificates.

Contact the National Transportation Safety Board, 800 Independence Ave. SW, Washington, D.C. 20594, Tel. 202-472-6100.

RAILROADS

The Federal Railroad Administration (FRA) administers and enforces federal railroad safety rules and regulations. It also administers federal assistance to the railroads for passenger and freight services. For further information contact the Department of Transportation, Federal Railroad Administration, 400 Seventh St. SW, Washington, D.C. 20590, Tel. 202-426-0881.

RAILROAD TRAVEL: PASSENGER

Most of the nation's intercity rail passenger service is provided by The National Railroad Passenger Corporation (AMTRAK), a quasi-federal agency created in 1970 to provide a nationwide rail transportation policy and system.

Local and regional passenger service not part of AMTRAK'S network is regulated by the Interstate Commerce Commission to ensure that consumers have adequate transportation service at reasonable rates. Consumer problems for non-AMTRAK passenger service should be referred to a consumer representative for the railroad company concerned or to the Consumer Assistance Office, Interstate Commerce Commission,

Washington, D.C. 20423, Tel., toll free 800-424-9312, or 202-275-7806.

Contact the local AMTRAK office for information about routes and ticket prices. For consumer problems, contact a consumer relations officer at the local AMTRAK office or AMTRAK, Office of Consumer Relations, P.O. Box 2709, Washington, D.C. 20013, Tel. 202-383-2121. AMTRAK's administrative offices are at 400 North Capitol St. NW, Washington, D.C. 20001, Tel. 202-383-3000.

REAL ESTATE AGENTS AND BROKERS

All states require that real estate agents and brokers be licensed. The agent license is the basic qualification in the business. Certification levels are based on years of experience and further training. Brokers are qualified to manage a real estate office, while agents are not.

To qualify for an agent's license, the applicant must be a high school graduate, must be at least 18 years old and must pass a written state examination. The examination includes questions on basic real estate transactions and on laws affecting the sale of property. In addition, most states require that candidates for the general license must complete at least 30 hours of classroom instruction.

In most states a broker's license requires 90 hours of formal training in addition to experience in real estate usually one to three years. The experience requirement may be waived for those with a bachelor's degree in real estate.

Contact the state real estate commission, usually located in the state capital, for specific licensure requirements.

REAL ESTATE: INTERSTATE LAND SALES

Certain developers who sell land through interstate commerce or the mails are required to register with the Office of Interstate Land Sales Registration. Such developers are also required to furnish each purchaser with a copy of an approved Property Report in advance of the time that they sign the sales contract. For further information contact the Department of Housing and Urban Development, Assistant Secretary for Neighborhoods, Voluntary Associations and Consumer Protection, Office of Interstate Land Sales Registration, HUD Building, Washington, D.C. 20410, Tel. 202-755-5860.

RECORDS: PUBLIC AND HISTORICAL

Public records such as land deeds, police arrests, birth certificates, and death certificates are available to the public generally at the county courthouse.

Census records are available from the Bureau of the Census.

Government files not dealing with matters of national security are available under the Freedom of Information Act.

See INFORMATION: FREEDOM OF

Income tax records and social security records are not available except to the individual involved.

See also specific entry records on the type of record involved.

See: CENSUS: POPULATION.

REHABILITATION

States generally have rehabilitation commissions that offer services to individuals who have a physical or mental disability which causes a substantial handicap to employment and for which vocational rehabilitation services may be reasonably expected to help employability. Examples of disabilities are mental illness, mental retardation, neurological disorders, amputations, speech or hearing limitations, heart ailments, epilepsy, cerebral palsy, diabetes, arthritis, tuberculosis, alcoholism, and drug addiction.

Services available include evaluation to determine the nature and degree of disability, assessment of work potential; counseling; interpreter services for the deaf; medical treatment; assistive devices such as artificial limbs, braces, wheelchairs, and hearing aids; training in a trade school, business school, college or university, on the job, or at home; room, board, and transportation during rehabilitation; placement and follow-up to ensure job success. Services may be available depending on economic need.

Contact the regional or state office of the state rehabilitation commission.

REHABILITATION COUNSELORS

Many jobs for rehabilitation counselors require a master's degree in rehabilitation counseling or vocational counseling, but some persons are hired with the B.A. degree if they have related work experience.

The Commission on Rehabilitation Counselor Certification offers certification for rehabilitation counselors. This is required by some private organizations who hire counselors. For further information contact the Commission on Rehabilitation Counselor Certification, 520 North Michigan Ave., Chicago, Ill. 60611, Tel. 312-236-4499.

RELIGION:

See specific denominations

REPUBLICAN PARTY

The central organization for the Republican Party is the Republican National Committee. It handles the national affairs of the party such as setting up conventions, assisting the Presidential election committee and helping state and local Republicans in election campaigns. The Committee is composed of three representatives from each state, the state chairman, a committeeman and a committeewoman. The Committee chairman is the head of the Republican Party when there is no Republican Party President. Each state has a Republican party organization with offices in capitals and major cities.

The Republican National Committee is located at 310 First St. SE, Washington, D.C. 20003, Tel. 202-484-6638.

RETIREMENT PLANS

Beginning in 1982 all Americans can set up their own retirement plans by setting aside a portion of their income in an Individual Retirement Account (IRA). These plans are independent of company pensions, social security, etc. Once in the fund, the money collects interest but neither the money nor the interest can be touched until the individual is 59 and one half years old without incurring substantial penalties. The money in the fund is not taxed until it is withdrawn, presumably at retirement, when the individual's income is smaller and tax burden, therefore, proportionately lighter.

Many savings institutions, banks, securities dealers, insurance firms, and trade and professional associations offer these plans. Information about the tax advantages is available from the local savings institutions, local Internal Revenue Service offices or from the Department of the Treasury, Internal Revenue Services Headquarters, Public Affairs Division, 1111 Constitution Ave. NW, Washington, D.C. 20224, Tel. (toll free) 800-492-4830.

REUNION

See FRANCE

RHODE ISLAND

Consumer complaints in Rhode Island can be referred to the Consumer Unit of the Public Protection Division within the Department of Attorney General. After the consumer contacts the Consumer Unit by phone or by mail, an investigator will evaluate the complaint and if it is under their jurisdiction, the investigator will forward a complaint form to the consumer. When the consumer returns the completed form, the investigator will send it to the business involved along with a letter from the Consumer Unit. The investigator will keep in contact with both parties in the dispute by phone and letter to help resolve the dispute.

If the problem is not resolved, the two parties will be asked to come to a consumer unit office to discuss the complaint with the Director of Medication and Arbitration to obtain a satisfactory informal resolution of the complaint. If Consumer Unit efforts fail to resolve the complaint, the office will advise the consumer to file in small claims court.

The Consumer Unit may file a class action suit on behalf of the complainants if there have been a number of complaints about a particular business.

The Consumer Unit also monitors virtually all advertisements in the state newspapers for possible violations of the Deceptive Trade Practices Act. When deceptive advertising is discovered, the business is contacted and given an opportunity to change promotional materials. If changes are not made voluntarily, the staff attorney in the Consumer Unit may decide to institute legal proceedings.

Contact the Consumer Unit, Department of the Attorney General, 72 Pine St., Providence, R.I. 02903, Tel. 401-277-3163. Regional offices are located in Woonsocket, Kent County, and South County.

The Department of Business Regulation in Rhode Island regulates certain businesses and professions operating in the state. The Department issues licenses, investigates and resolves consumer complaints, and is responsible for enforcement of statues pertaining to licensing.

The department issues the following licenses for businesses and professions: Accountants, autobody repair shops, automobile wrecking and auto salvage yards, surplus line brokers, insurance appraisers and solicitors, burglar alarm businesses and alarm installers, travel agencies and agents, credit unions, loan companies, savings banks, trust companies, general lenders, second mortgage lenders, small loan lenders, loan and investment companies, securities brokers and salesmen, franchisers, charitable organizations, insurance agents and sub-agents, insurance brokers, insurance solicitors, insurance adjusters, brewery manufacturers, wholesale beer and wine dealers, wholesale liquor

dealers, wineries, marine vessel, alcoholic beverage dispensers, liquor salesmen and agents, real estate brokers, real estate salesmen, interstate land sales, upholstery manufacturers, upholstery supply dealers, upholstery repairers, second-hand dealers, hearing aid dealers and fitters.

The Department regulates these businesses and professions primarily to insure the protection of the public in its general business affairs. It ensures that persons issued licenses are qualified to practice their business specialty before the public. Direct inquiries or complaints to the Rhode Island Department of Business Regulation, Office of the Director, 100 North Main St., Providence, R.I. 02903.

Rhode Island has enacted several state business tax incentives. Out of state sales are eliminated in the formula to determine taxable income. An investment tax credit of 2% is allowed on the cost of tangible personal property and other property including buildings used in the production process of manufacturing. Corporations are allowed an operating loss deduction similar to that indicated under Section 172 of the Internal Revenue Code of 1954. An elective deduction for new research and development facilities allows the entire cost to be written off in one year. Domestic International Sales Corporations (DISC) are treated as they are under federal income tax laws, sales tax elimination on manufacturers' machinery and equipment, and local property tax elimination. For further information about Rhode Island corporate taxes, contact the Rhode Island Division of Taxation, Corporations Section, 289 Promenade St., Providence, R.I. 02908. Tel. 401-277-3061.

Rhode Island currently has a state income tax of approximately 19% on individuals, proprietorships, partnerships and other unincorporated businesses. Domestic corporations are subject to one of three taxes: net income, new worth, or corporate franchise, whichever yields the highest amount. The corporate franchise tax does not apply to foreign corporations.

Net income of corporations is taxable at 8%, corporate net worth is taxable at $4.00 per $1,000, and corporate franchise is taxable at $2.50 per $10,000 of authorized capital stock.

In Rhode Island a 6% sales tax is applied to retail sales of tangible personal property, with the principal exceptions of grocery foods, clothing, manufacture, periodicals, drugs, gas, electric, water and fuel bills for residential use and certain items subject to special tax such as gasoline or cigarettes.

Employers in Rhode Island must pay unemployment insurance tax of 3.7% on the first $6,000 paid in wages to each worker in a calendar year, temporary disability tax of 1.5% of the first $4,800 in wages paid to each worker in a calendar year.

The Business and Industry Division of the Rhode Island Department of Economic Development provides a management consulting and advisory service to small business firms in Rhode Island, including principal who wish to start a new business venture. Write or call the Department of Economic Development, One Weybosset Hill, Providence, R.I. 02903, Tel. 401-277-2601. Contact the Chamber of Commerce at 206 Smith St., Providence, R.I. 02908, Tel. 401-272-1400.

Tourist information can be requested from the Tourist Promotion Division, Department of Economic Development, One Weybossett Hill, Providence, R.I. 02903, Tel. 401-277-2614.

RIDING: DISABLED PERSONS

The North American Riding for the Handicapped Association, Inc. promotes horseback riding as a therapeutic and recreational tool for the handicapped. The organization brings together medical professionals, riding instructors, teachers and interested people of all backgrounds as well as the handicapped people who participate in the program. For further information contact the Association at P.O. Box 100, Ashburn, Va. 22011, Tel. 703-471-1621.

RIFLERY

The National Board for Promotion of Rifle Practice, an agency of the U.S. Army, provides free and low-cost ammunition to junior rifle clubs and also lends them rifles. To qualify the club must be a legitimate rifle club with at least ten members from 12 to 19 years of age. The club must have three adult leaders who can pass a low-level national security check. It must also have access to a rifle range. College rifle clubs also qualify and undergraduates may participate regardless of age.

For further information contact the National Board for Promotion of Rifle Practice, Director of Civilian Marksmanship, Pulaski Bldg., Rm. 1205, 20 Massachusetts Ave. NW, Washington, D.C. 20314, Tel. 202-272-0810.

ROMAN CATHOLIC CHURCH

The Roman Catholic Church is the largest single Christian body in the United States with almost 50 million members. It is organized hierarchically into parishes and dioceses. The head of the church is the Pope in Rome. The National Conference of Catholic Bishops coordinates national and interdioscesan activities. For further information contact the organization at 1312 Massachusetts Ave. NW, Washington, D.C. 20005, Tel. 202-659-6600.

ROMANIA

A passport and a visa are necessary for U.S. citizens traveling to Romania for a stay of up to two months. Visas may be obtained either at a Romanian consulate or at the border upon arrival. For business travelers a visa is necessary along with a letter from their company detailing the nature of business to be conducted and confirming financial responsibility for the visa applicant. There are no health requirements for entry but typhoid shots are recommended. Pets may be brought into Romania with a veterinarian's health certificate. The local currency is the leu (or plural—lei). The import or export of lei is strictly prohibited. There is no limit, however, on the amount of foreign currency that may be taken in or out of the country. The official language is, of course, Romanian, but some English, French and German are also spoken. To drive a car, an International Driving License is required.

Foreign trade is government controlled by the State Foreign Trade Enterprises. These organizations deal directly with foreign companies and are also responsible for issuing import licenses which are required for all goods. They receive foreign currency from the Ministry of Foreign Trade to pay for imported goods. Those planning to do business with Romania can contact the Office of the Economic Counselor of the Romanian Embassy at 200 East 38 St., New York, N.Y. 10016, Tel. 212-682-9120.

The Embassy of Romania is located at 1607 23rd St. NW, Washington, D.C. 20008, Tel. 202-232-4748.

For further information contact the Romanian National Tourist Office 573 Third Ave., New York, N.Y. 10016, Tel. 212-697-6971.

ROWING

The National Rowing Foundation financially supports Americans participating in international regattas. The foundation sends a full national team to European and world championship regattas. Contact the foundation at P.O. Box 6030, Arlington, Va. 22206, Tel. 703-379-2974.

RUGBY FOOTBALL

Rugby football in the United States is governed by the United States of America Rugby Football Union Ltd. (USARFU), which was formed in Chicago in 1975. Four territorial unions comprise the USARFU: the Eastern Rugby Union of America, Inc.; the Midwest Rugby Football Union; the Pacific Coast Rugby Football Union; and, the Western Rugby Football Union of the United States. Each of the territorial unions has from between three and 13 local unions. The local clubs have a total of about 850 members. Each territorial union elects four directors to the USARFU board of directors and has four votes at all meetings. Each territorial union also has one of its directors as an officer and member of the executive committee.

The USARFU has regulatory power but does not set rules for the game. Rules are developed by the International Rugby Football Board. However, the USARFU sets rules for tours by domestic and visiting rugby teams, for tournaments and for national championships. National championships are conducted at three levels: the National Club championship; the National Collegiate championship and the National Military championship. The USARFU also governs the inter-territorial championship between the four member unions. The USARFU has an office at 27 East State St., Sherburne, N.Y., 13460, Tel. 607-334-9946.

RUNAWAYS

Operation Peace of Mind offers 24 hour message relay services to runaways. Runaways can call the toll-free number without any obligation and ask that a message be called to their parents. Operation Peace of Mind also provides runaways with referral information on medical assistance and shelter. The program is funded by the State of Texas but operates throughout the United States. Call 800-231-6946; in Texas call 800-392-3352; in Alaska and Hawaii call 800-231-6762.

The Department of Health, and Human Resources Funds a free and confidential private service to runaways and parents 24 hours a day. The toll-free telephone number is 800-621-4000. In Illinois call 800-972-6004.

S

SAFETY: AT WORK

Occupational Safety and Health Administration (OSHA) regulations require that all employees have the right to receive information on safety and health hazards at work. They are also entitled to access to the employer's log of job-related injuries and illnesses. Medical records of toxic exposure must be preserved and access granted to employees for five years after the duration of employment.

Employee complaints about safety and health hazards at work or the refusal of employers to provide access to their records of job-related injuries and illnesses should be reported to OSHA. Employees can file a formal complaint and request an inspection of their workplace. If the agency finds a violation, it asks for immediate correction. Failure to act will result in daily files for noncompliance. Generally, OSHA is concerned only with hazards that may cause physical hardship or death. If OSHA decides not to investigate, employees have the right to request a hearing. Complaints by workers are kept confidential.

Contact OSHA at one of its regional offices located in major cities throughout the country or through the Department of Labor, 200 Constitution Ave. NW, Washington, D.C. 20210, Tel. 202-523-8165.

See also: WORKER'S COMPENSATION

SAFETY: CONSUMER PRODUCTS

The Consumer Product Safety Commission (CPS) is responsible for establishing mandatory product safety standards and giving the public information on product safety for over 10,000 objects in and around the home. The agency also regulates the safety packaging of certain hazardous household products and drugs. The agency does not regulate medicine, automobiles, food, drugs, cosmetics, airplanes, tobacco, firearms, alcohol or pesticides. The CPS does not act on individual consumer complaints. Complaints are put into a data base. If a product receives enough complaints, the agency will investigate and ask for a national recall if necessary. The agency also gives information on how to use products safely. For further information contact the Consumer Product Safety Commission, 111 Eighteenth St. NW, Washington, D.C. 20207. The agency maintains a Toll-free number for complaints: 800-638-8326.

See also: PRODUCT SAFETY: RETAILERS' RESPONSIBILITY; POISON PREVENTION PACKAGING

SAFETY: JOB
See SAFETY: AT WORK; WORK-ER'S COMPENSATION

SAILING
See BOATING: RECREATION-AL, YACHT RACING.

ST. BARTHELEMY
See FRENCH WEST INDIES

ST. LUCIA
Proof of citizenship is required for travel to St. Lucia as well as a return ticket and sufficient funds for the stay. Neither a passport or visa is necessary. Business travelers may need a work permit obtainable from the Ministry of Labour, Government Headquarters, Castries, St. Lucia. The fee for this permit is 10 East Caribbean dollars (the local currency). There are no health requirements if arriving from the U.S. or another Caribbean island, but smallpox vaccinations are needed if coming from another area and a yellow fever innoculation if arriving from an infected area. All pets are subject to quarantine on the island. There are no restrictions on the amount of currency allowed in or out of St. Lucia, but business travelers must declare all funds upon arrival. Travelers can drive on the island with an International Driving License. The official language is English.

Trade with St. Lucia is conducted under a general import license which covers most items.

There are few foreign exchange restrictions.

The government of St. Lucia has no embassy in Washington but there is a mission in New York. The St. Lucia Permanent Mission to the U.N. is located at 41 East 42nd St., New York, N.Y. 10017, Tel. 212-697-9360. For further tourist information contact the St. Lucia Tourist Board at the same address, Tel. 212-867-2950. The St. Lucia National Development Corp. is also at that address; Tel. 212-867-2952.

ST. MARTIN
See FRENCH WEST INDIES

ST. PIERRE & MIQUELON
See FRANCE

ST. VINCENT
Proof of citizenship is required for travel to St. Vincent as well as a return ticket and sufficient funds for the stay. Neither a passport or visa is necessary. There are no health requirements if arriving from the U.S. or other Caribbean islands, but smallpox vaccinations are needed if coming from another area and a yellow fever innoculation if traveling from an infected region. All pets are subject to quarantine on the island. The monetary unit used in St. Vincent is the East Caribbean dollar. There are no restrictions on currency allowed in or out of the island, but business travelers must declare all money upon arrival. English is the official language. Travelers can

drive in St. Vincent with an International Driving License.

Trade with St. Vincent is conducted under a general import license which covers most items. There are few foreign exchange restrictions.

The only representative of the government of St. Vincent in the United States is the St. Vincent Mission, 41 East 42 St., Suite 606, New York, N.Y. 10017, Tel. 212-687-4490.

For further tourist information contact St. Vincent Tourist Information, 220 East 42 St., New York, N.Y. 10017, Tel. 212-986-9370.

SALESMEN: DOOR-TO-DOOR

The Direct Selling Association adjusts complaints against its members and will try to deal with problems involving nonmembers. It also provides a listing of firms belonging to the Association, which has a strong code of ethics. For further information contact the Direct Selling Association, Code of Ethics Administrator, 1730 M St. NW, Washington, D.C. 20036, Tel. 293-5760.

SAVINGS AND LOAN ASSOCIATIONS

State-chartered savings and loan associations are regulated and supervised by a state savings and loan department, which is usually part of the state finance commission.

The department initiates corrective measures against savings and loan associations or their officers found in apparent malpractice or violation of the law.

Contact the state banking division, savings and loan department for complaints or further information.

SAVINGS AND LOAN ASSOCIATIONS: REGULATION

The Federal Home Bank Board regulates savings and loan associations. It also operates the Federal Savings and Loan Insurance Corp. (FSLIC) which insures savings accounts in FSLIC insured institutions. The Board, through the Federal Home Loan Bank System, provides reserve credit for the savings and loan associations, as the Federal Reserve System does for banks. For further information contact the Director, Office of Communications, Federal Home Loan Bank Board, 1700 G Street NW, Washington, D.C. 20552, Tel. 202-377-6680.

SAVINGS BONDS

The United States Government promotes the sale of savings bonds to the public. They can be purchased from post offices in areas where there are no banks or other issuing agencies. Contact a local bank or post office for information about the purchase of U.S. Savings Bonds. For further information contact the Treasury Department, United States Savings Bonds Division, 111 20th St. NW, Washington, D.C. 20226, Tel. 202-634-5350.

SCHOOL LUNCH PROGRAM

The federally funded School Lunch Program provides financial assistance to public and non-profit private schools in all grades through high school to operate non-profit school lunch programs. The intention of the program is to provide meals to all school children, with meals available free or at reduced cost to children from needy families.

The School Breakfast Program supports schools in providing nutritional breakfasts, especially for students from needy families, who receive meals free or at reduced costs. For further information contact the Department of Agriculture, Food and Nutrition Service, 14th St. and Independence Ave. SW, Washington, D.C. 20250; 202-447-9065.

SCHOOL RECORDS: PARENT'S ACCESS TO

Under the Family Rights and Privacy Act of 1974, if a school receives funds from the Department of Education (which most schools and colleges do) parents and students over age 18 have the right to see the child's school record. If the record contains inaccurate or unfair comments, the parent can ask to have them removed. If the school is unwilling to make the change, the parent can request a hearing with a school official who was not involved in the placement of the comments on the record. The parent can also write a rebuttal to the comments which must be included in the record and be attached to the disputed material.

If parents have no success getting the school to comply with the Family Rights and Privacy Act, they should write the Department Health and Human Services, Room 514 E., South Portal Building, Washington, D.C. 20201, Tel. 202-245-7488.

SCHOOLS: ADMISSION, EXCLUSION AND EXPULSION

In the United States it is generally the duty of the parents to enroll a child in a school at age six as required by state law. The child may go either to a public school as directed by the school district, or to a private school. In many school districts the parents have the option of enrolling the child in public kindergarten at or near age five.

If the family moves out of the area served by a particular school, the child may be transferred either by notifying the former school to send school records, or by going to the new school to enroll and requesting that the new school request the child's school records.

Children may be required to attend a school in the same city but out of the neighborhood so that school integration can be achieved. In order for the child to attend public school, the child must attend the school directed by the school district. Individual school districts make policy regarding expulsion or suspension from school. Children generally are required to have immunizations before they can enroll in school.

Check with the local school district superintendent's office for policy questions.

SCHOOLS: MANAGEMENT

In the United States local school districts have management authority for their schools. Educational policy is set by the local school board, which directs the school district. The federal government, however, has authority over the local schools in a number of areas. The Department of Education provides federal funds to local districts. If the school districts refuse to comply with federal guidelines, the Department of Education can cut off federal funds.

In the case of school integration, the U.S. Supreme Court has intervened to assure compliance with federal laws even in states where segregated schools were allowed by state law.

State laws also affect local schools, setting minimum standards for teacher education, building facilities, etc.

Schools are subject to state health department inspections, and can be closed if the lavatories, kitchens and other facilities constitute a health hazard. Schools are also subject to local fire codes and can be closed if they do not

comply with them. Contact the local school district, state education department or the Department of Education, Federal Office Building 6, 400 Maryland Ave. SW, Washington, D.C. 20202, Tel. 202-655-4000.

SCHOOLS: PRIVATE

General policies of private schools are regulated by the state board of education and the U.S. Department of Education. Schools not receiving public funding, however, do have considerable freedom in the curricula and course content. They cannot discriminate on the basis of sex, race or national origin in admissions or treatment of students. Complaints about discrimination can be made either to the state board of education or the U.S. Department of Education.

A public school counselor may be able to offer suggestions about local private schools.

The Advisory Service on Private Schools is a private agency that can supply in-depth information on a private school's academic character, curriculum, class sizes, faculty, extracurricular activities and type of students. The Advisory Service will, upon request, send a questionaire to interested families on factors important to the family. It will then provide information about suitable schools at no cost to the family.

Contact The Advisory Service on Private Schools Inc., 500 Fifth

Ave., New York, N.Y. 10036, Tel. 212-944-6200.

SCOTLAND
See UNITED KINGDOM

SCUBA DIVING AND SKIN DIVING

All scuba and skin divers and instructors must be certified. Those interested in scuba divers on instructors should contact the Professional Association of Diving Instructors (PADI), 2064 N. Bush St., Santa Ana, Calif., 92706, Tel. 714-547-6996, or the National Association of Underwater Instructors Association (NAUI), P.O. Box 630, Colton, Calif. 92324, Tel. 714-824-5440, both of which certify instructors and maintain lists of local facilities which use certified instructors. Local authorized scuba facilities offer divers' certification through training programs.

The national organization for recreational scuba and skin diving is the Underwater Society of America (USA), 732 50th St., West Palm Beach Fla. 33407, Tel. 304-844-1124. The USA sponsors national competitions and awards scholarships. They also publish a quarterly newsletter, the Underwater Reporter.

SECURITIES: GOVERNMENT

The U.S. government offers for sale Treasury bills, notes and bonds through a Federal Reserve Bank or branch or through the Department of the Treasury, Bureau of the Public Debt. Securities can also be bought through financial institutions, such as banks, brokers and other dealers in government securities. They can be bought either at the time of issue or after issue but before maturity. Securities sold before maturity are sold at the prevailing market price.

Treasury bills are sold as short-term obligations, which mature in 13 weeks to one year. The bills are sold on a discount basis, which means that the buyer pays less than the face value of the bill but collects the face value at maturity. They are generally offered in $10,000 minimum issues.

Treasury notes mature in one to 10 years, and bonds after 10 years. Some longer-term bonds redeemable before maturity at the option of the U.S. Treasury. Notes maturing in less than four years are usually offered in minimum issues of $5000. Notes maturing in more than four years and all bonds are usually available in minimum issues of $1000.

Treasury bills, notes and bonds can be bought directly from the government at auction. Applicants submit bids either competitively or noncompetitively. Competitive bidders submit bids or tenders in terms of an annual interest rate yield such as 7.11%. Noncompetitive bidders do not specify a price, but agree to purchase the notes or bonds at the weighed average yield of accepted competitive bids. The actual interest rate of the securities, therefore, is not selected by the government but is set by the market through the auction process. Most individuals who do not follow the Treasury securities market closely submit noncompetitive bids or buy through a financial institution such as a bank or a broker.

Tender or bid forms for Treasury securities are available through any Federal Reserve Bank or branch, or at the Bureau of the Public Debt. Tender forms should be sent to the nearest Federal Reserve Bank or branch or to the Bureau of the Public Debt. Treasury securities may be redeemed at maturity for face value at any Federal Reserve Bank or branch, or at the Bureau of the Public Debt.

For further information contact the Office of Public Affairs, Board of Governors, Federal Reserve System, Washington, D.C. 20551, Tel. 202-452-3204; or the Department of the Treasury, Bureau of the Public Debt, Washington, D.C. 20226; Tel. 202-376-0249 or one of the Federal Reserve Banks in the following cities:

Boston, Massachusetts: 600 Atlantic Ave. 02106

New York, N.Y.: 33 Liberty St. (Federal Reserve P.O. Station) 10045

Philadelphia, Pa.: 100 North Sixth St. (P.O. Box 90) 19105

Cleveland, Ohio: 1455 East Sixth St. (P.O. Box 6387) 44101

Richmond, Va.: 701 East Byrd St. (P.O. Box 27622) 23261

Atlanta, Ga.: 104 Marietta St. NW, 30303

Chicago, Ill.: 230 South La Salle St. (P.O. Box 834) 60690

St. Louis, Mo.: 411 Locust St. (P.O. Box 442) 63166

Minneapolis, Minn.: 250 Marquette Ave. 55480

Kansas City, Mo.: 925 Grand Ave. (Federal Reserve Station) 64198

Dallas, Texas: 400 South Akard St. (Station K) 75222

San Francisco, Calif.: 400 Sansome St. (P.O. Box 7702) 94120

SECURITIES INDUSTRY

The Securities and Exchange Commission regulates the selling of stocks, bonds and other types of securities. The agency supervises the stock exchanges and persons in the security business as well as investment counselors. The SEC publishes data on the exchanges and industry and compiles financial reports and other information about the securities traded. The SEC's Office of Consumer Affairs assists investors with questions about their rights in the market and dealings with brokers. Complaints about possible fraud in the sale of securities should be addressed to the commission or its regional offices. However, like most federal agencies, it does not generally investigate individual complaints. If a pattern of improper action develops the agency will investigate a firm and, if it finds improper action take appropriate action. These actions include obtaining court orders to prevent continuation of fraudulent practices, revoking licenses of securities dealers, expelling from the exchanges those found guilty of fraud and revoking the privilege of practicing law before the Commission. For further information contact the SEC at 500 North Capitol St. NW, Washington, D.C. 20549, Tel. 202-272-2000.

See also: SECURITIES: SALES WORKERS

SECURITIES: SALES WORKERS

Most states require persons who sell securities to be licensed. Applicants for licensing generally must pass an examination and furnish a personal bond. In addition, sales workers must generally register as representatives of their firms according to the regulations of the security exchanges where they do business or the National Association of Securities Dealers Inc. To qualify for registration the worker must pass the Securities and Exchange Commission's General Securities Examination or examinations prepared by the exchanges or the National Association of Securities Dealers. For further information consult the state securities board or commission, the particular exchanges or the National Association of Securities Dealers, 1735 K St. NW, Washington, D.C. 20006, Tel. 202-833-7200.

Stock brokers and dealers who sell securities over the counter must register and are regulated by the Securities and Exchange Com-

mission. Contact the Securities and Exchange Commission, 500 North Capitol Street, Washington, D.C. 20549, Tel. 202-755-4846.

Complaints about securities dealers can be referred to the National Association of Securities Dealers which will attempt to resolve the case, or if necessary, turn it over to the proper government regulatory agency. For further information contact the National Association of Security Dealers, 1735 K St. NW, Washington, D.C. 20006, Tel. 202-833-7200.

SECURITIES REPORTS

Corporation reports and statements filed with the Securities and Exchange Commission can be obtained from the Securities and Exchange Commission, Public Reference Section, 1100 L St. NW, Washington, D.C. 20549, Tel. 202-523-5360.

SEPARATION

A couple, on its own, cannot enter into a valid agreement to dissolve their marriage. However, they can make a separation agreement which is generally given full force by courts in most states, providing there is no fraud or duress. Usually a separation agreement can encompass everything a court would consider in issuing a divorce decree: provisions for living apart without interference from the other spouse, property settlement, arrangements for support payments and child custody, etc. A separation agreement must be by mutual consent. If one party fails to agree to the separation, only a court, with proper grounds, can force a separation. Generally separation agreements reached by mutual consent are more simple to expedite and are more flexible than court issued separation orders during which grounds for the separation must be proved. No such grounds are needed in a mutual consent separation agreement.

A separation agreement does not obligate either party to eventually obtain a divorce. A separation agreement should be looked upon only as a temporary remedy unless a person's religious beliefs prohibit divorce. Then it may be considered among the parties as a permanent solution. It does not free either party to remarry. Terms of separation agreements may be incorporated in later divorce proceedings.

Both parties are advised to have legal counsel in drafting a separation agreement.

See also: DIVORCE

SENEGAL

A valid passport and a visa are required for U.S. citizens traveling to Senegal. To obtain a visa travelers will need three photos and a return ticket. The fee is $5.10. The visa is good for a stay of up to three months. A yellow fever shot is required for entry; and protection against cholera, typhoid and malaria is advisable. Pets can be brought into the country but re-

quire proof of a rabies shot. The local currency is the CFA franc. Its import or export is limited to 25,000. Any amount of foreign currency may be brought into the country, but it must be declared and no more taken out than was brought in. French is the official language of Senegal; Wolof and Fulani are among the local languages also spoken there. To drive a car an International Driving License is required.

Foreign trade is usually handled through local agents or French companies with representatives in Senegal. Some imports require licenses and exchange controls are in effect.

The Embassy of Senegal is located at 2112 Wyoming Ave. NW, Washington, D.C. 20008, Tel. 202-234-0540. There is a consulate in New York but it does not issue visas.

The U.S. Embassy in Senegal is located at B.P. 49, Avenue Jean XXIII, Dakar, Senegal, Tel. 20206.

SEVENTH-DAY ADVENTISTS

The Seventh-Day Adventists have over three million adult members in 21,000 organized churches with 9,000 ordained ministers.

Officers and departmental directors of the World Headquarters are elected every five years in general session of the world delegates. The church is divided into 11 divisions, each with its own officers and departmental secretaries, also elected at the general session. The divisions are: North American,

Africa-Indian Ocean, Afro-Mid-eastern, Australasian, Euro-African, Far Eastern, Inter-American, Northern European, South American, Southern Asian, Trans-African.

Each division is comprised of two or more union conferences. In the United States, unions cover a state or several states, depending on the number of church members. Unions are then divided into conferences, which have direct responsibility for church and evangelistic work within the area. Officers of the conferences are elected biennially by delegates from the churches within its territory. There are now 60 conferences in the North American Division. Congregations govern themselves through officers nominated by a committee and elected by the members of the church. Ministers are appointed by the conference.

The church World Headquarters is at 6840 Eastern Ave. NW, Takoma Park, Washington, D.C. 20012, Tel. 202-722-6000.

SERVICE CORPS OF RETIRED EXECUTIVES (SCORE)
See BUSINESS: ADVISORY SERVICES

SHIP RATES AND SANITATION
See CRUISE SHIPS: RATES; CRUISE SHIPS: SANITATION

SHIPS: SAFETY
The Coast Guard is responsible for enforcing safety standards for the design, construction and maintenance of commercial vessel in United States waters. It also investigates all marine accidents involving these vessels. For further information contact the local Coast Guard office or the U.S. Coast Guard, Washington, D.C. 20593, Tel. 202-426-2158.

SINGAPORE
A valid passport and a round trip ticket are required for U.S. citizens traveling to Singapore for a stay of up to two months. There are no health requirements for entry unless arriving from an infected area. Pets are subject to quarantine if brought into the country. The local currency is the Singapore dollar. There are no limits on the amounts of local or foreign currency that may be taken in or out of Singapore. Many languages are spoken; the official ones are Malay, Mandarin Chinese and Tamil. In addition, English, various Chinese dialects and a number of Indian and Pakistani dialects are used. To drive a car, an International Driving License is required. Travelers should note that males with long hair may be denied entry into Singapore.

Trading with Singapore is generally handled through local agents. There are no licenses required and there are no exchange controls.

The Embassy of Singapore is located at 1824 R St. NW, Washington, D.C. 20009, Tel. 202-667-7555.

The U.S. Embassy in Singapore is located at 30 Hill St., Singapore, Tel. 30251.

For additional tourist information contact the Singapore Tourist Promotion Board, 342 Madison Ave., New York, N.Y. 10017, Tel. 212-687-0385.

For business information contact the Singapore Trade Office, 745 Fifth Ave., New York, N.Y. 10151, Tel. 212-421-2207.

SKATEBOARDING

The International Skateboard Association (ISA) standardizes rules of the sport, promotes safety in skateboarding and disseminates information on skateboarding. It also maintains a library on skateboarding information. Contact the International Skateboard Association, 5466 Complex St., Unit 207, San Diego, Calif. 92123, Tel. 714-565-1616.

SMALL BUSINESS ADMINISTRATION

See BUSINESS: ADVISORY SERVICES; BUSINESS: COMPLIANCE LOANS; BUSINESS: LEASE GUARANTEES; BUSINESS: MINORITY FEDERAL ASSISTANCE; BUSINESS: OVERSEAS; BUSINESS: PROCUREMENT ASSISTANCE; BUSINESS LOANS: RURAL; BUSINESS LOANS: SMALL BUSINESS

SMALL CLAIMS COURTS

Small claims courts are a judicial forum for the resolution of disputes involving small amounts of money. The limit of a suit in small claims court varies from a low of $100 to around $3000, depending on state law, with the average being $500. Anyone can be sued in a small claims court as long as the person or business lives or does business in that state.

Procedures in a small claims court are simple, inexpensive and informal. Neither party in a suit needs an attorney, and in some courts attorneys are not allowed. In most cases individuals must sue through the small claims court in the county precinct where the person or the business being sued is located, but there are exceptions, such as if the person performs work or services in another county.

Court fees range from $2 to $15. The filing fee is sometimes refunded if the suit is successful. The trial in a small claims court consists of the presentation of evidence by the plaintiff and the defendant. Both sides have a right to question all witnesses. The judge may also ask questions. Though court procedures are informal, the ruling of the court is binding, just as in any other court.

If the defendant loses the case and refuses to pay voluntarily, the plaintiff may have to go back to court to ask for the judge's order to be enforced. After a grace period the court can order that some of the defendant's property be seized by law enforcement officers and be sold to pay the judgment. The court may also order the defendant's employer to deduct money from each of the defendants paychecks until the judgment is paid.

Check the local telephone directory for small claims courts under the municipal, county or state government headings.

SOAPBOX DERBY

The Soapbox Derby is a series of local and regional races in handbuilt cars propelled only by the force of gravity. The cars are built by participants either from approved kits or from scratch. The first Soap Box Derby was held in Dayton, Ohio in 1933, and the final has been held in Akron, Ohio annually since 1934.

Races are held for two age groups: the junior division is for boys and girls 10-12 years of age, and the senior division is for those 12-15. Twelve-year-olds may participate in either group depending on their experience and skills. Winners of the International finals receive scholarships and trophies. Trophies, cash prizes and scholarships are also awarded on the local and regional levels.

The Soap Box Derby program is administered world-wide by the All-American Soap Box Derby, 789 Derby Downs Drive, Akron, Ohio 44306, Tel. 216-733-8723.

SOARING

The Federal Aviation Administration sets requirements for private glider ratings. The sailplane pilot must have passed a written test and a flying test after at least 20 aero-tow flights and seven hours of solo time in a sailplane. Regulations are somewhat different for persons who hold private pilots licenses. Requirements for a commercial glider pilot's license are more stringent. For further information contact the regional FAA office or the Department of Transportation, Federal Aviation Administration, 800 Independence Ave. SW, Washington, D.C. 20591, Tel. 202-426-1960. Many of those interested in soaring as a sport belong to the Soaring Society of America. Contact that organization for information about soaring clubs and schools and soaring techniques and safety regulations. The address is Soaring Society of America, Box 66071, Los Angeles, Calif, 90066, Tel. 213-390-4447.

SOCCER

The organizing body for professional, amateur and indoor soccer in the United States and Canada is the U.S. Soccer Federation. It promotes soccer with clubs, youth leagues, schools and associations. It also sets the standard rules of play, sanctions, tournaments, assigns and licenses officials and awards annually the Challenge Cup and the National Junior Cup. For further information contact the association at 350 Fifth Ave., New York, N.Y. 10001, Tel. 212-736-0915.

On the college level, the Intercollegiate Soccer Association of America (ISAA) promotes the

Social Security Benefits

sport. It annually sponsors several national tournaments and names the best offensive and defensive players and the regional champions. For further information contact the Intercollegiate Soccer Association of America, Marist College, North Rd., Poughkeepsie, N.Y. 12601, Tel. 914-471-3240.

Professional soccer is represented by the North American Soccer League, which is currently composed of 16 professional teams. For further information contact the North American Soccer League, 1133 Ave. of the Americas, New York, N.Y. 10036, Tel. 212-575-0066.

Indoor soccer is an Americanized version of the sport, combining elements of soccer and hockey. It is regulated by the Major Indoor Soccer League, One Bala Cynwyd Plaza, Bala Cynwyd, Pa. 19004, Tel. 215-667-7070.

SOCIALIST LABOR PARTY

The national office for the Socialist Labor Party is located at 914 Industrial Ave., Box 10018, Palo Alto, Calif. 94303.

SOCIAL SECURITY BENEFITS

Social security benefits are available to all Americans who have made sufficient contributions through payroll deductions and who have reached retirement age or who qualify under special circumstances. Benefits are paid through a federal agency, the Social Security Administration. Monthly cash benefits can be paid by the Social Security Administration to people in the following categories: (a) disabled, insured workers under age 65, (b) retired, insured workers at age 62 or over, (c) spouses of retired or disabled workers entitled to benefits who are age 62 or over or who have care of the worker's child under age 18 who is entitled to social security benefits, (d) divorced wives (in some cases) of retired or disabled workers entitled to benefits if age 62 or older and married to the worker for at least 10 years, (e) dependent, unmarried children of retired or disabled workers entitled to benefits or of deceased, insured workers if the child is under age 18, age 18-22 and attending school full-time, or age 18 or over but under a disability that began before age 22, (f) surviving spouses of deceased, insured workers if the spouse is age 60 or older, (g) disabled, surviving spouses of deceased, insured workers, if the spouse is age 50-59 and meets certain eligibility requirements, (h) surviving spouses of deceased, insured workers if caring for an entitled child of the deceased if the child is under 18 or is disabled, (i) dependent parents of deceased, insured workers at age 62 or over.

Insured workers are those U.S. citizens who have paid part of their salaries into the Social Securities system for a required period of time. In 1981, 6.65 percent of each worker's salary was withheld for Social Security payments up to a maximum of $1,975 per year per individual. Workers are fully insured if they have paid deductions into Social Security system for at least one quarter for each calendar year after age 21 and before age 62. Anyone who has paid, or who has had Social Security coverage for 40 quarters of years or 10 years consecutively is fully insured for Social Security for life. Also, a person is currently insured by the Social Security system if he or she has payed contributions to the Social Security system for at least six out of the last 13 quarters in which he or she dies, becomes disabled, or becomes entitled to retirement insurance benefits.

Contributions to the Social Security system are not voluntary. Nine out of 10 workers in the United States are in employment that requires deductions to be paid for Social Security insurance. Those not required to pay and thus not eligible for Social Security benefits (unless they have qualified by employment in the past) are federal civilian employees covered under another U.S. retirement system, employees of state and local governments who have not been covered by a federal-state agreement, certain agricultural and domestic workers and employees of certain nonprofit organizations that have not arranged for Social Security coverage for their employees.

The full monthly benefit paid was $660 in the first half of 1981. The minimum monthly benefit at that time was $153. The monthly benefit goes up each July by a percentage equal to cost of living increases as measured by the Consumer Price Index. The amount of monthly benefits is based on the individual's monthly earnings averaged over his or her working lifetime. The actual monthly benefits are computed by the Social Security Administration by a complicated formula.

Recipients of Social Security benefits are allowed to earn a certain amount of money per year without having their Social Security benefits affected. In 1981 the amount for persons aged 65–71 was $5500. Those under age 65 had a ceiling of $4,080, and there was no ceiling on earnings for those over 71. Benefits are reduced $1 for each $2 earned above these ceilings.

Any individual can check on his or her benefit earnings record maintained by the Social Security Administration by filing a Form 7004, "Request for a Statement of Earnings," available at any Social Security office and mailing it to the Baltimore office. If there is an error or suspected error, the individual can ask the Social Security office to have the record corrected. These records are important because they will be used eventually to determine any benefits the individual may be entitled to receive.

Claims for Social Security benefits can be filed at any Social Security office. U.S. citizens residing in Canada should file claims at the nearest border Social Security office, or in the Philippines with the Veterans Administration office in Manila. In other foreign countries claims can be filed at the nearest U.S. Foreign Service post. If any claimant is dissatisfied with any action taken regarding benefits, he or she can request a reconsideration of the decision, a hearing before a presiding officer or a review by the Appeals Council.

Social Security benefit checks are mailed by the U.S. Treasury department, but problems with checks should be referred to a Social Security office. Checks are usually mailed for receipt on the third day of the month following the month for which the payment is due, except when that day is a Saturday, Sunday or a holiday. In that case the checks are mailed for receipt on the preceding day on which financial organizations are usually open. If a check is not received within three days after its normal day of receipt, or if the check has been stolen, lost, destroyed or forged, the Social Security office should be notified promptly.

The Social Security Administration is part of the U.S. Department of Health and Human Resources. Regional offices are located in Atlanta, Boston, Chicago, Dallas, Denver, Kansas City, New York, Philadelphia, San Francisco and Seattle. Local offices are in more than 1300 cities in the United States and territories. For further information contact the Division of Public Inquiries, Social Security Administration, 6401 Security Blvd., Baltimore, Md. 21235, Tel. 301-594-1234. From recipients residing abroad inquiries can also be directed to P.O. Box 1756, Baltimore, Md. 21203.

See also: AID TO FAMILIES WITH DEPENDENT CHILDREN; SOCIAL SECURITY NUMBERS; SOCIAL SECURITY BENEFITS: DIRECT DEPOSIT

SOCIAL SECURITY BENEFITS: DIRECT DEPOSIT

Recipients of Social Security benefits can request that the checks be directly deposited to an account in a financial institution, such as a bank, savings bank, savings and loan association or a federal- or state-chartered credit union. The recipient should make arrangements with the financial institution and fill out a form, which is forwarded by the financial institution to the Social Security office.

Direct deposit is not possible to foreign banks, but a power of attorney procedure is available for foreign bank deposits.

Contact any Social Security office for details.

SOCIAL SECURITY NUMBERS

To obtain a social security number apply at the nearest social security office (listed in the local telephone directory). Individuals must show identification to establish age, and citizenship or alien status. Social security numbers are needed by persons whose incomes are covered by the social security program and also by those whose income is reported to the Internal Revenue Service.

Persons who have lost their social security card can apply for a duplicate at the nearest social security office.

SOCIAL SERVICES

Social services are provided in all states, the District of Columbia, Puerto Rico, Guam, and the Virgin Islands to persons who receive the federally aided assistance programs. Those programs include the Supplemental Security Income Program (SSI) and the Aid to Families with Dependent Children program (AFDC). Other families with limited income may qualify for social services. These services are financed from federal Social Security Administration, state public welfare, and local funds.

Application for social services should generally be made to the state department of public welfare.

Home Help Services are available to SSI recipients who temporarily or permanently require assistance with household tasks or personal needs. The program is aimed at helping persons remain in their homes rather than forcing them into nursing homes.

Day Care for Adults is provided to those SSI recipients who would

otherwise require nursing home care. It offers people who need care and supervision a place to go during the day while relatives are away at work.

Foster Care for Adults is provided for SSI recipients who cannot live alone but do not require full time nursing home care.

Other social services for SSI recipients include: programs designed to protect adults from abuse, exploitation, and neglect; employment training, and transportation in special situations.

Day Care for children is provided for AFDC recipients and participants in the Work Incentive Program. It may be provided in a center or in the home. The program is offered to adults who need to work, but have small children, or to those who are physically or mentally unable to care for their children.

Other programs for AFDC recipients include job training, employment services, homemaking services, housing services, and home management and consumer education services.

Family Planning Services including birth control information, counseling, and related medical services are available to many people who ask for them, not just recipients of assistance programs.

State public welfare offices also make referrals to other social service organizations who may help those not eligible for the above programs.

See also CHILD DAY CARE; CHILDREN: AID TO FAMILIES WITH DEPENDENT CHILDREN; CHILDREN: SOCIAL SECURITY BENEFITS; DAY CARE: MEAL PROGRAMS; FOSTER PARENTS; ELDERLY: HOME CARE; ELDERLY: HOME HEALTH CARE; ELDERLY: NUTRITION; ELDERLY: PUBLIC TRANSPORTATION (HALF FARES); FAMILY PLANNING; FOOD PROGRAMS: MEALS ON WHEELS; FOOD STAMPS; FOOD: SUPPLEMENTAL PROGRAM; MEDICAL CARE: MEDICADE; MENTAL HEALTH: STATE SERVICES; REHABILITATION; SCHOOL LUNCH PROGRAM; SUPPLEMENTAL SECURITY INCOME (SSI).

SOCIAL WORKERS: LICENSING

The minimum qualification for a social worker is generally a bachelor's degree in social work (B.S.W.) or in a closely related field. Many employers prefer a master's degree in social work for more responsible positions.

The following states and jurisdictions require the registration or licensing of social workers: Oregon, Arkansas, Illinois, Michigan, Tennessee, South Carolina, Maryland, New York, Rhode Island, California, Idaho, Utah, South Dakota, Kansas, Oklahoma, Louisiana, Alabama, Kentucky, Virginia, Massachusetts, Maine, Puerto Rico, Colorado, and Delaware. The agencies licensing or

registering social workers have different names in different states, but can be contacted through the licensing agency listed in the individual state entry.

All of the above states or jurisdictions require the applicant to pass an examination except: Puerto Rico, Rhode Island, South Carolina, Michigan, Arkansas, Oregon, and Tennessee. All require at least two years of experience except Rhode Island, South Carolina, and Arkansas. Tennessee requires five years experience for licensing as an independently practicing social worker or master social worker.

All of the states or jurisdictions listed above require that applicants for licensing or registration have a master's degree in social work (M.S.W.). The following states grant licenses or registration for positions such as associate social worker on the B.S.W. level: California, Oklahoma, Illinois, Maine, Michigan, Utah, Kansas, Kentucky, Arkansas, South Dakota, Maryland, Colorado, Idaho, Alabama, Massachusetts.

In the following states or jurisdictions employees of a private agency are exempt from licensing requirements: Puerto Rico, Virginia, Illinois, Louisiana, South Dakota, Maryland, Idaho, Alabama, Oregon, and Massachusetts.

The following states have reciprocity for social workers licensed in other states: New York, Virginia, Illinois, Maine, Michigan, Louisiana, Utah, Kansas, Kentucky, Maryland, Colorado, Idaho, Delaware, Alabama, and Massachusetts. Consult the licensing or registering agency in the states above for specific information about how state laws affect social workers.

The National Association of Social Workers allows social workers to use the ACSW title (Academy of Certified Social Workers) who have had at least two years of post master's degree work experience and who have passed the ACSW examination. Such certification is an additional professional qualification, indicating a certain level of competence in the field.

For information about ACSW certification, contact the National Association of Social Workers, 1425 H St., NW, Suite 600, Washington, D.C. 20005, Tel. 202-347-9893.

SOCIALIST WORKERS PARTY

The national office for the Socialist Workers Party is located at 14 Charles Lane, New York, N.Y. 10014, Tel 212-242-5530.

SOUTH AFRICA, REPUBLIC OF

A passport valid for one year beyond the stay and a visa are required for U.S. citizens traveling to South Africa for a period of up to three months. Tourists also need a return ticket and/or a copy of their itinerary; businessmen need a letter from their company detailing the nature of their business and confirming financial responsibility. Cholera and yellow fever shots are required if coming from an infected area. Pets are allowed into the country if accompanied by rabies and health certificates from a veterinarian and a South African permit. To obtain a permit, write to the Department of Agriculture, Division of Veterinary Services, Private Bag, X138 Pretoria 0001. The local currency is the rand. Up to 50 rands may be taken in or out of the country. Any amount of foreign currency may be imported but it must be declared and no more taken out than was brought in. The official languages of South Africa are English and Afrikaans. Zulu and Xhosa are the most commonly spoken local dialects. To drive a car an International Driving License is required. Driving conditions are variable throughout the country and frequently hazardous. The price of gasoline is very high and so is the accident rate. The import of narcotics, pornography and objectionable political literature is prohibited.

Foreign trade is handled mostly through local agents or branch offices of foreign companies in South Africa. Exchange controls are in effect and most imports require licenses.

The Embassy of the Republic of South Africa is located at 3051 Massachusetts Ave. NW, Washington, D.C. 20008, Tel. 202-232-4400. There are consulates in New York, Chicago, Houston and Los

Angeles.

The American Embassy in South Africa is located at Thibault House 225, Pretorius St., Pretoria, South Africa, Tel. 484226. There are U.S. consulates in Capetown, Durban and Johannesburg.

For further business information contact the South African Commercial Office, 4801 Massachusetts Ave. NW, Washington, D.C. 20016, Tel. 202-966-1650.

For additional tourist information contact the South African Tourist Corp., 610 Fifth Ave., New York, N.Y. 10020, Tel. 212-245-3720.

SOUTH CAROLINA

The consumer protection agency in South Carolina is the Department of Consumer Affairs, Box 5757, Columbia, S.C. 29250, Tel. 803-758-2040. The Department accepts consumer complaints and attempts resolution by contacting the businesses concerned. When there is a pattern of complaints of deceptive or unfair business practices, the Department will investigate, hold hearings, and take appropriate action such as seeking court restraining orders.

Occupations and professions in South Carolina are licensed through a number of licensing boards which review applicants, issue licenses, and investigate any complaints about licensees. Inquiries about licensing or complaints can be sent to the Department of Consumer Affairs listed above, which will send the letter on to the proper licensing board.

Businesses can request consulting services from the South Carolina State Development Board, 1301 Gervais Street, Columbia, S.C. 29202, Tel. 803-758-3332 or contact the Chamber of Commerce, 1002 Calhoun St., Columbia, S.C. 29201, Tel. 803-779-6270.

South Carolina offers state, city, or county revenue bond financing for industry in the state.

The corporate income tax in South Carolina is 6% for business corporations, 4.5% for banks, and 8% for financial associations. The state sales tax is 4%.

The individual income tax rate in South Carolina ranges from 2% for income less than $2,000 to 7% for income over $10,000.

Tourist information can be requested from the Department of Parks, Recreation, and Tourism, Edgar A. Brown Building, Columbia, S.C., Tel. 803-758-2279.

SOUTH DAKOTA

In South Dakota most consumer affairs matters are handled by the Attorney General's Office, Division of Consumer Affairs. These include: deceptive trade practices, warranty violations, fair credit, motor vehicle recalls, multi-level distribution plans, and small claims questions.

The South Dakota Division of Consumer Affairs will investigate and mediate consumer complaints, and recommend to the Attorney General legal action against companies alleged to be engaged in unfair business practices. The Division cannot act as a private attorney for consumers, but will act to protect consumers of the state from unfair business practices.

Consumers can contact the South Dakota Division of Consumer Affairs by calling the Toll-free telephone number, 800-592-1865, or write the Division of Consumer Affairs, Insurance Building, Pierre, S.D. 57501.

Professional and occupational licensing in South Dakota is handled by individual boards with an overall administrative office, Division of Professional Licensing, Department of Commerce, State Capitol, Pierre, S.D. 57501, Tel 605-773-3177, Toll-free 800-592-1865 in South Dakota. State Boards in South Dakota license: abstracters, accountants, barbers, chiropractors, cosmetologists (beauticians), dentists, electricians, engineers and architects, funeral directors, hearing aid dispensers, medical and osteopathic doctors, nurses, nursing home administrators, optometrists, pharmacists, plumbers, podiatrists, real estate agents and brokers, social workers, and veterinarians.

These Boards exist to regulate the quality, quantity, and variety of services provided by the professions and occupations to the consumer of the services. They regulate by establishing standards and prescribing qualifications. The boards will accept consumer complaints, investigate, hold hearings when appropriate, and repri-

mand, place on probation, or revoke licenses.

The Industrial Development and Expansion Agency offers assistance to businesses interested in moving to or expanding in South Dakota. Their staff will help prospective businesses find a location and supply other assistance such as marketing information. The Agency can be reached at 221 South Central, Pierre, S.D. 57501, Tel. 605-773-5032, or Toll-free in South Dakota 800-925-3625.

Further business information about South Dakota can be requested from the Greater South Dakota Association, P.O. Box 190, Pierre, S.D. 57501.

South Dakota has no corporate income tax, no personal income tax, and no personal property tax. The state bonding law offers a financing method for industries locating in South Dakota. Industrial Revenue Bonds have interest rates that are usually much lower than conventional financing rates. The bonds can be issued for a period of 30 years and are tax exempt for the purchaser.

The state sales tax in South Dakota is 4%, with production equipment exempt from the tax.

Tourist information can be requested from the Division of Tourism, Joe Foss Building, Pierre, S.D. 57501, 605-399-6779.

SOUTH KOREA

A valid passport and visa are necessary for U.S. citizens traveling to South Korea. A visa application must be accompanied by one picture and a passport and is good for one month. Business travelers must have a letter from their company detailing the nature of their business and confirming financial responsibility for the applicant. There are no health requirements, but travelers must have smallpox and/or cholera innoculations if arriving from an infected area. Pets are not allowed. The currency of South Korea is the won. Won may not be taken in or out of the country, but any amount of foreign currency is·allowed provided it is declared on arrival. Up to $3,000 worth of won may be reconverted when departing but receipts of all exchange transactions must be shown. The official language of Korea is Korean, but there is also some English and Japanese spoken. To drive a car, an International Driving License is required. There is an airport departure tax of 1,500 won.

Trading with South Korea is handled through agents, importers and distributers. Licenses are required for all imports and are automatically granted for any item not on the banned list. Items on this list must be decided on a case by case basis. Personal contact is considered important in the Orient and is recommended. Exchange controls are in effect.

The Embassy of Korea is located at 2370 Massachusetts Ave. NW, Washington, D.C. 20008, Tel. 202-483-7383. There are consulates in Atlanta, Chicago, Hono-lulu, Houston, Los Angeles, New York and San Francisco.

The U.S. Embassy in Korea is located at Sejong-Ro, Seoul, Korea, Tel. 722601.

SOVIET UNION

A valid passport and a visa are required for U.S. citizens traveling to the Soviet Union. Tourists and businessmen can arrange for their visas through one of the American travel agencies that does business with Intourist, the official Soviet tourist agency. Tourist travel is generally limited to approved pre-paid tours through cities which have Intourist facilities for foreign travelers. Marked deviation from a travel itinerary is not recommended. Visas for private trips to visit a relative, for example, can be applied for at Soviet diplomatic mission. The relative in the Soviet Union must likewise apply for permission. Business travelers will need three photos, a letter from their company detailing the nature of their business, their itinerary, length of stay, dates of arrival and departure, the name of the organization(s) to be visited and a confirming invitation from that organization. Travelers' passports should be valid for at least three months from their scheduled date of departure from the Soviet Union. There are no health requirements if arriving from North America, but if arriving from an infected area, the appropirate shots are necessary. The Russian currency is the ruble. It is strictly prohibited to take rubles in or out of the country. There is no limit on the amount of foreign currency travelers can take in, but all money and valuables must be declared on arrival and receipt of all exchanges kept. More money cannot be taken out than was brought in. The official language of the USSR is Russian, but some English and German are spoken. Most tourists will generally not have an opportunity to drive inside the Soviet Union, but businessmen can rent cars with an International Driving License. Caution must be taken to travel only on approved Intourist routes.

Trade with the Soviet Union is government controlled by the Ministry of Foreign Trade. Within this ministry organizations called Foreign Trade Corporations handle individual items. All imports require licenses. The Bank for Foreign Trade handles all foreign exchange transactions.

The Consular Division of the Soviet Embassy is located at 1609 Decatur St. NW, Washington, D.C. 20011, Tel. 202-332-1466.

The U.S. Embassy is located at Ulitsa Chaykovskogo 19/23, Moscow, USSR, Tel. 252-0011. There is a U.S. consulate in Leningrad at Ulitsa Petra Lavrova 15, Tel. 725-217. Americans traveling or residing in the Soviet Union have the right to communicate with an American consular officer in case of difficulty with the Soviet government. Americans in trouble should insist upon calling the American Embassy in Moscow or the consulate in Leningrad. Americans not traveling in group tours and Americans born in territory now under the control of the USSR are urged to register their visits with the American Embassy in Moscow or the consulate in Leningrad.

Travelers may purchase souvenirs and artifacts at special stores for tourists. Antiques and artifacts purchased at regular Soviet stores may be confiscated at customs inspection if they have not been assessed by Soviet cultural authorities—a lengthy process.

SPAIN

A valid passport but no visa is required for U.S. citizens traveling to Spain for a stay of up to six months. There are no health requirements for entry unless arriving from an infected area. Pets are allowed into the country with a veterinarian's health and rabies certificate validated by a Spanish consular official. The local currency is the peseta. Up to 50,000 pesetas may be brought into the country and up to 3,000 may be taken out. There are no limits on the amount of foreign currency that may be imported or exported. The official language is, of course, Spanish, and other languages are not commonly spoken. To drive a car, an International Driving License is required.

Trade with Spain is usually

handled through resident agents. Few import licenses are required, and there are few exchange controls in effect. Foreign exchange is handled by government authorized banks.

The Embassy of Spain is located at 2700 15th St. NW, Washington, D.C. 20009, Tel. 202-265-4939. There are consulates in Boston, Chicago, Coral Gables, Houston, Los Angeles, New Orleans, New York and San Francisco.

The U.S. Embassy in Spain is located at Serrano 75, Madrid, Spain, Tel. 276-3400. There are U.S. consulates in Barcelona and Bilbao.

For additional business information contact the Spain-U.S. Chamber of Commerce, 405 Lexington Ave., New York, N.Y. 10017, Tel. 212-661-4959.

SPECIAL OLYMPICS

The Special Olympics is a program for mentally retarded children and adults which includes programs of physical fitness, sports training, and athletic competition. Individual competitors are assigned to "competition divisions" based on age and actual performance, and athletes in all the divisions may advance to the International Games. Currently almost 1 million mentally retarded children and adults compete.

The Special Olympics is operated by Special Olympics Inc., a non-profit organization located at 1701 K St. NW, Suite 203, Washington, D.C. 20006, Tel. 202-331-1346. State organizations administer a year round program within their geographic areas.

Participants in the Special Olympics are 8 years of age or older. There is no upper age limit. Most have an IQ score of 75 or less. Athletes who are members of regular interscholastic or intramural teams are not eligible for the Special Olympics, but participants in Special Olympics are encouraged to move on to compete in regular sports programs.

The sports included in the Special Olympics are: track and field, swimming, diving, gymnastics, ice skating, basketball, volleyball, soccer, softball, floor hockey, bowling, Frisbee Disc, Alpine and Nordic skiing, and wheelchair events.

Over 10,000 local competitions are held each year in a number of countries of the world. Chapter and National Games are scheduled in May and June of each year. Over 100,000 athletes compete each year in Chapter Games in the U.S. alone. The International Games are held every four years.

Special Olympics Inc. and Chapter organizations offer assistance to local programs in the form of program materials, medals, and ribbons, and insurance coverage.

For information about Special Olympics events contact the Local Chapter organization or the Special Olympics Inc. at the Washington address above.

SPEECH PATHOLOGISTS AND AUDIOLOGISTS

Speech pathologists generally diagnose and treat speech defects, while audiologists deal with hearing impairments. Many states require that speech pathologists and audiologists have a master's degree in their field. More than half of the states require that speech pathologists and audiologists be licensed when they practice outside the public schools. Some states require that speech pathologists and audiologists have a teacher's certificate to work in the schools. Information about licensing for independent practice can be obtained from the state licensing board. Information about requirements for a teacher's certificate can be obtained from the local school board or state education department.

The American Speech and Hearing Association (ASHA) awards a certificate of Clinical Competence, which can be obtained by ASHA members and nonmembers by meeting specific requirements such as a master's degree or its equivalent, one year of internship approved by the association and passing a national examination given by ASHA. The ASHA Certificate permits the holder to practice independently in states that do not require licensing. It also attests that the holder may supervise the clinical practice of student trainees and clinicians who do not hold certification. The certificate is held by over 28,000 professional speech pathologists and audiologists.

For information about certification contact the American Speech Language and Hearing Association, 9030 Old Georgetown Rd. Rockville, Md. 20014, Tel. 301-897-5700.

SQUASH

The United States Squash Racquets Association (USSRA) represents both men and women interested in the game of squash racquets in the U.S. The USSRA is governed by a board of directors appointed by the member districts and by officers and regional vice presidents elected annually be the board.

The USSRA schedules and sanctions all national squash racquet championships in both singles and doubles and in all age groups from the 12-and-under junior group to the 60-and-over senior group. A full-time director and staff are employed. The USSRA has offices at 211 Ford Rd., Bala-Cynwyd, Pa., 19004, 215-667-4006.

STAMPS: COLLECTING

The U.S. Postal Service Stamps Division sells United States postage stamps of selected quality. It also sells commemorative, airmail, special delivery, special handling, postage-due and migratory-bird hunting stamps. Send a self-addressed stamped envelope to the division to get a list of items available for sale. For further information contact the U.S. Postal Service Stamp Division, Philatelic Sales Division, 401 M St. SW, Washington, D.C. 20265, Tel. 202-245-4000.

For enquiries about history, design, engraving and first day city sales of stamps, contact the Treasury Department, Bureau of Engraving and Printing, Management Services Division, 14th St. and C Sts. SW, Washington, D.C. 20228, Tel. 202-447-0261.

STATISTICS, POPULATION

See CENSUS: POPULATION

STOCK BROKERS

See SECURITIES: SALES WORKERS

STOCK CAR RACING

The National Association for Stock Car Auto Racing, Inc. (NASCAR) is the sanctioning and regulatory body for professional stock car racing in the U.S. Participating tracks and cars must meet NASCAR safety requirements. It sponsors a number of competitions in the U.S. including the Winston Cup Series, the Late Model Sportsman's Division, the International Sedan Series and the weekly tracks, which are smaller tracks.

The National Association for Stock Car Auto Racing, Inc. is located at 1801 Valusia Ave., Daytona Beach, Fla. 32015, Tel.

904-253-0611.

STOCK PURCHASE: BORROWING

The borrower as well as the lender—bank, broker-dealer or other lending institution—must comply with government rules relating to the use of credit in purchasing securities, even when the credit is obtained outside the United States.

The Federal Reserve sets a limit on the amount of funds that banks, broker-dealers, and others may lend on stock and convertible bonds. This limit is less than the market value of the securities that are pledged as collateral. In effect, the Federal Reserve sets a minimum down payment that must be made in a transaction. Both borrowers and lenders are subject to prosecution if the violation of the law is willful. Further information about borrowing can be obtained from the Board of Governors, Federal Reserve System, 20th St. and Constitution Ave. NW, Washington, D.C. 20551, Tel. 202-452-3204.

STORE OPENING HOURS

Shop opening hours are generally voluntary except where a local authority or city council has instituted regulations for closing certain types of businesses during certain hours. These include "blue laws" for closing businesses on Sundays. Businesses that sell alcoholic beverages may also have their operating hours regulated. See also: LIQUOR LICENSES.

STREET MUSICIANS

Local authorities make regulations governing street musicians. In some cities they are permitted as long as they do not obstruct foot or street traffic. In other cities street musicians must obtain a license, generally from the local consumer protection agency. For specific information contact the mayor's office or the office of the city executive.

STREET TRADING

Most cities require that peddlers obtain a license from the appropriate office in city hall to pursue their trade. In many cases those peddling food will be licensed by the department of health and those selling general merchandise by the consumer protection agency. For specific information call the mayor's office or the office of the city executive.

STUDENT CULTURAL EXCHANGE

The American Field Service is a private, non-profit organization that has an international scholarship program designed to exchange students between the United States and nations in Europe and Asia. Students must be between 16 and 18 years of age. They come for either a summer or a full school year and live with a family in the host nation. The local chapters of the American Field Service make the selection of students and families in the program. For further information contact the local chapter (listed in the telephone directory) or the American Field Service, 313 East 43rd St. New York, N.Y. 10017, Tel. 212-661-4550.

SUDDEN INFANT DEATH SYNDROME

See CRIB DEATH SYNDROME

SUICIDE

Most cities have one or more telephone counseling centers where people can call for help when they are depressed or contemplating suicide. They are listed as crisis center, suicide prevention center, or HELP. Check the telephone yellow pages under social service agencies; centers also are listed in the front of some phone books. If one is not listed, call another social service organization or the police and ask for the number of a telephone counseling center.

The American Association of Suicidology, 2459 S. Ash, Denver, Colo. 80222, Tel. 303-692-0985, is an organization with some 200 suicide prevention and crisis intervention centers as members. The association can help advise and train those interested in operating or improving a crisis or suicide prevention center.

SUPPLEMENTAL SECURITY INCOME (SSI)

The federal government through the Supplemental Security Income (SSI) program makes monthly payments to the aged, blind and disabled who have little or no income or resources. SSI is administered through the Social Security Administration, but SSI is not the same as Social Security. Those who are eligible for SSI are 65 or older, blind or disabled and have limited income and resources. The person must also be a U.S. citizen or an alien lawfully admitted for permanent residence, and must reside in the United States or the Northern Mariana Islands. Blind or disabled individuals qualify for SSI regardless of age, so young children who are blind or disabled may also qualify.

In determining eligibility, support by relatives is not generally assumed. The law does assume, however, that a husband and wife who life together share income and resources and that a child shares in the income and resources of his or her parents. To qualify for SSI an individual may have assets of up to $1,000. A couple may have resources of up to $2,500. The parents' assets are considered to be the child's, so for a child to qualify for SSI the family may not have assets greater than $2500. Resources include real estate, personal property, household goods, savings and checking accounts, stocks or bonds. The home and adjacent land that is the applicant's principal residence is not counted as asset, however, regardless of its value. Personal effects or household goods up to a value of $2000 are allowed, but the excess counts as resources.

An individual with more than the allowed assets may qualify if he or she sells the excess assets within a specified time. SSI payments made while waiting for the sale may have to be returned after the sale of the excess assets for the recipient to continue to qualify for SSI. An individual income of less then $228 or a family income of less than $357 a month may qualify for SSI. In 1981 the maximum federal SSI payment was $228 a month for an individual and $357 for a couple, but payment levels increase with the cost of living.

Apply for SSI at the nearest Social Security office. If the applicant appears to meet the requirements for SSI and is in need of immediate assistance because of an emergency, the Social Security office may issue an emergency check. The emergency money is then deducted from the first regular SSI check. Any applicant or beneficiary of SSI has the right to appeal any decision about benefits. Ask the social Security Office for help in the four step appeal process: reconsideration, hearing, appeals council review and federal court action.

Contact the Social Security Administration, Division of Public Inquiries, 6401 Security Blvd., Baltimore, Md. 21235, Tel 301-594-1234.

SURGERY: SECOND OPINION

Many individuals seek a second medical opinion before consenting to a nonemergency operation. Both Medicare and Medicaid programs make partial payments for second medical opinions on the advisability of surgery. Private medical plans vary in the amount of the cost of a second opinion they will pay.

The Health Care Financing Administration (HCFA) has a toll-free telephone line to provide referral information to citizens who want a second opinion on the advisability of surgery. Call 800-638-6833, or 800-492-6603 in Maryland to obtain the name and phone number of a local medical referral center.

See also: MEDICAL CARE: MEDICADE; MEDICAL CARE: MEDICARE

SURVEYORS

Land surveyors are responsible for locating and describing physical and legal land boundaries. All states require their licensing or registration. Requirements for such licensing or registration are usually very strict, because a surveyor can be held legally responsible for his work. Requirements vary from state to state, but most states ask both three to eight years experience in surveying and passing an examination. Some states also require a bachelor's degree in a subject related to surveying, such as mathematics or engineering. Civil engineers sometimes want to become licensed surveyors for part of their professional qualifications.

For specific information about licensing, contact the state licensing agency listed under the individual state entry. For additional information about surveying as a profession contact the American Congress on Surveying and Mapping, 210 Little Falls St., Falls Church, Va. 22046, Tel 703-241-2446.

SWAZILAND

A valid passport but no visa is required for U.S. citizens traveling to Swaziland for a stay of up to two months. Persons wishing to stay longer must apply for a Temporary Residence Permit within Swaziland. A cholera shot is required for entry if travelers are arriving from South Africa. It is recommended that they have, in addition, a yellow fever shot and protection against malaria. Pets are allowed into the country with a certificate of good health from a veterinarian. The local currency is the lilageni. The South African rand also circulates freely in Swaziland. Up to 50 lilageni may be brought in or out of the country. There are no limits to the amount of foreign currency that may be brought in or out but no more may be taken out than was brought in. Siswati and English are the two national languages. Driving conditions in the country are generally good. An International Driving License is required.

The import requirements and exchange controls are similar to those in South Africa. The import of any weapons requires a special import license.

The Embassy of Swaziland is located at 4301 Connecticut Ave. NW, Washington, D.C. 20008, Tel. 202-362-6683. There is a consulate in New York.

The U.S. Embassy in Swaziland is located at Embassy House, Allister Miller St., P.O. Box 199, Mbabane, Swaziland, Tel. 2272.

SWEDEN

A valid passport but no visa is required for U.S. citizens traveling to Sweden for a stay of up to three months. There are no health requirements for entry. Pets brought to the Swedish border are subject to quarantine in Sweden. The local currency is the krona (Kr). Up to Kr 6,000 may be taken in or out of the country. There are no limits on the amount of foreign currency that may be imported or exported, but no more may be taken out than was brought in. Although Swedish is the national language, English is widely spoken. To drive a car, an International Driving License is required.

Trade with Sweden is conducted through resident agents. Few imports licenses are necessary, and there are no exchange controls. Foreign exchange is authorized by the Central Bank of Sweden.

The Embassy of Sweden is located at Watergate 600, 600 New Hampshire Ave. NW, Washington, D.C. 20037, Tel. 202-298-3500. There are consulates in Los An-

geles, San Francisco, Minneapolis, Chicago, New York and Houston.

The U.S. Embassy in Sweden is located at Strandvagen 101, Stockholm, Sweden, Tel. 630520. There is an American consulate in Gothenburg.

For further tourist information contact the Swedish National Tourist Office, 75 Rockefeller Plaza, New York, N.Y. 10019, Tel. 212-582-2802. For additional business information there is the Swedish Trade Office, 1 Dag Hammarskjold Plaza, New York, N.Y. 10017, Tel. 212-593-0045.

SWIMMING

The Amateur Athletic Union is the governing body for amateur swimming in the United States. It sponsors developmental programs and competitions, including Olympic trials. For further information contact the Amateur Athletic Union, 3400 West 86th St. Indianapolis, Ind. 46268, Tel. 317-872-2900.

The National Collegiate Athletic Association is the sanctioning body for collegiate swimming. For further information contact the National Collegiate Athletic Association, U.S. Highway 50 and Nall Ave., P.O. Box 1906, Shawnee Mission, Kan. 66222, Tel. 913-384-3220.

SWISS BANK ACCOUNTS

All Swiss bank accounts are secret under Swiss law. Exceptions are carefully defined by the

Swiss Civil or Criminal Codes. These include actions involving inheritance, bankruptcy, debt collection, and all criminal cases. Foreign governments can obtain information about Swiss bank accounts only under multilateral conventions and only when the alleged offense is a crime under Swiss law. Failure to declare or to pay taxes is not a crime in Switzerland, so bank accounts cannot be investigated if that is the only alleged crime.

Bank accounts in Switzerland can be opened under a number rather than a name, but the identity of the person opening the account must be revealed to the bank or the account will not be opened.

U.S. citizens who open Swiss bank accounts must report the account and the amount of money in it to the Internal Revenue Service.

See also: BANKS: ACCOUNTS IN FOREIGN BANKS

SWITZERLAND

A valid passport but no visa is required for travel to Switzerland for a stay of up to three months. There are no health requirements unless arriving from an infected area. Pets are allowed into the country, but a veterinarian's health certificate is required. The local currency is the Swiss franc. There are no limits on the amounts of local or foreign currency that may be taken in or out of the country. German, French or Italian are spoken. English is often understood. To

drive a car, an International Driving License is required.

Trade with Switzerland is conducted either through local agents or through direct contact with Swiss retailers or distributors. Few import licenses are required, and there are no foreign exchange controls.

The Embassy of Switzerland is located at 2900 Cathedral Ave. NW, Washington, D.C. 20008, Tel. 202-462-1811. There are consulates in Chicago, Los Angeles, New Orleans, New York and San Francisco.

The American Embassy in Switzerland is located at Jubileaumstrasse 93, 3005 Bern, Switzerland, Tel. 437011. There are American consular representatives in Geneva and Zurich.

For further information contact the Swiss National Tourist Office at 608 Fifth Ave., New York, N.Y. 10020, Tel. 212-757-5944.

For additional business information contact the Commercial Section of the Swiss Embassy or a consulate.

T

TABLE TENNIS

The U.S. Table Tennis Association is the sanctioning body for the sport in the United States. It conducts tournaments, including the U.S. Open, forms leagues and runs clinics for players from beginners to professionals. It also selects the U.S. teams for the Olympic and Pan American games. For further information contact the Association at Olympic House, 1750 East Boulder, Colorado Springs, Colo. 80909, Tel. 303-632-5551.

TAIWAN

Since the U.S. government recognized Communist China, it has not had normal diplomatic relations with Taiwan. However, Americans can still travel there; the United States does maintain an Interests Section on the island. A valid passport and a visa are required for entry. There are various types of visas—transit, tourist and commercial. These are good for multiple entries within a four year period. The transit visa is good for stays of up to two weeks, the tourist visa is good for stays of up to six months with an extension available. The application for a commercial visa must be accompanied by a letter from the representative's company stating the reason for the visit. Business visas are good for stays of up to two months with extensions available. All applications for visas must be accompanied by three photographs, a travel ticket or confirmation from the travel agency or business firm. There are no health requirements for entry except for smallpox or cholera if arriving from an infected area. To bring a pet travelers must mail a certificate of vaccination against rabies,

a veterinarian's health certificate and three whole body color photos of the pet (4 inches) to the National Health Administration, P.O. Box 58668, Taipei, Taiwan, Republic of China to get a written permit. The local currency is the Taiwan dollar; its import or export is limited to NT$8,000. There are no restrictions on the amount of foreign currency, but travelers may not take out more than $1,000 cash unless it has been declared on arrival. The national language is Mandarin, but Taiwanese (a Fujian dialect) is also spoken. Japanese and English are also spoken on the island. To drive a car, an International Driving License is required. Items bearing a label from the People's Republic of China may be confiscated until departure. Pornography and Communist or leftist literature may be seized by customs.

Trading with Taiwan is usually done through local agents. Most imports require licenses. Authorization of availability of foreign exchange is necessary before licenses are granted.

More information about Taiwan can be obtained from the Coordination Council, 801 Second Ave., New York, N.Y. 10017, Tel. 212-697-1250.

The U.S. Interests Section in Taiwan is located at 7-9, Lane 134, Hsin Yi Rd., Section, Taipei, Taiwan, Tel. 7084150.

TAXES: FEDERAL INCOME

The Internal Revenue Service is responsible for administering and enforcing the internal revenue laws, except those relating to alcohol, tobacco, firearms and explosives. The IRS offers taxpayers information on compliance and will assist individuals in filling out their tax returns. For those with incomes of under $20,000 coming primarily from wages, tips and salary, the IRS will compute the tax. It will not, however, guarantee the accuracy of the return. Tax payers can obtain advice from the IRS either by visiting the local office or over the telephone. See the local telephone directory for the nearest office.

The IRS is also responsible for collecting deliquent taxes. Generally taxpayers get four notices before the service will employ forcible methods. Taxpayers who cannot pay should contact the local IRS office which will arrange payment terms.

Taxpayers who have problems obtaining refunds should contact a local IRS office. If they do not get satisfaction, they should call the Problem Resolution Officer at that branch. As a last resort call the District Director, IRS District Office. If the taxpayer feels he or she is being harassed about payment, he should write to the Assistant Regional Commissioner, Inspection. Problems about audits should be taken in writing to the Chief, Audit Division, IRS District Office; Collection problems to the Chief, Collections, IRS District Office. The local IRS office can give the address for the above.

For further information contact the Department of the Treasury, Internal Revenue Service, 1111 Constitution Ave. NW, Washington, D.C. 20224, Tel. 202-566-5000.

TAXES: PROPERTY

Property taxes have been the principal source of local revenue virtually since the founding of the Union, until more recent years when income and sales taxes have been added. Property taxes generally fall into two large categories: real and personal property. Real property consists mainly of land, buildings and other improvements of a permanent nature. Personal property includes all property not considered real property, and it can be further divided into tangible and intangible personal property. Among the more common types of tangible personal property are automobiles, boats, home furnishings, livestock and farm equipment. Intangible personal property includes stocks and bonds, promissory notes and bank accounts.

Administration of property tax collection varies from state to state, but is largely on a county basis. Real property is assessed usually about every two to four years while personal property is normally assessed annually. The taxing district, frequently the county, determines the assessed value of real or personal property and then bills the owner at the rate established by the governing legislative body: county board, city council, school board, etc. The owner then pays the tax to the district assessor who then distributes it to the appropriate government entity. Tax appeal boards are generally operated locally for those property owners who feel that they have been taxed excessively.

TAXES: STATE INCOME

Nearly every state now has some form of income tax or tax based on the worth of the individual. Those that do not are: Florida, Nevada, South Dakota, Texas, Washington and Wyoming. State revenue services are responsible for educating the public about the taxes, aiding taxpayers in filling out the forms and collecting back taxes. Questions about the tax should be addressed to the nearest branch of the agency, usually found in large cities, or the main office, located in the capital.

TAXICAB DRIVERS

Taxicab drivers usually must have a chauffeur's (commercial) driver's license and special taxicab operator's license issued by the local police, safety department or public utilities commission. Requirements for the special license vary from city to city, but may include a written examination, health requirements and the like.

Consult a local taxicab company, city government office or the above agencies to locate the appropriate licensing body for taxicab drivers.

TAX RETURNS: COPIES

Individuals may obtain copies of their previous tax returns from the Internal Revenue Service. Call the local branch office for the appropriate forms.

TEACHER EXCHANGE

The U.S. Department of Education offers grants for qualified American teachers to work in elementary and secondary schools abroad. To be eligible an applicant must have at least three years of full-time teaching experience and be a U.S. citizen. Grants provide round trip transportation to most countries participating and a maintenance allowance based on the host country's cost of living. For further information contact the Department of Education Teacher Exchange Section, Division of International Education, ROB-3, Seventh and D Streets, SW, Washington, D.C. 20202, Tel. 245-9692.

TEACHERS: ENGLISH LANGUAGE

The Teachers of English to Speakers of Other Languages is an organization of high school, college and adult education teachers who teach English as a second or foreign language, as well as students and professionals in the field. The organization serves as a clearinghouse for information on the subject and compiles a list of all those teaching in the field. For further information contact the Teachers of English to

Speakers of Other Languages, School of Languages and Linguistics, Georgetown University, Washington, D.C. 20057, Tel. 202-625-4301.

TEACHERS: KINDERGARTEN, ELEMENTARY SCHOOL AND SECONDARY

All states require teachers in public, kindergarten, elementary and secondary schools to be licensed, and a few states require licenses for private school teachers for those grades.

To qualify a teacher must have at least a bachelor's degree from an institution with an approved teacher education program. Course work is required in specific areas, including teacher education and student teaching. A number of states also require a teacher to pursue post-graduate work to a master's degree or a fifth year of study. Local school districts may have additional requirements.

Questions or complaints about teachers in a local school district should be referred first to the department chairman or principal and then to the superintendent of schools in that district. Contact the state department of education, usually located in the state capital for further information or policy guidelines.

TELECOMMUNICATIONS

The federal agency with responsibility for telecommunications is the National Telecommunications and Information Administration in the U.S. Department of Commerce. NTIA is mandated to formulate policies for development, growth, and regulation of telecommunications, information, and related industries. It also provides telecommunications facilities grants to public service users.

Contact the Public Information Officer, National Telecommunications and Information Administration, Dept. of Commerce, 1325 G Street NW, Washington, D.C. 20005, Tel. 202-724-3361.

TELEGRAMS

To order a telegram contact Western Union at the address or toll free telephone number listed in the local telephone directory. Questions or complaints should be addressed to the customer service representative or supervisor of the office, or write Western Union, One Lake Street, Upper Saddle River, N.J. 07458.

TELEPHONE ATTACHMENTS

Any attachments placed on a telephone such as an answering machine must be reported to the telephone business office. Give the 14-digit registration number to the business office as proof that the attachment is approved by the Federal Communications Commission.

TELEPHONE CALLS: OBSCENE

State and federal laws prohibit obscene or harassing telephone calls. In the event of an obscene

288

telephone call hang up immediately. If the calls do not stop notify the business office of the telephone company, which will contact the police department if necessary.

TELEPHONE DIRECTORIES

Telephone subscribers are entitled to a free copy of the local directory and a free listing in the "white pages," the alphabetical listing of subscribers. There are charges for extra listings. A number can be unlisted, which means that it will not be printed in the directory or given out by directory assistance. There may be an additional charge for this service.

Businesses and professionals generally have their telephone numbers listed in the "yellow pages," a listing by subject. Charges for such listing can be obtained from the telephone company business office.

Questions and complaints about telephone directories can be referred to the local telephone company business office. The address and telephone number is found in the front of the telephone directory or by calling telephone information.

TELEPHONES

Telephone service customers can either use instruments provided by the telephone company or can purchase instruments from the phone company or a private company.

The telephone company must be notified when a purchased telephone is to be used by a customer. The customer must provide the company with the 14-digit federal registration number, which is marked on each telephone licensed by the Federal Communications Commission. Telephone companies have a base charge for telephone service to customers, but the monthly bill is reduced in cases where the customer provides his own telephone.

TELEPHONE SERVICE: BILLING

The state public utilities commission requires the telephone company to include enough information on bills for the customer to determine if they are accurate. For example, they must contain the time period covered by the bill, a clear listing of all charges due, an itemized list of long distance calls and charges and a separate listing of local service charges. Customers disputing bills should first report their complaint to the customer service department of the telephone company. If a telephone inquiry is not sufficient, they should write a letter to the customer service department and request the results of the investigation of the bill. The utility cannot cut off service to a customer disputing a bill, provided that charges not in dispute are paid. A consumer can report a billing error to the state public utilities commission, but this agency does not generally investigate individual complaints. It is better to contact the local consumer affairs office or Call for Action.

See also: CALL FOR ACTION

TELEVISION AND RADIO: LIVE SHOWS

To secure tickets to live television and radio shows write well in advance to the network producing it. Availability of tickets varies from show to show.

TELEVISION STATIONS

The Federal Communications Commission licenses television stations. Each station must renew its broadcast license every three years. In order to obtain a renewal, the FCC must determine that the station's programming is "in the public interest." It does this, in part, by reviewing letters sent by listeners to the station over the three year period. Consumers can also write directly to the FCC regarding a particular station. It is very rare, however, that the FCC revokes a license, regardless of complaints. For further information contact the Federal Communications Commission, Office of Public Affairs, Consumer Assistance and Information Division, 1919 M St. NW, Washington, D.C. 20554, Tel. 202-632-7000.

TELEVISION: CHILDREN'S PROGRAMMING

Television programming is regulated by the Federal Communica-

tions Commission (FCC), which requires stations to present some programming especially designed for children. A portion must educate and inform as well as entertain. The FCC also evaluates a station's adherence to the industry codes limiting the amount of commercial time per hour and the content of commercials shown on children's programs. Parents wishing to comment or complain about children's programming should write directly to the station, which is required to keep letters on file for inspection by the public and the FCC at time of license renewal. They can write the program sponsor if they object to the commercials or the content of the program. As a last resort they can contact the FCC, but the agency does not investigate individual complaints. Contact the Federal Communications Commission, Consumer Assistance Office, 1919 M St. NW, Washington, D.C. 20554, Tel. 202-632-7000.

Action for Children's Television has led the fight for improvement in programming and commercials. For information about its program or developments in this area contact Action for Children's Television, 46 Austin St., Newtonville, Mass. 02160, Tel. 617-527-7870.

TENNESSEE

The Tennessee Consumer Affairs Division of the Tennessee Department of Agriculture and the State Attorney General jointly administer the Tennessee Consumer

Protection Act which protects consumers from unfair and deceptive trade practices. The Act allows for civil penalties up to $1,000 for each offense, recoverable by the state of Tennessee, and restitution in the amount of triple damages may be obtained in a court action brought by an individual.

Consumer complaints in Tennessee can be reported to the Consumer Affairs Division Toll-free by calling 800-342-8385. The consumer will be mailed a short complaint form to fill out and return. The staff of the Consumer Affairs Division will contact the person or business against whom the complaint was filed to get their position on the complaint and attempt to negotiate a satisfactory settlement. If it appears to the Division that the person or business against whom the complaint was filed has engaged in conduct contrary to the Consumer Protection Act, the matter will be referred to the legal staff for appropriate action.

Information about business and industry in Tennessee can be obtained from the Department of Economic and Community Development, 1007 Andrew Jackson State Office Building, 500 Deaderick St., Nashville, Tenn. 37219, Tel. 615-741-1888, or the State Chamber Division, Tennessee Taxpayers Association, 1970 Capitol Hill Building, Nashville, Tenn. 37219, Tel. 615-242-1854.

Corporations doing business in Tennessee pay a corporate income tax or excise tax of 9% on banks and 6% on net earnings of corporations, foreign and domestic, on the portion of income arising from business done in Tennessee. All taxes are deductible in determining the state excise tax base except income taxes paid to the federal government. Manufacturers are allowed an investment tax credit for a percentage of the cost of industrial machinery purchased after July 1, 1980.

All retail sales are subject to a state sales tax rate of 4½% and a local rate of 1% to 2¼% (combined is usually 6%). Industrial machinery, manufacturers' use of energy fuel and water is subject to a reduced tax.

The Department of Economic and Community Development administers industrial revenue bond, general obligation bond, and other state programs of assistance for new or expanding businesses in the state.

Tourist information can be requested from the Tourist Development Division, 1028 Andrew Jackson Building, Nashville, Tennessee 37219, Tel. 615-741-2158.

TENNIS

The United States Tennis Association is the sanctioning body for tennis in the United States. It conducts educational programs in the sport and oversees numerous tournaments for amateurs and professionals including the Davis Cup. For further information contact the United States Tennis Association, 51 East 42nd St., New York, N.Y. 10017, Tel. 212-949-9112.

TEXAS

The consumer protection agency in Texas is the Attorney General's Office, Consumer Protection Division, Austin, Tex. 78711, (512) 475-3288. Citizens who write in with a complaint will be mailed a standard complaint form. When the form is returned, a copy is mailed to the business concerned with the Division's request that the business attempt to settle with the consumer. The Division may also advise the consumer to contact the Better Business Bureau or a private attorney.

A number of state agencies license businesses in Texas. Professions and occupations licensed include: accountants, architects, lawyers, barbers, cosmetologists, morticians, chiropractors, psychologists, dentists, surveyors, engineers, veterinarians, securities brokers, insurance agents and brokers, landscape architects, hearing aid dispensers, private investigators, polygraph examiners, nurses, nursing home administrators, medical doctors, optometrists, pharmacists, physical therapists, plumbers, podiatrists.

For information about licensing for these occupations or for complaints, contact the state board of the occupation or profession, or contact the Texas Industrial Commission which will refer you to the appropriate licensing board. The Industrial Commission is located at 410 East 5th St., P.O. Box 12728, Capitol Station, Austin, Tex. 78711, Tel. 512-472-5059.

The main purpose of the Industrial Commission is to promote business and industrial growth in the state. The Commission provides services to businesses interested in moving to the state and helps community leaders organize their own industrial development programs. The Commission administers the state's industrial revenue bond program which provides financial assistance to new or expanding businesses through limited low-interest financing available to communities for selected industrial projects.

There is no personal or corporate income tax in Texas, but there is a business franchise tax for corporations. The tax is $4.25 per $1,000 of the corporation's capital plus its surplus and undivided profits or the minimum tax of $55 per year, whichever is greater.

The state sales tax is 4% on sales, rentals, leases, and use of most tangible personal property. Exemptions are grocery food products and prescription medicines, property which will be consumed in manufacturing or processing, property sold for resale, and many items used exclusively on ranches and farms.

Request tourist information from the Texas Tourist Development Agency, Box 12008, Capitol

Station, Austin, Tex. 78711, Tel. 512-475-4326 or the State Department of Highways and Public Transportation, Texas Highway Building, 11th and Brazos Streets, Austin, Tex. 78701, Tel. 512-475-2081.

THAILAND

A valid passport and a return ticket are required for U.S. citizens traveling to Thailand for a stay of up to 15 days. For longer stays travelers must apply in person to a Thai consulate with three photos, a valid passport and a return ticket. There is also a fee of $10. A tourist visa is good for 60 days. Business travelers also require a visa. Three photographs, a valid passport and a letter from their company plus $15 are needed for a visa good for 90 days. Smallpox and cholera vaccinations are required for entry; yellow fever innoculation is required if a traveler is arriving from an infected area. Pets are allowed into the country with a veterinarian's health certificate which has been validated at a Thai consulate before leaving the United States.

The Thai currency is the baht and only 500 may be taken in or out of the country. There is no limit to the amount of foreign currency that may be brought in or out but it may be have to be declared on arrival. Thai is the official language. Lao, Malay, various Chinese dialects and some English are also spoken. The transliterated signs that exist in the country use several different systems and may be spelled several ways. To drive a car, an International Driving License is required. Thailand prohibits the export of pre-18th century artifacts. The export of later antiques require the permission of the Foreign Trade Department. This is usually arranged by local shopkeepers. Pornography, narcotics and firearms cannot be brought into the country.

Trading with Thailand is usually conducted through local agents. Some licenses are required for imports and there are no exchange controls.

The Embassy of Thailand is located at 2300 Kalorama Rd. NW, Washington, D.C. 20008, Tel. 202-667-1446. There is a consulate in Los Angeles and a U.N. Mission in New York.

The U.S. Embassy in Thailand is located at 95 Wireless Rd., Bangkok, Thailand, Tel. 2525040.

TOURISM: STATE ASSISTANCE

See individual state entries

TOXIC SUBSTANCES CONTROL

The Environmental Protection Agency, Office of Assistant Administrator for Toxic Substances is responsible for developing national strategies for control of toxic substances. It sets rules and procedures for industry reporting and regulates the control of substances deemed hazardous. It also develops criteria for determining what substances are indeed hazardous to man or the environment. The agency cannot prosecute offenders. Legal action is handled by the Department of Justice, Land and Resources Division. For further information contact the Public Information Center, Environmental Protection Agency, 401 M St. SW, Washington, D.C. 20460, Tel. 202-755-0707 and the Department of Justice, Land and Natural Resources Division, 10th St. and Constitution Ave. NW, Washington D.C. 20530, Tel. 202-633-4169.

TOYS

Children's toys are regulated by the federal government through the Consumer Product Safety Commission (CPSC). Toys are not tested for safety by the CPSC before marketing, but those found to be dangerous are removed from stores. Many toy manufacturers make real efforts to pretest toys and not to put dangerous toys on the market, but each year many toys are still identified as dangerous and removed from sale.

If an individual toy is defective in manufacture or hazardous in design, contact first the store, then the manufacturer. The state consumer protection agency (see individual state entry) can mediate unresolved complaints. The Federal Consumer Product Safety Commission cannot investigate each consumer complaint but maintains records for use in monitoring the safety of toys and for future investigations.

Contact the commission at 1111 18th St. NW, Washington, D.C. 20207, Tel. 202-634-7700. The commission also maintains a toll-free line for the Consumer Product Safety Commission: 800-638-2666.

See also SAFETY: CONSUMER PRODUCTS; PRODUCT SAFETY: RETAILER'S RESPONSIBILITY

TRACK AND FIELD

The Amateur Athletic Union is the governing body for amateur track and field in the United States. It sponsors developmental programs and competitions, including annual championships and Olympic trials. For further information contact the Amateur Athletic Union, 3400 West 86th St., Indianapolis, Ind. 46268, Tel. 913-384-3200.

Collegiate track and field events are governed by the National Collegiate Athletic Association, U.S. Highway 50 and Nall Ave. P.O. Box 1906, Shawnee Mission, Kan. 66222, Tel. 913-384-3220.

TRADEMARK

A trademark is defined by an act of Congress as any word, name, symbol or device adopted and used by a manufacturer or merchant to identify goods and distinguish them from those manufactured or sold by others.

Trademarks are registered in the Patent and Trademark Office, Department of Commerce. Rights to a trademark are acquired only by use of the trademark in commerce. Registration of a trademark is simply recognition by the government of the right of the owner to use the mark in commerce to distinguish his goods from those of others. A trademark is registered for 20 years and may be renewed for 20-year periods if still used in commerce.

The Patent and Trademark Office maintains a digest of registered marks that is open to the public for inspection. In the digest word marks are arranged alphabetically and a set of visual marks—symbols, birds, animals, etc.—are arranged according to the classification of the goods or services for which they are used. The *Trademark Official Gazette,* contains current information about trademarks and is published weekly. Copies may be obtained from the Government Printing Office.

A booklet *General Information Concerning Trademarks* may be obtained from the Government Printing Office, North Capitol and H Streets NW, Washington D.C. 20401, Tel.: 202-275-2051. Applications for trademarks may be obtained from the Commission of Patents and Trademarks, Patent and Trademark Office, Washington, D.C. 20231, Tel. 703-557-3158.

TRAFFIC ACCIDENTS

State laws require that drivers stop vehicles involved in traffic accidents in which there is property damage or bodily injury. They must give their names and addresses to each other person involved. Failure to stop at the scene of an accident can lead to a criminal complaint of hit and run. The accident must be reported to the appropriate law enforcement agency within 24 hours, usually the city police within city limits. Outside city limits, the agency is generally the state police.

TRAVEL AGENTS: CERTIFICATION

In order to do business, a travel agency must be able to issue tickets for air travel, cruise ships and forms of land travel. The travel agent must join certain conferences to do so. For example, the agent must join the Air Traffic Conference to be able to sell airline tickets. The Air Traffic Conference and other travel conferences impose membership requirements such as minimum working capital and minimum management experience of two years in travel work.

There is a national trade association which sets standards for its member agents: The American Society of Travel Agents (ASTA). In order to be accepted as a member of ASTA the applicant must satisfy certain requirements such as being in business for a minimum of three years.

Consumers with complaints strictly with the travel agent, should first try to resolve the problem with the agent. If the agent is a member of ASTA, the consumer can contact its Consumer Affairs Department. If not satisfied, the consumer can contact the state attorney general or take the agent to small claims court.

If the complaint is with an airline, hotel or other business with which the travel agent has made arrangements, ASTA recommends that the consumer first try to resolve the problem with that business. ASTA offers its services as an intermediary, so the consumer can send complaints to the address below. The consumer can also contact the regulatory agency for that business such as the Civil Aeronautics Board for the airlines. There is no national government regulatory agency for travel agents. Several states are considering legislation requiring state licensing of travel agents, but none yet have passed.

For consumer complaints contact ASTA Consumer Affairs Department, 711 Fifth Ave., New York, N.Y. 10022, Tel. 212-486-0700. Specific licensing requirements can also be requested from ASTA at the same address and telephone number.

See also: AIR TRAVEL, CRUISE SHIPS, etc.

TRAVEL, EMERGENCIES ABROAD

The Department of State, Bureau of Consular Affairs maintains a telephone number for Americans wishing to report emergencies that friends or relatives may have abroad. These include the arrest of an American citizen, the need for repatriation of a destitute U.S. national, the medical evacuation of a U.S. citizen, the death of a U.S. citizen or the need to search for a citizen who has not been heard from for an undue length of time and/or about which there is a special concern. The office will also transmit emergency messages to U.S. nationals abroad. In an emergency call 202-632-5225.

TRAVEL, INNOCULATIONS

Innoculation requirements vary from country to country. The United States Public Health Service recommends that travelers have only those shots that are really necessary in order to avoid the risks of being vaccinated against a disease to which they will not be exposed. Most countries will not refuse admittance to travelers without required vaccinations. They may require vaccination upon entry, give the traveler a medical follow-up card or, in rare cases, put the traveler in isolation for the incubation period of the disease for which he was not vaccinated. It is best, however, for travelers to be vaccinated for the proper diseases for their own protection. Vaccinations must be recorded on the approved forms available from the public health office or the passport agency. The form must be kept with the passport. For specific information on vaccinations see individual country entries.

See also: specific country

TRAVEL: PROMOTION

The United States Travel Service promotes travel to the United States by preparing and distribuing materials abroad. It also makes available basic source material for the international travel industry and the general traveling public. In addition the agency promotes domestic tourism by working with other state and federal groups as well as private travel agencies. For specific travel information write the agency describing the material desired at: Department of Commerce, U.S. Travel Service, Main Commerce Bldg., Washington, D.C. 20230, Tel. 202-377-4752.

See also individual state entries

TRAVEL ARRANGEMENTS: COMPLAINTS

If the consumer has a complaint about a travel agent, he should first try to resolve the problem with the agent. If the agent is a member of the American Society of Travel Agents (ASTA), the consumer can contact the Consumer Affairs Department of ASTA, the trade association for travel agents. The address is: ASTA Consumer Affairs Department, 711 Fifth Ave., New York, N.Y., Tel. 212-486-0700. If appropriate, the consumer can contact the local consumer complaint agency or take the agent to small claims court.

If the complaint is with an air-

line, hotel, or other business with which the travel agent has made arrangements, ASTA recommends that the consumer first try to resolve the problem with that business. ASTA offers it services as an intermediary, so the consumer can send his complaint to the above address.

TRAVELERS AID

Individuals who are stranded can obtain services from numerous social service organizations. The Travelers Aid Society, with offices in most major cities and frequently at major airports, is among those groups that offer assistance. The headquarters of the Travelers Aid Association of America is located at 701 Lee Street, Des Plaines, Ill. 60016, Tel. 312-298-9390.

TRINIDAD AND TOBAGO

A valid passport and a return ticket are required for U.S. citizens traveling to Trinidad and Tobago for tourism purposes for a stay of up to two months. Business travelers must apply for a business visa. First time applicants are requested to make a personal appearance at a diplomatic mission with two photographs, a letter from their company detailing the nature of business to be conducted, and with whom, the proposed length of stay and a passport valid for at least six months beyond the date the visa is issued. The cost of the visa is $4.80. There are no health requirements for entry, but if arriving from an infected area cholera and yellow fever shots are necessary. It is advisable to have been innoculated against typhoid and yellow fever. It is probably a good idea not to take a pet since permission is required from the Trinidad and Tobago government beforehand. This takes a long time, and even with the permission, the animal is still subject to quarantine on the islands. The local currency is the Trinidad and Tobago dollar. There is no limit on the amount of local currency that can be brought into the islands but only about TT$48 can be taken out. Any amount of foreign currency can be taken in or out of the islands but it may have to be declared. English is the official language of the islands although some Indian languages are also spoken.

Trade with Trinidad and Tobago is handled either through local agents or directly with distributors. Few licenses are required and foreign exchange transactions are authorized by the Central Bank.

The Embassy of Trinidad and Tobago is located at 1708 Massachusetts Ave. NW, Washington, D.C. 20036, Tel. 202-467-6490. There is a consulate in New York.

The U.S. Embassy in Trinidad and Tobago is located at 15 Queen's Park West, P.O. Box 752, Port-of-Spain, Trinidad.

For additional tourist information contact the Trinidad and Tobago Tourist Board, 400 Madi-

son Ave., New York, N.Y. 10017, Tel. 212-838-7750. At the same address is the Trinidad and Tobago Industrial Development Corp. for additional business information, Tel. 212-755-9360.

TUNISIA

A passport but no visa is required for U.S. citizens traveling to Tunisia for a stay of up to four months. There are no health requirements for entry, but smallpox, cholera and yellow fever shots are needed if coming from an infected area. Typhoid and paratyphoid shots are recommended. Pets may be taken into the country if accompanied by a veterinarian's health certificate. The local currency is the Tunisian dinar. Taking dinars in or out of the country is prohibited. There is no limit to the amount of foreign currency that can be taken in or out, but it is advisable to change only what is needed since it may prove difficult to reconvert Tunisian currency. The official language is Arabic, and French is widely spoken. English is not so common. To drive a car, an International Driving License is required.

Trade with Tunisia is handled by direct contact with suppliers or through resident agents. The government holds monopolies on the import of certain items. All imports require licenses, and a license guarantees the availability of foreign exchange.

Travelers are advised that evidence of a planned or past trip to

Israel may prevent their entry into Tunisia. Tunisia, although a Muslim country, is one of the less restrictive ones. Travelers can bring up to one liter of alcohol into the country, and there are bars in most large hotels. Life in the large cities is comparatively informal and non-Muslims can visit the local mosques.

The Embassy of Tunisia is located at 2408 Massachusetts Ave. NW, Washington, D.C. 20008, Tel. 202-234-6644.

The U.S. Embassy in Tunisia is located at 144 Avenue de la Liberte, Tunis, Tunisia, Tel. 282566.

For further information contact the Tunisian National Tourist Office, 630 Fifth Ave., New York, N.Y. 10020, Tel. 212-582-3670.

U

UNEMPLOYMENT INSURANCE

Persons who become unemployed are eligible for partial income replacement for a limited period through the Unemployment Insurance Program funded by the federal government and administered by the states.

Individual states determine who may receive unemployment benefits, how each worker can qualify for benefits, the amount of the weekly unemployment benefit, and the maximum number of weeks for which unemployment insurance benefits can be paid.

To qualify for benefits, the unemployed worker must generally register for work at a public employment office and file a claim for benefits (usually at the state employment agency located in most cities).

The worker must have worked previously at a job that was covered by the unemployment insurance in that state; most jobs are covered except certain agricultural and domestic employment. He or she must have worked a prescribed length of time during the "base period," generally a year, prior to the time benefits are claimed; or must have earned a prescribed amount during the base period.

To qualifty for unemployment insurance the worker must be able to work, although if illness occurs after the claim is established in some states payments will be made as long as no offer of suitable work is refused.

Claimants may be disqualified from benefits if a job was left voluntarily without good cause, or the person was discharged for misconduct, or became unemployed because of a labor dispute.

The amount of the weekly benefit to qualified claimants varies in each state, but is usually about half the worker's full-time weekly pay within top and bottom limits. All states except Montana pay partial benefits for partial unemployment. The length of payment of benefits ranges from one to 39 weeks, but payments may be extended during periods of high unemployment. A worker who has been employed in several states or has moved to a new state and is out of a job, should apply for benefits in the same way he or she would if he had been working in the state all the time.

If a worker gets a full time job, he or she is no longer eligible for benefits.

UNITARIAN UNIVERSALIST CHURCHES

The Unitarian Universalist Association, with headquarters in Boston, Massachusetts, is an association of lay-led churches and fellowships in communities where no Unitarian Universalist Church exists. There is also the Church of the Larger Fellowship for those who are not able to reach a church or fellowship. It has members in 40 countries.

Information about the Unitarian Universalist movement can be obtained from local churches and fellowships or from the Unitarian Universalist Association, 25 Beacon St., Boston, Ma. 02108, Tel. 617-742-2100.

UNITED KINGDOM (England, Wales, Scotland, Northern Ireland)

A valid passport but no visa is required for U.S. citizens traveling to the United Kingdom for a stay to be determined by the Immigration Authorities. There are no health requirements except smallpox immunization, if coming from an infected area. Pets taken to the country are subject to a quarantine for a minimum of six months. The local currency is the pound sterling. There are no limits on the amount of currency, local or foreign, which may be taken in or out of the country. English is, of course, the official language, but some Welsh and Gaelic are also spoken. An International Driving License is required to drive a car.

Trade with the United Kingdom is conducted either through agents, or through distributors, wholesalers or retailers. For a list of imports requiring licenses write the *Open General Licenses* to Her Majesty's Stationery Office, 49 High Holborn, London WC1. There are no exchange controls.

The British Embassy is located at 3100 Massachusetts Ave. NW, Washington, D.C. 20008, Tel. 202-462-1340. There are consulates in Atlanta, Chicago, Houston, Los Angeles, New York and San Francisco.

The American Embassy in England is located at 24-32 Grosvenor Square, London W1A 1AE, England, Tel. 499-9000. There are U.S. consulates in Belfast and Edinburgh.

For further tourist information contact the British Tourist Authority, 680 Fifth Ave., New York, N.Y. 10019, Tel. 212-581-4700. At the same address and telephone number is the office of Executive & Travel Trade.

For additonal business information contact the British Trade Development Office, 150 East 58 St., New York, N.Y. 10155, Tel. 212-593-2258.

UNIVERSITIES AND COLLEGES: ACCREDITATION

Accreditation is a voluntary process in which an organization or agency recognizes a college or university or a specific program within an institution as meeting that agency's predetermined qualifications or standards. Approximately 84% of American colleges are accredited.

General colleges and universities are accredited by the following regional agencies:

Middle States Association of Colleges and Secondary Schools
225 Broadway, Room 4003
New York, N.Y. 10007

New England Association of Colleges and Secondary Schools
50 Beacon St.
Boston, Mass. 02108

North Central Association of Colleges and Secondary Schools
5454 South Shore Dr.
Chicago, Ill. 60615

Northwest Association of Colleges and Secondary Schools
Commission on Colleges
M302 Miller Hall
University of Washington
Seattle, Wash., 98105

Southern Association of Colleges and Schools
795 Peachtree St. NE
Atlanta, Ga. 30308

Western Association of Schools and Colleges
Mills College
Oakland, Calif. 94613

Professional programs such as social work, business administration, medicine and pharmacy have separate accrediting agencies.

URUGUAY

A passport and a round trip ticket are required for U.S. citizens traveling to Uruguay for a stay of up to three months for purposes of tourism or business. There are no health requirements for entry, but typhoid and paratyphoid shots are recommended. Pets require a permit from a Uruguayan diplomatic mission. A veterinarian's certificate of good health that is validated by the U.S. Department of Agriculture must be presented to obtain the permit. The cost is $10.50. The local currency in Uruguay is the Uruguayan peso. There are no limits on pesos or foreign currency that can be taken in or out of the country. The official language is Spanish, and English is not widely spoken. To drive a car a permit good for 90 days must be obtained from the Town Hall in Montevideo.

Trade with Uruguay is conducted through local agents. All imports must be authorized by the Bank of the Republic. There exist large duties for imports.

The Embassy of Uruguay is located at 1918 F St. NW, Washington, D.C. 20006, Tel. 202-331-1313. There are consulates in Chicago, New Orleans, New York, Philadelphia and San Francisco.

The U.S. Embassy in Uruguay is located at Calle Lauro Muller 1776, Montevideo, Uruguay, Tel. 409051.

For further business information contact the Uruguayan Govt. Trade Bureau, 301 East 47 St., New York, N.Y. 10017, Tel. 212-751-7137.

UTAH

In Utah the consumer protection agency is the Department of Business Regulation, which accepts consumer complaints and mediates between the complainant and the business concerned.

The Utah Department of Business Regulation also licenses the following occupations and businesses: accountants, architects, barbers, cosmetologists, chiropractors, chiropodists, dentists, dental hygenists, embalmers, funeral directors, physicians and surgeons, naturopathic physicians, nurses, obstetricians, osteopathic physicians and surgeons, plumbers, pharmacists, prophylactic sales, shorthand reporters, veterinarians, nursing and convalescent homes, sanitarians, physical therapists, psychologists, money order vendors, sprinkler and irrigation fitters, pharmaceutical manufacturers, landscape architects, electricians, social workers, controlled substances, marriage and family counselors, electronic service dealers, recreational therapists, speech pathologists and audiologists, occupational therapists and assistants, engineers and land surveyors, and cemetery authority. Requests for licensing requirements for the above occupations and businesses can be directed to the State of Utah Department of Business Regulation, 330 East 4th South, Salt Lake City, Utah 84111.

Complaints about licensees or other businesses can be sent to the above address of the Department of Business Regulation. After investigation, complaints which appear to have substance will be the subject of a formal or informal hearing. The Department does have the power to revoke licenses.

Businesses needing consulting services because they are considering a move to Utah or are expanding in the state can contact the Department of Business Regulation.

Utah offers city or county revenue bond financing to help industry moving into the state.

The corporate income tax rate is 4% with the minimum amount being $25. The state sales tax is 4%.

The state individual income tax rates range from 2.25% for amounts up to $750 to 7.75% for amounts over $4,500.

For tourist information about Utah contact the Utah Travel Council, Council Hall, Capitol Hill, Salt Lake City, Utah 84114, Tel. 801-533-5681.

UTILITIES: BILLING

The local utility company is generally required by the state public utilities commission to include enough information on the bills for the customer to judge if they are accurate. For example, if the meter is read by the company, the date and the reading of the meter at the beginning and end of the billing period must be shown on the bill. The total amount charged, the date due, the total due after addition of any penalty for nonpayment within a designated period also must be indicated. If the bill is estimated, the bill must be clearly marked as such. Service charges should be listed separately from basic costs.

Report any dispute about a bill to the customer service department of the utility. Customers who do not get satisfaction from the company should contact the local consumer protection agency. The utility cannot discontinue service if a customer formally protests a bill, provided that the customer continues to pay undisputed portions. The consumer can contact the public utilities commission with a complaint but this is frequently ineffective. Most state commissions do not deal with individual problems, and many are closely allied with the utilities they control.

See also: UTILITY DEPOSITS

UTILITIES: DEFERRED PAYMENT PLAN

Many public utility companies in the United States offer deferred payment plans to customers who are unable to pay a particularily large utility bill in full. The amount of that particular bill is spread out over several months. The customer and the utility company must agree upon a payment plan and both are then required to abide by the agreement. If the customer fails to make the deferred payments as agreed, the company can cut off service. The company, however, cannot cut off service as long as the customer meets the deferred payment plan. Check with the customer service department of the utility for information about deferred payment plans.

UTILITIES: DEPOSITS

Public utility companies are allowed to charge deposits in order to protect themselves from customers who do not pay their bills. The amount of the deposit and the conditions under which it is charged is regulated by the state public utilities commission.

In most cases a deposit is not required if the applicant has a good credit record that can be verified easily by the utility company, or if he or she has a good payment record with the same or another utility company offering the same services. If service was terminated because of nonpayment of bills, the amount due the utility generally must be paid before service can be resumed at that or another location.

Public utility companies are required to return the customer's deposit plus interest when the service is disconnected. The amount of interest paid is regulated by the state public utilities commission. Any payments due the utility are subtracted before the deposit is refunded.

A deposit can also be refunded when the customer has maintained a good payment record with the company for a specified period of time.

UTILITIES: DISCONNECTIONS

To have the utilities disconnected in home or office, the consumer should contact the business office of the utility from which he is purchasing. If the consumer is moving he should give a forwarding address to which the final bill can be mailed. If a deposit was made with the utility when service was begun, it can be returned or sent to a forwarding address less the unpaid balance.

UTILITIES: METER RECHECK

A consumer may request a meter recheck if he thinks that the bill is too high to be accurate. The utility company can check the meter to make sure it is not defective, do an energy audit to determine what appliance is causing the high usage, and check the wiring to see if it is wasting electricity. The company may charge for the above services unless the meter is found to be defective,

though some companies may offer services such as energy audits without charge. Contact the business office of the public utility.

UTILITIES: REFUSAL OF SERVICE

Public utilities generally have the right to refuse service to individuals who do not meet the conditions of the utility company that have been approved by the state public utilities commission or fail to comply with conditions established by the regulatory agency itself. Grounds for refusal of service that are recognized by most state regulatory commissions are: inadequate facilities (faulty wiring or plumbing), indebtedness to the company or to another company that provides the same service (unless the bill is in dispute), or refusal to pay an authorized deposit to the company.

The public utility is required to inform an applicant for service of the reason for refusal. If the applicant feels that the refusal is unjust, he may complain to the state public utilities commission.

A utility company cannot refuse service because of delinquency in payment by a previous occupant of the premises. Check with the public utilities commission for further information about the grounds for refusal of service.

UTILITIES
See also GAS LEAKS

V

VENERAL DISEASE CONTROL

State health departments generally have a venereal disease control division which provides local services for VD patients through free clinics. Examination and treatment is confidential and voluntary. Physicians discovering a case of venereal disease are required to report it to health authorities who contact the sexual partners of the victim to prevent the spread of the disease.

VENEZUELA

U.S. citizens traveling to Venezuela for tourist purposes are required to have a valid passport, a round trip ticket and a tourist card which is issued by airlines serving Venezuela for a stay of up to 60 days. Business travelers must apply for a visa good for a 60-day stay. Applicants need a health certificate from their doctor, a letter of good conduct from a local Police Department, a letter from their company detailing the nature of business to be conducted and confirming financial responsibility and one photograph. There are no health requirements for entry if arriving from the United States, but yellow fever and cholera shots are advised. Pets may be brought into the country with the appropriate certificate of good health which has been validated by a Vene-

zuelan consulate. The local currency is the bolivar. There are no limits on the amount of local or foreign currency which may be taken in or out of Venezuela. The official language is Spanish, and other languages are not commonly spoken. To drive a car, an American drivers license will suffice.

Trade with Venezuela is conducted through local agents. Import licenses are needed for most items but there are no exchange controls. There is a duty-free zone on the island of Margarita.

The Embassy of Venezuela is located at 2445 Massachusetts Ave. NW, Washington, D.C. 20008, Tel. 202-265-9600. There are consulates in Baltimore, Boston, Chicago, Houston, Los Angeles, Miami, Mobile, New Orleans, New York, Philadelphia, Portland, San Francisco and Savannah.

The American Embassy in Venezuela is located at Avenida Francisco Miranda y Avenida Principal de la Floresta, Caracas, Venezuela, Tel. 284-7111.

For further tourist information contact the Venezuelan Government Tourist Bureau, 450 Park Ave., New York, N.Y. 10022, Tel. 212-355-1101. At the same address is the Venezuelan Institute of Foreign Trade for additional business information, Tel. 212-421-3360.

VERMONT

In Vermont consumers can direct complaints about businesses to the Consumer Protection Division of the Office of the Attorney General. The division will, after receiving a consumer complaint, contact the business being charged and mediate an agreeable resolution between both parties.

If the business presents a different version of the facts and is unwilling to resolve the complaint, the role of the division ends. However if there are numerous consumer abuse complaints brought against a particular business, the division has the power to sue the business.

Consumers in Vermont can contact the division through their in-state Toll-free number, 800-642-5149, or contact the Consumer Protection Division, State of Vermont Office of the Attorney General, 109 State St., Montpelier, Vt. 05602. Local phone 802-828-3171.

Licensing of occupations and professions in Vermont is made through a number of licensing boards and commissions. Inquiries are directed to the Secretary of State Office, Pavilion Building, Montpelier, Vt. 15602, which will direct the inquiry to the correct licensing board.

Assistance is offered to businesses which may be interested in moving to or expanding in Vermont by the Department of Economic Development, Montpelier, Vt. 05602, Tel. 802-828-3221. Contact the Chamber of Commerce at P.O. 37, Montpelier, Vt. 05602, Tel. 802-223-3443.

The Vermont Industrial Development Authority provides low-cost loans, mortgage loans and tax exempt bonds for industrial sites, buildings and corporate capital to businesses locating in Vermont in a manner compatible with its economic and environmental goals. Information may be obtained from the Director, Industrial Development Authority, Pavilion Office Building, Montpelier, Vt. 05602, Tel. 802-828-2384.

Corporation income taxes are 5% of of the first $10,000 with increasing percentages of larger amounts up to 7½% for net income of over $250,000.

Request tourist information from the Office of Information, Agency of Development and Community Affairs, 61 Elm St., Montpelier, Vt. 05602, Tel. 802-828-3236.

VETERANS: EDUCATIONAL AID

The Veterans Administration (VA) provides two types of educational aid for veterans. Those who entered active duty between February 1, 1955 and January 1, 1977 and served on active duty for at least 181 days may receive benefits through the GI Bill. Those who entered the military on or after January 1, 1977 can receive assistance under a contributory plan.

In order to receive benefits, the veteran must attend an educational institution approved by the VA. It can be a public or private elementary, high, vocational, correspondence or business school, junior or teachers college, college or university, professional, scientific or technical institution or any other institution furnishing education at the secondary school level or above. The VA provides educational and vocational counseling on request.

Each veteran qualifying for aid under the GI Bill is entitled to assistance for one and one-half months or the equivalent in part-time training for each month or fraction of a month served on active duty up to a maximum of 45 months. A veteran who has served at least 18 months is entitled to 36 months of educational aid.

Veterans educational aid under the GI Bill must be used within 10 years of release from active duty, or before December 31, 1989, which ever is first. An exception is made for those who are prevented from beginning or completing their chosen program because of a physical or mental disability not the result of their own willful misconduct. The GI Bill also makes available educational loans regardless of the date the veteran entered active duty. The amount of the loan depends on financial aid.

Under the contributory plan, the VA matches the contribution of the veteran at a rate of $2 for every $1 contributed. To qualify for this program the veteran must have been released under conditions other than dishonorable or continue on active duty but have completed his or her obligated period of service and have contributed a required amount to the program. Contributions consist of monthly deductions from salary. Benefits are paid monthly for the number of months the service person contributed to the fund or for 36 months, whichever is less. Unused contributions can be refunded.

Applications for assistance can be obtained from any VA office or from the Veterans Administration, 810 Vermont Ave. NW, Washington, D.C. 20420, Tel. 202-393-4120.

VETERANS: NURSING HOMES

The Veterans Administration operates nursing homes for veterans who are not acutely ill and in need of hospital care but who require skilled nursing care and related medical services. Eligibility requirements are generally the same as for Veterans Administration hospitals. Transfer of a veteran in a VA hospital to a nursing home is made upon the recommendation of his physician. Other veterans may apply through the nearest VA medical facility.

VETERANS: VOCATIONAL REHABILITATION

Veterans who have a service related disability are eligible for vocational rehabilitation assistance. Costs of tuition, books, fees, and training supplies are covered, as well as a subsistence allowance in addition to disability compensation. The training period lasts up to four years and must be completed within nine years following the date of discharge from the service. Extensions of benefits are made in some cases.

Application forms are available from any VA office, or the Veterans Administration, 810 Vermont Ave. NW, Washington, D.C. 20420, Tel. 202-393-4120.

VETERANS HOSPITALS

U.S. Veterans Administration (VA) Hospitals treat veterans who have been discharged or released from active military service under conditions other than dishonorable. Admission is on a priority basis for the space available. Veterans needing hospitalization because of injuries or disease incurred or aggravated on active duty in the Armed Forces have first priority. The second priority goes to veterans discharged or retired for a disability incurred or aggravated on active duty, or who are receiving a veteran's pension, or would be receiving a pension except for receipt of retirement pay. They are considered a second priority because they are requesting treatment for a medical problem not incurred or aggravated during active duty.

Third priority admissions are for veterans who were not discharged or retired due to disability incurred or aggravated during military service. These third priority admissions must be unable to pay for medical treatment elsewhere and must be willing to take an oath to that effect. Any veteran or who is 65 years of age or older, who is in receipt of a veteran's pension or

who is eligible for Medicaide is eligible regardless of ability to pay.

Hospital care includes medical expenses while in the veterans hospital and transportation and incidental expenses for veterans who are unable to pay such costs. In special cases medical care is available for the spouse or child of a veteran who has a permanent and total service-connected disability. It may also be available for the spouse or child of a veteran who died of a service-connected disability. Outpatient care is also available at Veterans Administration hospitals and clinics for eligible veterans.

Application for either inpatient or outpatient care can be made at any VA hospital, outpatient clinic or regional office. A ruling on eligibility is made the same day if the veteran applies in person and usually within a week if he or she applies by mail.

Contact the Veterans Administration, 810 Vermont Ave. NW, Washington, D.C 20420, Tel. 202-393-4120.

VETERINARIANS

All states require that veterinarians have a license to practice medicine. Applicants for licenses must have a Doctor of Veterinary Medicine (D.V.M. or V.M.D.) degree from an accredited college of veterinary medicine. They must also pass both written and oral proficiency examinations given by the state board of veterinary medicine or other state board licensing veterinarians.

A professional organization for the promotion of veterinary medicine is the American Veterinary Medical Association, 930 N. Meacham Road, Schaumburg, Ill. 60196, Tel. 312-885-8070.

VIRGINIA

The consumer protection agency in Virginia is the Office of Consumer Affairs, Washington Building, Richmond, Va. 23219, Tel. Toll-free 800-552-9963. The office receives and mediates consumer complaints. It cannot investigate each complaint, but where patterns of complaints appear, it initiates investigations. Whenever appropriate the office refers evidence of unfair or deceptive practices to the Attorney General's Office for prosecution.

In Virginia the Department of Commerce performs administrative functions for the following state regulatory boards and licensing programs: accountants, alcoholism counselor certification committees, architects and land surveyors, athletic commissions, audiology and speech pathologists, barbers, behavioral science, collection agencies, commerce, contractors, commercial driver training schools, drug counselors, employment agencies, professional hairdressers, hearing aid dealers and fitters, librarians, nursing home administrators, opticians, pilots, polygraph examiners, private security services, profession-

al counselors, psychologists, real estate brokers, sanitarians, social workers, water and wastewater works operators. Licensing requirements for the above professions and occupations can be obtained from the Department of Commerce, 2 South Ninth Street, Richmond, Va. 23219.

Complaints about licensees must be submitted in affidavit form to the Department of Commerce at the above address. The Chief Investigator reviews all complaints to determine if they fall under the licensure law. If so, an investigation is conducted and the complainant is notified. If the case is civil in nature, however, the complainant is advised to contact an attorney.

The Department of Health Regulatory Boards licenses health related professions which include the following boards: dentists, funeral directors and embalmers, medicine, nurses, optometrists, pharmacists, and veterinarians. Complaints or inquires about licenses in these occupations can be sent to the Commonwealth of Virginia, Department of Health Regulatory Boards, Seaboard Building, Suite 453, 3600 West Broad St., Richmond, Va. 23230, Tel. 804-257-0345.

The Department of Commerce in Virginia offers consultant services to businesses considering a move to or expanding in the state. Interested businesses should contact the Department of Commerce, 2 South Ninth Street, Richmond,

Va., 23219, Tel. 804-786-2161.

Personal income tax rates start at 2% for the first $3,000 and increase to 5.75% for income over $12,000. It is based on the individual's federal adjusted gross income. The state sales tax is 3%, with a local sales tax of 1%.

The corporate income tax rate is 6% of the state's taxable income.

Virginia has city or county revenue bond financing available for businesses. Consult the Division of Industrial Development for information.

Request tourist information from the Virginia State Travel Service, 6 North Sixth Street, Richmond, Virginia 23219, Tel. 804-786-2051.

VISA

See individual country entries

VOCATIONAL APTITUDE TESTS

Most state employment offices offer vocational aptitude, proficiency and interest tests designed to help individuals select an appropriate field for employment. For further information contact the local state employment agency or the Labor Department, Employment and Training Administration, United States Employment Service, 601 D St. NW, Washington, D.C. 20213, Tel. 202-376-6289.

VOLLEYBALL

The United States Volleyball Association is the governing body for the sport in the United States. It conducts tournaments leading to the National Championships and trains and selects the teams for the Olympics and the Pan American games. For further information contact the United States Volleyball Association, P.O. Box 77065, San Francisco, Calif. 94117, Tel. 415-982-7590.

Collegiate volleyball is governed by the National Collegiate Athletic Association, U.S. Highway 50 and Nall Ave., P.O. Box 1906, Shawnee Mission, Kan. 66222, Tel. 913-384-3220.

VOLUNTEERS IN SERVICE TO AMERICA (VISTA)

Vista volunteers serve up to two years in the United States, working among the poor in urban areas, small towns and rural sections in an effort to help communities solve problems and reduce poverty. Assignments and specific programs are controlled by the program's regional directors. For further information contact ACTION, 806 Connecticut Ave. NW, Washington, D.C. 20525, Tel. 202-254-7376.

VOLUNTEER PROGRAMS: GOVERNMENT

ACTION is the federal agency responsible for federal volunteer service. It controls six programs: the Peace Corps, VISTA, Foster Grandparents, RSVP, Senior Companion Program and University Year for Action. The Reagan Administration has drastically cut

310

funding to this agency, and its future is in doubt. For general information contact ACTION, 806 Connecticut Ave. NW, Washington, D.C. 20525, Tel. 800-424-8580.

See also: individual programs

W

WAGES: MINIMUM

The Wage and Hour Division of the Department of Labor enforces the law requiring that covered employees be paid the minimum wage specified and not less than one and one half the regular rate of pay for overtime. The minimum wage as of January 1, 1981 was $3.35 an hour. The law covers most workers employed in enterprises engaged in interstate commerce. Professional, executive, administrative and certain sales employees are exempted as are babysitters and companions to the elderly. The Wage and Hour Division investigates suspected violations. Willful violations can be prosecuted criminally. The agency can also force employers to pay back wages.

Complaints and questions about the minimum wage law should be directed to the regional or area offices of the Department of Labor, Wage and Hour Division listed in the local telephone directory under U.S. government. Or contact the Department of Labor, Employment Standards Administration, Office of Information and Consumer Affairs, 200 Constitution Ave. NW, Washington, D.C. 20210, Tel. 202-523-8743.

WARDS OF COURT

Children may become wards of the court if they have no surviving relatives, or if the court decides that the parents are not providing a fit home for the child because of neglect or abuse. The local child welfare agency or child protective service is frequently the agency which will bring a child to the notice of the court.

Children who are wards of the court are generally placed in foster homes or group homes supervised and licensed by the state.

In some cases children become temporary wards of the court when the child welfare agency or child protective service has removed the child from the home but there is hope that the child can be returned to the home when the problems are worked out.

See also CHILD ABUSE; ABANDONED CHILDREN; ADOPTION; FOSTER PARENTS

WARRANTY

A warranty is a promise by a manufacturer or a seller to stand behind its product. In addition to written warranties, products are covered by implied warranties such as the "warranty of merchantability," which means that the seller promises that the product is good for the ordinary use of the product. For example

311

lamps must illumine, irons must iron, cooking stoves must provide heat for cooking unless the seller specifically states in writing that it gives no warranty at all. As protection regarding warranties falls under both state and federal law, the consumer has several options of recourse.

If the amount of money is substantial and the product was manufactured after July 4, 1975, the manufacturer can be sued under federal law for failure to honor a warranty. If the amount of money is small the consumer may want to sue through a local small claims court. Warranty violations can also be reported to the Federal Trade Commission. The FTC cannot investigate cases of individual warranty violation but maintains files, and numerous complaints about a particular product or company may cause it to initiate an investigation.

Contact the Federal Trade Commission, Pennsylvania Ave. at Sixth St. NW, Washington, D.C. 20580, Tel. 202-523-3625.

WASHINGTON, STATE OF

Consumer complaints in the state of Washington can be referred to the Consumer Protection Division, Attorney General's Office, 1366 Dexter Horton Building, Seattle, Wash., 98104, Tel. Toll-free in Washington, 800-552-0700, or tel. 206-464-6684. Offices are also located in Spokane, Tacoma, and Olympia.

Complaints received in writing will either be processed by the Consumer Protection Division or will be sent to another agency with jurisdiction over that particular problem. If the Consumer Protection Office does handle the complaint, it will assign the complaint to a investigator who will send a copy to the firm involved and request a response. In many cases, the firm will then adjust the complaint to the customer's satisfaction.

The Consumer Protection Division does not have the authority to force adjustments, but attempts to provide the information about alternative avenues of complaint, such as the small claims court. See SMALL CLAIMS COURT.

If the Consumer Protection Division receives numerous complaints about unfair or deceptive businesses practices by a particular firm, the Attorney General's office may file a lawsuit against the firm.

The Department of Licensing is responsible for licensing and regulating functions for many professions and businesses in Washington: accountants, architects, barbers, charities, chiropractors, collection agencies, cosmetologists, debt adjusters, dentists, drugless healers, employment agencies, engineers/land surveyors, firearm records, funeral directors/embalmers, hearing aid fitters, landscape architects, massage midwives, notary publics, nursing home administra-

tors, ocularists, opticians, optometrists, osteopathic physicians, physicians and surgeons,
physicians assistants, physical
therapists, podiatrists, psychologists, practical nurses, registered
nurses, registered sanitarians,
veterinarians. For information
about licensing requirements or
complaints in the above professions and occupations, contact
the Department of Licensing, Professional Licensing Division, P.O.
Box 9649, Olympia, Wash., 98504,
200-753-6838.

If a complaint, upon investigation, is found to have merit, it is
brought before the Director of the
appropriate licensing board which
has the power to revoke licenses.
In each case the license has the
right to a hearing.

The following agencies in Washington also regulate licenses:

Plumbers, contractors, and
electricians: Department of Labor
and Industries, Building and
Construction Safety Inspection
Services Division, 520 South Water
St., Olympia, Wash. 98504 Tel. 206-
753-1587.

Emergency medical personnel
and health care institutions and
facilities: The Board of Pharmacy,
319 East 7th, Olympia, Wash.
98540, Tel. 206-753-6834; State
Board of Accountancy, 210 E.
Union, Olympia, Wash. 98504, Tel.
206-753-2585; Department of Social and Health Services, 12th and
Franklin, Olympia, Wash. 98504,
206-753-5874.

Insurance Commissioner, Insurance Building, Olympia, Wash.
98504.

The Department of Commerce
and Economic Development helps
businesses get established ini-
tially in Washington State, improve their marketing opportunities, provide information for future
operations, and solve problems
involving governmental regulations. Interested businesses
should contact the Department of
Commerce and Economic
Development, 101 General Administration Building, Olympia, Wash.
98504, Tel. 206-753-5630.

Washington state offers city
and county revenue bond financing to businesses moving to or
expanding in the state. It also
offers state incentive programs for
locating industry in areas of high
unemployment.

State excise taxes depend upon
the type of business and range
from .125% to .1%. The retail
sales tax is 4.5%. Counties and
unincorporated cities and towns
have the option of a .5% sales tax.

There is no personal income tax
in the state of Washington.

Tourist information is available
from the Travel Development Division, Department of Commerce
and Economic Development,
General Administration Building,
Olympia, Wash., 98504, Tel. 206-
753-5610.

WATER SUPPLY: SAFETY
The state health departments
generally inspect and test water

supply systems to ensure that they meet existing standards. They also maintain chemical and bacteriological records on water samples taken periodically from every system in the state. Health departments also review and approve plans for new water systems, train water system operators and certify their competence.

Suspected contamination of the water supply should be reported to the nearest office of the state health department.

See also: HAZARDOUS MATERIALS: ACCIDENTS AND SPILLS, RIVERS AND CANALS.

WEATHER CHARTS: MARINE

The National Ocean Survey issues marine weather charts periodically for various coastal and Great Lakes areas. The charts are available at local marinas and marine chart dealers or write the Commerce Department, National Oceanic and Atmospheric Administration, Distribution Division, 6501 Layfayette Ave., Riverdale, Md. 20854, Tel. 301-443-8708.

WEATHER SERVICES

The National Weather Service of the National Oceanic and Atmospheric Administration (NOAA), describes, monitors and predicts conditions of the atmosphere, ocean, sun and space environment. It issues warnings of impending natural events and studies the beneficial and adverse effects of environmental modifications. It also provides weather forecasts for the general public and for aviation and marine traffic, for agricultural, forestry and urban environments.

A recorded Weather Service forecast is available in most cities. It can be located in the telephone directory under: U.S. Government. Further information can generally be obtained by calling NOAA listings for administrative offices. Pilots can contact the Civil Air Patrol office at local airports.

Contact the National Weather Service, National Oceanic and Atmosphere Administration, 6010 Executive Boulevard, Rockville, Md. 20852, Tel. 301-655-4000.

WEIGHTLIFTING

The Amateur Athletic Union conducts training programs and competitions in weightlifting in the United States. It also governs the trials for the Olympic and Pan American games. For further information contact the Amateur Athletic Union, 3400 West 86th St., Indianapolis, Ind. 46268, Tel. 913-384-3200.

WEIGHTS AND MEASURES

Each state has an office of weights and measures that enforces state regulations for commercial transactions. These offices monitor the weights of packaged goods sold in that state and the accuracy of supermarket scales, gasoline pumps, taxi meters and rental car odometers.

A consumer who has purchased a short-weight package or who

thinks that a weight or measuring device used by a store is inaccurate can contact the state or local weights and measures office. These can be found listed in the telephone book under: Weights and Measures, Standards, Consumer Protection or Consumer Affairs headings in the city or county sections.

WEST VIRGINIA

The Office of the Attorney General, Consumer Protection Division, in West Virginia, enforces the state's unfair and deceptive practices law. The division accepts and mediates consumer complaints. When there is a pattern of complaints about a particular business or trade practice, the division initiates an investigation. It has the power to hold hearings, subpoena witnesses and records, seek court orders for restitution and court restraining orders. Send complaints to the Consumer Protection Division, Office of the Attorney General, 3412 Staunton Ave. SE, Charleston, West Virginia, 25304, Tel. 304-348-8986.

There is no central licensing agency for professions and occupations in West Virginia. Instead, individual boards determine qualifications for licensing, license applicants and review any complaints. Inquiries about licensing or complaints about licensees can be sent to the Consumer Protection Division listed above which will forward the letter to the proper licensing board.

The State of West Virginia offers tax incentive programs designed to aid industrial concerns relocating or expanding within the State. Credits against business taxes are allowed for the purchase or improvement of real or personal property first placed into service. Low interest loans are offered for similar purposes by the West Virginia Economic Development Authority. A detailed description of tax incentive programs can be supplied to prospective industrial concerns. Contact the Tax Department of West Virginia, Charleston, West Virginia 25305, or the Governor's Office of Economic and Community Development, Capitol Building, Charleston, West Virginia 25305, Tel. 304-348-0190.

The corporate income tax rate in West Virginia is a flat 6%. The state sales tax is 3%.

The individual income tax rates range from 2.1% on amounts less than $2,000 to 9.6% for income in excess of $200,000.

Request travel information about West Virginia from the Travel Development Division, Governor's Office of Economic and Community Development, State Capitol Complex, Charleston, West Virginia 25305, Tel. 304-348-2286.

WHEELCHAIR BASKETBALL

The National Wheelchair Basketball Association provides opportunities for the physically disabled to participate in national basketball. It sponsors competitions, awards trophies and keeps statistics on the game. The organization works closely with the National Wheelchair Athletic Association in sponsoring international competition. For further information contact the National Wheelchair Basketball Association, 110 Seaton Bldg, University of Kentucky, Lexington, Ky. 40506, Tel. 606-257-1623.

WILDLIFE: CONSERVATION

The Fish and Wildlife Service of the Department of Interior is responsible for the preservation and restoration of wildlife and its environment. It also conducts research and is responsible for animal damage control. For further information contact the Department of the Interior, U.S. Fish and Wildlife Service, C St. between 18th and 19th Sts. NW, Washington, D.C. 20240, Tel. 202-343-5634.

See also: ENDANGERED SPECIES

WILLS

A will is a legal document by which an individual disposes of property at death according to his or her own plan. A will must generally be written and must conform to the minimum requirements of the particular state's law. An oral will is recognized only in extreme circumstances that are carefully regulated by state law.

Signatures of two witnesses are generally required when signing a will. One or more executors should be named in the will to carry out the terms of the will. After the individual's death, the will is offered for probate in court. Probate is the process of proving before a court that the will is genuine and valid. If the will is in order the court will authorize the executors to administer the estate.

Consult a lawyer.
See also: PROBATE

WISCONSIN

Wisconsin has two main consumer protection agencies. The Department of Justice Office of Consumer Protection enforces state consumer laws and has programs in four main areas: investigation and prosecution, complaint mediation, consumer advocacy and consumer information and education. The Department of Agriculture, Trade and Consumer Protection Division administers unfair business practice, deceptive advertising, product safety, minimum mark-up, trading stamp and weights and measure laws. It also mediates consumer complaints and provides consumer information and education.

The two agencies work closely together and complaints can be sent to either.

Each complaint received by one of the above offices is reviewed to determine if the complaint falls within the statutory jurisdiction of the Office of Consumer Protection. If it does not, it is referred to another state or federal agency and the consumer is notified where the complaint has been sent. Usually, the business or person complained against is contacted for its side of the dispute. Frequently a resolution is reached by the state office through mediation.

Contact the Department of Justice, Office of Consumer Protection at 114 East, State Capitol, Madison, Wis. 53702, Tel. 608-266-1852 or at the Milwaukee State Office Building, 819 N. 6th St., Rm. 520, Milwaukee, Wisconsin 53203, Tel. 414-224-1867.

Contact the Department of Agriculture, Trade and Consumer Protection Division at 801 West Badger Road, P.O. Box 8911, Madison, Wisconsin 53708, or call the toll free hot line 800-362-3020. Regional offices are located in Altoona, Green Bay, and Milwaukee.

The Wisconsin Department of Regulation and Licensing licenses the following occupations and businesses: certified public accountant, animal technician, architect, barber, cemetery salesperson, chiropractor, cosmetology instructor and operator, dentist, dental hygenist, designer, private detective, electrologist, embalmer, engineer, funeral director, hearing aid dealer and fitter, land surveyor, manicurist, nurse, nursing home administrator, optometrist, pharmacist, physical therapist, physician, physician's assistant, podiatrist, psychologist, real estate broker and veterinarian.

The Department will supply information about licensing requirements upon request and also will process complaints against licensees. Each board has the power to revoke licenses when misconduct has been proved. The Division of Enforcement within the Department has a staff of attorneys and investigators who follow through on complaints filed with the Department.

Contact the Department of Regulation and Licensing at 1400 E. Washington Avenue, Madison, Wisconsin 53702, Tel. 608-267-7211.

Tourist information about Wisconsin can be requested from the Division of Tourism, Department of Business Development, 123 W. Washington Ave., Madison, Wisc. 53702, Tel. 608-266-2161.

WORKER'S COMPENSATION

All states have worker's compensation laws that ensure either prompt medical care and cash benefits to a worker injured in connection with a job, or cash benefits to dependents if the worker is killed. In most states all employers covered by the law are required to provide worker's compensation insurance. Not all jobs are covered, and the extent of coverage varies from state to state. Some states cover only work that is considered dangerous; others cover only employers with more than a certain number of employees.

Employers meet the cost of worker's compensation by buying

insurance, usually either from a private insurance company or, in the case of large companies, from themselves. In some states employers have the option or obligation to insure with the state.

Most states cover injuries that arise out of and in employment, including some or all diseases attributable to the worker's occupation. Most states exclude injuries due to the employees intoxication, willful misconduct or gross negligence. The amount of the payments is based on the worker's wages at the time of the injury, with maxmum and minimum weekly limits. Some states limit the number of weeks for payment of expenses, and/or the total amount payed in a given case. Most states provide death benefits to a widow throughout her life unless she remarries, and to surviving children until they reach a given age. States are now beginning to pay benefits to widowers as well.

Worker's compensation covers medical care expenses for injured employees, although some states limit the length of time or the total cost of such care. Most states provide benefits to help meet burial expenses of employees killed on the job.

Application for benefits can be made directly to the worker's compensation board located in most cities. If the worker is taken to the hospital because of an injury, the hospital should be notified that the injury is work-related. The hospital will then inform the worker's compensation board.

The federal government provides worker's compensation to employees engaged in certain industries. Contact the district or national offices of the Worker's Compensation Programs, Employment Standards Administration, Department of Labor, 200 Constitution Ave. NW, Washington, D.C. 20210, Tel. 202-523-8165.

WRESTLING

The Amateur Athletic Union governs amateur wrestling in the United States. It sets the rules for competition, conducts developmental programs and sponsors competitions including the Olympic trials. For further information contact the Amateur Athletic Union, 3400, West 86th St. Indianapolis, Ind. 46268, Tel. 913-384-3200.

Professional wrestling is sponsored and controlled by individual promoters.

WYOMING

The main consumer protection agency in Wyoming is the Consumer Affairs Division in the Attorney General's Office. It enforces the state's unfair and deceptive trade practice law, investigates consumer complaints, obtains restraining orders and seeks court orders for restitution to consumers. Contact the Consumer Affairs Division, Office of the Attorney

General, State Capitol, Cheyenne, Wy. 82002, Tel. 307-777-7841.

There is no central licensing department for occupations and professions in Wyoming. Individual boards and commissions set requirements for licensing, issue licenses and investigate any complaints against licensees. Inquiries about licensing or complaints about licensees can be sent to the Consumer Affairs Division mentioned above which will refer the letter to the proper licensing board or commission.

Wyoming has no personal income tax, no corporate income tax and a maximum sales tax of 3%. There is also no personal property tax on inventories or in-transit goods.

The Wyoming Department of Economic Planning and Development offers advisory services to businesses moving into the state. They feel that due to the low business and personal taxes in the state, they do not need to offer further incentives to encourage businesses to move into Wyoming. Industrial revenue bonds are offered on a local level to help with construction or land purchase. The Wyoming Department of Economic Planning and Development can be contacted at Barrett Building, Cheyenne, Wyoming 82002, Tel. 307-777-7284.

Request travel information about Wyoming from the Travel Commission, Etchepare Circle, Cheyenne, Wyoming 82002, Tel. 307-777-7777.

Y Z

YACHT RACING

The United States Yacht Racing Union is the coordinating organization for the sport in the United States. It sponsors the U.S. Sailing Championship and other races and supplies educational information on the sport. For further information contact the United States Yacht Racing Union, P.O. Box 209, Newport, R.I. 02840, Tel. 401-849-5200.

YUGOSLAVIA

A valid passport and a visa are required for U.S. citizens traveling to Yugoslavia. A visa is easily obtainable by presenting a valid passport at a Yugoslav consulate. It is good for one year for a stay of up to 90 days. There are no health requirements for entry if arriving from the United States. Pets may be brought into the country with a certificate of good health and rabies from a veterinarian. The local currency is the new dinar. Up to 1,500 dinars may be taken in or out of the country. There are no limits on the amount of foreign currency that can be taken in or out. There are three national languages in Yugoslavia—Serbo-Croat, which is the most widely spoken, Slovenian and Macedonian. In some sections of the country, the Cyrillic alphabet is used. English and German are the most commonly spoken foreign lan-

Yugoslavia

guages. To drive a car, an International Driving License is required.

Trade with Yugoslavia is generally handled through resident agents. Few goods require licenses and there are few exchange controls.

The Embassy of Yugoslavia is located at 2410 California St. NW, Washington, D.C. 20008, 202-462-6506. There are consulates in Chicago, New York, Pittsburgh, Cleveland and San Francisco.

For additional tourist information contact the Yugoslav State Tourist Office, 630 Fifth Ave., New York, N.Y. 10020, Tel. 212-757-2801. For further tourist business information contact the Yugoslav Chamber of Economy Trade Promotion Office, 488 Madison Ave., New York, N.Y. 10022, Tel. 212-355-7117.

O'LEARY LIBRARY UNIVERSITY OF
LOWELL